£6·25

D1256304

STUDIES IN IRISH HISTORY, SECOND SERIES

edited by

T. W. MOODY
Professor of Modern History
University of Dublin

J. C. BECKETT
Professor of Irish History
Queen's University, Belfast

T. D. WILLIAMS
Professor of Modern History
National University of Ireland

VOLUME VII
THE IRISH EDUCATION EXPERIMENT

STUDIES IN IRISH HISTORY, SECOND SERIES

THE
IRISH EDUCATION
EXPERIMENT

The National System of Education
in the Nineteenth Century

by

DONALD H. AKENSON

LONDON: Routledge & Kegan Paul
TORONTO: University of Toronto Press
1970

First published in Great Britain in 1970
by Routledge and Kegan Paul Ltd
and in Canada and the United States of America
by University of Toronto Press
Printed in Great Britain by
Cox & Wyman Ltd
London, Fakenham and Reading
SBN 7100 6647 3
UTP SBN 8020 1671 5

To
M.E.R.A.

CONTENTS

ABBREVIATIONS

~~~~~~

M.C.N.E.I. Minutes of the Commissioners of National Education
            in Ireland.
N.L.I.   National Library of Ireland.
P.R.O.N.I. Public Record Office, Northern Ireland.
P.R.O.I.   Public Record Office, Republic of Ireland.
P.R.O.L.   Public Record Office, London.
S.P.O.D.   State Paper Office, Dublin.

ACKNOWLEDGEMENTS

~~~~~~

I AM MORE THAN MERELY GRATEFUL for the kindness and guidance of a number of generous individuals. This book was begun as a Ph.D. thesis in the Graduate School of Arts and Sciences, Harvard University, under the direction of the late Professor David E. Owen and of Dean Theodore R. Sizer. Professor John V. Kelleher read and criticized the early drafts in detail, a gift whose value will immediately be recognized by anyone in Irish studies.

The following persons in Ireland and England were of assistance in a variety of ways: Rev. Robert Allen, Professor D. A. Binchy, Sr Helen M. Connolly, Fr Donald F. Cregan, Professor Myles Dillon, Professor R. Dudley Edwards, Mr Thomas McElligott, Professor Roger McHugh, Dr T. Ó'Raifeartaigh, Professor J. V. Rice, and Mr Nicholas Wheeler-Robinson. Special thanks are due the duke of Bolton for granting access to those family manuscripts dealing with Thomas Orde's Irish educational activities.

The librarians and staffs of the following institutions made research not only profitable, but often enjoyable: the Bodleian Library, the British Museum, the National Library of Ireland, the Presbyterian Historical Society of Ireland, the Public Record Office of Great Britain, the Public Record Office of Northern Ireland, the Public Record Office of the Republic of Ireland, Queen's University, Belfast, the Representative Church Body, the Royal Irish Academy, the State Paper Office of Ireland, Trinity College, Dublin, University College, Cork, University College, Dublin, and Widener Library, Harvard University.

Acknowledgements

Research expenses for this study were partially underwritten by a grant from the Milton Fund, Harvard University.

The Provost of Yale University and the Dean of Yale College have generously provided a grant in aid of publication.

Most important, I wish to express my appreciation to two people who have served in the combined roles of research assistants, typists, and critics: my secretary, Nancy Di Benedetto, and my wife, Mary E. R. Akenson.

DONALD H. AKENSON

Davenport College
Yale University
June, 1968

I

THE IRISH NATIONAL SYSTEM AS AN EDUCATIONAL SURPRISE

~~~~~~~~~~~~~~~~~~~~~~~~~~~~~~~~~~~~

I

DURING THE LAST CENTURY the Irish national system of education, founded in 1831, was highly controversial, widely denounced, and imperfectly understood. Contemporaries seldom agreed in their definitions of the nature and purpose of the system. 'That system', Dr Blake, the Roman Catholic bishop of Dromore stated,

. . . provides . . . first, the great desideratum, a good moral education for the whole community, supplying excellent class-books, excellent teachers, and excellent inspectors. Secondly, it invites all the youth of the whole country into its schools. Thirdly, it takes care that the great principles of morality and religion, which are suggested by the law of nature, and are admitted by all Christians of every denomination in Ireland, shall be diligently inculcated in its books and by its teachers.[1]

In contrast, John MacHale, Roman Catholic archbishop of Tuam, saw the system as the entering wedge of a government conspiracy. 'From the extraordinary power now claimed by the state over a mixed education, it would soon claim a similar despotic control over mixed marriages, and strive to stretch its net over all ecclesiastical concerns.'[2] During the system's early

[1] *Royal commission of inquiry into primary education (Ireland)*, vol. I, pt. I: Report of the commissioners, p. 123 [C 6], H. C., 1870, xxviii, pt i.

[2] *Dublin Evening Post*, 24 Nov. 1838.

I

years the clergy of the established church were among the chief opponents of the national board. Yet, the protestant archbishop of Dublin served as one of the commissioners of national education and stoutly defended the system in Dublin and in Westminster. In the system's early years members of the synod of Ulster believed it to be such an evil that they harassed national schoolmasters and on occasion burned schoolhouses; yet in later years the members of the synod became the strongest advocates of the system.

Because the national system of education was such a volatile and emotion-laden topic, it is important that the assumptions and methods with which the subject is here approached be made as explicit as possible. The first of these is that attention should be focused upon the 'top' of the national system, that is, upon the system's political and administrative arrangements. This is not to say that what happened in the individual schoolrooms is unimportant, but merely that it is of second priority; only after the outlines of the bureaucracy of national education are accurately defined and the political influences upon that outline determined, will it be appropriate for the historian to turn to filling in the gaps with material gathered from individual national school classrooms.

Second, the emphasis upon the top of the system means that considerable attention will have to be paid to ecclesiastical history, for the twisting and shaping of the system was chiefly the work of religious authorities. Admittedly, church history can be dull, but in the case of the Irish national system the scorn twentieth-century man may feel for ecclesiastical debate is badly misdirected. The important issues concerning nineteenth-century Irish education were defined by nineteenth-century Irishmen as religious problems. If we refuse to immerse ourselves in their way of thinking about the schools it will be impossible to understand the development of the Irish national system of education. Moreover, it is important to realize that when we are discussing Irish clerics of the last century—and most especially the prelates of the Roman Catholic church—we are not dealing with men as devoid of secular power as are most twentieth-century European clerics. Quite the opposite—it might be argued that what cabinet members were to England, the Irish Roman Catholic bishops were to Ireland, at least after 1850. Certainly Cardinal Cullen had as much impact upon everyday Irish life as did W. E. Gladstone.

Third, our primary attention will be focused directly upon the national system and upon the development of the system. Considerably less attention will be placed upon the effect the system had upon the Irish nation. Again, this is a matter of priority. The national system played an important role in shaping the minds of Irish peasantry and working classes during the last century, but attempts to describe that role in any depth will have to wait until the system itself is first studied in detail.

Given this perspective, a triad of major themes will emerge. First, the Irish national system of education was unusual because it appeared seemingly before it should have. As formed in 1831, the system involved control by the central government of schools erected under its auspices or placed under its supervision. The state entrusted formal control of the system to the 'commissioners of national education'. This board of unpaid dignitaries was served, and sometimes dominated, by a phalanx of civil servants. The commissioners paid the salaries of all school teachers, possessed the right to dismiss individual schoolmasters, and controlled the use of textbooks and lesson materials in the national schools. Local managers were responsible for the maintenance of the schools and for the hiring of masters. The crucial point to be made about these arrangements is that they involved the creation and provision of a system of popular education by the central government. Considerable responsibility and power devolved upon local authorities, but this should not obscure the fact that, in 1831, the government created a state system of schools in Ireland.

When we pursue the matter we will discover that the creation of the system can be explained only by reference to a series of circumstances and personalities unique to Ireland. In the years before the system's founding Ireland underwent no industrial revolution, no significant urbanization, no breakdown in the agrarian order and family structure, and did not experience any of the other forms of social revolution that usually presage the creation of state systems of formal education. Thus, the question, 'why was the national system created at such an early date?'

becomes an especially intriguing one and is worth considerable attention.

A second major strand of events involves the national system's religious arrangements. Originally the system was intended to be 'non-denominational' in the sense that children of all faiths were to attend the same school, and in the sense that religious material of a dogmatic nature was to be excluded while children assembled for combined literary instruction. For a number of reasons, however, the system that was founded as a non-denominational one in 1831 was, by 1851, a denominational one in practice, if not in law. The reasons for this development are complex and involve intricate dealings between the commissioners of national education and the three major Irish denominations. Demographic considerations and a series of compromising errors by the commissioners of national education also played a part.

A third important sequence of events involves a change in the men at the controls of the national system. The original group of commissioners was composed of vigorous and distinguished individuals, such as the archbishops of Dublin of the Anglican and the Roman Catholic churches. In their first twenty years the commissioners had a nearly free hand to run their system any way they pleased. After mid-century, however, things turned sour. The giants of the early years were gradually replaced by faceless men. The treasury slowly, but inexorably, cut away at the commissioners' freedom of action. The Roman Catholic hierarchy became a taskmaster that the commissioners had to satisfy. Thus, by the end of the nineteenth century the system, while controlled in theory by the commissioners of national education, was actually run according to the dictates of the treasury and the bishops of the Roman Catholic church in Ireland. The change in the control of the national system was of course a mirror of the rapidly shifting balance of power within Ireland in the nineteenth century. When the system was founded the country was still heavily influenced politically by the established church. The catholics had only recently received emancipation. The Roman Catholic bishops were still grateful for mere toleration and were far from demanding. During the century, however, a religious revolution occurred. Power slipped gradually from the anglican hands and, after disestablishment in 1871, was gone almost entirely. The Roman Catholic church,

4

on the other hand, became ever stronger and increasingly aggressive. The catholic church's position was immeasurably strengthened by the famine since the subsequent population decline removed the financial burden of a large number of poverty-stricken peasants from its shoulders. Almost simultaneously the arrival of Paul Cullen in Ireland, first as archbishop of Armagh and then of Dublin, breathed a new and rigid order and a sense of righteous aggressiveness into the clerical ranks. The Irish religious revolution, when combined with a policy of increasing treasury intervention in Irish affairs, inevitably meant a transformation in the way the affairs of the commissioners of national education were conducted.

2

To grasp fully our first theme—that the Irish system appeared at an unusually early date—we must not look immediately at Ireland, but rather turn first to the greater political entity within which Ireland was set, the United Kingdom of England, Scotland, and Ireland. How unusual the national system was becomes clear only when we view it within the context of British history and realize that Ireland possessed a system of popular education almost four decades before England, its ostensibly more advanced neighbour. Clearly, the educational history of the British isles forms the proper context for a study of the Irish national system of education; this perspective will suggest to the insular Britisher that the English and Scottish pattern of educational development was not the only possible pattern, and to the parochial Irishman that his country's educational history is noteworthy.

English events during the last century and a half form the classic pattern of a society undergoing economic, social, and educational transformation. The first of the world's nations to embrace fully the modern pattern of industrial culture, England deserves attention in any discussion of educational growth. G. M. Young and W. D. Handcock suggest that 'the central theme of Victorian history, which can be described as that of the response of the institutions and traditions of an old, vigorous, and highly integrated society to the twin impacts of industrialism and democracy, has more than a national, even something of an ecumenical significance'.[3] Strangely, although England and Ireland followed sharply divergent paths of economic and social development in the nineteenth century, their educational systems evolved along strikingly similar lines.

It is convenient, if overly simple, to think of English social and economic patterns of the last two hundred years as having occurred in a series of layers. The basic, and potentially most revolutionary, layer has consisted of the rapid growth of the English nation's population. A second stratum of change has been the nation's transformation from an agrarian to an industrial economy. Paralleling these developments has been the growth of large towns, with the concomitant shift in the residence of the average Englishman from the country to the city. Another layer has been the growing involvement of the state in attempts to control the less desirable aspects of industrialization and urban growth. Political developments such as the extension of the franchise, the granting of female suffrage, and the emergence of working class associations have comprised another layer of change. Educational developments may be viewed as a final layer of change, paralleling the underlying strata of political, social, and governmental development. Each of the basic layers of change has had an important influence upon the educational structure of the English nation, and the country's educational network has been as thoroughly transformed during the last two centuries as have the nation's other institutions.

If we use administrative developments as our terms of reference, it appears that English educational events have followed a path of logical and predictable development. At the turn of the nineteenth century England was a nation dependent on informal means of education for the civilization of the bulk of its population. Granted, the upper classes were already using the formal institutions of the grammar or public school and the university, but the majority of their inferiors received scant formal training. The education of the lower and agricultural classes took place chiefly within the individual family. Colquhoun estimated that, in 1806, 2,000,000 children in England and Wales were receiving no schooling whatsoever. Alexander Murry claimed that in 1810 three-quarters of the nation's farm

[3] G. M. Young and W. D. Handcock (ed.), *English historical documents, 1833–1874* (London, 1956), p. 3.

6

labourers were unable to read. The returns of 1819 revealed that the number of children attending schools was only one-fifteenth of the entire population.[4]

If early nineteenth-century England remained a country dependent upon informal means of education, these informal means were rapidly being displaced by formal mechanisms, as informal institutions crumbled before the onslaught of social change. The obvious example of the breakdown of informal methods is the transformation of the family from an agrarian economic unit into a series of almost autonomous members, all working at different jobs in different places, in the city. A less obvious example is the rapid decline of apprenticeship during the latter half of the eighteenth century and the early nineteenth century. If we view the apprenticeship system as an arrangement in which the master was a surrogate father to the apprentice, it becomes apparent that the apprenticeship system was a replication of home education. Like the family, it was an informal mechanism of education, for the training of the apprentice was only a secondary accomplishment of an activity that was essentially economic rather than educational. Sixteenth- and seventeenth-century legislation required that a seven-year period of apprenticeship be compulsory for those who wished to enter most industrial callings. During the eighteenth century the system broke down in certain branches of the woollen trade and by the last quarter of the century in all departments of the woollen, knitting, and calico trades. The apprenticeship clauses regarding the wool trade were set aside permanently in 1809, and following the report of an investigatory committee appointed in 1812, the statute of artificers was repealed for all trades in 1814.[5]

Early nineteenth-century England, then, was a nation largely dependent upon informal methods of educating its young, methods that were becoming less and less effective. As informal ways of education declined, formal methods came to the fore. A number of voluntary societies arose, intent on providing formal schooling for the working classes. The prototype of these

[4] Elie Halevy, *England in 1815* (New York, 1961, originally published, 1913), p. 532.
[5] O. Jocelyn Dunlop, *English apprenticeship and child labour* (London, 1912), passim.

societies was the Society for Promoting Christian Knowledge, founded in 1699. For our purposes the significance of the Society for Promoting Christian Knowledge lies in its attempt to use schooling as an antidote for disorder and heathenism among the poor.[6] The rapid rise of the Sunday schools in the years after 1780 provides another instance of the provision of formal educational institutions by voluntary bodies. Although hardly a new idea, the idea of schooling children on Sunday became a popular idea only after Robert Raikes, sole proprietor and editor of the *Gloucester Journal*, used his paper to publicize his educational efforts with local children. The idea spread with extraordinary rapidity. By 1795 the Sunday School Society claimed 1,012 schools and 65,000 scholars.[7] It was calculated in 1820 that 477,225 children were attending Sunday schools in England and Wales.[8]

The most important voluntary societies, however, were neither the Society for Promoting Christian Knowledge, nor the Sunday school unions, but the British and Foreign School Society and the National Society for Promoting the Education of the Poor in the Principles of the Established Church throughout England and Wales. The British and Foreign School Society was an outgrowth of the work of Joseph Lancaster, the popularizer of the 'monitorial system'. After Lancaster lost control, between 1812 and 1814, of the society that he had founded, the society became increasingly identified as the educational society of the dissenting churches.

As its name implies, the National Society, founded in 1811, served as the established church's educational arm. The growth of these societies was rapid, and roughly 1,000,000 children were thought to be under education in schools of the voluntary societies in the early 1830s.[9] Thus, by 1830, formal schooling for large numbers of the working classes had become an established fact of English social life.

Up to 1833 the schools of the voluntary societies were sup-

---

[6] See, M. G. Jones, *The charity school movement, a study of eighteenth-century puritanism in action* (London, 1964, originally published, 1938), passim.

[7] Alfred Gregory, *Robert Raikes, journalist and philanthropist* (London, 1877), p. 104.

[8] Halevy, p. 528; Young and Handcock, p. 847.

[9] Young and Handcock, p. 847.

ported solely through private philanthropy. In that year the government took a major step and granted aid to each of the two major voluntary societies. The state's financial commitment grew sharply, rising from £20,000 in 1833 to £836,920 in 1859.[10] With government money came indirect government control. A committee of council on education was created in 1839 to supervise the grant. The committee's rudimentary inspectorial powers were greatly enhanced by the revised code of 1862 under which grants were allocated according to student performance on standard examinations. The state, through its grants policy, gained indirect control over the content of the curriculum of the voluntary schools. All through the middle years of the nineteenth century the voluntary societies continued to grow with the help of government money: in 1867 the established church's day schools had about one and a half million children on their books.[11]

Having granted aid to, and having assumed indirect control over, the schools of the voluntary societies, the state took, in 1870, the next logical step: it began to supplement the voluntary schools with schools of its own. The Forster act of 1870 required that in areas in which the voluntary schools were inadequate, school boards were to be created. These boards were empowered to establish public elementary schools and to strike a school rate. The school attendance act of 1880 introduced compulsory attendance for children between the ages of five and ten. In 1891, a government fee grant of ten shillings per student made elementary education effectively free. The result of the introduction of free and compulsory schooling was to guarantee that eventually the voluntary schools would become less important than the state schools. The flood of children implied by compulsion and by the ten shilling fee grant almost swamped the voluntary schools. The board schools, on the other hand, spread with the tide, since their support came from rate aid, a source of income much more elastic than the subscriptions of the

[10] H. C. Barnard, *A history of English education, from 1760* (London, second ed., 1961), p. 69. Besides growing in size, the grants came to be available to other voluntary societies in addition to the two original recipients.

[11] G. Kitson-Clark, *The making of Victorian England* (London, and Cambridge, Mass., 1962), p. 174.

voluntary schools. In 1880, 14,181 of the 17,614 elementary schools in the country were voluntary. Yet by 1900, the voluntary schools taught only forty-six per cent of the total elementary school population.[12]

By 1900 the trend of events was clear. The state was gradually displacing the voluntary schools with state schools, just as surely as the voluntary schools had displaced the informal means of education. The Balfour act of 1902 was a landmark in this process. It provided for the supervision of all board schools and state-aided voluntary schools in a given county or county borough by a local education authority established for that area. For the first time, the local education authorities were empowered to provide rate aid to the voluntary schools. In return for their money, the local education authorities obtained the right to nominate one-third of the managers of each of the voluntary schools under its jurisdiction. The education act of 1918, and especially the education act of 1944, extended the control of the state over the voluntary schools. The 1944 act gave the financially pressed voluntary schools two options: they could become 'controlled schools' and cede all financial obligations to the local education authorities, along with their right to appoint teachers (except religious teachers) or they could become 'aided schools', keeping almost all of their old manager's rights, but receiving in most cases only a fifty per cent grant from the state for building expenses. Most voluntary schools opted for the former status.

We have seen that a slow revolution in English education has occurred within the last two hundred years. This revolution was gradual and logical. Informal education was slowly supplanted by formal institutions. At first, schools were provided solely by voluntary societies. Later the state granted aid to the voluntary schools, exacting some degree of control in return for its money. The next step was the supplementing of the voluntary schools with state institutions. Finally, both voluntary and board schools were united in a single network. In this network almost all of the school revenue comes from the state and almost all educational control belongs to it.

At this point it is logical to ask, 'what relationship does this pattern have to the layers of social and economic change we

[12] Barnard, p. 168.

mentioned earlier'? One form of relationship is that of correlation: the pattern of educational events has paralleled that in some of the other areas. For example, for the state to intervene increasingly in the education of the nation's children is similar to the tendency for the state to intervene more and more in everyday economic and social life. The professionalization of the civil service is paralleled by the professionalization of all levels of educational endeavour. And the greater availability of school places to children of the lower social classes is an analogue to the extension of political enfranchisement to adults of the working class.

Correlation does not prove causation. Nevertheless, it is reasonable to suggest that educational developments, beside paralleling fundamental changes in English society, were caused by these events. A number of cases may be pointed to as confirming this common-sense conclusion. For instance, the fact that a number of factory acts, notably those of 1833 and 1844, contained compulsory education clauses indicates that the problems raised by industrialization sometimes forced recourse to educational solutions. Similarly, the fact that the school boards rose most swiftly in the urban areas points to a casual relationship of urbanization and increasing state involvement in education. Robert Lowe's emphasis on the need to educate the classes enfranchised by the 1867 reform act suggests that the forces producing political democracy had educational effects as well. Surveying the changes which took place in nineteenth- and twentieth-century England, it appears that as the nation has become more advanced, its educational system has become increasingly formal, and more and more a department of the state.

At this point a Scot might well object that his homeland possessed a network of schools long before it became an industrial nation, and that Scotland presents a crushing contrast to the English pattern of educational growth. At first glance he would seem to have a good case, for Scotland was covered with a blanket of parish schools by the early eighteenth century, the maintenance of these schools being required by statute. If we examine the situation more closely, however, we will find that the parish schools were nearer to being extensions of the family than to being instruments of the central government's social policy. Further, we will find that the schools were the concern and a responsibility of the presbyterian church rather than of a secular government. Thus, at most, the parish schools were voluntary schools coordinated by the agency of the general assembly in much the same way that the English voluntary schools were coordinated by the various voluntary societies.

It is customary, and correct, to point to the demands of the presbyterian religion as the source of much of the early Scottish concern with education. An educational imperative was built into the Scots' faith, for presbyterianism demands both a learned clergy and literate laity. Formal schooling was an inevitable part of the Church of Scotland's social policy. John Knox's Book of Discipline, issued in 1560, enunciated an elaborate plan for four levels of education to be built upon the foundations abandoned by the church of Rome. In every upland and rural area a school was to be taught by the reader or minister of the parish. Two years of schooling, from six to eight years of age, were to be given. In the larger villages a grammar school was to be created and a schoolmaster hired to teach grammar and Latin, for children ages eight to twelve. Every major town was to be the seat of a high school or college providing a four-year course in the liberal arts. Finally, boys of high ability were to pass to one of the universities for an eight-year course, lasting from age sixteen to age twenty-four.[13]

Little came of the plan, but in 1616 the privy council commanded that a school be established in each parish. This decree was not enforced. In 1633 the decree was passed as a statute, but continued to be ineffective, as were the education acts passed during the civil wars. Finally, in 1696, a workable statute made the presbyterian dream of an educated polity an actuality. A school was required to be maintained in each parish. The maintenance of the school was paid from a tax divided evenly between the occupiers of the land and the owners. If the heritors failed to create a school the presbytery could apply to the shire authorities to enforce the tax.[14] As a result of this act the nation possessed a surprisingly advanced scheme of education: schools

[13] Alexander Morgan, *Rise and progress of Scottish education* (Edinburgh, 1927), pp 50–1.
[14] George S. Pryde, *Scotland, from 1603 to the present day* (London, 1962), pp 5, 35–6.

were systematically planted throughout the country, rate aid was made available, and central government sanctions were brought to bear on recalcitrant parishes.

We should note, however, that the system in some way appeared more sophisticated than it actually was. The parish, whose responsibility it was to create the schools, should not be equated with a modern unit of local government, such as a county or county borough council. It should be viewed more as a social and a religious unit than as an administrative entity. It is as true of pre-industrial Scotland as of pre-industrial England that the parish was a nexus of persons related by blood or marriage, and that it could be viewed as one large extended family. The Scottish clan system reinforced the kinship nature of the parish. Hence, in voting a rate to aid education, the Scottish parishes were not serving the purposes of the distant central government but were simply moving to take care of their own children.

If the parish was a family unit, it was also a religious one. Here it must be underscored that in social matters—notably poor relief and education—the parish authorities were agents of the Church of Scotland, and that the British parliament allowed the church's control to continue until the disruption of 1843.[15] Thus, the church acted as a voluntary body, coordinating education in much the same way as was done by voluntary bodies in England. Unlike the English voluntary bodies the Scots' kirk very early received state aid, through rates, and the power to invoke state processes in dealing with recalcitrant parishes.[16]

Another indication that the Scottish parochial system was not

---

[15] George S. Pryde, *Central and local government in Scotland since 1707* (London, 1960), p. 16.

[16] In addition to Morgan and to Pryde's *Scotland, from 1603 to the present day*, see William J. Gibson, *Education in Scotland, a sketch of the past and present* (London, 1912), pp 39–90; Anthony J. C. Kerr, *Scottish education, school and university, from early times to 1908* (Cambridge, Eng., 1910), pp 196–206; Henry M. Knox, *Two hundred and fifty years of Scottish education, 1696–1946* (Edinburgh, 1953), pp 3–13; Stewart Mechie, *The church and Scottish social development, 1780–1870* (London, 1960), pp 136–9; John M. Reid, *Scotland, past and present* (London, 1959), pp. 87–94; Alexander Wright, *The history of education and of the old parish schools of Scotland* (Edinburgh, 1898), pp 57–64, 82–178.

as advanced as it appears at first glance is found in the fact that the system disintegrated when faced with social and industrial change. We do not need to describe the Scottish social revolution of the nineteenth century in detail, but should note that the pattern of developments was similar to the English pattern. Like England, Scotland has undergone a continuing expansion of its population. From 1,608,420 in 1801 the population grew to 4,472,103 in 1901[17] to 5,178,490 in 1961.[18] Industrial change affected Scotland as much as it affected England, centring first in the cotton industry and then, after 1830, in the metal industries. As in England, the population became largely urban and increasingly concentrated in the lowlands. The population of the highlands and the western isles declined from one-fifth of that of Scotland (about 300,000) in 1801 to one-twentieth (about 293,000) in 1931.[19] By 1931 the country's population was slightly more than eighty per cent urban.[20] One result of the Victorian economic and social revolution was that the old parochial form of government proved incapable of dealing with new social problems. The situation became acute after the disruption of 1843 when the splits in the church reduced it from a national church to a collection of sectarian bodies. Hence, the civil powers of the ecclesiastical parish had to be gradually withdrawn.[21]

When it became clear that the parish schools were unable to cope with the needs of an industrial population the government created 'sessional schools' to supplement them. Over one hundred of these were serving the children of Edinburgh, Glasgow, and other large towns in the first quarter of the nineteenth century.[22] In 1834 the central government began aiding Scottish education by providing £10,000 annually to aid the building and maintenance of parish schools. An act of 1838 extended the parish school to the *quoad sacra* parishes (parishes created for ecclesiastical purposes in ill-served urban areas). Under

---

[17] Newman A. Wade, *Post-primary education in the primary schools of Scotland, 1872–1936* (London, 1939), table I, p. 12.

[18] *Britain, an official handbook* (London, 1964), p. 17.

[19] Charles, L. Mowat, *Britain between the wars, 1918–1940* (London and Chicago, 1955), p. 469.

[20] Wade, table II, p. 15.

[21] Pryde, *Central and local government in Scotland since 1701*, p. 16.

[22] Pryde, *Scotland, from 1603 to the present day*, p. 164.

the act the government provided the teacher's salary. There were 695 of these 'parliamentary schools' built between 1839 and 1864.[23] The disruption resulted in the withdrawal of numerous free church children from the parish schools and the creation of a rival set of schools to those of the established church.

The chaos caused by the concentration of the population in the cities, and by the subsequent overloading of the parochial network, coupled with the undercutting of that network by the disruption, made it inevitable that the state would have to step in with more than money. Finally, in 1872, an act similar to England's Forster act removed from the established church the last of the local session's civil functions: education. The act created school boards with rating power, introduced compulsory schooling and placed the school boards under a committee of the privy council known as the Scotch Education Department. Thereafter, education acts of 1901, 1918, 1929, and 1945 brought the Scottish system into groove with the English.[24] Scotland, then, developed an advanced system of education only when faced with the problems of an advanced nation.

When we return to Ireland after having seen that the English and the Scots obtained state systems of mass education only after undergoing economic and social revolutions, we can only be surprised to find Ireland in possession of a state system of schools almost a full four decades before either of its neighbours. Ireland before the famine was an 'underdeveloped country', even if no one had yet thought to use the term. It was swamped with a tide of rising population. The majority of its people were farmers, barely surviving by subsistence farming. Agricultural productivity throughout the country was low, and the system of landholding effectively prevented agrarian improvements. Industry was only a minor sector of the economy. The average income of the people was low, and they lived under extremely poor housing conditions. It would be folly, therefore, to try to explain

[23] Ibid., p. 267.
[24] On nineteenth- and twentieth-century Scottish educational developments, see Gibson, pp. 91–149; J. Kerr, pp 182–206, 274–93; Knox, pp 23–68, 107–20, 175–92, 208–42; Mechie, pp 138–53; Morgan, pp 164–211; Pryde, *Scotland, from 1603 to the present day*, pp 163–4, 206, 267–70, 309–10; Wade, pp 40–252.

Irish educational events by referring to the patterns of industrial and urban development advanced to explain educational progress in other countries.

The following two chapters will examine the constellation of circumstances that made possible the creation of the Irish national system of education in 1831.

II

THE EIGHTEENTH-CENTURY
BACKGROUND

~~~~~~

I

IT IS IMPOSSIBLE TO find a single, simple reason why the Irish
national system appeared at such a relatively early date as 1831.
Instead, we must look for a combination of reasons. In this
chapter and the succeeding chapter five factors will be discussed, each of which was contributory—and probably necessary—to the creation of the system. The first strand of the
explanation concerns the government of Ireland. Ireland, whatever its formal status throughout the eighteenth and nineteenth
centuries, was governed as a crown colony. Legislative intervention in everyday life occurred much more freely than in
England, often dealing with matters about which it would have
been unthinkable to legislate in England in the same period.
Second, Ireland had a tradition of legislative intervention in
educational affairs that considerably antedates the English
parliament's first faltering steps of 1833.

Given, then, that the government in Ireland intervened with
impunity in everyday affairs, and that it had a considerable
history of passing education legislation, a third important pre-
condition for the establishment of the Irish national system of
education will be discussed: the Irish peasantry showed a
striking desire for their children to be schooled, and thus a
willingness to support any reasonable educational arrangement

17

the central government might provide. Fourth, the next chapter will suggest that in the first three decades of the nineteenth century an official consensus emerged about the way a state system of schools should be constructed. Into this consensus were woven the opinions of M.P.s, Castle officials, and catholic prelates. Hence, unlike England, Ireland in the first third of the nineteenth century possessed a body of educational opinion that could be easily crystallized into an educational structure that would be readily accepted by the majority of the nation's power brokers. Finally, the roles of individual personalities in the complicated business of bartering and lobbying that led to the creation in 1831 of the national system will be discussed.

The government of Ireland in the eighteenth century was characterized by two qualities: confusion and a colonial mentality. Confusion in this case does not refer to administrative inefficiency, although the government was nothing if not inefficient. Rather, it refers to a situation in which the governmental structure was crazy, complex, and so dependent upon long defunct statutes and concepts that an economical and coherent discussion of the Irish administration is impossible. The root of this confusion was the method by which the government of Ireland came to rule the country of Ireland. Until 1603, English civil administration was securely established only in the Pale, and it was only in the last decade of the seventeenth century that English control held firm throughout the country. After the whole of Ireland fell under English control laws and procedures that had been shaped to meet the conditions of the Pale were extended to the entire nation. Needless to say, the laws that worked reasonably well in the Pale did not work as well in the rest of the country. Unfortunately for historical clarity, the outdated laws and procedures remained on the books, and although the Ireland of the eighteenth century was not the Ireland of the sixteenth century, many of the laws, and the vocabulary of those laws, were still those of the sixteenth century. This fact should serve as a warning to those who think that they can discover what Irish government was like in the eighteenth century simply by reading formal statements of practice and procedures, and also to those who wish to look at the country's eighteenth-century government in twentieth or, for that matter, even nineteenth-century terms. In such a situation, where the

18

formal and legal statements of laws and procedures did not correspond to the reality of everyday practice, and in which no scholar has yet fully defined the actual procedures and the operative laws, we must work under a shadow of obscurity that ranges from mild ambiguity to complete ignorance.

The one pattern of behaviour that can be unhesitatingly ascribed to the eighteenth-century Irish administration may be described in the term 'colonial mentality'. C. T. Grenville wrote the duke of Rutland in 1784 that 'Ireland is too great to be unconnected with us, and too near us to be dependent on a foreign state, and too little to be independent'.[1] An examination of the governmental arrangements of pre-Union Ireland provides ample evidence of the peremptory manner in which Ireland was treated. The king of England was the king of Ireland simply because Henry VIII had decided that he preferred to be king of Ireland rather than 'lord'. When the statutes altering the succession to the throne were passed in England they were not re-enacted in Ireland, but merely accepted. The king had considerably greater powers in Ireland than in England. A much larger proportion of the Irish revenue was granted to the crown in perpetuity than in England; hence, the crown's financial position was relatively stronger than in England. Irish judges were under royal appointment and held office only during the king's pleasure.

The king's representative in Ireland was the lord lieutenant, under whom the remainder of the Irish administration, headed by the chief secretary, served. Nowhere is the colony mentality of Ireland's rulers so clearly seen as in the fact that prior to the union the lord lieutenant, the head of the Irish executive, was not responsible to the Irish parliament but to the English parliament. Without the ability to overthrow an executive of which it disapproved, the Irish nation lacked any semblance of responsible government. Not only was Ireland ruled by a virtually unshakable English executive, but the Irish parliament was subjugated to the English privy council. Under the Poynings' Law system, bills had to be submitted by the Irish privy council to the English privy council for its approval, rejection, or amendment. The bill was then returned to the Irish parliament where the

[1] Edith M. Johnston, *Great Britain and Ireland, 1760–1800, a study in political administration* (Edinburgh, 1963), p. 1.

version of the bill handed down by the English privy council had either to be accepted or rejected in full. Amendment was forbidden, but while parliament was sitting new 'heads of bills' might be transmitted to London for approval by the English privy council, and if approved might be enacted into law by the Irish parliament. Irish parliamentary subordination to England was extended by the declaratory act of 1719, which affirmed the right of the British parliament to make laws for Ireland and denied the appellate jurisdiction of the Irish house of lords. Although the declaratory act was repealed in 1782, and Poynings' Law so modified as to forbid the origination, altering, or suppression of bills by either the Irish or the English privy council, this meant little. Before any bill became law it still had to be approved by the lord lieutenant, over whom the Irish parliament had no control. In any event, freedom of legislation would have been meaningless, since the executive branch of the Irish government was responsible only to the English cabinet.[2]

Because England ruled Ireland as if it were a colony fiat measures were not only permissible, but were usual. Time and time again the English government forced measures upon Ireland which would never have been approved in the home country. Moreover, legislation initiated in Ireland often dealt with matters untouched by the law in England. Education was one of the areas in which the Irish parliament, with English approval, legislated long before the beginning of the nineteenth century. By the end of the eighteenth century the Irish parliament had aided all levels of schooling, from primary schools to intermediate institutions to university foundations. A recognition of this tradition of state provision in Irish education is essential to an understanding of the creation of the national school system. None of the state's attempts prior to the union to provide schools could be described as successful, but that is not the point; the point is that a legislating tendency in educational matters existed in Ireland and that this tendency was not extinguished by the union with England.

Michael Sadler, in one of his 'special reports' published in the

[2] J. C. Beckett, 'The Irish parliament in the eighteenth century', *Belfast Natur. Hist. Soc. Proc.*, series 2, iv (1950–55), pp 17–37; J. G. S. MacNeill, *The Irish parliament; what it was and what it did* (London, third ed., 1886), pp 31–68.

late nineteenth century, claimed that 'national education in Ireland began in 1537, when the Irish parliament established parochial schools . . .'.[3] Although one may question Sadler's claim that Henry VIII's educational efforts were the beginning of 'national' education, we can certainly agree that educational legislation at such an early date is noteworthy. Under Poynings' Law, no bill could be considered by the Irish parliament until it had been approved by the English privy council, of which the king was the dominant figure. When the Irish parliament passed the parish schools measure (28 Henry VIII, c. 15), it was enacting a piece of legislation approved by the English government as part of its Irish policy. The act was not a product of random circumstances, but a considered instrument of that policy.

The act may be divided into four parts. The first, the preamble, established the act's purpose as indicated in the following extract:

The king's majestie, our most gracious and redoubted sovereigne lord, prepending and waying by his great widsom, learning, and experience, how much it doth more conferre to the induction of rude and ignorant people to the knowledge of almighty God, and of the good and virtuous obedience which by his most holy precepts and commandments they owe to their princes and superiors, then a good instruction in his most blessed laws, with a conformitie, coincidence, and familiarity in language, tongue, in manners, order, and apparel, with them that be civil people, and do profess and knowledge Christ's religion, and civil and politique orders, laws, and directions, as his grace's subjects of this part of this his land of Ireland, that is called the English Pale, doth most graciously, considering that there is again nothing which doth more conteyne and keep many of his subjects of the said land in a certain savage and wilde kind and manner of living, then the diversitie that is betwixt them in tongue, language, order, and habit.[4]

The next segment provided that the Irish manner of dress and of wearing the hair should be discontinued. The subsequent section required:

[3] Michael E. Sadler, 'The history of the Irish system of elementary education', Michael E. Sadler (ed.), *Special reports on educational subjects, 1896-97* (London, 1897), p. 211.

[4] Quoted in *Report from the commissioners of the board of education in Ireland; eleventh report, parish schools*, p. 269, H. C. 1813-14 (47), p. v; originally printed, 1810-11 (107), p. vi; also reprinted, H. C. 1821 (743), p. xi.

That every person or persons the king's true subjects inhabiting this land of Ireland, of what estate, condition, or degree he or they may be or shall be, to the uttermost of their power, cunning, and knowledge, shall use and speake commonly the English tongue and language; and that every such person and persons having childe or children, shall endeavour themselfe to cause and procure his said childe and children to use and speake the English tongue and language, and according to his or their abilitie, cunning, and power, shall bring up his said childe and children in such places where they shall or may have occasion to learn the English tongue, language, order, and condition.[5]

In order to effect the provisions regarding the English language, spiritual promotion was, with certain exceptions, to be limited to those speaking English. Further, all those taking orders were to take an oath to endeavour to learn English and to read and teach it to all under their jurisdiction, and to preach in English. Most important, all those taking orders were required to keep, or cause to be kept, an English school within the vicarage or rectory in which they were situated. Thus, a network of schools, one to each parish, was to be created.

Several points should be made about the parish schools act. In the first place the act is obviously noteworthy because of its early date. The Scottish parish schools act was not passed until 1696, and the English parliament did not enact a local schools statute until 1870. Second, it is important to underscore the fact that the Tudor statute applied only to the Pale and its marches. Like the statutes of Kilkenny, with which it can be usefully compared, it was a fundamentally defensive measure aimed at preserving the loyalty of the Anglo-Irish and at recapturing that of the fallen-away 'rebel English', especially those of the poorer classes. It was not aimed at the native Irish. Third, with the extension of firm English control to the entire country of Ireland during the seventeenth century, the law was extended to the entire country but with significant modifications in its provisions. Fourth, we should be very chary of making dogmatic statements about the specific workings of the parish schools act because on a number of points precise information is lacking. For instance, it is unclear to what extent an organized parish system existed in Tudor Ireland and also uncertain when it was completed in the

[5] Ibid., pp 269–70.

remainder of the country. Further, although it is certain that the ecclesiastical parish was the axis of the statute in Tudor times, and that the civil parish had replaced the ecclesiastical parish by 1800, it cannot yet be known when and by what process the one was replaced by the other. The act's working should be surveyed with these cautions in mind.

Inertia was the system's early enemy. Despite the threat of a scale of fines and the possibility of loss of benefice for failure to comply with the law, the parish clergy did not budge. R. Barry O'Brien doubted if any parish schools whatsoever were built in Henry VIII's reign and questioned if any serious effort was made to enforce the legislation during his reign or, indeed, until the Restoration.[6] Some of the clerical reluctance to carry out the act's provisions can be ascribed to the wretched circumstances plaguing many of the clergy. Plundered by adventurers and bled by the higher clergy, the lower clergy of the established church in Ireland retained few of the resources of the old Roman Catholic church. Hence, the government found it necessary to pass further legislation to shore up the mythical system.

The Tudor statute was renewed in 1695 by the Irish parliament (7 Will. III, c. 4). Parliament enacted 'that the act of Henry VIII, whereby it was provided that every incumbent should keep or cause to be kept an English schoole, should thenceforth be strictly observed and put into execution.'[7] A later Irish statute (8 Geo. I, c. 12) entitled 'An act for the better enabling of the clergy having cure of souls, to reside upon their respective benefices; and for the encouragement of protestant schools within this kingdom of Ireland' enabled clergy and higher clergy to grant land in each parish for the endowing of a resident protestant schoolmaster. Archbishops and bishops were allowed to make an absolute grant to the churchwardens of each parish of two acres, the lesser clergy a grant of one acre. The right of nominating the schoolmaster was retained by the person

---

[6] R. Barry O'Brien, *Fifty years of concessions to Ireland, 1831–1881* (London, 1885), i, 16.

[7] Quoted in Thomas Wyse, *Speech of Thomas Wyse, Esq., M.P., in the house of commons on Tuesday, May 19, 1835, on moving leave to bring in a bill for the establishment of a board of national education, and the advancement of elementary education in Ireland* (Dublin, 1835), p. 31.

making the grant, and the schoolmaster was to be licensed by the archbishop or bishop of the diocese. The last eighteenth-century statute containing provisions dealing with parish schools (5 Geo. II, c. 4) allowed holders of certain tenancies to grant an acre of thirty shillings yearly value to the church-wardens to support parish education. Parish schools finally began to appear in the early years of the eighteenth century but did not become common until the middle of the century. As the system emerged it became increasingly clear that the eighteenth-century reality did not match the sixteenth-century theory. This was because the conditions referred to in the 1537 act had all but vanished along with the distinction between the Pale and the mere Irish. Whereas the Tudor statute focused upon the teaching of the English language and customs, the renewing acts emphasized the advancement of the Protestant religion. As the schools became identified as proselytizing agencies, catholics grew reluctant to enroll their children.[8]

If we examine the statistical evidence on the parish schools, it quickly becomes apparent that at best they were pitifully few. A report of 1791, based on returns for the year 1788, revealed that of the 838 benefices reporting, only 361 contained operative parish schools. In seventy-four of the benefices the clergymen paid the salary of forty shillings yearly to someone who did not keep school. In the rest of the benefices the clergy neither paid a schoolmaster's salary nor caused a school to be kept. The same returns estimated that roughly 11,000 children were being educated in parish schools.[9] A return of 1810 covered 736 of the 1,125 benefices in Ireland. Five hundred forty-nine parish schools were reported. Only about half of these schools, how-ever, were granted the luxury of being conducted in a school-house of their own. Slightly more than 23,000 students were enrolled.[10] A later report, based on information obtained in

---

[8] James Godkin, *Education in Ireland; its history, institutions, system, statistics and progress, from the earliest times to the present* (London and Dublin, 1862), p. 21; O'Brien, i, 16–17; Philip O'Connell, *The schools and scholars of Breifne* (Dublin, 1942), p. 224; *Report from the commissioners of the board of education in Ireland: eleventh report, parish schools*, pp 271–2.

[9] Cited in *Report from the commissioners of the board of education in Ireland: eleventh report, parish schools*, p. 273.

[10] Ibid., pp. 273, 277.

1823, stated that the number of parish schools had grown to 782. Some 36,498 children were enrolled, 21,195 of whom were protestant, 15,303 of whom were catholic.[11] By 1823 the Irish population had soared past the six million mark. Against such a background the parish school enrollment seems small indeed.

The eleventh report of the commissioners of the board of education stands as the best available contemporary judgement of the parish schools. The report concluded as follows:

First, That for the original objects of their institution, namely, the introduction and diffusion of the English language in Ireland, the parish schools can no longer be deemed necessary.

Second, That for the purposes to which they were afterwards converted, namely, the advancement of the protestant religion, and the education of the lower classes, they have proved in a certain degree useful, where they have been continued, but in both respects inadequate, on account of the extent and population of the several parishes . . .

But we are fully persuaded of their inadequacy, as a system of general education of the poor, even if it were practicable to establish an effective one in every union . . .[12]

The concern of the Tudors with educational legislation had not ended with the passage of Henry VIII's parish schools act. During Elizabeth's reign the Irish parliament created another set of educational institutions, the 'diocesan schools'. In England the founding or refounding of grammar schools was a common practice during the sixteenth century. Similar foundations were urged for Ireland. Hugh Brady, protestant bishop of Meath, founded a free school at Trim and was a powerful advocate of further foundations. Adam Loftus, protestant archbishop of Dublin, Sir Henry Sidney, the lord deputy, and Chancellor Weston, gave their support to the cause. Hence, a petition was addressed to the Queen and a draft bill was prepared for submission to the Dublin parliament for the establishment of a system of free grammar schools. The bill was rejected by the

[11] *First report of the commissioners of Irish education inquiry, appendix*, pp. 14–15, H.C. 1825 (400), xii.

[12] *Report from the commissioners of the board of education in Ireland:* eleventh report, parish schools, pp 275–6.

February–March 1569 sitting of the Irish parliament. Apparently, opposition to the bill came from those who would have to pay for the schools. The bill was slightly revised and reintroduced when parliament reconvened in late May 1570.[13]

The act (12 Elizabeth I, c. 1), like the parish schools act of Henry VIII, was essentially defensive, in this case being intended to shore up the drifting allegiance of the Anglo-Irish middle classes. Like the 1537 act of Henry VIII, it began with a denunciation of those who lived in 'rude and barbarous states, not understanding that almighty God hath by his divine laws, forbidden the manifold and haynous offences, which they spare not dailey and hourely to commit and perpetrate'. It was therefore enacted 'that there shall be from henceforth a free schoole within every diocesse of this realm of Ireland, and that the schoolmaster shall be an Englishman, or of the English birth of this realm'.[14] The right of nominating schoolmasters in their dioceses was to be maintained by the archbishops of Armagh and of Dublin, and by the bishops of Meath and of Kildare. In all other dioceses the lord deputy was to exercise the right of nomination. Schoolhouses were to be built in the principal town of each diocese and where schoolhouses were not already extant the cost was to be spread upon the entire diocese.

The diocesan schools began with a handicap, since the Irish parliament was far from enthusiastic about them and had passed the diocesan schools act only under mild duress. Diocesan schools did not spring immediately into bloom; Quane quotes the lord deputy that, in 1584, the schools were 'for the most part, not kept or maintained'.[15] Nevertheless, a number eventually came into being, although it is difficult to determine their number or quality before the restoration. The diocesan school system, like the parish school system, had to be buttressed by additional legislation. An amending act of 1662 provided for the transfer of schools from inconvenient places. The Williamite act to restrain foreign education (7 William III, c. 4) referred to the

[13] Michael Quane, 'The diocesan schools—1570–1870', *Journal of the Cork Historical and Archaeological Society*, 2 ser., lxvi (Jan.–June, 1961), pp 26–31.
[14] Quoted ibid., p. 30.
[15] Ibid., p. 31.

Elizabethan statute and required that all previously enacted education statutes be enforced. In 1725, members of the protestant hierarchy were empowered to set apart sites of one acre apiece for diocesan schools, provided such provision had not already been made, and, in 1755, grand juries were empowered to tax their respective counties for the building and repair of diocesan schools. Neither of these powers seems to have been much used.[16] Parenthetically, the provision for grand jury involvement in education is significant for it points to an increasing separation of ecclesiastical and civil institutions during the eighteenth century, as well as to an increasing subservience of the church to the state in matters of importance.

Unlike the parish schools, the diocesan schools taught higher subjects as well as elementary literacy, and, in contrast to the parish schools, the few diocesan schools that did exist were usually peopled with children of the middle classes. The report of 1791 revealed that of the thirty-four dioceses, only eighteen possessed schools, educating a total of 324 students.[17] The commissioners of the board of education found seventeen diocesan schools in operation in 1808–1809. Eleven of these schools had their own separate schoolhouses, of which one was in a 'ruinous state', another 'begun twelve years ago, but never finished', a third a thatched cabin, 'in tolerable repair'. Four hundred thirty-two students were enrolled, thirteen of them free scholars. One of the schools boasted one student, another six.[18] A return of 1831 showed twelve diocesan schools, enrolling 419 students of whom seventy-four were free scholars.[19]

The early Stuarts followed Tudor precedent and dabbled in education. Their efforts, centring on the 'royal schools', were

[16] Ibid., pp 33–4; O'Brien, i, 19.

[17] Wyse, p. 33.

[18] *Report from the commissioners of the board of education, fourth report, diocesan free schools, appendix*, pp 116–17, H. C. 1813–14 (47), v; originally printed 1810 (174), x.

[19] *A return from the different diocesan and other endowed schools under the superintendence of the commissioners of education in Ireland; of the number of scholars taught in each school, at the period of January 1831; specifying the number of those from whose education, board and lodging, payment is made from private means and the number of those who are free scholars taught gratuitously at each school; with an account or the salary and emolument attached to such schools from their foundation or establishment*, p. 1, H. C. 1831 (106), xv.

ultimately as fruitless as those of their predecessors. As part of the scheme of settling Ulster, James I aimed at a system of grammar schools in the plantation counties. The 'project for the plantation' required that a free school be founded in each of the counties of Armagh, Cavan, Derry, Donegal, Fermanagh, and Tyrone, and land was to be reserved in each county for the maintenance of these schools. Despite the government's intentions, the Ulster colonists made little effort to found free schools. Hence, in 1612, James directed the lord deputy to see that the lands marked for school sites were immediately conveyed to the respective bishops. Once again, nothing was done, and in 1614, James again wrote the lord deputy this time ordering that the lands be given over to the archbishop of Armagh who was to select the school sites. Letters patent of 20 April 1616 confirmed this order. In 1618 James was still complaining that the lands had not been conveyed to the archbishop, although the primate had by that time appointed several of the schoolmasters. Eventually, by 1621, four schools were established in counties Tyrone, Derry, Fermanagh, and Cavan. The Derry royal school never came into existence but a free school was founded at Derry by a private benefactor, Matthias Springham, of London. The school for Tyrone failed. Schools for Armagh and Donegal were established about 1625.[20]

On James I's wobbly foundation, Charles I attempted to build. In 1626, he made re-grants of the land his father had given for educational endowments. The grants in the counties of Armagh, Tyrone, Fermanagh, Donegal, and Cavan were once again made to the archbishop of Armagh and his successors in perpetuity. Charles made no grant to Derry since there was some indication that the London Irish Society there may have intercepted the endowment originally intended for the Derry foundation. In 1629, Charles created a second set of royal schools by granting lands for schools in the boroughs of Banagher in King's County and of Carysfort in County Wicklow.

[20] O'Brien, i, 21–4; O'Connell, p. 80; James I to Chichester, 30 Jan. 1612, quoted in Timothy Corcoran, *Education systems in Ireland, from the close of the middle ages* (Dublin, 1928) p. 22; T. W. Moody, *The Londonderry plantation, 1609–41* (Belfast, 1939), pp 34, 35, 172, 188–9, 198, 205, 207, 219–20.

Three years later another school was founded at Clogher in County Tyrone.[21]

The royal schools appear to have been reasonably well maintained throughout the seventeenth and eighteenth centuries, although they did not grow in number. The report of 1791 noted a total of 211 pupils in the royal schools, thirty-eight of whom were free scholars. The report revealed that there was not a single scholar in the school at Banagher, that the master of Carysfort had never kept school since his appointment in 1784, and that the Raphoe schoolmaster had done no teaching since 1785.[22] Things improved somewhat thereafter, a return of 1831 indicating that the Carysfort, Raphoe, and Banagher schools were once more in operation. In that year 343 students were enrolled, seventy being free scholars:[23] this from a total endowment of 13,672 acres which in 1831 produced £5,800 per annum.[24] (This works out to a little less than £17 per student, a figure clearly indicating that a good deal of educational graft was occurring.)

The parish, diocesan, and royal schools were created by legislation and endowed through government grants. Another form of government educational provision was illustrated by the charter schools, to which the government granted a charter and which it aided through parliamentary grants. The Irish charity school movement began early in the eighteenth century. In most instances, the schools enrolled both protestant and catholic children of the lower classes, but instruction was in the protestant religion only. Bible reading and catechizing monopolized most of the children's time. Financial support was raised through committees of subscribers, and after 1710 some support came

---

[21] O'Brien, i, 23–5; *Report from the commissioners of the board of education in Ireland; first report, free schools of royal foundation*, p. 1, H.C. 1813–14 (47), v; originally printed, 1809 (142), vii.

[22] Cited in O'Brien, i, 28.

[23] *A return from the different diocesan and other endowed schools under the superintendence of the commissioners of education in Ireland; of the number of scholars taught in each school, at the period of January 1831; specifying the number of those from whose education, board and lodging, payment is made from private means, and the number of those who are free scholars taught gratuitously at each school; with an account or the salary and emolument attached to such schools from their foundation or establishment*, p. 1.

[24] Wyse, p. 34.

from the trustees of the Linen Board. There were three protestant charity schools in Dublin in 1706 and fifteen therein in 1717. Dr Henry Maule, later protestant bishop of Meath, was the early leader of the Irish charity school movement. He was the chief founder, in 1717, of a Society in Dublin for Promoting Christian Knowledge whose purpose was the general establishment of charity schools. By 1725 the society was returning 163 schools, containing 3,000 pupils. Thereafter, advance slowed as financial support failed to grow sufficiently.[25]

When the financial shoe began to pinch, Hugh Boulter, protestant archbishop of Armagh, sought new means of support for the schools. Although requests for a crown charter which would allow the society to draw on a wider variety of subscribers had twice previously been denied, Boulter, in concert with most of the higher clergy and a number of nobility and gentry, petitioned the English government in 1730, stating:

That in many parts of the kingdom there are great tracts of mountainy and coarse lands of ten, twenty or thirty miles in length and of a considerable breadth, almost universally inhabited by papists; and that in most parts of the same and more especially in the provinces of Leinster, Munster, and Connaught the papists far exceed the protestants of all sorts in number. That the generality of the popish natives appear to have very little sense or knowledge of religion, but what they implicitly take from their clergy, to whose guidance in such matters they seem wholly to give themselves up, and thereby are kept, not only in gross ignorance, but in great disaffection to your sacred majesty and government, scarce any of them having appeared to be willing to abjure the pretender to your majesty's throne; so that if some effectual method be not made use of to instruct these great numbers of people in the principles of true religion and loyalty, there seems to be little prospect but that superstition, idolatry, and disaffection will, from generation to generation, be propagated among them.

Among the ways proper to be taken for converting and civilizing these poor deluded people, and bringing them (through the blessing of God) in time, to be good christians and faithful subjects, one of the most necessary, and without which all others are like to prove in-

[25] M. G. Jones, *The charity school movement, a study of eighteenth century puritanism in action* (London, 1964; originally published, 1938), pp 223–8; O'Connell, pp 223–6; Roland Savage, *A valiant Dublin woman, the story of George's Hill* (1766–1940) (Dublin, 1940), pp 37–8.

effectual, has always been thought to be that a sufficient number of English protestant schools be erected and established, wherein the children of the Irish natives might be instructed in the English tongue, and the fundamental principles of true religion, to both of which they are generally great strangers.

. . . .

To the intent thereof that the youth of this kingdom may generally be brought up in the principles of true religion and loyalty in all succeeding generations, we, your majesty's most dutiful and loyal subjects, most humbly beseech your majesty, that out of your great goodness you would be pleased to grant your royal charter for incorporating such persons as your majesty shall think fit, and enabling them to accept of gifts, benefactions and lands to such a value as your majesty shall think to be proper; that the same may be employ'd under such rules and directions as your majesty shall approve of for the supporting and maintaining such schools as may be erected in the most necessary places where the children of the poor may be taught *gratis*.

And we are the more encourag'd to make this humble application, from the good success which the same method has already had, and (through God's blessing) we hope will further have among your majesty's subjects of north Britain, and also in some measure by what we have seen already done in this kingdom, in some few places where such schools have been erected and maintained at the private expense of charitable persons.[26]

The charter was duly granted in 1733, the group being enrolled as the 'Incorporated Society in Dublin for Promoting English Protestant Schools in Ireland'. The society's executive committee was empowered to establish and maintain whatever number of English Protestant schools they thought necessary and to educate the children of the poor therein free of charge. The executive committee was to appoint schoolmasters who would instruct the children in the English tongue and in the protestant religion. Secular learning was to be limited to those skills necessary for the menial arts and for husbandry.[27]

[26] *A humble proposal for obtaining his majesty's royal charter to incorporate a society for promoting christian knowledge among the poor natives of the kingdom of Ireland* (1730), quoted in Jones, pp 233–5.

[27] *Report from the commissioners of the board of education in Ireland; third report, the protestant charter schools*, p. 15, H.C. 1813–14 (47), v. Originally printed 1809 (142), vii.

For a time the magic of the royal charter did its work. Subscriptions rose, and the society became the recipient of a number of valuable estates. Nevertheless, funds remained insufficient and in 1738 the lord primate petitioned the crown for a grant. The king replied by subscribing £1,000 annually, a grant which did not cease until 1794.[28] Parliamentary support for the schools began in 1747 when the licensing duty on hawkers and peddlers was assigned to the society. Until the 1780s, when the duty became almost wholly unproductive, it brought the society more than £1,100 a year.[29]

It was only a small step for parliament to pass from granting duty revenues to making an outright grant to the society, and under the leading of Lord Dorset, the viceroy, £5,000 was granted the society. In the first decade of parliamentary grants, 1751–60, the society received an average of £3,500 a year. By the last decade of the eighteenth century the average was £11,850 a year, and in the first seven years of the nineteenth century, almost £20,000 a year.[30] The grant exceeded £38,000 in 1818,[31] but thereafter it declined sharply and ceased in 1831. Altogether, it is estimated that a total of more than a million and a quarter pounds sterling were voted to the society from public funds.[32] Certainly the Dublin parliament had set an expensive precedent, when before adjourning in 1747, 'it made the first parliamentary grant to elementary education in the history of the United Kingdom'.[33]

What did the Incorporated Society give in return for such extensive support? For one thing it treated the Irish public to the spectacle of a curious and thoroughly inefficient administrative structure. Around the executive committee revolved four satellite groups: the committee of fifteen (which transacted most

---

[28] M. G. Jones, p. 236, *Report from the commissioners of the board of education in Ireland: third report, the protestant charter schools*, p. 16.

[29] *Report from the commissioners of the board of education in Ireland: third report, the protestant charter schools*, p. 16.

[30] Ibid.

[31] *A statement of the grants voted by parliament on account of miscellaneous services for Ireland in 1818; of the estimates for the like services laid before parliament in 1819; and of the sums voted thereupon; with a comparative view of the increase and decrease under each head in those years; and the total decrease upon the whole*, p. 1, H. C. 1819 (515), xv.

[32] O'Connell, p. 248.   [33] Jones, p. 238.

ordinary business of the society), the committee of accounts, the law committee, and the committee for examining teaching candidates. In addition, a local committee was established in every district in which there was a school.[34] Such a structure would look fine on a modern organization chart, but it still would be an absurdity, for, despite the various committees, the control of what actually went on in the classroom appears to have been left almost entirely in the hands of individual teachers.[35] The society could influence individual schools through the provision of textbooks and through its rare inspections, but such methods could only slightly reduce the enormous opportunities for malfeasance open to the teachers. A Taj Mahal built on quicksand, the elaborate central administration was swallowed up by local incompetence and abuse.

The society's educational gifts to Ireland were even of more dubious quality. Children aged four to six were admitted into the society's nurseries, those six to ten into its regular schools where they remained until apprenticed.[36] The children's educational diet was threefold, consisting of the three Rs, the established church catechism, and the sweat of their own brow. The reading, writing, and arithmetic require no comment, but the religious education is worth note. From its founding, 'the charter-school system was ultra-fanatic—it was formed for the purpose of fanaticizing the country—it out-churched the church; it was determined to educate outright into protestantism, and carry the nation by a *coup de main*'.[37] Originally the schools were open to protestants, but by resolutions of 15 March 1775 and of 4 December 1776 the society confined admission to children born of popish parents, and this policy continued until rescinded in May 1803.[38]

In order to perform more efficiently the task of proselytizing the popish Irish, the society created a number of boarding schools, thus allowing it to remove children entirely from parental influence. The society developed a practice of

[34] O'Brien, i, 53–4.

[35] Patrick J. Dowling, *The hedge schools of Ireland* (London, 1935), p. 36.

[36] *Report from the commissioners of the board of education in Ireland: third report, the protestant charter schools*, p. 19.

[37] Wyse, p. 15.

[38] *Report from the commissioners of the board of education in Ireland; third report, the protestant charter schools*, p. 19.

'transplanting' children from one of its schools to another when circumstances warranted it. Justifiable circumstances in the society's eyes included the necessity of promoting children from nurseries to the regular schools and of balancing the distribution of children among schools. A child could also be transplanted in another instance:

The avowed object of the society being to educate the children entrusted to its care in the established religion, whenever this object is likely to be interrupted by the interference of the parent, the child is removed from the neighbourhood of the parent's residence to a more distant school.[39]

One of the society's own publications affirms this policy: 'For obviating the great danger of the children relapsing, the society are very careful to transplant them originally to schools remote from their popish parents and relations.'[40] The finishing touches to the proselytizing process came when a child left school and was apprenticed to a protestant master.[41]

One of the striking features of the charter school education was the amount of manual labour performed by the children, especially in the society's early years. Garden and farm labour occupied the boys, spinning and cloth manufacture the girls. At the Stradbally school the boys, without adult help, cleared, plowed, and planted five acres of land to flax, and cut and sorted forty cartloads of hay.[42]

A further activity of the society should be mentioned, in addition to its educational pursuits: the society undertook to feed and clothe children under its protection as well as boarding students. Abuses were inevitable, since such services were provided by the schoolmasters at a flat rate under contract with the society.

No public scrutiny threatened the society's activities until 1784 when John Howard, a philanthropist and prison reformer, visited a number of the schools and published an account of the

[39] Ibid., p. 20.

[40] *A brief review of the rise and progress of the Incorporated Society in Dublin for Promoting English Protestant Schools in Ireland, from the opening of his majesty's royal charter, February 6th, 1733 to November 2nd, 1748* (Dublin, 1748), p. 10.

[41] *Report from the commissioners of the board of education in Ireland: third report, the protestant charter schools*, p. 21.

[42] Jones, p. 240.

abuses he had seen. He repeated his inspection in 1787 and was called to testify before a committee of the Irish house of commons formed in 1788 to investigate Irish education. 'The children, in general,' he averred, 'were sickly, pale and such miserable objects, that they were a disgrace to all society; and their reading had been neglected for the purpose of making them work for the masters.'[43] Sir Jeremiah Fitzpatrick, inspector general of prisons, who had visited twenty-eight of the charter schools, was also brought before the committee. He testified that the children therein were puny and below normal standard of health, generally ill-clothed and filthy. At Castle-Carberry school there were twenty-four ragged shirts and shifts in stock, though fourteen boys and eighteen girls were in the school. The window was partially stuffed with dung. Only two of the children could read.[44]

The commissioners of the board of education in their report of 1809 were far from enthusiastic about the schools and recommended several revisions in the society's operations. But it was not until the *First report of the commissioners of Irish education inquiry* (1825) that the schools came in for a thorough official roasting. After cataloguing a massive collection of abuses, the commissioners declared:

But however great and numerous the instances of mismanagement and abuse which prevail in these establishments, it appears to us, that the main objection arises from the mistaken principles on which they are founded. A system of education which separates children from their kindred, and which turns them out into life when just arrived at maturity, without friends or relations, and without that practical experience which children under ordinary circumstances insensibly acquire, by witnessing the realities of life around them, does not appear to us likely to attain the benefits expected from these establishments.

We are convinced that if a thousand children educated in charter schools were to be compared with an equal number who had remained in the apparently wretched cabins inhabited by their parents, but who had attended orderly and well regulated day schools, it would be found, not only that the latter had passed their years of instruction far more happily to themselves, but that when arrived at the age of manhood, they would upon a general average

[43] Quoted in *First report of the commissioners of Irish education inquiry*, p. 7.
[44] Ibid., p. 7.

be in every respect more valuable and better instructed members of society. . . .[45]

Nearly worthless in terms of educational quality, the Incorporated Society's schools were not significant in number of students. In the society's early years, before it became known as a remorselessly proselytizing agency, and before it began transplanting children from their parents' neighbourhoods, it was besieged with applications from catholic parents who were only too happy to have their children promised proper food and clothing. Parental support quickly disappeared when the intentions and practices of the society became well known. Throughout the second half of the eighteenth century the society had a difficult time filling its schools. The commission of 1788 found that although the society claimed 2,100 children under its charge, only 1,400 could be produced.[46] Thirty-four schools were operated by the society in 1824, enrolling somewhat more than 2,150 children.[47] Fifteen hundred children were enrolled in 1828, 1,099 in 1829, and 834 in 1830.[48]

We have seen then, that in four instances—those of the parish, diocesan, royal and charter schools—the Irish government attempted to provide or to aid the provision of public educational institutions.[49]

[45] Ibid., p. 29.   [46] Ibid., p. 7.   [47] Ibid., p. 14.

[48] *Return of the total number of children in the charter schools of Ireland in the years 1826, 1827, 1828, 1829, and 1830*, p. 1, H.C. 1831 (157), xv.

[49] In addition to the instances of state provision or aid of elementary and secondary schools mentioned in the text, brief mention should be made of the Irish government's early activity in higher education. For example, in the spring of 1592 when Trinity College, Dublin, was being founded, the lord deputy and council on behalf of the government sent a circular letter to the principal gentlemen in the country asking for subscriptions. Queen Elizabeth granted confiscated lands worth a hundred pounds per year to the college in 1594–5. Another hundred pounds per year was added in 1596 from the Queen's Irish revenue. These donations were confirmed by a letter from the Queen and by letters patent in 1600, when £200 per year was added from the royal revenues. Large grants were later made to the college from the confiscated lands of O'Neill and his Ulster allies. See, Anthony Gallagher, *Education in Ireland* (Washington, D.C., 1948), pp 165–7; J. P. Mahaffy, *An epoch in Irish history, Trinity College, Dublin; its foundation and early fortunes, 1591–1660* (London, 1903), pp 90–1; Constantia Maxwell, *A history of Trinity College, Dublin, 1591–1892* (Dublin, 1946), pp. 15–16; Harold Murphy, *A history of Trinity College, Dublin from first foundation to 1702* (Dublin, 1951), pp 28–38.

From our present vantage point in time the government's motivation in establishing or aiding these institutions appears far from commendable, especially in so far as the measures were aimed at undercutting the Roman Catholic faith. Nevertheless, we should not allow the impercipient nature of the government's motives to obscure the fact that the state did intervene in Irish educational affairs at a much earlier date than elsewhere in the United Kingdom, and that long before the nineteenth century began, the provision of public education institutions was an accepted weapon in the Irish state's arsenal of social control devices. Failure to recognize this tradition of state provision and intervention in Irish education would make an understanding of the creation of the national system of education impossible.

Our discussion of the eighteenth-century educational background began with the assertion that Ireland before the union with England was ruled by people who functioned as colonial governors and by institutions that were appropriate for control of a subjugated province, not an independent country. This mentality and these institutions made it easy for the state to intervene in matters such as education and, indeed, made it probable that such intervention would take place. In concluding this section it is important to emphasize that the union with

---

The founding and underwriting of Maynooth College by the Irish government, although for much different reasons than the aiding of Trinity College, was another example of intervention in Irish education. Established in 1795, Maynooth College was intended to take the place of continental seminaries for the education of Irish priests. The 1795 act that created the institution provided £8,000 for initial building expenses. Annual grants to the school were made by parliament throughout most of the nineteenth century. The grants for the first twenty-one years of the college's existence averaged about £8,000 a year. See *Eighth report of the commissioners of Irish education inquiry*, pp 5–6, H.C. 1826–7 (509), xiii; Gallagher, pp 205–6.

In 1814 the government granted £1,500 a year to the Royal Belfast Academical Institution, much of whose work was of university calibre. Peel stopped the grant in 1817, but it was restored in 1828, the salaries of the arts professors being paid from 1828 until the founding of the Queen's Colleges. Later grants were made to cover building expenses and salaries of medical professors. See John Jamieson, *The history of the Royal Belfast Academical Institution, 1810–1960* (Belfast, 1959), pp 24–35, 46–7, 205; T. W. Moody and J. C. Beckett, *Queen's Belfast, 1845–1949; the history of a university* (London, 1959), i, xlviii–xlix.

England did not destroy, or even moderate, the colonial mentality under which Ireland was governed. Whatever the constitutional theory of the union, Ireland continued to be run as an English crown colony, open to the imposition of coercion, fiat rule, and state interference in all aspects of everday life.

As part of the treaty of union, Ireland was allotted one hundred seats in the house of commons and thirty-two in the lords. These members were swamped, however, by the hordes of English and Scottish representatives and could act decisively on Irish issues only if they became obstreperous, a policy not adopted until Parnell's time. As important as the fact that Irish M.P.s still did not legislate for Ireland is the fact that the Irish executive remained an adjunct to English politics, rather than a servant of the Irish populace. The direction of Irish affairs was shared by a triumvirate of the lord lieutenant, the chief secretary for Ireland, and the secretary of state for home affairs. Theoretically, the home secretary was superior to the viceroy who in turn was superior to the chief secretary. In actual practice, the home secretary had little to do with Ireland, while after the union the status of the chief secretary rose to that of the viceroy's equal; and on occasion the chief secretary was a cabinet member while the viceroy remained outside. These offices were part of the English political structure and incumbents and policies shifted with the ripples of English electoral politics rather than with the tides of Irish opinion. As the post of chief secretary became more important the holder tended to spend increasing amounts of time in parliament as the government's Irish spokesman. In his absence the civil government of Ireland was run by him through the Irish Office in London. The act of union produced little immediate change in the Irish administrative structure. In the three succeeding decades, however, most of the patronage appointments in the civil service were eliminated, and the civil service became a reasonably efficient instrument of the executive's will. The Irish departments came to be broken into two groups: those concerned solely with Irish affairs, which reported to the chief secretary's office, and those, such as the treasury, which were satellite branches of their English counterparts.

The colonial approach to Irish affairs was further facilitated by the lack of viable institutions of local government in Ireland: the Irish parish never assumed the administrative functions characteristic of the English and Scottish parish. Almost all county affairs were thrust upon the often corrupt grand juries composed of leading land-owners. Beginning in 1817, a series of acts gradually reformed the county administration, but county affairs never aroused the same interest or degree of participation as in England. The Irish boroughs were notorious for their political venality. John J. Webb calculated that of the 117 parliamentary boroughs extant in 1800, eighteen did not possess a corporation, while thirty-six of the corporations disappeared immediately after losing their parliamentary seats as a result of the union. Of the remaining sixty-three, thirty-six corporations did 'practically nothing', and the other twenty-seven 'comparatively little, and that inefficiently'. After as well as before the union, Ireland was governed by men and methods of a colonial stripe, and often the devices and attitudes of the English rulers of Ireland—such as coercion acts—were of the sort normally reserved for dealing with marauding aboriginals. Fortunately, if England could rule its Irish colony with the brutal imposition of coercion, it could also exert itself in social and economic matters in Ireland with considerably more ease than in England itself. It is to England's credit that in some instances it exercised its colonial prerogatives by intervening to better the economic, social, and educational condition of its Irish subjects.[50]

2

We have seen that the state, motivated partially by religious considerations, made several attempts to provide public educational institutions in eighteenth-century Ireland. This same religious motivation produced another sort of governmental intervention in educational affairs: the attempt to suppress Roman Catholic educational enterprise. The penal measures concerning education are interesting in themselves as further examples of the readiness of the Irish state to intervene in education, but are

[50] R. B. McDowell, 'Ireland on the eve of the famine', in R. Dudley Edwards and T. Desmond Williams (ed.), *The great famine* (Dublin, 1956), pp 19–22; R. B. MacDowell, *The Irish Administration, 1901–1914* (London and Toronto, 1964), pp 2–6; R. B. McDowell, 'The Irish executive in the nineteenth century', *Irish Historical Studies* ix (Mar. 1955), p. 266; R. Barry O'Brien, *Dublin Castle and the Irish people* (London, 1909), p. 22; John J. Webb, *Municipal government in Ireland, medieval and modern* (Dublin, 1918), pp 154–237.

more important for their consequences, for in Newtonian fashion, the state action brought a catholic reaction. Largely because of the penal laws the catholic peasantry came to support their own 'hedge schools' with a tenacity born of desperation. One of the necessary preconditions for the establishing of the national system of education in 1831 was a readiness of the catholic lower classes to accept and support a system of popular schools. This readiness was one of the few blessings that we may attribute to the penal code.

The penal laws on education were merely one segment of a considerable number of statutes constituting the Irish penal code. The code was a logical mess. It consisted of a snarl of overlapping statutes that were neither codified nor evenly enforced. The primary purpose of the laws, however, was clear: to eradicate popery in Ireland. The laws also served as a bulwark of the ascendancy's monopoly on social and economic privilege. Although penal codes were not uncommon in seventeenth-century Europe, they usually represented attempts of a majority group to suppress a religious minority. In contrast, the vast majority of the Irish people came under the code's penalties. Analytically, the penal laws fell into three categories. The first of these were the statutes directed at the suppression of the Roman Catholic hierarchy and at hobbling the priesthood. All popish archbishops, bishops, vicar-generals, deans, and all regular clergy were required to leave the country. Anyone who returned was guilty of high treason and was to suffer accordingly. Without bishops ordination was, of course, impossible. Foreign-trained clergy were banned. All catholic secular priests were required to register with the government. Rewards were placed on the heads of illegal ecclesiastics: fifty pounds upon conviction to anyone who reported a higher clergyman and twenty pounds for every lower cleric who was not registered.

A second category of laws disabled the Roman Catholics from participating in a number of trades and professions. Entrance into all governmental franchises, into trade guilds, and into the professions was made contingent upon oaths abjuring the temporal authority of the pope, transubstantiation, and other Roman Catholic doctrines. The 'test' of taking the sacrament according to the rites of the Anglican communion was later added as a condition of entry into the corporations and professions. Clearly, no faithful Roman Catholic could take the oath or undergo the test. Hence, the catholic population was excluded from all but the most menial of economic activities and from participation in the government of the nation.

A third type of penal measure was punitive in nature, penalizing the catholic laity simply because it was popish. Under this heading come such provisions as those which prohibited the practice of primogeniture among the catholics. The land of catholic parents dying before the heir reached his majority could be held in guardianship only by protestants. No papist was to act as ward to any child, the children of popish parents being parcelled out to the nearest protestant relation. Should the eldest son of a catholic landowner turn protestant, his parents were, upon the enrolling of a certificate in the court of chancery by the local anglican bishop, to become mere tenants for life upon the family estate. The extent to which the penal enactments were enforced is still unsettled. Certainly portions went uneffected, but just as certainly other segments were used to hound catholic priest and peasant. It is clear that the code seriously affected discipline in the Roman Catholic church, diminishing the hierarchy's control over an increasingly unruly and often ignorant clergy.[51]

For our purposes it will be sufficient to describe the penal laws on education and to note that they had considerable in-

---

[51] The discussion of the penal code is based on, R. E. Burns, 'The Irish penal code and some of its historians', *Review of Politics*, xxi (Jan. 1959), pp 276–99; R. E. Burns, 'The Irish popery laws: a study of eighteenth-century legislation and behaviour', *Review of Politics*, xxiv (Oct. 1962), pp 485–508; William E. H. Lecky, *A History of Ireland in the eighteenth century* (London, new impression, 1912), i, 145–71; P. R. Madden, *Historical Notice of penal laws against Roman Catholics, their operation and relation during the past century: of partial measures of relief in 1779, 1782, 1793, 1829, and of penal laws which remain unrepealed, or have been rendered more stringent by the latest so-called emancipation act* (London, 1865), pp 1–12; *The report of a committee appointed by the Society of United Irishmen of Dublin 'to enquire and report the popery laws in force in this realm'* (Dublin, 1792), passim; Denys Scully, *A statement of the penal laws which aggrieve the catholics of Ireland; with commentaries* (Dublin, 1812), i, passim; Maureen Wall, *The penal laws, 1691–1760* (Dundalk, 1967, originally published 1961), passim.

It should be noted that the test act of 1704 applied to dissenters as well as to Roman Catholics. The act in so far as it applied to dissenters was repealed in 1780.

fluence upon the educational efforts of the catholic peasantry. The serious attempts to grind the catholic Irish into illiteracy did not begin until after the English revolution of 1688. A Williamite statute of 1695, entitled, 'An act to restrain foreign education' (7 William III, c. 4), began the attack:

> In case any of his majesty's subjects of Ireland shall go or send any child or other person to be resident or trained up in any priory, abbey, nunnery, popish university, college or school or house of jesuits or priests in parts beyond the seas in order to be educated in the popish religion in any sort to profess the same, or shall send money or other thing towards the maintenance of such person gone or sent, or as a charity for the relief of a religious house, every person so going, sending or sent shall on conviction be disabled to sue in law or equity or to be a guardian, executor or administrator, or take a legacy or deed of gift, or bear any office, and shall forfeit goods and chattels for ever and lands for life.[52]

The act's domestic provisions were even more sinister:

> ... be it enacted that no person whatsoever of the papist religion shall publicly teach school, or instruct youth in learning ... upon pain of £20 and also being committed to prison with bail or main prize for the space of three months for every offence.[53]

Queen Anne's reign saw the continuation of the Williamite tradition of suppression of catholic education. An act of the second year of her reign (2 Anne, c. 6) affirmed the Williamite statute and added:

> Where any two justics of the peace suspect that any child has been sent into foreign parts, they are required to convene any relation who had care of the child, to produce the child within two months; and if good proof is not given that the child is resident not beyond the seas, then such child shall incur all the penalties in the act to restrain foreign education.[54]

[52] Quoted in O'Connell, p. 202.

[53] Quoted in Savage, p. 28. Portions of 7 William III, c. 4 are also quoted in Corcoran, *Education systems*, p. 30; Corcoran, 'Enforcing the penal code on education', *The Irish Monthly*, lix (March 1931), pp 149–50; Corcoran, *Some lists of catholic lay teachers and their illegal schools in the later penal times* (Dublin, 1932), p. 15; *Report . . . Society of United Irishmen*, pp 3, 5–8.

[54] Quoted in Corcoran, *Education systems*, p. 30; Corcoran, 'Enforcing the penal code on education', p. 150; Corcoran, *Some lists*, p. 15.

Other sections of the act are quoted in Gallagher, p. 37; O'Connell, p. 203; *Report . . . Society of United Irishmen*, p. 8.

In 1709 an act with the title, 'Act for explaining and amending an act Entitled "An act to prevent the further growth of popery"'became law (8 Anne, c. 3). Among its provisions was the following:

Whatever person of the popish religion shall publicly teach school, or instruct youth in learning in any private house within this realm, or be entertained to instruct youth as usher, or assistant by any protestant schoolmaster, he shall be esteemed a popish regular clergyman, and prosecuted as such . . . and no person, after November 1, 1709, shall be qualified to teach or keep such a school publicly or instruct youth in any private house, or as usher, or assistant to any protestant schoolmaster, who shall not first, at the next general assizes or quarter sessions of the place where he resides, take the oath of abjuration, under a penalty of 10 £ for every such offence—a moiety to go to the informer.[55]

A Hanoverian statute (I Geo. 2, c. 20), forbade converts to protestantism to educate their children in the popish religion, lest the children be subject to the penalties imposed upon the catholics. Later, any protestant knowingly permitting his children to be educated as catholics became subject to the penalties of the popery laws himself (I Geo. 2, c. 6).[56]

There is good evidence that the laws concerning catholic education were enforced in the first half of the eighteenth century and that they remained a threat for a considerable time thereafter. Although judicial records are sparse, Corcoran found a number of cases in representative counties of prosecution of popish schoolmasters. For example, his list of education prosecutions taken from the Limerick grand jury presentment book shows nineteen indictments against popish schoolmasters in the years 1711–1722.[57]

Fortunately, the penal code was too evil to last forever. Minor ameliorative measures were passed in the early 1770s, and in 1778 the Irish parliament passed 'An act for the relief of his majesty's subjects professing the popish religion' (17 and 18

[55] Quoted in Gallagher, p. 39. Portions of the act's educational provisions also quoted in, Corcoran, *Education systems*, pp. 30–1; Corcoran, 'Enforcing the penal code on education', p. 150; Corcoran, *Some lists*, pp 15–16; *Report . . . Society of United Irishmen*, p. 4; Savage, p. 28.

[56] *Report . . . Society of United Irishmen*, p. 9.

[57] Corcoran, *Education systems*, pp 53–4.

Geo. III, c. 49). The statutes allowed catholics to lease lands for 999 years and abolished the right of converted popish children to force their parents to become tenants for life. The Irish parliament framed a further relief bill in 1781 under which catholics taking an oath of allegiance were enabled to hold and dispose of land in the same manner as were protestants. The relief act of 1782 (21 and 22 Geo. III, c. 62), known as 'Gardiner's act', further removed penal restraints but at the same time codified the remaining penal measures. Almost all of the remaining penal legislation was, however, abrogated by the catholic relief measure of 1793. The 1793 act opened the professions and civil offices to catholics on the condition of their taking an oath of allegiance, gave them the right to possess arms, and removed most of the restrictions upon the exercise of the catholic religion.[58] It must quickly be added that the repeal of the penal laws did not solve the catholics' problems overnight. The entrenched protestant monopolists were not immediately shaken from their position and the attitudes of inferiority bred into the formerly oppressed Catholics were not easily discarded. In ridding themselves of these attitudes the catholics naturally tended to overcompensate, and, for decades, indeed generations, after the repeal of the penal laws, large segments of the catholic population were highly aggressive and often intolerable on matters of privilege and prerogative.

The educational provisions of the penal code were repealed by Gardiner's act of 1782:

Whereas several of the laws made in the kingdom relative to the education of papists or persons professing the popish religion, are considered too severe, and have not answered the desired effect: be it enacted that so much [of the acts 7 Will. III, c. 4; 8 Anne, c. 3] as subjects persons of the popish religions, who shall publicly teach school, or who shall instruct youth in learning in any private popish house with in this realm, to the like . . . penalties and forfeitures as any popish regular convict, shall be . . . repealed.[59]

Repeal was made conditional upon the popish schoolmaster taking the oath of allegiance and upon his not receiving into his school anyone of the protestant religion. The act introduced a

[58] Madden, pp. 12–25.
[59] Quoted in Corcoran, *Education systems*, p. 76.

new penal educational element, however, in that it forbade the endowing of any popish educational foundation in Ireland. Moreover, before a catholic teacher could set up a school he was required to obtain a license from the Anglican bishop of his diocese, a license which could be withdrawn at will.[60] This latter provision seems not to have been strictly enforced. In 1792 the licensing requirement was abolished, and the relief act of 1793 provided that 'persons professing the popish or Roman Catholick religion . . . shall not be liable to any penalties . . . save such as . . . subjects of the protestant religion are liable to'. Thus, save for the forbidding of catholic endowments, the educational provisions of the penal code had disappeared by the beginning of the nineteenth century.[61]

3

Although the penal laws relating to education seem to have gone off the statute books with legislative ease, their educational consequences lingered. In response to the attempts to suppress catholic educational endeavours, the catholic peasantry created a patchwork of 'hedge schools', institutions that they continued to support well into the nineteenth century. While the penal laws were enforced catholic schoolmasters taught as members of a quiet but widespread conspiracy. Their fellow conspirators were the students who formed their classes and the peasant parents who sheltered them and paid their fees. In many rural areas a hedge school was literally that: a collection of students and a teacher holding class in a ditch or hedge row, with one of the pupils serving as look-out for law officers. As the penal laws were relaxed the schoolmasters were able to make themselves a bit more comfortable. The comparative luxury of a sod hut replaced the ditch as the master's classroom, and the master could stay in one area as long as the children's parents would pay his fees, not, as formerly, as long as the local grand jury left him in peace.

[60] Timothy Corcoran, 'Catholic teachers and the penal law of 1782', *The Irish Monthly*, lix (July 1931), pp. 423–5; Corcoran, *Education systems*, pp 76–77; Dowling, pp. 24–5.
[61] Corcoran, 'Education in the Dublin acts of 1792–93', *The Irish Monthly*, lix (Sept. 1931), pp 544–5.

In the nineteenth century, 'pay schools' became a synonym for 'hedge schools'. The oft-quoted testimony of A. R. Blake provides the best-known definition of the schools:

'Do you mean by pay schools what usually are called hedge schools?'

'They are usually called hedge schools.'

'Are they called pay schools because the children pay for their own instruction?'

'Yes; and they are distinguished as "pay schools" in the reports which we made in 1825 and 1826.'

. . . .

'Will you explain further what you mean by pay schools?'

'I mean by pay schools, schools in which the masters receive some small stipend from the children who attend them; schools set up on private speculation; schools that received no aid either from the state or from any society established for the promotion of education. The masters received 1d. a week or so from the children; sometimes more and sometimes less. The schoolmasters, I thought, in those schools were of a very inferior class.'[62]

An understanding of the hedge schools depends more on catching their flavour than on reviewing their statistics. Probably the best reporter of the hedge school phenomenon was William Carleton, himself a hedge school graduate and a some-time hedge schoolmaster.[63] Carleton was born near Clogher, County Tyrone, in 1794. He received his earliest significant schooling in one of the less common forms of hedge schools: one run by a woman. The mistress of the school and her daughter conducted the establishment in one of the larger barns in the neighbourhood. The mistress, Mrs Dumont, led a life of polite mendicancy, teaching classes for young ladies ages five to eighteen in one barn one year, in a similar building in another town the next. Younger boys were occasionally allowed to attend her school, Carleton being so favoured. Young William spent

[62] *Report by the select committee of the house of lords on the plan of education in Ireland, with minutes of evidence*, p. 54, H.C. 1837 [543-1], viii, pt i.

[63] For Carleton's life see Benedict Kiely, *Poor scholar: a study of the works and days of William Carleton (1794-1869)* (London, 1947); David J. O'Donoghue, *The life of William Carleton: being his autobiography and letters; and an account of his life and writings, from the point at which the autobiography breaks off*, 2 vols (London, 1896).

little time there, indeed only a week, since he spent his time kissing a girl with whom he had fallen in love, rather than learning his ABCs. Much more important than the child's brief dalliance in Mrs Dumont's establishment was his encounter with Pat Frayne, hedge schoolmaster. Carleton had met Patrick Frayne momentarily before his experience in the girls' school, when he had enrolled in Frayne's school and had returned home having learned the entire alphabet in a single day. Unfortunately, only three scholars had appeared for the opening of Frayne's hedge school, and Frayne promptly made his first day of teaching his last day in the town. Frayne was a relation to young Carleton, and when he returned four or five years later Carleton eagerly joined his flock. This time a sod schoolhouse was built for the master and within a month he had garnered about a hundred pupils, mostly boys, but a number of girls as well. An amiable, if thoroughly unpredictable disciplinarian, Pat was not above taking advantage of his students. He managed to get more butter from his students than any five families like his could consume; it was known that his wife Nancy sold a great deal of butter in Clogher markets, although it was generally well known that they had no cow. Whatever his faults, Carleton was greatly taken with Frayne and immortalized him as Mat Kavanagh in his story 'The Hedge School', of which 'The abduction of Mat Kavanagh, the hedge schoolmaster' comprises the major portion.

The Kavanagh story is worth our attention because it reveals a great deal about the pattern of hedge school education. For instance, the fact that the villagers went so far as to kidnap a schoolmaster is itself a comment upon the high value the Irish peasant placed upon securing schooling for his children. Once settled in the village of his captors, Kavanagh set out to advertise his learning in his finest copperplate hand. He modestly mentioned forty-nine subjects, plus assorted works, that he was capable of teaching. In addition to the more conventional subjects he professed to teach stereometry, gauging, dialling, astrology, austerity, glorification, physic (by theory only), and ventilation.[64] Dressed in a torn black coat and a white cravat,

---

[64] William Carleton, 'The hedge school', in *Traits and stories of the Irish peasantry* (London, tenth ed., 1854), ii, 296. J. J. Campbell makes the fascinating, if undocumented, assertion that Kavanagh's prospectus of

his charges huddled around him, he conducted lessons with a large broad ruler clenched in his hand, the symbol of his executive justice. On a typical afternoon, one corner of the classroom was taken up with children playing 'Fox and Geese', or 'Walls of Troy' on their slates, in another a set was playing 'fighting bottles' by smashing bottles against each other to see which broke first, a third playing a game with pins. Others ranged themselves on the floor copying from their lesson books, others doing sums, and still others being examined by the master. Bookkeepers, Latinists, Grecians, all worked simultaneously.

Kavanagh, like his prototype Frayne, had come to teaching through the apprenticeship of being a wandering student. In 'The poor scholar', Carleton depicted the life of those wandering searchers after knowledge who were a common part of the Irish social landscape. In that story a northern lad sets south after receiving his basic education, his parents' blessing, and his neighbours' contributions, in order to study under the famed masters of Munster. Throughout most of his travels he was provided with food and lodging gratis by local peasants: 'his satchel of books was literally a passport to their hearts'.[65] Hospitality to poor scholars was especially warm because the student was commonly intending to become a priest and there was particular blessing on those who helped support him. Through several years of his Munster residency he went home night after night, in rotation, with one of his schoolmates. Eventually, he entered Maynooth and was ordained.

Not all scholars, however, entered the priesthood. A number became hedge schoolmasters. According to Carleton, those who entered the schoolmastering profession bound themselves to a long training. Whenever a student felt he had learned all he

[65] William Carleton, 'The poor scholar', in *Traits and stories of the Irish peasantry*, ii, 288.

---

subjects was really intended to be a parody of the suggested program outlined in the education report of 1791. J.J. Campbell, 'Primary and secondary education', in Theodore W. Moody and J. C. Beckett (ed.), *Ulster since 1800, a social survey* (London, 1957), p. 182. Attractive as the suggestion is, it ignores the fact that, as we shall document later, the 1791 report was never printed and existed in handwritten copy only in the files of the board of education for endowed schools until printed by a parliamentary commission that did not meet until after Carleton had written his story.

could from his hedge schoolmaster he penned him a formal challenge to meet in a public literary contest. If the master was victorious the student resumed his studies under the master; if the lad won he went out to seek a contest with a more renowned schoolmaster. Eventually he affixed the epithet 'Philomath' after his name and became a master himself.[66] Although we may question the universality of the ritual that Carleton describes, it is clear that a lively underground intellectual life did exist in portions of peasant Ireland.

Both the friends and the enemies of the Irish hedge schools agreed that the peasant Irish possessed a striking avidity for learning. Sir Robert Peel, hardly an enthusiast for things Irish, said in Westminster on 27 February 1816, that he could 'state, as a fact within my own knowledge that the greatest eagerness and desire prevails, among the lower orders in Ireland, for the benefits of instruction'.[67] The commissioners of the board of education in their fourteenth, and summary, report concluded: 'from the facts here stated, we conceive it clearly to appear, that the lower class of the people in Ireland are extremely anxious to obtain instruction for their children, even at an expense, which though small, very many of them can ill afford'.[68] Edward Wakefield wrote in 1812, 'I do not know any part of Ireland so wild, that its inhabitants are not anxious, nay, eagerly anxious for the education of their children'.[69] An Irish landlord declared of the peasantry: 'they set so high a value on learning, that the poorest labourers will often appropriate a part of their scanty earnings to the education of their children'.[70]

Such enthusiasm for learning can be largely ascribed to the penal laws which, by attempting to suppress the education of the Roman Catholics, affirmed its importance. The almost fanatical grasping for educational straws by the Irish peasantry

[66] Carleton, 'The hedge school', pp 272–6.

[67] *Hansard 2*, xxxii, 929.

[68] *Report from the commissioners of the board of education in Ireland: fourteenth report, view of the chief foundations, with some general remarks, and result of deliberations*, p. 328, H.C. 1812–13 (21), vi; reprinted, H.C. 1813–14 (47), v, and H.C. 1821 (744), x.

[69] Edward Wakefield, *An account of Ireland, statistical and political* (London, 1812), ii, 397.

[70] *An essay on the population of Ireland* (London, 1803), quoted in Corcoran, *Some lists*, p. 62.

was not, however, simply a perverse attempt to thwart the English government. A much more subtle and complicated mechanism was at work. In its attempts to conquer the Irish catholics, the English realized that they had to reduce them to a cultural level as low as that of a preliterate society. To effect such a brutalization the extinction of catholic educational institutions was a requirement. Significantly, the Roman Catholic peasant clung to education for the same reason that the protestants attempted to suppress it: without schooling the catholics would be ground into economic helplessness, permanent social inferiority, and religious ignorance. Although it is questionable whether the individual Roman Catholic peasant thought in terms of preserving the catholics in Ireland as a group from pulverization, he doubtlessly realized as an individual that his own family's survival depended upon his children obtaining certain forms of useful or prestigious knowledge. Thus the penal laws brought a hidden blessing, for they underlined the fact that only by preserving some semblance of learning could the Irish people preserve themselves from cultural extinction.

In turning from the accepted fact of the peasant Irishman's support of the hedge schools to an attempt to evaluate the quality and quantity of these schools, we enter an area of considerable historical uncertainty.[71] Ultimately, we wish to obtain a tentative answer to the basic question, 'How good were the schools?' To answer this major question we must ask a number of small questions about the hedge schools, while remembering that an air of tentativeness must characterize our findings. One query deserving attention is, 'What subjects were taught in the hedge schools?' The three Rs, of course, formed the backbone of the curriculum in all such schools. The parochial returns of 1824 revealed that of the 262 male teachers in Kildare and Leighlin on whom information about the subjects they taught was returned, only five were found to teach less than all three Rs.[72]

[71] For a discussion of some of the problems of the historiography of the hedge schools, see William J. Bradley, 'Sir Thomas Wyse – Irish pioneer in education reform' (unpublished Ph. D. thesis, University of Dublin, 1947), pp 7–18.

[72] Martin Brenan, *Schools of Kildare and Leighlin*, A.D., *1775–1835* (Dublin, 1935), p. 79.

There is no reason to assume that these figures were atypical, or that the average hedge school taught less than the three rudiments of literacy. On the other hand, if McEvoy's observation of County Tyrone, that, 'from the age of six or seven, to that of ten or eleven years, is the usual time for children to be kept at school',[73] reflects the national pattern, then it is also clear that there was time to teach the average child little more than these fundamentals, with perhaps a smattering of other subjects as sweetening. It is important to note that, by the beginning of the nineteenth century, English was rapidly replacing Irish as the medium of instruction in the hedge schools, and that elementary literacy was usually an attainment of the English, rather than of the Irish language. The lack of printed books in Irish was partially responsible for this result. The switch to English was also a product of the use of English in most business affairs, and of the apparent carelessness of the parents in transmitting a knowledge of Irish to their children.[74]

Children were taught to read from any of a number of primers and spelling books of the standard varieties, whereafter they were allowed to read just about anything they could lay their hands upon. Dutton listed the following as common among the hedge school fare for those past the universal spelling book stage (the comments are his):

History of the seven champions of christendom
History of Montelion, knight of the oracle
History of Parismus and Parismenes
History of Irish rogues and rapparees
History of Freney, a notorious robber, teaching them the most
    dexterous mode of robbing
History of the most celebrated pirates
History of Jack, the bachelor, a noted smuggler
History of Fair Rosamond and Jane Shore, two prostitutes
History of Donna Rosina, a Spanish courtezan
Ovid's Art of Love
History of witches and apparitions

[73] John McEvoy, *Statistical survey of the county of Tyrone, with observations on the means of improvement; drawn up in the years 1801 and 1802, for the consideration, and under the direction of the Dublin Society* (Dublin, 1802), p. 164.
[74] Dowling, pp 53, 71–3.

The devil and Dr Faustus
Moll Flanders, highly edifying no doubt
New system of boxing by Mendoze[75]

Coloured as Dutton's list may be, it is clear that some very strange books often served as the second readers for the Irish young.

Arithmetic, even more than reading, was the backbone of the hedge school curriculum. Parents expected to be dazzled by the master's magic with numbers and were suspicious of any schoolmaster who underplayed the subject. Practical applications were emphasized with surveying and bookkeeping being the most common forms of advanced arithmetical instruction. History and geography were often taught to the more advanced students. A surprisingly sympathetic article on the hedge schools in the *Dublin University Magazine* noted the following sources of historical instruction in the schools the author had visited: 'An odd volume of a history of France at the period of Anne of Brittany, an odd volume of "Clarissa Harlowe", "Castle Rackrent", "Buffon's Natural History", "Baron Munchausen", Boyse's "Pantheon", a volume of the "Universal History", and the "Life of Baron Trench".'[76]

The classics, too, appear to have entered the curriculum of some hedge schools. Certainly great respect was paid to possessors of classical learning of any sort, and Latin tags were a major item in the hedge teacher's intellectual kit. The best indication of the extent of classical teaching is found in Brenan's study in which sixteen of the 262 teachers upon whom he had information were conducting schools with enough Latin taught to be classified by him as 'classical schools'.[77]

Another important subject taught in the schools was religion. A number of the pay schools were founded by Roman Catholic bishops or priests, and the appointment of masters in several additional schools occurred only with approval of the parish priest. Hence, it is not surprising that in many instances the

[75] Hely Dutton, *Statistical survey of the county of Clare, with observations on the means of improvement; drawn up for the consideration and by direction of the Dublin Society* (Dublin, 1808), pp. 236–7.
[76] 'An Irish hedge school', *Dublin University Magazine*, lx (Nov. 1862), p. 601.
[77] Brenan, p. 87.

master worked closely with the priest, teaching catechism and doctrine.[78] In summary, it appears that the curriculum of the hedge schools, while admitting of notable exceptions, was essentially elementary in nature, providing elementary literacy and arithmetical knowledge and passing on the elements of the catholic faith from generation to generation.

When we ask the question, 'how may we characterize the methods used in the hedge schools?' the most general answer is that enlightened chaos seems to have been the common approach to classroom organization. As the earlier references to Carleton indicate, the hedge school classes usually had as many different things going on at once as there were levels of pupils. The schoolmaster, like the head of any one-room school, had to be the ringmaster of myriad varieties of intellectual animals. In most schools the student's day appears to have been broken into alternate periods of lesson-learning and examination by the master thereby keeping several different groups of children busy at their respective activities. Since the more advanced scholars brought whatever book they could acquire for their reading lesson, and since 'rehearsing' lessons aloud was a common method of teaching reading, cacophony was often the result. One commissioner of the 1824–26 education inquiry visited a school in Sligo where children were all reading aloud, simultaneously, their respective copies of 'The forty thieves', 'The Pleasant Art of Money-catching', the New Testament, and the mutiny act.[79] Carleton indicates that some form of the monitorial system was used in the hedge schools considerably before it was promulgated by Bell and by Lancaster.[80]

'How well qualified for their tasks were the hedge schoolmasters?' it is next logical to ask. One fact is clear: they were not men educated in universities or even in grammar schools. Rather, they were products of educational incest, men trained in hedge schools to teach in hedge schools. The records and traditions of the hedge schoolmasters are highly distorted because the hedge schoolmaster depended upon his ability to

---

[78] Brenan, pp 65–9; P. J. Dowling, 'The catholic clergy and popular education in Ireland in 1825', *The Tablet*, clxi (27 May 1933), pp 654–5; Jones, p. 261.

[79] *First report of the commissioners of Irish education inquiry*, p. 44.

[80] 'The hedge school', pp 306–7.

convince parents that he was a savant in order to obtain employment. Immoderate claims and a touch of charlatanry were often matters of economic necessity. Traditionally, the hedge schoolteacher was a man, but even this point is uncertain. Although Dowling states that the hedge schools were, with very few exceptions, taught by men,[81] Brenan's study of the parochial returns of 1824 reveals that of the teachers mentioned on the returns, 275 were male, ninety-six female.[82] It would of course be possible to define away the question as to whether or not a significant number of women taught hedge schools by simply stating that all schools taught by women were dame schools and hence not worthy of the elevated title of hedge school. Brenan's data, however, show that fifty-four per cent of those women teachers upon whom he could obtain information taught at least the three Rs, or more,[83] figures that suggest that most of these schools were of a scholastic level equal to the male-run hedge schools.

The intellectual attainments of the masters ranged from the possession of bare literacy to inflated pedantry to genuine scholarly achievement. Bishop Doyle wrote Sir Henry Parnell that 'in the counties of Carlow, Kildare, and the Queen's County, very nearly all the Roman Catholic children attend school during the summer and autumn, are taught reading, writing, and arithmetic, but their masters, in many instances, are extremely ignorant'.[84] Most masters appear to have been possessors of at least some knowledge beyond the three Rs. A by-product of the masters' possession of more knowledge than was possessed by most peasants, and of the master's need to make a living through school fees, was the masters' indulgence in intellectual showmanship and pedantry. 'That a great deal of ludicrous pedantry generally accompanied this knowledge is not at all surprising, when we consider the rank these worthy teachers held in life and the stretch of inflation at which their pride was kept by the profound reverence excited by their

---

[81] Dowling, *The hedge schools of Ireland*, p. 107.

[82] Brenan, pp 79, 86.

[83] Ibid., p. 86.

[84] 22 Apr. 1821, quoted in, William J. Fitzpatrick, *The life, times and correspondence of the Right Rev. Dr Doyle, bishop of Kildare and Leighlin* (Dublin, 1861), i, 168.

learning among the people'.[85] Still, it is hard not to admire the Latinate vocabulary of Mat Kavanagh who could wake with a dreadful hangover and cry, 'I'm all in a state of conflagration; and my head—by the sowl of Newton, the inventor of fluxions, but my head is a complete illucidation of the centrifugal motions, so it is'.[86] And one cannot but be a trifle awed by a man who could rebuke students who were making noise while he spoke with a visitor, with the threat, 'I'll castigate yez in dozens: I can't spake to this dacent women, with your insuperable turbulentiality'.[87]

The following piece of philomath poetry tells a good deal about the intellectual kit of most hedge schoolmasters. Its Latinate quality is especially noteworthy, both English and Latin having been book-learned by a native Irish speaker:

COLLEEN RUE

As I roved out on a summer's morning, aspeculating
    most curiously,
To my surprise I soon espied a charming fair one
    approaching me.
I stood awhile in deep meditation, contemplating
    what I should do,
Till at last recruiting all my sensation, I thus
    accosted the Colleen Rue.

Are you Aurora, the Goddess Flora, Artemidora or
    Venus bright?
Or Helen fair beyond compare whom Paris stole from
    Grecian sight?
Oh, fairest creature, you have enslaved me, I'm
    intoxicated in cupid's clew,
Your golden sayings are infatuations that have
    ensnared me, a Colleen Rue.

Kind Sir, be aisy, and do not tease me with your
    false praises most jestingly,
Your dissimulation and invocation are vaunting praises
    alluring me,

---

[85] Carleton, 'The hedge school', p. 275.
[86] Ibid., p. 292.   [87] Ibid., p. 308.

I'm not Aurora, the Goddess Flora, but a rural
  female for all to view,
That's here condoling my situation, my apellation
  the Colleen Rue.

Oh, were I Hector the noble victor who died a
  victim to Grecian skill,
Or were I Paris whose deeds are various, an
  arbitrator on Ida's hill,
I'd range through Asia, likewise Arabia,
  Pennsylvania seeking for you,
The burning regions like Sage Orpheus to see
  your face my sweet Colleen Rue.[88]

A few truly distinguished scholars did teach in hedge schools. Walsh mentions the case of one of the later hedge schoolmasters whose classical achievements were so high that the University of Dublin offered him an honorary degree.[89]

The moral qualities of the average hedge schoolmaster were indeterminate. Probably their morals were no worse, nor no better, than those which prevailed among the peasantry as a whole. Wakefield contended that most schoolmasters were priestly drop-outs: 'The common schoolmaster is generally a man who was originally intended for the priesthood, but whose morals had been too bad or his habitual idleness so deeply rooted, as to prevent his improving himself sufficiently for that office.'[90] On the other hand, the parochial returns of 1824, filed in almost all cases by the parish priests, indicated, at least in Brenan's sample, that most of the masters had the moral approval of the local priests, hardly an indication of rampant vice or indolence.[91] It appears that the peasantry were much more interested in learning than in saintliness in their masters, and they looked upon minor vices as a desirable sign of the master's humanity. Carleton recalled asking a peasant why he sent his children to a schoolmaster who was a notorious drinker

[88] Edward Sheehy, 'The philomath sings', *Ireland Today*, i (Aug. 1936), pp 22–3.
[89] Louis J. Walsh, 'Some Irish schoolmasters', *The Catholic World*, cxxxv (Aug. 1932), p. 584.
[90] Wakefield, ii, 398.   [91] Brenan, pp 61–2.

rather than to a sober master who taught in the same neighbourhood:

'So,' I said, 'you think that a love of drinking poteen is a sign of
talent in a schoolmaster?'

'Ay, or in any man else, sir,' he replied.[92]

The schoolmasters, the curriculum, and the teaching methods
of the hedge schools were clearly of a mixed sort. The same tentativeness and awareness of variety that characterized our discussion of the qualitative aspects of the schools must extend to
estimates of enrollment. During the era when the penal laws
were being strictly enforced the hedge schools were, by definition, clandestine operations, impossible to enumerate. In 1731,
a *Report on the present state of popery* was prepared from information submitted by prominent persons in each diocese. Although
the reporters undoubtedly failed to uncover every popish school,
the number reported, 549, is strikingly large.[93] Bishop Coppin-
ger of Cloyne and Ross prepared a catholic school census in
1807, providing the basis for an estimate in 1809 by Major
Newenham that in these districts there were 316 unendowed
schools containing 21,892 children, mostly Roman Catholics.[94]
The school census of 1824 provided two sets of figures on the
number of pupils and schools throughout the country, one set of
returns being provided by protestant clergy, the other by those
of the catholic faith. According to the protestant returns, there
were 10,387 day schools in the country, containing 498,641
pupils, of whom 357,249 were catholic. The catholic return
enumerated 10,453 schools, with a total of 522,016 pupils,
397,212 of these being Roman Catholic.[95] It is safe to assume
that the great majority of the catholic children were being
educated in hedge schools and hence to conclude that by the
mid-1820s, between 300,000 and 400,000 children were being
educated in such institutions.

If much about the hedge schools remains unknown that is

[92] Carleton, 'The hedge school', p. 272.
[93] 'Report on the state of popery, Ireland 1731', *Archivium Hibernicum*,
i (1912), p. 11.
[94] Thomas Newenham, view of Ireland (London, 1809), p. xix, quoted
in Corcoran, *Some lists*, p. 42.
[95] First report of the commissioners of Irish education inquiry, pp
101–2.

inevitable. For an understanding of the creation of the national system of education, their existence is their most important characteristic. Willingness on the part of the bulk of the Irish common people to support popular educational institutions is one of the chief reasons Ireland was to come to possess the first state system of popular schools in the English-speaking world.

III

AN ADMINISTRATIVE
GENEALOGY

~~~~~~

I

IN 1831 E. G. STANLEY, the chief secretary for Ireland,
established the Irish national system of education; to the average member of parliament it must have seemed as if Stanley
fashioned the system upon his own initiative and from his own
ideas. Such was not the case. In reality, Lord Stanley merely
crystallized into administrative form the ideas of an Irish
educational consensus that had been forming for almost fifty
years before his administration began. The emergence of the
Irish educational consensus is best traced through a series of
official government reports on education. Although the individual documents in the series were often dull and repetitive,
their cumulative effect was important and deserves considerable
attention. Significantly, the Irish educational consensus was
achieved at a remarkably early date, indeed, nearly four decades
before the parallel consensus was reached in England.

The chain of events that produced the national system began
in the pre-union Irish parliament with Thomas Orde's introduction of a plan of education into the Irish parliament of 1787.
It is noteworthy that educational thought in official circles after
the union maintained a remarkable continuity with its pre-
union antecedents. The commissions of 1806–12, 1824–7, 1828
and 1830 all built upon pre-union foundations. Because

59

parliaments both before and after the union did not hesitate to meddle in Irish educational matters, it was nearly inevitable that a parliament would eventually replace the illiberal and almost useless educational system of Henry VIII, of Elizabeth I, and of the charter school zealots, with a new system of its own. When that happened, the basic ideas were sure to be drawn from the accepted educational wisdom of the day.

John Hely-Hutchinson, provost of Trinity College, Dublin, was a proponent of parliamentary reform and of relief of catholic disabilities who also concerned himself with educational matters. In late October 1783, he stated, during a short discussion of education in the house of commons of the Irish parliament, that he had long seen the necessity of the creation of two or more 'great public schools' in Ireland, similar to Westminster and Eton. He briefly mentioned a scheme for establishing such schools in Ireland that he intended to propose to the house at a future date.[1] Hely-Hutchinson made a detailed outline of the plan, and sent it in December 1785 to Thomas Orde, then chief secretary for Ireland. 'The want of good schools in this kingdom,' Hely-Hutchinson declared, 'has long been the subject of general complaint. There never was greater cause for it than at present. The learned languages are very ill taught; and young men are not trained to composition in any language. The defects in school education essentially affect the knowledge, taste, and manner of the people.'[2] He proposed that two great schools be established in Ireland under the authority of the legislature. The schools were to be founded and supported by public expense, and these arrangements were to be sanctioned by an act of parliament. Hely-Hutchinson intended that the schools, at least in their early stages, would each consist of one master, three assistants, and thirty-four boys. The boys were to be on the foundation and called 'king's scholars' and were to receive 'education, dinner, supper and dormitory, without any expense'. The school course was to last seven or eight years. King's scholars were to be chosen by public examination, a test that

---

[1] *The parliamentary register* (Dublin, 1784), iv, 57.
[2] Bolton Manuscripts, 29/24, 17 Dec. 1785. 'Outline of a plan for a great school connected with the University and some thoughts on school education in Ireland' (in the possession of the Right Hon. Lord Bolton, Bolton Hall, Leyburn, Yorkshire).

was to include composition in Latin verse and prose. Two hundred pounds a year for the headmaster, one hundred pounds for any under-masters, and fifty pounds for assistants were suggested salaries. Masters and assistants were to be from Eton, Westminster, or Harrow. Significantly, Hely-Hutchinson saw these schools as model schools upon which other schools throughout the country would pattern themselves: 'The greatest advantage which will attend a scheme of this nature remains to be mentioned. It will raise the spirits and invigorate the exertions of the rising generation, to see that education is become an object of public attention and solicitude, in Ireland, and that by the cheering countenance of royal favour and protection it is to receive legislative encouragement, and support.'[3]

Perhaps the most important result of Hely-Hutchinson's proposals was that they alerted Thomas Orde to the need for educational legislation. Orde was a member of the Irish parliament for Rathcormack from 1784 to 1790. He also served as member of the English parliament from 1780 to 1796. As chief secretary for Ireland under the duke of Rutland, from 1784 to 1787, he concerned himself at first with proposals for the commercial union of England and Ireland. Hely-Hutchinson's plan, however, intrigued him. He thought the general system proposed was good, and he was sufficiently interested to show the plan to the lord lieutenant.[4] On 6 April 1786, Orde addressed the commons about the improvement of education, and moved two resolutions which the house unanimously adopted. He stated that he was aware that there were already several endowed schools in the country, some of them very rich, but he felt that their very opulence was the chief cause of the defeat of their founders' intentions, for some of the masters were content to receive their salaries without doing any work at all. The best remedy, he felt, was not to endow additional schools in a manner that only benefited the masters but to provide assistance to the students as well. He then moved 'that the national foundation of one or more public schools, with regulations adapted thereto, for

---

[3] Ibid.
[4] T. Orde to J. Hely-Hutchinson, 26 Dec. 1785, *Historical Manuscripts Commission, twelfth report, appendix, part IX, Manuscripts of the duke of Beaufort, K.G., the earl of Donoughmore and others*, p. 316 [C. 6338–I], H.C. 1890–1891, xlvi.

facilitating and extending to the youth of this kingdom the means of good education, would be of great public utility'.[5] Appropriately, Hely-Hutchinson seconded Orde's motion. The commons resolved that an address was to be presented to the lord lieutenant requesting that his grace give directions for the preparing of necessary plans for the creation of such schools. Thus, somewhat less than three years after Hely-Hutchinson raised the educational question, the Irish commons was on record as favouring government provision of endowed schools and as demanding action on the part of the lord lieutenant.

The lord lieutenant returned the commons' volley in his message to the house at the opening of the January 1787 session of parliament. Significantly, in telling the commons what he expected of them in educational matters, the lord lieutenant made it clear that he wished them to prepare a plan not only for endowed schools, but for Irish education generally: 'I hope some liberal and extensive plan for the general improvement of education will be matured for an early execution.'[6] Meanwhile, the chief secretary had been busy. Sometime in late 1786 or in early 1787 he began making notes of various matters concerning schools.[7] He eventually produced two notebooks in which he outlined his plan of education. One of these was an eighteen page proposal entitled 'system of education, college of visitors and inspectors', a cautious document whose contents were no more dramatic than its title.[8] But in his second notebook, Orde indulged in none of the timidity that characterized his essay on the college of visitors. His subject was nothing less than a plan of education for all Ireland.[9] By April 1787 he was ready to

[5] *The parliamentary register* (Dublin, 1786), vi. 448. See also the *Journals of the house of commons of the kingdom of Ireland from the nineteenth day of January, 1786, inclusive, to the eighteenth day of April, 1788, inclusive, in the reign of his majesty George the Third* (Dublin, 1792), p. 138.

[6] *The parliamentary register* (Dublin, 1787), vii, 12.

[7] See Bolton Manuscripts, 29/26, 29/28-35.

[8] Bolton Manuscripts, 29/36.

[9] A notebook of sixty-two pages contains the outline of Orde's plan (Bolton Manuscripts, 29/37). Orde later produced a polished version of the plan, contained in two volumes of 86 pages each. (Bodleian Library, MSS Top Ireland, d.2, d.3). Three points are worth noting about the dating of the various Orde notebooks: first, since none of them are dated, any reconstruction of the chain of events must be conjectural; second, the college of visitors notebook and the plan of education notebook are

present it to parliament for its approval. On 12 April he arose and called the attention of the house to that part of the lord lieutenant's message dealing with education, and upon Orde's suggestion the commons resolved itself into a committee to consider the matter of education. Orde then opened the committee debate with a long speech in which he outlined his plan of education. He imputed 'all the violent and atrocious acts which had too often disgraced this nation' to a want of education and consequently to a want of obedience to the laws.[10] Orde pressed

[10] The *parliamentary register* vi, 486–7. See also the *Journals of the house of commons* for 12 April 1787, and also John Giffard, *Mr Orde's plan of an improved system of education in Ireland: submitted to the house of commons, April 12, 1787, with the debate which arose thereon* (Dublin, 1787). Giffard should be treated with somewhat more caution than the other two sources on the debate, since he was evidently in Orde's pay: a letter from Giffard to an unnamed member of Orde's staff dated 22 October 1787, indicates that Orde underwrote Giffard's publication (Bolton Manuscripts, 29/22).

closely related. For instance, the college of visitors notebook took for granted the idea of a 'new university' which is mooted in the plan of education essay. One should not assume, however, merely because some ideas of the plan of education essay are part of the framework for the college of visitors piece, that the plan of education essay was necessarily completed before its companion piece. The extremely timid tone of the college of visitors notebook, when compared with the experienced, confident tone of the plan of education outline, argues that the college of visitors piece could well have been written first. Lacking any conclusive evidence, it is best merely to note that the two notebooks were products of a single thought process, and to abandon any attempt to establish the precise sequence of Orde's ideas. Third, the reason for placing the production of both notebooks in late 1786 or early 1787, is Orde's statement to the Irish commons on 12 April 1787, that 'the state of his health had not allowed him to consider the subject till the present session had commenced' (*The parliamentary register*, vii, 500). The session began 18 Jan. 1787. 'The subject' probably refers specifically to his own plan of education, not to the topic of education in general, since in April 1786, he had moved resolutions on the subject of endowed schools. Despite Orde's statement that he had worked on the plan only during 1787, one wonders if he did not actually begin late in 1786. The fact that the lord lieutenant instructed parliament to produce a general plan of education for Ireland in his January speech opening parliament is suggestive in this regard since Orde, and not the lord lieutenant, had previously handled the government's educational dealings. A reasonable guess would be that the lord lieutenant made his suggestion to the commons at the chief secretary's urging, and that the chief secretary had been doing some planning some time before the January opening of parliament.

upon the committee the case of the neglected Irish peasantry who, though blessed with minds as vigorous as those of any nation, were apparently considered by the legislature as weightless in the political scale and hence were ignored. Far from believing them weightless or worthless, Orde was aggrieved 'that they have been suffered to remain as a rich metal in the mine, which no fashioning hand of an artist has hitherto attempted to polish into beauty, and upon which no stamp of instruction has been set to give an acknowledged worth and currency'.[11]

But were there not already institutions of education in the country bending to the task? There were, the chief secretary admitted, but they were largely inefficient and ineffective altars from which the incense had been robbed. The situation could be saved only by old institutions being purified and new ones being created alongside. The first part of Orde's plan involved breathing life into Henry VIII's parish schools act by requiring incumbents to actually make the prescribed educational donations, in amounts ranging from forty shillings a year for the less well-paid clergy, to above three pounds a year for those with livings worth more than two hundred pounds annually. Further imposts were to be made if the rectors received rectorial and impropriate tithes. After this amount was collected, the remaining amount needed to fully support a parish school was to be assessed, at the discretion of the vestry, upon the more prosperous proprietors of the parish. The second aspect of Orde's plan involved the creation of four great schools, one in each province, similar to Christ's Hospital in London. These were to be supported by funds previously allocated to the charter schools from which they were to be gradually withdrawn. The great schools were to teach the technical arts, navigation, mercantile knowledge, agriculture, modern languages, and similar useful subjects. Orde suggested that one of the schools might be formed by enlarging the Blue Coat Hospital in Dublin and that the needs of two provinces might be served by locating a large institution in the buildings at New Geneva which were already public property. The estimated cost of operating these schools was 11,000 pounds to 12,000 pounds per annum. Third, Orde proposed to improve the diocesan schools. He did not elaborate

[11] *The parliamentary register,* vii, 487.

greatly upon this, but made it clear that the protestant bishops would be required to contribute liberally towards their improvement. Twenty-two operational diocesan schools providing a foundation in classical learning was his goal.[12]

Orde's fourth object was to establish two 'great academies' that would serve as preparatory schools for the university. To support these, and also to aid the diocesan schools, he proposed that part of the revenue of lands given to the state for the endowment of schools—land that had largely fallen into private hands—be reclaimed and applied consonant with the donors' intentions. In order to provide an educational ladder for boys of genius to climb, exhibitions and other incitements to merit were to be created throughout the system, and especially at the two highest academies. Fifth, he proposed a second university for Ireland, this one to be located in the northwest portion of the country. He thought that several of the endowed schools of the northwest could be blended together to form a university. This object, he admitted, could not be achieved for several years. Finally, Orde proposed that a college of visitors be created, as sketched in his early notebook on the subject. He concluded by offering resolutions recording the house's approval of his proposals. In the resolutions he made two important additions to his plan: he moved that it was expedient for parliament to create an annual fund, to be known as the 'lord lieutenant's school fund', to be applied to purchasing and building schools and providing for free instruction for the poor. He also moved that parliament at its next session should take steps to carry the foregoing resolutions into full effect.[13]

Parliamentary reaction was notably mild. Messrs Stewart, Browne, and Wolfe expressed stupefaction; the plan was simply too grand and complex to comprehend at a moment's notice, much more to criticize intelligently. Hely-Hutchinson seconded the resolutions, but demurred, as one would expect the provost of Trinity to do, from the idea of a second university. The debate meandered along much the same course when resumed on April sixteenth. Arthur Browne (Trinity College) moved that the resolution that another university might be useful be amended by adding the words 'or might not'. This amendment was

12 Ibid., pp 487–92.
13 Ibid., pp 492–6.

defeated, and without further objection the resolutions passed unanimously.[14] If Orde's correspondence is any indication, the reception of the plan outside of parliament seems to have been equally benign. The grand jury of the county of the city of Limerick returned their thanks to Orde for a plan that 'must not only reform the morals of the people, but furnish the nation with a new and most useful body of industrious men'.[15] One correspondent denominated it 'a glorious plan of civilization for the country'.[16] The protestant archbishop of Cashel wrote that 'if the day be approaching when we shall see a well digested plan of education permanently established throughout Ireland, I shall congratulate my country on having obtained one of the greatest blessings which providence can bestow on a people'.[17]

Although the Irish commons approved Orde's plan with only minor hesitation, the dissenting protestants and Roman Catholics were not pleased with the religious arrangements implied by Orde's proposals. The plan introduced the principle, crucial to developments of the succeeding century, that the benefits of education should be equally available to all children, without regard to their religious denomination. We should not, however, regard the plan as extremely liberal, for Orde postulated that children who were maintained and educated at state expense should be brought up in the established religion. Also, the superintendence and staffing of the institutions were to be under established church control. Orde felt that those who were objecting, notably the presbyterians, would 'readily perceive and acknowledge the evident propriety of forming these public establishments, thus made in general open to all disciples of all religions, upon the *single basis* of the established church'.[18] Certainly the idea of resuscitating the parish and the diocesan schools was an attempt to breathe new life into the establishment's educational structures. When Sir Francis Hutchinson protested that Orde's plan would be a fatal blow to the prot-

[14] Ibid., pp 496–504, 507–11.
[15] John Ferrar to Thomas Orde, 16 Apr. 1787, Bolton Manuscripts, 29/6.
[16] Dr Allott to Thomas Orde, Oct. 1787, Bolton Manuscripts, 29/19.
[17] Michael Cox to Thomas Orde, undated, Bolton Manuscripts, 29/3.
[18] Giffard, p. 121.

estant religion in Ireland, the chief secretary replied that 'he wondered that such an idea could have entered the mind of the honourable baronet; for surely if ever any plan more strong than another in support of the established religion, had been proposed, it was present'.[19] In fairness to Orde, we must note that if he favoured increasing the educational prerogatives of the state church, he also proposed increasing the responsibility borne by the church in educational matters. In exchange for the benefits such a system would bring the church, its clergy were to fulfil the educational duties they had long neglected.

Richard Griffith expressed the situation clearly in debate when he stated bluntly of the plan, 'it does not extend to the education of the Roman Catholic and presbyterian youth of this country. It may be answered, that they are not directly excluded; but I say they are virtually so, unless pastors of their own persuasion are appointed to instruct them'.[20] The matter of the Ulster university was especially troubling to the presbyterians, for they wanted not a university in the north run by the established church, but a presbyterian foundation supported by government money. In February 1787, the synod of Ulster had petitioned parliament for 'ample and permanent' support for an academy or academies for educating their youth for the ministry, these institutions to provide a sufficiently advanced education to obviate the need for presbyterians to send their ministerial candidates to foreign universities.[21] James Stewart, who had presented the Ulster petition in February, mentioned this request during the debate on Orde's bill, but did not press the matter. The catholic reaction was more bitter, if less well organized. Archbishop Egan of Tuam wrote to Archbishop Troy at Dublin in February 1788:

I have, on receipt of your most esteemed favour, written to the prelates of this province of Tuam. Our thoughts on Mr Orde's scheme of education are that it is a deep-laid and hostile plan against the interests of the catholic religion. Nor is it to be supposed from motives of persecution: but from a political view of strengthening the hands of government, by increasing the members of the established church. For what other can be the design in establishing protestant

19 *The parliamentary register*, vii, 500.
20 Ibid., pp 503–4
21 Ibid., p. 169, 14 Feb. 1787.

schoolmasters in every parish, to the exclusion, no doubt, of catholic teachers, and with so many inducements to the poor to send their children there: the youth will there be fitted for different employments, in which protestants alone are trusted, and all these motives will be carefully and artfully insinuated and displayed before their eyes.[22]

Whatever its virtues or vices, Orde's plan was never implemented. Despite its resolve to return to the subject of its implementation in their next session, the Irish parliament never again discussed Orde's proposals. The lord lieutenant (the duke of Rutland) died, and Orde left office in October 1787. The plan was abandoned, and the pressures of the French war and the regency crisis prevented its being reintroduced. Nevertheless, Orde's work was a touchstone in the evolution of the core of ideas from which the national system of education was eventually to be fashioned. Orde was the first legislator to realize that Ireland's educational institutions should be treated as a system, rather than as a collection, of schools. This system, he believed, should not be limited to the middle and upper classes but should also extend to the teaching of the peasantry. Orde's plan implied the provision and control of schools by the central government. And narrow though Orde's religious prejudices may seem to the modern observer, his plan deserves notice for postulating that any state system of education should be open to all Irish children irrespective of their religious affiliations.

Thomas Orde's educational legacy was not limited to the expression of new ideas which parliament promptly forgot; he was chiefly responsible for setting afoot a series of educational investigations that continued in progress and influence long after he had resigned as chief secretary. John Howard visited Ireland in 1784 and in 1787 and inquired into the prisons and charter schools, on the latter of which he reported most unfavourably. A good deal of discussion occurred, and in 1786 and 1787, Sir Jeremiah Fitzpatrick, the inspector-general of prisons, visited a large number of charter schools.[23] These tours excited consider-

[22] Quoted, but not cited, by Corcoran, 'The Dublin education bill of 1787', *The Irish Monthly*, lix (Aug. 1931), p. 499.

[23] *Report of her majesty's commissioners appointed to inquire into the endowments, funds, and actual condition of all schools endowed for the purpose of education in Ireland*, p. 16 [2336–I], H.C. 1857–8, xxii, pt. i.

able interest among M.P.s. Hely-Hutchinson had suggested, in the outline of his own plan for two great schools which he sent to Orde and dated 17 December 1785, that the state and management of the charter schools bore looking into. Orde commented in the margin, 'This should really be attended to.'[24] Orde was concerned about the royal and diocesan schools and other foundations as well as about the charter schools, and in April 1786, when moving his resolutions about the creation of one or more public schools, also moved that returns be ordered from the registrars of the several dioceses, and also that returns on the royal and diocesan schools, their numbers, endowments, and enrolment be prepared. To this the house unanimously agreed.[25] Among the resolutions passed concerning Orde's plan of education during the following year was one that the lord lieutenant be addressed and requested to have exact returns prepared of the number and state of the parish schools, to have all facts concerning their endowment and financial arrangements returned. In another resolution his grace was also asked for returns on the charter schools, and the Erasmus Smith schools. A third resolution asked for returns of diocesan schools.[26] These resolutions were the only ones touching on Orde's plan to be carried into effect.

Orde's successor as chief secretary, Alleyne Fitzherbert, was interested in educational matters, and, on 13 March 1788, he followed Orde's lead by introducing a bill to enable the lord lieutenant to appoint commissioners to inquire into the funds and revenues, both of public and private donation, given for the endowment of schools, and also into the condition of the schools. The bill was given an immediate first reading, a second reading on the next day, and was debated in committee on the nineteenth of March, before passing the third reading on the twentieth. The lords reported their agreement on the twenty-fifth and it received the royal assent on the eighteenth of April.[27] Fitzherbert himself was one of the commissioners

[24] Bolton Manuscripts, 29/24.
[25] *Journals . . . house of commons . . . nineteenth day of January, 1786 . . . to the eighteenth day of April, 1788*, p. 138, 6 Apr. 1786.
[26] *The parliamentary register*, vii, 493–4, 12 Apr. 1787.
[27] *Journals . . . house of commons . . . nineteenth day of January, 1786 . . . to the eighteenth day of April, 1788*, pp 402, 411, 413, 419, 427.

appointed, along with John Hely-Hutchinson.[28] The commissioners proceeded with great dispatch; the *Wexford Herald* of 4 December 1788, reported that the commissioners were nearly done with their investigations.[29] It is probable that they issued a report of some kind in late 1788 or early 1789, although no copy has survived.[30] This report was probably a preliminary document, as the commission's warrant was extended until they could complete their work in 1791. Like the 1788–9 document, the 1791 report was not published. Although referred to by the education commissions of 1806–12 and of 1838, it was not printed until the endowed schools commission discovered and published a copy in 1858.[31]

[28] The other members were Denis Daly, Isaac Corry, John Forbes, Thomas Burgh, Edward Booke and Robert Hobart. Hobart joined in 1789, when appointed chief secretary, in place of Fitzherbert who resigned from the commission upon leaving office (*Evidence taken before her majesty's commissioners of inquiry into the state of the endowed schools in Ireland*, ii, p. 366 [2336–III], H.C. 1857–8, xxii, pt iii).

[29] Quoted in Michael Quane, 'The diocesan schools—1570–1870', *Journal of the Cork Historical and Archaeological Society*, 2 ser., lxvi (Jan.–June 1961), pp 35–6.

[30] The endowed schools commission of 1858 conducted a thorough search for the 1788/9 report. It reported that 'according to the record commissioner, this document was obtained from the secretary of state's office by the commissioners of education inquiry, 1807–1812. It is mentioned among their minutes of evidence. The committee of the house of commons on foundation schools of 1838 mentions a report of 1788, but the passage quoted is from the final report of 1791. The 1788/9 report was, unfortunately, never published and although transferred to the care of the secretary of the commissioners of education for Ireland, could not be found' (*Report of her majesty's commissioners appointed to inquire into the endowments, funds, and actual condition of all schools endowed for the purpose of education in Ireland*, p. 17).

[31] 'Copy of report of commissioners appointed by his excellency the lord lieutenant of Ireland, in 1788, under the provision of an act, 28th Geo. III, c. 15 (Irish), entitled "An act to enable the lord lieutenant and other chief governors of this kingdom to appoint commissioners for inquiry into the several funds and revenues granted by public and private donations for the purpose of education in this kingdom, and into the state and conduct of all schools in this kingdom on public or charitable foundations, and of the funds appropriated for the maintenance and support thereof, and for the other purposes herein mentioned"', in *Evidence taken before her majesty's commissioners of inquiry into the state of the endowed schools in Ireland*, ii, 341–79.

The 1791 report attacked its subject in much the same manner in which Thomas Orde had proceeded. The commissioners first surveyed the parish schools of Henry the VIII and found the Tudor act defective because it failed to stipulate the salary to be paid to schoolmasters by the incumbent; a general usage prevailed in more than half the Irish benefices of paying only forty shillings yearly for school keeping. The act was also declared ineffective for not providing for the education of the children of the poor. The requirement that the incumbent must conduct the school himself if he did not hire a schoolmaster was considered by the commissioners to be degrading to the clerical order. The commissioners recommended, therefore, that all clergy be required to contribute forty shillings yearly and that their parishioners should raise an equal sum. They proposed that the parish clerk be the schoolmaster and that he be paid at least twenty pounds yearly for his educational and ecclesiastical duties. Nine hundred parish schools, it was thought, would be sufficient for the whole kingdom.

The commissioners made a very radical suggestion for the eighteenth century: namely, that the visitors or governors of these schools should be the incumbent, the churchwardens and four laymen. The laymen, two protestants and two catholics, were to be named by the Anglican vestry. Equally important, the incumbent was to be obliged to fill only two major duties in connection with the school: to report yearly to a central board of control on the state of the school, and to instruct those children of the protestant faith in the religion of the established church. Thus, the incumbent was to share his formerly exclusive control over the parish school with a board of laymen, two of whom were to be Roman Catholics, and was to be limited in his catechizing to teaching children of the protestant faith. Even more striking was the commissioners' statement that, 'it is our opinion that the children of Roman Catholics and protestants should be admitted indiscriminately into the schools, and that the clergy of each persuasion should attend for the purpose of instructing the children belonging to their respective communions

On the discovery of the report see *Report of her majesty's commissioners appointed to inquire into the endowments, funds, and actual condition of all schools endowed for the purpose of education in Ireland,* p. 17.

in the principles of religion; a mode practiced, as we are informed, with great success in the school of Saint Andrew's, Dublin, and of Saint Peter's, Drogheda'.[32] As an inducement for parents, especially the poor, to send their children to school, the commissioners suggested that no person should be entitled to an exemption from paying the hearth-money tax or be eligible to receive any grants from parish charity unless they sent their children to the parish school.

The diocesan schools were next discussed, or, rather, the confusion surrounding the diocesan schools was discussed. To bring order into the situation, the commissioners desired that the lord lieutenant and council appoint a schoolmaster for each of the thirty-two dioceses. (They had found evidence of schools in only twenty of the dioceses.) Although the Elizabethan act creating the diocesan schools had laid the entire expense of building and maintaining the schools, as well as the cost of hiring the schoolmaster, upon the ordinary and clergy, the commissioners made the important additional suggestion that all building and repair expenses, plus one half of the teacher's salary, be borne by the county. The commissioners then surveyed the condition of each of the five royal schools, but they made no suggestions save that salaries ought to be reduced and the savings put towards the foundation of a 'great' or 'collegiate' school to be connected with the university. The collegiate school plans were clearly a modified restatement of Hely-Hutchinson's and Orde's proposals for the founding of public schools on the English model. Also clearly based on Orde's proposals were the plans for the creation of one or more professional academies to teach the useful arts, sciences, and languages. Next, the commissioners scrutinized ten assorted schools of public and private foundations, but it was only the protestant charter schools which drew their full wrath. They listed seven 'evils' responsible for the 'wretched condition of these schools and nurseries'. These evils ranged from the utterly insufficient allowance of only two pence a day to maintain each child, to the 'ignorance, gross neglect, and frauds of the masters and mistresses' to the number of charter schools being greater than their funds could support.[33] Their remedies involved a complete revolution in the society's handling of its affairs.

[32] Ibid., p. 343.   [33] Ibid., pp 357–8.

The commissioners' final suggestion deserves special attention: the creation of a board of control. This board, to be created by an act of parliament, was to receive all complaints made about the conduct of masters and ushers of schools on public and private foundation, or about the misapplication of funds, and was to have summary jurisdiction to redress complaints. Appeal from the board's sentence could be made to the court of chancery. In the case of schools with no visitors or where the founder had given no instructions on the plan of education to be followed, the board of control was to be empowered to determine the course of education to be pursued. It was also to be authorized to require periodic accounts from schoolmasters, and to be allowed to visit any of the schools under their jurisdiction to examine masters and ushers under oath. The proposal that a state board with considerable power over educational institutions be created represents an important addition to Thomas Orde's proposals and a major step towards a plan of national education. The committee began the last paragraph of its report on a note of restrained optimism: 'We have now submitted to your excellency such a plan of education as we have been able to digest from the information that has been laid before us, from which we are able to decide with perfect certainty that a plan of national education is not, as has been supposed by many, impracticable in this kingdom'.[34]

The 1791 report was a remarkable document especially for eighteenth-century Ireland: it propounded that the control of local parish schools should be taken from the iron grasp of the local protestant vicar and placed in the hands of a body composed chiefly of laymen; it suggested that Roman Catholics be admitted to the body of laymen controlling each of the local parish schools; it implicitly attempted to prevent proselytizing by suggesting that clergy of all denominations be allowed into the parish schools to teach religious doctrine to any child of their faith; and it proposed the creation of a board of control by the central government with supervisory power over almost all of the nation's educational institutions. Unfortunately, the report's immediate fate was as undistinguished as its contents were remarkable. The report was never published and was not presented to parliament. The document may well have been the

[34] Ibid., p. 366.

victim of its own vigour; one reason suggested for the report's suppression is that its findings, especially those regarding the charter schools, were too strong to be made public.[35] Yet, despite the suppression of the document, it eventually had a significant impact upon Irish educational development, since it was exhumed and studied by the commissioners of education inquiry, 1806–12. Thus, the report served as an almost invisible link in the evolving chain of Irish education thinking.

With the exception of the catholic relief act of 1793 which removed the remaining catholic education disabilities, and excepting the establishment of Maynooth in 1795, the Irish parliament did not spend much time on education during most of the 1790s. It ceased its educational slumbers for a brief moment in 1799 when, on the eighth of February 1799, the commons resolved that an address be presented to the lord lieutenant asking that the 1791 report be laid before the house.[36] At the same time the house prayed that a committee be appointed to inquire into the state of the education of the lower orders of the people and the means of improving their education.[37] Richard Lovell Edgeworth deserves credit for re-opening the education question. His *Practical education*, in three volumes, appeared in the autumn of 1798 and attracted a great deal of attention to the subject of education. It was owing to his personal efforts that the select committee of February 1799 was appointed, Edgeworth himself being the chief member of the committee.[38] The committee sprinted through its paces and reported on 22 February 1799. Speaking for the committee, Edgeworth read six resolutions the committee had passed. First, that in their opinion the

---

[35] Quane, p. 36.

[36] *Journals of the house of commons of the kingdom of Ireland from the twenty-second day of January, 1799, inclusive, to the first day of June, 1799, inclusive; being the second session of the sixth parliament of Ireland in the reign of his present majesty George III* (Dublin, 1799), p. 19. The endowed schools commission of 1858 could not find any trace that the application was complied with (*Report of her majesty's commissioners appointed to inquire into the endowments, funds and actual condition of all schools endowed for the purpose of education in Ireland*, p. 19).

[37] *Journals . . . house of commons . . . twenty-second day of January, 1799 . . . to first day of June, 1799*, p. 19.

[38] Desmond Clarke, *The ingenious Mr Edgeworth* (London, 1965), p. 169.

present state of education of the lower orders was highly defective and required the interposition of the legislature. Second, that the establishment of one or more schools in every parish would be useful to the public. Third, that masters of these new parish schools should undergo examination, receive certificates of morals and ability, and be licensed annually. Fourth, that the payment of such masters should consist partially of a fixed salary and partially of rewards proportioned to their exertion and success. Fifth, that the books used in the schools to be created in each parish be chosen by persons specially appointed for that purpose. Finally, that one or more visitors be empowered to inspect these and all other parish schools once in every year.[39] Edgeworth, unlike Thomas Orde and unlike the 1791 commissioners, envisaged a system of lower class education apart from schools of the middle sort and apart from any ladder of university entrance.

The house debated the subject in committee on the twenty-fifth of February, and again on the twenty-sixth. On the conclusion of the debate the commons resolved 'that it is the opinion of the committee, that the house should be moved for leave to bring in a bill pursuant to the said report'.[40] Edgeworth, Sir John Freke, John Staunton Rochfort, and Arthur Browne were appointed to prepare the bill. Edgeworth presented the bill to the house on 28 March 1799, when it was read the first time. Although the house had resolved on the twenty-eighth that the bill was to be read a second time tomorrow,[41] this was never done. Precisely why the 1799 bill was dropped so precipitously remains a mystery, although the politics of the coming union with England doubtless were generally responsible. The exact contents of the bill are also a mystery, for no copy remains; certainly the bill followed the guidelines set down by the select committee's resolutions, but we have no indication of the precise details.

Thus, when the British parliament took over responsibility for Irish education in 1800, it inherited not only the problems of Irish education, but a considerable amount of detailed

---

[39] *Journals . . . house of commons . . . twenty-second day of January, 1799 . . . to first day of June, 1799,* p. 32.
[40] Ibid., p. 42.
[41] Ibid., p. 88.

information on the educational system, and a stock of suggested solutions. The united parliament ignored neither the problem of Irish education nor the backlog of possible answers. Typically, the government seems to have walled off Irish problems from similar English questions. The matter of Irish education was dealt with solely as an Irish matter, and the answers provided were treated as solely applicable to Ireland. Ironically, while Irish educational policy was evolving in isolation from English politics, it was steadily developing towards a consensus; meanwhile educational discussions in England itself was balked by a series of religious disputes. In 1806, apparently at the bequest of Newport, chancellor of the exchequer for Ireland in the Ministry of All the Talents, and William Stuart, protestant archbishop of Armagh, a statutory commission of inquiry on Irish education was created.[42] The commission was, quite explicitly, a revival of the 1788–91 commission, the act of parliament under which it operated being, 'An act to revive and amend an act made in the parliament of Ireland, for enabling the lord lieutenant to appoint commissioners for inquiring into the several funds and revenues granted for the purposes of education, and into the state and condition of all schools in Ireland'.[43] Under the provisions of the act the lord lieutenant was to appoint up to six commissioners, and the commissioners of charitable bequests were to appoint up to five of their own body as commissioners. The commissioners appointed by the lord lieutenant formed a link with pre-union educational thinking, Isaac Corry (one of the 1788–91 commissioners) and Richard Lovell Edgeworth being among them. The lord lieutenant's other nominees were Robert Stearne Tighe, William Disney, Henry Grattan, and William Parnell. The appointees of the commissioners of charitable donations and bequests were William Stuart, the protestant archbishop of Armagh, Charles Agar, earl of Normanton and archbishop of Dublin, James Verschoyle, dean of St. Patrick's and later bishop of Killala, George Hall, the provost of Trinity College, and James White-

---

[42] R. B. McDowell, *The Irish administration, 1801–1914* (London and Toronto, 1964), p. 234.

[43] *Report from the commissioners of the board of education in Ireland: first report, free schools of royal foundation,* p. 1, H.C. 1813–14 (47), v, originally printed 1809, H.C. (142), vii.

law, minister of St Catherine's, Dublin.[44] The commissioners first met in Dublin Castle on 21 October 1806. From the first, it was clear that the clerical members would be dominant, for at that meeting the archbishop of Armagh presided. At all subsequent meetings one of the archbishops or the provost took the chair.[45]

The commissioners worked from October 1806 until October 1812, producing fourteen reports. The first thirteen of these reports need not concern us here for they dealt with the now familiar topics inevitably covered by Irish education commissions: royal schools, diocesan schools, charter schools, parish schools, classical schools, and various schools of public and private foundation. The fourteenth report, in contrast, deserves detailed study, for it greatly influenced Irish educational practice during the century following its appearance. In that report, the commissioners concluded, hardly surprisingly, that the opportunities for education among the poor were insufficient. To bring order out of the chaos of 'ill-taught and ill-regulated schools' that plagued the kingdom, the commissioners suggested that a permanent body of education commissioners be created. The initial duty of such commissioners would be to inquire more closely into existing establishments. Thereafter the commissioners were to administer parliamentary grants, using them to create new schools where necessary, such schools to be under their control. The report mentioned this idea so casually that it is easy to miss the point that it is really a recommendation for massive state intervention in education, and for the provision of a system of education for the poorer classes. Another major idea mentioned by the commissioners was that there be a series of training institutions created for the proper training of teachers. Third, and most important, the fourteenth report enunciated a principle that was to be pivotal in all later Irish education discussions:

We conceive this to be of essential importance in any new establishments for the education of the lower classes in Ireland, and we venture to express our unanimous opinion, that no such plan however wisely and unexceptionably contrived in other respects, can be carried into effectual execution in this country, unless it be explicitly avowed, and clearly understood, as its leading principle, that no attempt shall

[44] Quane, p. 39.   [45] Ibid., p. 39.

77

be made to influence or disturb the peculiar religious tenets of any sect or description of christians.[46]

The report contained a fourth major suggestion, concerning the curriculum of the schools: the new education commissioners were to have control over all texts used in their schools, and they were also to draw up selections of extracts from the scriptures containing religious and moral instruction of a general sort. The volume of sacred extracts was apparently to be used during normal classroom hours. The inquiry commissioners felt it would 'form the best preparation for that more particular religious instruction which it would be the duty, and we doubt not, the inclination also, of their several ministers of religion to give, at proper times, and in other places, to the children of their respective congregations'.[47] Here was the germ of the principle that was to be the heart of the national system, namely that of keeping ordinary classroom literary and moral instruction separate from the study of dogmatic religion. The former was the province of the state, the latter of the local clergyman, and neither was to encroach upon the other.

Ironically, one immediate effect of the report was the establishment of a board of education almost precisely opposite in structure to that which the fourteenth report had suggested. In recommending substantial state intervention in the education field the commissioners had suggested creating a board of education that would specialize in lower class elementary education, and that would not interfere with established endowments: 'The check which the existing schools would receive, were the superintendence of them to be transferred to the proposed commissioners . . . induce us strongly to recommend that the institutions which now exist should remain under their present managers; and that the spirit of improvement already manifested among them should be left to operate undisturbed, under the influence of that emulation which the new establishments would naturally excite'.[48] Instead, a board of education

---

[46] *Report from the commissioners of the board of education in Ireland: fourteenth report, view of the chief foundations, with some general remarks and result of deliberations*, p. 2, H.C. 1821 (744), xi, originally printed in 1812–13, H.C. (21), vi; also printed in 1813–14, H.C. (47), v.

[47] Ibid., p. 7.   [48] Ibid., p. 5.

was created that dealt exclusively with endowed schools, already existing institutions catering mainly to the middle classes, the board thus dealing mostly on the secondary school level. This event was not so much a rejection of the commissioners' fourteenth report as the working out of variant conclusions from the commissioners' information. Wellesley Pole, chief secretary for Ireland, introduced a bill to regulate endowed schools on 15 May 1811. His speech indicates that he was moved largely by the evidence found in the reports of the commissioners of 1806–12.[49] The bill was not proceeded with, but a similar bill was passed in 1813. Certainly, the act was at least within the spirit of the fourteenth report in involving the intervention of the state in educational affairs.

Any slight the 1806–12 commissioners may have felt must have been smoothed over by the appointment of some of their number to the new board of education. Thomas Elrington, provost of Trinity, who had replaced William Disney as one of the 1806–12 commissioners, was appointed to the new board, as was John Leslie Foster, who had replaced William Parnell as an 1806–12 commissioner. John Corneille, former secretary to the 1806–12 commissioners, was appointed secretary.[50] The new board of education 'had a long and undistinguished history'[51] largely because the charter schools, Erasmus Smith's schools, parish schools of Henry VIII and all schools of private foundation under the control of visitors appointed by charter or act of parliament, and all schools of private foundation for children of any other than the established religion were exempted from their domain. This left the royal schools and a few educational odds and ends. The commissioners further cut their own effectiveness by maintaining that their power to visit schools did not imply a right to inspect, but rather only to operate in a judicial capacity.[52] For what it was worth, Ireland had a board of education in 1813; we should not be too surprised

[49] *Hansard* 1, xx, 146–150.
[50] *The report of the commissioners of education in Ireland to his excellency, the lord lieutenant of the proceedings of their board, from the 18th of November 1813 to the 25th of March 1814*, p. 1, H.C. 1814–15 (29), vi; Quane, p. 39.
[51] McDowell, p. 236.
[52] Ibid., p. 236; *Report of her majesty's commissioners appointed to inquire into the endowments, funds and actual condition of all schools endowed for the purpose of education in Ireland*, p. 21.

when we find that a nation that had a board of education as early as 1813 had a national system of education as early as 1831.

2

At this point we must turn our attention from the administrative genealogy that we have been tracing to the activities of a number of voluntary bodies on the Irish educational scene. During the last years of the eighteenth century and the first three or four decades of the nineteenth, a 'second reformation' was attempted in Ireland. The protestant denominations made a concerted effort to wean the Irish from Romanism. Bible societies and all manner of missions to the popish Irish flourished. Most important for our purposes were the protestant education societies. They had the unexpected effect of weaving the opinions of the Roman Catholic hierarchy into the Irish educational consensus. The actual chain of events leading to the result are complex and must be described in detail. The basic mechanism, however, was fairly simple: first, the protestant societies threatened the Roman Catholic church through their proselytizing activities; second, the Irish administration gave financial aid to some of the societies; third, as the only politically attainable alternative to state-aided protestant schools, the Roman Catholic hierarchy pressed for a state system of schools that would be religiously neutral.

The prototype of all protestant education societies was the charter school society. By this time, however, the charter school society itself was useful as a precedent and little else. The 1791 report had shown the society to be a wobbly association, and after the union it was tottering badly, supported mainly by government money. New societies had to be founded if the protestants were to turn the bulk of the Irish nation from its catholic faith.

The first of the new societies was the Association for Discountenancing Vice and Promoting the Knowledge and Practice of the Christian Religion. The society was founded by three members of the established church who met in October 1792, to parry the 'rapid progress which infidelity and immorality are making throughout the kingdom'. They decided to band together because, 'as many may be disheartened by considering the impotence of separate attempts to discountenance vice, and to promote the cause of religion and piety, it appears to us advisable to associate for that laudable purpose'.[53] During its early years the society seems to have accomplished little. Its income between 1792 and 1800 was wholly from subscriptions and amounted to only £1,989 13s 8d. This amount was spent mostly in the purchase of Bibles and prayer books, of moral tracts, and on the distribution of premiums for promotion of catechetical examinations. The society was incorporated in 1800, however, and soon thereafter received a parliamentary grant of £300.[54] This grant was renewed annually, rising to £9,084 in 1823.[55] It fluctuated considerably after that date, the proposed grant for 1830 being £5,000.[56] The grant was discontinued in 1831.

The flow of parliamentary money changed the society from pamphleteers to large-scale educators. The society was under the exclusive control of clergymen of the established church, and was for many years the closest thing the church had to an official educational arm. The association gave money towards the establishment of schools and towards the payment of teachers. Titles to such schools were vested in the local church wardens and the Anglican minister, the minister having the sole power of appointing and dismissing the schoolmaster. Before granting money in aid of teachers' salaries the association demanded the provision of a proper site for the schools. It also demanded that the school managers refuse all annual pecuniary aid from other public institutions, that the master and mistress be of the established church, and that all children of sufficient proficiency read the scriptures. The association forbade the use of any catechism other than that of the Church of England and refused to allow any book to be used of which the association disapproved. The harshness of the religious rules was lessened

[53] *First report of the commissioners of Irish education inquiry*, p. 31, H.C. 1825 (400), xii.

[54] Ibid., p. 31.

[55] *The report of the Association Incorporated for Discountenancing Vice and Promoting the Knowledge and Practice of the Christian Religion* (Dublin, 1826), p. 43.

[56] *Estimate of miscellaneous services for the year 1830*, p. 2, H.C. 1830–1 (11), vi.

by the association's opening their schools to children of all denominations, but requiring only the children of the established faith to attend catechetical instruction. Catholic children were, however, required to read the authorized version of the Bible. The association's schools contained a fair proportion of catholics during the first two decades of the nineteenth century (of the 8,828 children returned in association schools in 1819, 4,460 were Roman Catholic), and we may infer that during its early years, the association kept proselytizing tendencies within bounds. During the early 1820s, however, the society became increasingly repugnant to catholic feelings, permitting in some cases the attendance of catholic children at the catechetical class. Further, whereas the society had previously eschewed publishing any works of a controversial nature, it gradually abandoned this principle. It became a vigorous proselytizing agency, with the result that Roman Catholic children withdrew from the association's schools in large numbers and the association shrank to unimportance.[57]

The dubious honour of being the most aggressive of the protestant proselytizing bodies went to the London Hibernian Society. The society originated in London in 1806 upon the most anti-catholic of principles:

The great body of the Irish wander like sheep, that have no faithful shepherd to lead them. Legendary tales, pilgrimages, penances, superstitions, offerings, priestly domination, the notorious habit of reconciling sanctimonious accents and attitudes with abandoned practices, and all that shocks and disgusts in the mummery of the mass house, cannot fail to fix a mournful sentiment in the heart of every enlightened and pious observer . . . The hope, therefore, that the Irish will ever be a tranquil and loyal people, and still more that piety and virtue will flourish among them, must be built on the anticipated reduction of popery.[58]

Despite such views, the society publicly disavowed proselytism, and in the schools that it aided controversial books and pamphlets were supposed to be banned, as were catechisms. The Bible, though, was required reading. The resident minister of

[57] *First report of the commissioners of Irish education inquiry*, pp 31–7; R. Barry O'Brien, *Fifty years of concessions to Ireland, 1831–1881* (London, 1885), i, 77–82.

[58] *First report of the commissioners of Irish education inquiry*, p. 66.

the established church superintended the society's schools, but ministers and priests of all denominations were, according to the printed rules, allowed to oversee the schools' concerns. Teachers did not have to be protestants. The society provided inspectors, and teachers were paid according to the results of the inspection.[59] It is difficult to discover how many children actually were taught by the society. The society claimed 32,000 in daily attendance in 1818,[60] 61,387 in day schools in 1823,[61] and that by September 1822, a total of more than 150,000 children and 7,000 adults had been educated in the society's day, Sunday, and evening schools.[62] Whatever the society's avowed intentions and despite its claims to educational revolution, it is clear that the majority of Roman Catholic priests recognized the society's proselytizing intentions and opposed the body from its founding. Opposition became most intense during the years 1823–4. A large number of the catholic children who had been in the schools were withdrawn, and the catholic masters who had been employed by the society in large part retired.[63]

Roman Catholic fear of the proselytizing societies was greatly increased by the subvention of some of the societies by parliament. The London Hibernian Society, unlike the Association for Discountenancing Vice and Promoting the Knowledge and Practice of the Christian Religion, did not receive direct grants from parliament but was given government money in two ways. The first of these was through subsidies given it by the Association for Discountenancing Vice.[64] The second source was through the lord lieutenant's school fund. The fund was created in 1819 following an appeal on behalf of the catholics by William Parnell. Parliament's original intention was to assist poor catholics in erecting schools, but in reality the fund became another establishment perquisite. The fund was managed by three

[59] *Report from the select committee on foundation schools and education in Ireland*, pp 10–11, H.C. 1837–8 (701), vii.

[60] *The Times*, 27 Oct. 1818.

[61] *First report of the commissioners of Irish education inquiry*, p. 67.

[62] [Illegible] Steven, on behalf of the London Hibernian Society, to Henry Goulburn, 16 Sept. 1822, P.R.O.I., Chief Secretary's Office, Registered Papers, carton 621, doc. 3688/1822.

[63] *First report of the commissioners of Irish education inquiry*, p. 59.

[64] Martin Brenan, *Schools of Kildare and Leighlin, A.D. 1775–1835* (Dublin, 1935), p. 121.

commissioners, Reverend James Dunn, James D. Latouche, and Major Benjamin B. Woodward. The commissioners received no instructions on the principles that were to govern their granting aid, so they were free to do as they liked.[65]

The grants under the commissioners' control were as follows:[66]

	£	s	d
1819	3,250	0	0
1820	3,250	0	0
1821	4,333	6	8
1822	4,333	6	9
1823	7,583	6	8
1824	10,833	8	6
1825-6	15,000	0	0

The amounts of these grants were large by the standards of the times (the English education vote of 1833 was £20,000) especially in view of the fact that the grant from the lord lieutenant's school fund was given in addition to large direct parliamentary grants to a number of educational foundations and societies. The catholic clergy had good reason to be worried about the use of money from the lord lieutenant's fund to support proselytizing schools. They also were bothered by the fund's commissioners making it very difficult for catholics to get any money from it. The commissioners required considerable pledges of financial aid from local sources before making a grant and this requirement, according to Major Woodward, led to the rejection of many catholic applications.[67] Another requirement was that the title to the land that was the site of an aided school had, in most cases, to be vested in the Anglican minister and churchwardens of the parish. Justifiably irked by such requirements, Bishop Doyle objected: 'no catholic can build a school to be thus disposed of; and yet it is most confidently and officially stated in parliament, that this fund is equally accessible to catholics and protestants.'[68] Thus, up to 1825, only twelve of the

[65] *First report of the commissioners of Irish education inquiry*, p. 59.

[66] *First report of the commissioners of Irish education inquiry*, p. 59; *Report from the select committee on foundation schools and education in Ireland*, p. 10.

[67] *First report of the commissioners of Irish education inquiry*, p. 59.

[68] James Doyle, *Letters on the state of Ireland; addressed by J. K. L. to a friend in England* (Dublin, 1825), p. 24.

481 grants made went to catholics.[69] The fund was extinguished after 1825 because of the adverse finding of the commissioners of Irish education inquiry. Before its demise it had the important effect of reinforcing the catholic hierarchy's disapproval of the connection between the government and the protestant societies and of helping stimulate the hierarchy's demands for religious neutrality in the expenditure of the state's educational resources.

For the sake of completeness, the activities of three other proselytizing societies should be mentioned in addition to those of the Association for Discountenancing Vice and of the London Hibernian Society. One of these was the Baptist Society for Promoting the Gospel in Ireland, founded in April 1814. The society is interesting because of its resolve to concentrate most of its energy on converting the native Irish through schoolmasters using the Irish language.[70] The Irish Society for Promoting the Education of the Native Irish through the Medium of their Own Language, founded in 1818, used similar methods. Neither the Baptist nor the Irish Society had any interest in preserving the Irish language, but rather used the language because it was the quickest vehicle for reaching the souls of the peasants. In the mid-1820s, the Baptist Society claimed ninety-five day schools, the Irish Society about fifty day schools.[71] A third unusual proselytizing society was the Sunday School Society for Ireland, an organization that derived considerable financial aid from the other proselytizing organizations. Except in its early years (it was created in 1809), the society limited its gifts to spelling books and books of religious instruction. It served, therefore, mostly as an agency for coordinating and encouraging local efforts at converting the catholics, efforts that must have been quite substantial, since the society claimed more than 150,000 children in its schools in 1825.[72]

All of the societies mentioned thus far were proselytizing societies in the strictest sense of the term, whatever some of their public pronouncements may have said to the contrary. In

[69] *First report of the commissioners of Irish education inquiry*, p. 60.
[70] *Second annual report of the Baptist Society, for promoting the Gospel in Ireland* (London, 1816), passim.
[71] *First report of the commissioners of Irish education inquiry*, pp 82–4.
[72] Ibid., pp 61–5.

contrast, the Society for Promoting the Education of the Poor in Ireland (usually known as the 'Kildare Place Society') was genuinely undenominational throughout its early years. In 1786 in Thomas's Court, Dublin, a school for the poor was established which was religiously neutral, or at least close to being so. The Bible was read daily, but doctrinal explanation was foregone. The school proved to be such a success that a large building was erected for it in which upwards of a thousand children were in daily attendance. This success caught the attention of a number of substantial Dublin citizens who eventually met to found the Society for Promoting the Education of the Poor in Ireland. The group passed six resolutions at their first meeting on 7 December 1811. The second resolution contained the kernel of the society's religious philosophy: 'That for the accomplishment of the "great work" of educating the Irish poor, schools should be upon the most liberal principles, and should be divested of all sectarian distinctions in Christianity.'[73] In practice, this meant that the Bible was to be read without note or comment, but that doctrinal matters were not to be raised.

It will be recalled that the fourteenth report of the commissioners of education of 1806–12 had recommended the creation of a national system of education for the poor. The recommendation had been shelved, but not forgotten. This meant that the Kildare Place Society was in an advantageous position in seeking government support, since its schools were undenominational, and because it specialized in education of the poor. Hence, when the society appealed for a parliamentary grant, its prayer was acceded to, and government money poured forth in increasingly large amounts. The annual parliamentary grants to the society from their inception in 1816 to their cessation in 1832 were as follows:[74]

1816	6,000	1821	10,000
1817	9,663	1822	10,000
1818	5,538	1823	14,000
1820	5,538	1824	22,000

[73] H. Kingsmill Moore, *An unwritten chapter in the history of education, being the history of the Society for the Education of the Poor of Ireland, generally known as the Kildare Place Society, 1811–1831* (London, 1904), pp 1–9.

[74] *Report from the select committee on foundation schools and education in Ireland*, p. 11.

1825	22,000	1829	25,000
1826	15,000	1830	18,750
1827	25,000	1831	30,000
1828	25,000		

The magnitude of these grants is apparent if we compare them to the English grants of 1833, the first parliamentary grants for English education, which totalled only £20,000.

To be national in any true sense in Ireland, a school system must have the approval of the Roman Catholic clergy and lay leaders; in the Kildare Place Society's early years, it came very close to being the basis of a successful national system, a fact usually ignored in most statements of Irish educational history. Daniel O'Connell was on the society's board of managers. Catholic gentry became patrons of individual schools, and the clergy of the catholic church gave cautious sanction to the society's activities.[75] The following figures, taken from the society's thirty-fifth report indicate that if the society never became the educator of most of the nation's children, it at least schooled a considerable number:[76]

Year	Number of schools	Number of scholars
1816	8	557
1817	65	4,527
1818	133	9,263
1819	241	16,786
1820	381	26,474
1821	513	36,657
1822	727	51,637
1823	1,122	79,287
1824	1,490	100,000
1825	1,395	102,380
1826	1,477	102,064
1827	1,467	98,063
1828	1,497	106,839
1829	1,553	124,449
1830	1,634	132,530
1831	1,621	137,639

[75] On early Roman Catholic approval see Isaac Butt, *The liberty of teaching vindicated* (Dublin, 1865), pp 23–4; *First report of the commissioners of Irish education inquiry*, p. 56; Michael A. Lynch, 'The Kildare Place Society (1811–1831)' (Unpublished M. A. thesis, University College, Cork, 1958), pp 204–6.

[76] Quoted in George L. Smyth, *Ireland: historical and statistical* (London, 1844), iii, 232.

Another fact often overlooked about the Kildare Place Society is that the society developed a number of educational techniques which were extremely advanced for the time and which were subsequently taken over by the framers of the national system. The central administrative arrangements of the society were hardly notable, it being run by a central committee and various sub-committees like most nineteenth-century educational societies. Nor were the teaching methods employed revolutionary, since the society relied in the main upon Lancasterian principles. The society did shine, however, in the publication of a complete set of books for their schools, plus an inexpensive library. The necessity of publishing a set of suitable related texts was a point that had previously escaped all other British educational societies. When the commissioners of national education put out their own series of books they were acting upon the Kildare Place Society's example and upon that society's recognition of the fact that a national system of schooling demanded a national set of textbooks. Another achievement was the operation of the male and female model schools at Kildare Place in which teachers were trained to man the Kildare Place Schools. Again, the recognition of the need for teachers to be trained and the creation of an institution for such training represents a major breakthrough by the society and was to be copied by the commissioners of national education. The third significant educational innovation that the society effected was the creation of an efficient inspectorial system. The idea of inspecting schools was hardly a new one, but the society was first in the field with a system of inspection that covered all the schools in its domain, and that made inspections a regular, rather than occasional, practice.[77]

It is obvious, then, that the Kildare Place Society was radically different from the proselytizing societies discussed earlier. Unlike the others it was truly undenominational in character. The support, or at the least benevolent neutrality, of the Roman Catholic clergy, combined with aid from parliament, meant that the society bid fair to be a national system of schooling for the Irish poor. Its administrative methods were not those of the

[77] Michael Breathnach, 'The infancy of school inspection', *The Irish School Weekly*, lv (7 and 14 Nov. 1953), pp 487–9; Moore, pp 214–36; *First report of the commissioners of Irish education inquiry*, pp 37–58.

petty proselytizers, but were suitable to a system of schools covering the entire nation.

But things turned sour. At the society's annual meeting in 1819, Daniel O'Connell attended and criticized the management of the society. O'Connell subsequently convinced the duke of Leinster and Lord Cloncurry, two of the society's patrons, that the rule regarding Bible reading should be modified in order to assure its acceptance by all Roman Catholics. The three then obtained an interview with the managing committee of the society in April 1819, at which the critics were invited to frame new rules, the only stipulation being that the new rules were not to undercut the society's principles. This O'Connell and his friends were unable to do; nevertheless O'Connell repeated his protest at the annual meeting of 1820. He moved that a committee of seven be appointed to inquire if the rules were really effective in guaranteeing non-interference in religious matters. The managing committee fought this resolution and won by a majority of about four to one. Thereupon O'Connell resigned from the society and the fight began in earnest.[78]

Why did O'Connell change from a supporter to a violent opponent of the Kildare Place Society? The answer lies mainly in changes that had previously taken place in the society itself. Up to 1819, the Roman Catholics had expressed only two objections to the society's operations: they did not approve of the overwhelming protestant majority upon the managing committee, and they were uneasy about the reading of the scriptures without note or comment.[79] The anxiety about scripture reading did not, during the society's early years, carry the emotional and theological weight it was to gain during the 1820s. If the questions of the scriptures and of the construction of the managing committee had remained as the catholics' only two objections, the society would probably have retained their support. The probability of continued connection, had not the society changed its policies, may be inferred from the fact that almost all the catholic schools connected with the society operated under what was known as the 'New Ross Plan', under which the week's scripture lesson was explained in chapel on Sunday by

[78] Moore, pp 74–82.
[79] Lynch, p. 208.

the village priest and under which Roman Catholic catechetical instruction was given during school hours, but outside the schoolroom. Thus, the catholic clergy were able to keep the letter of the society's rules, without violating their own religious principles.[80]

The society's managers disturbed this peaceful state of affairs by beginning, in 1820, to grant a part of their income to the various protestant proselytizing societies. In 1824, there were fifty-seven schools of the Association for Discountenancing Vice, 340 schools of the London Hibernian Society, and thirty Baptist Society schools receiving aid from the Kildare Place Society.[81] Further, after 1820, local protestant clergy and landlords quite freely violated the society's rules by providing exposition of the scripture lessons.[82] It is hardly surprising that the Roman Catholic leaders became disenchanted with the society, since it gradually became just another protestant agency.

For the sake of convenience it is easiest to mention the catholic lay opposition to the society and catholic clerical opposition as separate topics, but it should be borne in mind that the anti-Kildare agitation was a combined lay-clerical operation of considerable strength. The focal point of catholic lay opposition was the Catholic Association, formed in April 1823, and its assorted predecessors and successors. The association was a response to catholic grievances, and its function was to complain and agitate loudly enough to bring reform. Prior to the creation of the Catholic Association, Daniel O'Connell's activities resulted in the establishment of the Irish National Society for Promoting the Education of the Poor in January 1821. The society, whose leadership the laymen shared with the catholic bishops, appears to have been intended as a catholic Kildare Place Society, and its rules were almost identical with those of the Kildare Society. The Irish National Society served chiefly as an agitating body, seeking the deposition of the Kildare Place hegemony, and a share of the parliamentary education grant for itself. Through the influence of Henry Parnell, M.P., the catholic society managed to obtain the approval of Charles Grant, then chief secretary, for their scheme. The society's hopes

[80] Ibid., pp 211–12.
[81] *First report of the commissioners of Irish education inquiry,* p. 56.
[82] Lynch, pp 208–9.

and the society itself collapsed when the administration changed.[83]

Lord Cloncurry led another lay attack upon the Kildare Society when, at the 1822 annual meeting of the Kildare Place Society, he attempted to have six catholics appointed to the society's managing board, the 'General Committee'. His method in this foray was important, for it bound the catholic clergy and laity together on the education issue: he read a request submitted jointly by Lord Fingal and Dr Troy requesting that the Roman Catholic archbishop of Dublin and five persons, clerical or lay, chosen by the archbishop, be appointed to the six posts. Cloncurry was, it is hardly necessary to say, unsuccessful.[84] The Catholic Association, when its time came, smashed the Kildare Place Society with considerable vigour and with tactical shrewdness. O'Connell used the education issue as a subject on which to bind the clergy to his larger aims: he enlisted their support in taking a survey of catholic education throughout the country. Among the petitions with which he flooded parliament were a number upon catholic education, praying, among other things, for state aid to catholic schools.[85] Significantly for later developments, O'Connell had a petition prepared praying parliament, before the voting of the increased grant to the Kildare Place Society in 1824, to appoint a committee to inquire whether the means of the society were best calculated to effect parliament's educational object.[86]

The catholic clergy, and especially the prelates, pulled their oar as well as the laymen. Reverend John MacHale served as the clerical equivalent of O'Connell on the Kildare Place question. In February 1820, while a priest at Maynooth, he began issuing a series of letters under the name of 'Hierophilos' warning the clergy of the insidious schemes of the Kildare Place Society. These letters continued for three years, and they focused clerical

[83] William J. Fitzpatrick, *The life, times and correspondence of the Right Rev. Dr Doyle, bishop of Kildare and Leighlin* (Dublin, 1861), i, 221–8; Michael MacDonagh, *Bishop Doyle: a biographical and historical study* (London and Dublin, 1896), pp 147–8.

[84] Lynch, p. 214.

[85] James A. Reynolds, *The catholic emancipation crisis in Ireland, 1823–1829* (New Haven, 1954), pp 68, 88, 89.

[86] *Dublin Evening Post*, 4 Mar. 1824 and 9 Mar. 1824.

attention upon the Kildare group's activities.[87] In 1819, Cardinal Fontana, prefect of propaganda, had sent a letter to the Irish bishops condemning the Bible societies.[88] This condemnation was repeated by propaganda in August 1820.[89]

The cause was also taken up by Bishop Doyle of Kildare and Leighlin. Doyle, unlike MacHale, was a liberal. He believed in children of protestant and catholic denominations being educated together, provided certain religious safeguards were erected, on the sensible premise that if children of different faiths were going to have to live together as adults, they should not be separated as children. He later summarized his views on the subject in the following manner:

I do not see how any man, wishing well to the public peace, and who looks to Ireland as his country, can think that peace can ever be permanently established, or the prosperity of the country ever well secured, if children are separated, at the commencement of life, on account of their religious opinions. I do not know any measures which would prepare the way for a better feeling in Ireland than uniting children at an early age, and bringing them up in the same school, leading them to commune with one another and to form those little intimacies and friendships which often subsist through life.[90]

Yet Doyle concluded that 'it is not lawful for any catholic to assist or co-operate with the Kildare Place Society in carrying into effect their system of education'.[91] From the condemnation of the society by both the conservative MacHale and the liberal Doyle, we can infer that the entire catholic hierarchy stood in condemnation of the system. Doyle, in addition to being active

---

[87] Bernard O'Reilly, *John MacHale, archbishop of Tuam: his life, times and correspondence* (New York and Cincinnati, 1890), i, 75–87; R. Barry O'Brien, i, 120–4; E. J. Quigley, 'Saints, scholars and others, some incidents in Ireland's story—III', *Irish Ecclesiastical Record*, series 5, xxiv (July 1924), p. 25.

[88] M. Comerford, *Collections relating to the diocese of Kildare and Leighlin* (Dublin, 1883), p. 97.

[89] *The Times*, 19 Oct. 1820.

[90] *Second report of evidence from the select committee on the state of the poor in Ireland*, pp 426–7, H.C. 1830 (654), vii, quoted in T. W. Moody and J. C. Beckett, *Queen's Belfast, 1845–1949, the history of a university* (London, 1959), i, lvi.

[91] James Doyle to Daniel Murray, 16 Sept. 1824, reproduced in Fitzpatrick, 8, 352.

on behalf of the abortive Catholic Education Society, followed MacHale's lead in writing letters to newspapers. In 1822, he wrote a series of letters to the *Dublin Evening Post* over the initials 'J.K.L.', on a variety of catholic matters, one of which was education. The letters scorched the proselytizing groups for the 'wild superstition which, under the name of Bible reading or Bible distributions, is now disturbing the peace of Ireland, and threatening the safety of the state'.[92]

Opinion was strong among the catholic prelates, and on 9 March 1824, the bishops had Henry Grattan present a petition to the house of commons. The petition, signed by Bishops Curtis, Murray, Kelly, Laffan, Murphy, Magauran, Doyle, and Marum, enumerated catholic grievances in education, ticking off the matters of lack of grants to catholic schools, the activities of the proselytizing societies, the rules of the lord lieutenant's education fund, and the large grants to the Kildare Place Society. When he introduced the petition, Grattan told the house that he would move for a committee to investigate the distribution of Irish education funds, as soon as some returns that Sir John Newport had moved for had been provided.[93] Newport himself raised the idea of an investigation into Irish education in late March of the same year and noted that there were two ways in which such an investigation could be made, either by a committee appointed by the house of commons, or through a commission appointed by the king. A committee of the house, he felt, would excite more unnecessary attention than a commission. In addition, a commission would be able to investigate the subject on the spot. Hence, 'amidst loud cheers', Newport moved that an address be presented to his majesty asking that he appoint a commission to investigate Irish education, including not only the Kildare Place Society but all schools maintained in any part from public funds. The commission was also to report on measures for extending educational benefits to the people. The motion was agreed to without a division.[94] Thus, the line of government reports which we traced in the early part of the chapter here joins with the concern aroused by the proselytizing societies among catholic leaders. There had

[92] Doyle, p. 128.
[93] *Hansard* 2, xl, 837–47.
[94] *Hansard* 2, xl, 1399–1413, 25 Mar. 1824.

been a number of education commissions prior to the one appointed in 1824. But the 1824 commission, unlike its predecessors, was a response to catholic demands, and was an opportunity for the government to weave catholic opinion into the emerging educational consensus, if it really wanted to do so.

3

The catholics called a cease-fire while the commission of inquiry was at work, but there is no doubt that they were disappointed in the appointment of a royal commission, rather than a committee of the house of commons. According to Bishop Doyle, Newport had originally desired that a parliamentary committee, rather than a commission, be appointed to investigate education, but the partisans of the education societies threatened so much opposition that he had to yield to them. 'Thus,' Doyle later wrote, 'all our hopes were blasted, and from that hour to this [September 1826] we looked with doubt and apprehension to whatsoever we have witnessed on the part of this commission, and to all that has emanated from it.'[95] The crown appointed Thomas Frankland Lewis, John Leslie Foster, William Grant, James Glassford, and Anthony Richard Blake as commissioners. Blake, the treasury remembrancer, was the first Roman Catholic in modern times to be appointed to a commission of inquiry,[96] and his presence might have reassured the catholics as to the commission's integrity were it not that all catholics who took office were suspect by their fellow religionists. In any event, Blake was limited by his duties as treasury remembrancer and could hardly pay full attention to the education inquiry. O'Connell denounced Blake's appointment as 'a mere delusion in order to make a show of great liberality; and whenever, in the future they may require to make such an appearance, they have only to put in the name of the catholic chief remembrancer, which will give a currency and sanction to those of a host of orangemen and exclusionists. As they had Mr Blake in harness they merely wanted to take a ride out of him.'[97]

Leslie Foster was a counsel for the revenue and had no catholic

[95] James Doyle, Pastoral letter of 4 Sept. 1826, quoted in Brenan, p. 6.
[96] Lynch, p. 230.
[97] *Dublin Evening Post*, 22 June 1824.

sympathies, having been elected for Louth on the basis of his opposition to catholic claims. Moreover, he was an active member of the Kildare Place Society. Grant and Glassford had hardly been heard of in Ireland previous to their appointment. The latter was a supporter of the London Hibernian Society, while the former was a Scotsman who had been chief secretary from 1818 to 1821. He opposed proselytizing, but was unable to understand the catholic position regarding scripture reading. Lewis had been one of the 1806–12 commissioners and subsequently one of the members of the government's board of education.[98]

The commission sat from June 1824, to June 1827, and poured forth nine reports. These publications were based on three major types of evidence: statistical evidence provided by the commissioners' extensive educational census, testimony and documents of assorted witnesses, and dealings with the Roman Catholic hierarchy. Besides examining the leading catholic bishops in official hearings, they met with a number of them in less formal sessions. On Thursday, 16 December 1824, the commissioners met with Dr Murray, Roman Catholic archbishop of Dublin. Upon being asked whether the catholics would object to 'common' literary instruction (i.e. instruction shared by Roman Catholic and protestant children) being received from a protestant master, Murray replied that there could be no possible objection. He also answered, in reply to the query of whether religious instruction for catholic children could be given by a Roman Catholic layman who was approved by the Roman Catholic prelates, that there could be no objection to such a procedure. Murray concurred with the commission's suggestion that schools might be established in each of which there would be both a protestant and a Roman Catholic lay teacher, both of whom would administer common literary instruction, and that the Roman Catholic teacher might give religious instruction to the Roman Catholic children (subject to the direction of their pastors) in a portion of time, one or two days a week, especially set aside for separate religious instruction. Murray refused to agree, however, to the suggestion that Roman Catholic and protestant children might read the scriptures, in their respective

[98] James J. Sullivan, 'The education of Irish catholics, 1782–1831' (Unpublished Ph.D. thesis, Queen's University, Belfast, 1959), pp 357–8.

versions, during the hours of common instruction. The scriptures, he felt, should be read only during the hours of separate religious instruction. He added, apparently without being prodded by the commissioners, that there would be no objection to a suitable harmony of the Gospels or a book of scripture extracts being used during the period of combined instruction.[99]

The commissioners followed their individual conference with Murray with a group interview on 7 January 1825, with the four archbishops: Curtis, Kelly, Laffan, and Murray. They read the minutes of 16 December 1824, and explained in detail what the passage about separate religious instruction meant. On 8 January, the three other archbishops joined Murray in expressing their approval of the views previously expressed by Murray.[100] These dealings appear a bit puzzling in view of the opinions expressed in the petition which had led to the creation of the commission, that 'in the Roman Catholic church the literary and religious instruction of youth are universally combined, and that no system of education which separates them can be acceptable to the members of her communion'.[101] The disparity makes sense, however, if we realize that the prelates were really engaged in a collective bargaining process. In public they stated their demand for a catholic system of education, underwritten by government money. In private, they admitted that they would be satisfied with a system of combined literary instruction and separate religious education.

The commissioners' first report was finished in late May 1825, the bulk of its contents being a lengthy survey of work of the various educational societies. As a result of their inquiries, the commissioners recommended that public aid be withdrawn from the Incorporated Society and that the Association for Discountenancing Vice should limit its activities to printing and distributing books and that its schools should be transferred to the control of a government board. The activities of the Kildare

[99] 'Minutes of a conversation between his majesty's commissioners of education inquiry and the Most Reverend Dr Murray, one of the archbishops of the Roman Catholic church in Ireland', reproduced in *First report of the commissioners of Irish education inquiry*, pp 95–6. The minutes were signed by Murray as well as by the commissioners.

[100] *First report of the commissioners of Irish education inquiry*, pp 96–7.

[101] Ibid., p. 1.

Place Society, its was suggested, should also be severely limited. It should cease giving grants to other societies, and, following the establishment of the proposed government education board, was to cease adding schools to its connection. Eventually, it was hoped that the schools to be founded under the new board of education would serve the nation's needs so well that most voluntary schools would transfer themselves to the management of the new board, those refusing to transfer gradually ceasing to receive public aid. Clearly, the report met the negative portion of the catholic aims, in condemning the protestant education societies and suggesting the reduction and eventual abolition of grants to these societies.

The commissioners made a number of constructive suggestions, the most important of which, as implied above, was that a new government board be created to superintend the management of 'schools of general instruction'. The schools of general instruction were to be established in each benefice. During literary instruction Roman Catholics and protestants were to study together. (Literary instruction, it should be emphasized, was not a synonym for 'secular' learning; it meant all forms of literary material and moral education, excluding only those matters likely to raise denominational scruples.) Two teachers were to be in charge, each of them a layman, and, in places where there were any considerable number of Roman Catholics in attendance, at least one of them was to be a Roman Catholic. In presbyterian areas, at least one teacher was to be presbyterian. One or two days a week school was to break early and the remainder of the day to be given to religious instruction. To that point the commission's plan seemed fair. They then stipulated, however, that the religious instruction of the protestants was to be given by established church clergymen or presbyterian ministers, but that the Roman Catholic children should be taught by a Roman Catholic lay teacher who had received the bishop's approval. By implication, the Roman Catholic priest was to be locked out of the school, while the protestant divines were to be allowed access.

Continuing, the commissioners suggested that protestant children be provided with the authorized version of the New Testament by the new board, and that Roman Catholic children should receive the Douay version. Such emphasis upon the Bible was certainly protestant in nature, but had the virtue at least of being doctrinally neutral, since the reading of the scriptures was restricted to the hours of separate instruction. Also, a volume of extracts suitable to all faiths was to be prepared from the Gospels, as well as a book of proverbs, and a collection of extracts from the Pentateuch. Although the commissioners' recommendation left the point uncertain, their minutes on the meeting with Murray made it clear that the volumes of extracts were to be used in the time of combined instruction. In order to maintain effective control of the educational system, the board was to hire inspectors, and, more important, it was to have control over all monies applied to the maintenance of the schools, from whatever source they were derived. The board was also to maintain title to the schoolhouses, and to have the sole authority for appointing and dismissing masters, and of admitting or rejecting books for general instruction.[102]

Seeing the report, Bishop Doyle, who had not been present when Murray's opinions were endorsed by the archbishops, objected, 'It appears that the commissioners' report not only differs from the opinion recorded of the catholic bishops, but it sets up for the teaching of the sacred scriptures to children a sort of person invested with a character hitherto unheard of in the christian world ... A person ... whose tenure in office and interest as well as whose passions would lead him to oppose the pastor of the people, and to profit by discord and apostasy.'[103] He wrote a public letter to Blake, saying of the report, 'on more than one occasion, whilst reading it, I could not suppress a feeling of regret that your name was affixed to it; I had rather it were the work, exclusively, of persons who had been bred up in the old no-popery system, and amongst whom no gentleman of honour or integrity had had a place'.[104] In contrast, catholic laymen, as represented by the Catholic Association, approved of the first report. Although the association deplored the 'delicacy' with which the Kildare Place Society had been handled, they were generally favourable to the volume and felt inclined

[102] For the first report's major recommendations, see ibid., pp 97–101.

[103] James Doyle, *Unpublished essay by Dr Doyle: an essay on education and the state of Ireland by an Irish catholic* (Dublin, 1880), pp 50–1.

[104] *Dublin Evening Post*, 16 June 1825.

to give the commissioners a greater amount of credit than they had expected to be able to do.[105]

Lay opinion, however, was really of little import, for the Catholic Association had things other than education to worry about, and O'Connell made the conscious decision to leave educational dealings in the hands of the Irish bishops.[106] The majority of the prelates were not as angry as was Doyle about the report, but could not approve of it in its entirety. On the twenty-third of January 1826, Archbishop Murray forwarded to the commissioners six resolutions unanimously passed by the catholic archbishops and bishops two days previously. The prelates resolved, first, that the combined literary instruction of protestants and catholics met with their approval under the existing circumstances, provided sufficient care was taken to protect the religious sensibilities of the Roman Catholic children and to furnish them with adequate means for religious instruction. Second, they resolved that all schools in which catholics were in a majority should be under a catholic master, and where there was a catholic minority, a catholic assistant was to be employed. In either case the catholic teachers should be appointed only with the approval of the Roman Catholic bishop of the diocese, and should be removable by him. In the third place the bishops demanded that a male and a female model school be established in each province and be supported at public expense, for the training of Roman Catholic masters and assistants. Fourth, the Roman Catholic bishops wished to have jurisdiction over the selection of books for separate religious education, and veto rights over books for common instruction. Fifth, the prelates objected to the suggestion that all property titles be transferred to the government board, and, finally, they stated that they would withhold their concurrence from any system of education that did not meet these requirements.[107]

Meanwhile, the commissioners kept plugging away at their investigatory duties, producing seven more reports on the various sorts of educational institutions. In addition, they were called upon to make two 'practical experiments', the one involving combined education, the other having to do with the

---

[105] *Dublin Evening Post*, 18 June 1825.
[106] *Dublin Evening Post*, 21 Jan. 1826.
[107] *The Times*, 17 Oct. 1827.

proposed scripture extracts. At the chief secretary's direction they were requested to commence for the lord lieutenant an experiment in conducting schools under the principles described in their first report.[108] The commissioners agreed.[109] They first turned, however, to preparing an edition of the Douay Testament for catholic children. At the commissioners' request, Dr Murray permitted the deletion of one or two expressions in the version's notes that the commissioners felt were calculated to raise religious animosity. The edition received the approbation of the Roman Catholic archbishops and went to press in April 1826.[110]

The commissioners then began the compilation of a harmony of the Gospels. They took 'White's Diatessaron', a volume that employed the text of the authorized version, and held a two day conference with the Roman Catholic archbishops on the topic of revisions. The results of this conference convinced the commissioners that no existing harmony would be satisfactory and they therefore sought the compilation of one especially for their purposes. To this end they applied to the protestant archbishop of Dublin who gave his approval to the production of such a work.[111] At the suggestion of the protestant archbishop of Armagh[112] a committee of divines, four or five in number, was appointed, and when the committee finished the volume it was passed on to Dr Murray. He rejected it as being exclusively compiled from the protestant version of the New Testament.[113]

[108] Henry Goulburn to the commissioners of education inquiry, 28 Nov. 1825, reproduced in *Ninth report of the commissioners of Irish education inquiry*, pp 4–5, H.C. 1826–7 (516), xiii; P.R.O.I., 14,439/1826.

[109] Commissioners of education to Henry Goulburn, 30 Nov. 1825, P.R.O.I., Chief Secretary's Office, Registered Papers, carton 1123, doc. 12,702/1826.

[110] *Ninth report of the commissioners of Irish education inquiry*, pp. 6–7.

[111] Ibid., p. 7.

[112] Lord John G. Beresford to T. Frankland Lewis, 31 Jan. 1826, reproduced ibid., pp 9–10.

[113] Daniel Murray to T. Franklin Lewis, 17 July 1826, reproduced ibid., p. 12.

The number and composition of the protestant committee is unknown. The protestant archbishop of Dublin mentioned that the committee was made up of five members (William Magee to T. Frankland Lewis, 8 July 1826, reproduced ibid., p. 11).

In the library of the Representative Church Body, Dublin (225.5),

An unnamed member of the commission prepared a work called 'Christian Lessons', extracted chiefly from the New Testament, which, with alterations, met with the approval of the Roman Catholic prelates.[114] The work was then submitted to the protestant archbishop of Armagh who would not approve the work, and who urged the protestant committee's book upon the commissioners.[115] A stalemate developed, with the Anglican clergy holding out for their version and the Roman Catholics for the 'Christian Lessons'. Despite several months' attempts to break the deadlock, the commissioners failed to thaw the ice even slightly. On 2 June 1827, they turned in their final report with a wistful note: 'if we have not succeeded in disengaging the

[114] *Ninth report of the commissioners of Irish education inquiry*, p. 12.
A reasonable guess would be that the 'unnamed member' was A. R. Blake, since he was the only catholic on the commission. An article published in a Church of Ireland organ in the 1830s stated that the writing of the version that was accepted by the catholic prelates was done by the only member of the commission of education inquiry who was (in the mid-1830s) a commissioner of national education: in other words, by Blake. *A review of the scripture lessons for the use of the Irish national schools* (Dublin, 1836), reprinted from the *Christian Examiner and Church of Ireland Magazine*, pp 2–3.
[115] Lord John G. Beresford to T. Frankland Lewis, 28 Aug. 1826, reproduced in *Ninth report of the commissioners of Irish education inquiry*, pp 14–17.

there is a copy of a work which is a harmony of the life of Christ taken from the scriptures, on the inside cover of which is inscribed the following:

Scripture extracts compiled at the primate's desire in 1827, with the view of forming a school manual for the joint use of protestants and Roman Catholics, by the following persons who were appointed a committee:
1 Rev. Ch. Elrington, D.D.
2 Rev. Wm. Phelan, D.D.
3 Rev. Geo Hamilton
4 Rev. H. Cotton, LL.D.
It was never published, and never had a title page:
it was printed in London in 1827. The plan failed,
this book being rejected by the R. Catholic [illeg].
Dr Murray, Mr A. Blake, etc.
[s] H. Cotton.

This inscription is confusing, for the book itself and the events narrated seem to be those of 1826. There is no record of any attempt by the dignitaries of the established church to compile a gospel harmony in 1827. Possibly, Cotton, in his declining years, became confused about the dates involved.

subject of general education in Ireland from the embarrassments with which it was surrounded when the inquiry was committed to our charge, we trust that the information we have collected may lead hereafter to more satisfactory results'.[116]

The major virtue of the work of the commissioners of education inquiry was their obvious failure to complete their job—which made another commission almost inevitable. The appointment of another commission was made certain when Thomas Spring-Rice, member for Limerick, became the spokesman in parliament for the catholic interests. On 11 March 1828, he moved that the 'reports on the subject of education in Ireland'—including by implication all previous reports, not just those of the commissioners of 1824–7—be referred to a select committee of twenty-one members, with power to report their observations and opinions to the house. The commons agreed without opposition.[117] Here, then, was a chance for a parliamentary body to review the chain of Irish educational thinking, and to distill a clear and comprehensive outline for future policy. Spring-Rice headed the committee; under his tutelage it made a quick study of the work, its report being printed in mid-May 1828.

Unlike all preceding reports on Irish education, the 1828 report was short, to-the-point, and unambiguous.[118] The committee called for the creation of a new system of united education in Ireland. Basic to such a system, the committee felt, was the creation of a new government authority that would control the foundation and management of schools and that would guard against any interference with the religious tenets of the scholars. This new board of education was to be appointed by the government, the members to be appointed without religious distinction, to receive salaries, and to hold office during the government's pleasure. The board of education was to receive all applications for aid to schools of general instruction and was to allocate all grants made by parliament for education in Ireland. The board was to superintend a model school and was to edit and print all books for the literary instruction of the pupils.

[116] *Ninth report of the commissioners of Irish education inquiry*, p. 28.
[117] *Hansard* 2, xviii, 1,119–24.
[118] *Report from the select committee to whom the reports on the subject of education in Ireland were referred*, H.C. 1828 (341), iv.

Significantly, the report suggested that the board also print all books for the separate religious instruction of the children, the books to be recommended by the episcopal authorities of the established church and by the Roman Catholic bishops. The report implied that the board of education was to have the right of approving or disapproving of the books suggested by the clerics. It is also noteworthy that the report stated that the board of education was to receive title to all schoolhouses built at public expense and receiving aid from the board.

Parliamentary money was to be granted to aid local parishes or societies in erecting schoolhouses, for gratuities to teachers, for providing books for combined literary instruction to the children at half price, and for school requisites and books for separate religious instruction at prime cost, for teacher training, and for the appointment of inspectors. No school was to be built unless the local citizens granted a site for the schoolhouse and underwrote one third of the building expenses and all of the maintenance and school furnishing costs. Local authorities were also to be required to buy all books for general instruction (at half price), books for religious instruction (at prime cost), and were to pay the master a permanent salary of not less than ten pounds. Teachers, the report stated, should be selected without religious distinction but should be required to be graduated from, or at least examined at the government model school, and should be required, before being engaged, to produce a certificate of moral conduct and character from a clergyman of whatever faith they professed.

The suggested educational arrangements were that combined 'moral and literary' instruction take place on four fixed days a week, and that two days a week be set aside for separate religious instruction. On the latter two days, the schoolhouse was to be set aside on one day exclusively for the religious education of Roman Catholics and on the other exclusively for the religious education of protestants. In contrast to the 1825 report's suggestions, the 1828 report was scrupulously fair on this point: religious instruction for each denomination was to be placed under the exclusive superintendence of the clergy of the respective denominations. The 1828 report also suggested that New Testaments be given each child and printed by the board, but that they were to be read only during times of separate religious instruction. Protestant children were to receive the Testament in the authorized version, Roman Catholics in the version that had their bishops' approval. The committee also stated that all children should be required to attend their respective places of worship on Sunday and that the scholars should produce certificates to prove their attendance.

Much to Spring-Rice's consternation nothing immediate was done about the report, although eventually it was to be rewritten by Lord Stanley as the instructions on which the national system of education was to be founded. The report was well received by the catholic prelates. Still optimistic in 1829, Spring-Rice wrote Doyle that 'the Roman Catholic prelates, in adopting as they did last year the principles of my report have in fact relieved the subject from many of its difficulties'.[119] Archbishop Murray visited the lord lieutenant, evidently with a view to effecting the report's recommendations, but received no encouragement.[120] The authorities of the established church and the supporters of the Kildare Place Society, on the other hand, vigorously opposed the select committee's recommendations. *The Christian Examiner and Church of Ireland Magazine*, in a blast that foreshadowed its later opposition to Lord Stanley's national education system, denounced the report as 'chiefly remarkable for one of those little attempts at *a sinister dexterity*, to which the public have of late years been much too accustomed'.[121] The editors especially objected to the separation of literary from religious instruction and strongly condemned the requirement that each child attend his place of worship every Sunday, a practice that would lead to protestants being forced to encourage attendance of popish children at their mass houses.

Spring-Rice did his best, but the combination of protestant opposition and government inertia was too much for him. He first approached Lord Gower, the chief secretary, about implementing the report, but he was unable to find out what the government's intentions were. He then turned to Lord Anglesey,

[119] Thomas Spring-Rice to James Doyle, 31 July [?] 1829, N.L.I., Monteagle Papers.

[120] Thomas Spring-Rice to James Doyle, 31 Aug. 1828, N.L.I., Monteagle Papers.

[121] 'Report of the select committee of the house of commons appointed to examine the reports on Irish education', *The Christian Examiner and Church of Ireland Magazine*, viii (July 1828), p. 45.

the lord lieutenant, who informed him, with commendable frankness, that his own wishes were to bring about a settlement of the entire educational question, but that his hands were tied regarding appropriations because the Kildare Place Society had previously entered into engagements that disposed of the entire education grant. Anglesey had given the Kildare Place people notice that they must not make such engagements in the future, but was unable to do anything in the present year. Spring-Rice next obtained an interview with the duke of Wellington who, after hearing the case, asked for the documents on the subject. Spring-Rice also wrote to Peel and to some of the men who had been members of his committee.[122] Nothing came of all this activity, but he kept on. As chairman of the select committee on the education of the poor he again called the government's attention to the necessity of implementing the 1828 report:

It appears that the principles contained in that report have been perfectly sustained by the results of a most interesting experiment tried by the Rev. Sir I. L. Blosse, a beneficed clergyman of the established church, and one of the Roman Catholic archbishops in Ireland, and that, with some slight modifications, those principles also meet the assent of Dr Chalmers. The entire body of the Roman Catholic hierarchy have, by petitions to both houses, intreated that the recommendation of the committee should be adopted.[123]

Copies of the proofs of the report of the select committee on the state of the poor were forwarded to Wellington by Spring-Rice immediately upon receiving them from the presses, but still to no avail.[124]

Within the government, Lord Anglesey attempted for several years to break the Kildare Place monopoly, but without success. Anglesey was caught in a crossfire between the Kildare Place supporters and the catholic bishops. The bishops approved the report of the select committee of 1828 and petitioned for the suggested reforms. The Kildare Place advocates countered with a petition of their own for continued support. Anglesey, although

[122] Thomas Spring-Rice to James Doyle, 26 Apr. 1829, N.L.I., Monteagle Papers.

[123] *Report from the select committee appointed to take into consideration the state of the poorer classes in Ireland*, p. 50, H.C. 1830 (667), vii.

[124] Thomas Spring-Rice to the duke of Wellington, 2 Oct. 1830, N.L.I., Monteagle Papers.

theoretically in control of the education grant, felt hedged in by parliamentary restrictions: 'Upon the subject of education money', he wrote Gower, the chief secretary, 'I should say that the lord lieutenant in this, as in many other cases, is placed in a false position. Why pass an act to give him unlimited authority and then tell him that he is not to use it?'[125] Clearly, he would have liked to clip the wings of the Kildare Place Society. On 15 August 1828, Gower had advised him that the Kildare Place Society was spending their money very fast and acting as if they were to draw the whole education grant of £25,000, after they had already received £15,000.[126] Anglesey replied, 'Although I return tomorrow, I think it right not to lose a day in expressing my desire that you should stop the Kildare Street Society from appropriating for uses of their own, money that is intended for more general purposes.'[127]

Anglesey felt the justice of the catholic bishops' demands and thought that they would have just reason to complain if they got no share of the remaining £10,000;[128] but he was perplexed about what to do and put off seeing a catholic deputation on the subject as long as possible. He wrote Peel about the matter and Peel returned a memorandum.[129] Evidently Peel refused to sanction grants to catholics for Gower wrote:

Under all the circumstances I fear that you will find it advisable to give Kildare St the money and have done with the subject of its disposal. This is a course which is much at variance with my own inclination, but the only one which I think is open to you . . . I have every reason to think that Mr Peel's opinion as to the understanding on which the grant was placed at your disposal is correct . . . and though I have not seen the solicitor genl. since I received Mr Peel's answer to my enquiry, I know he is very much of the same opinion . . . I think the addition of his authority should set your

[125] Lord Anglesey to Lord Gower, 1 Sept. 1828, P.R.O.N.I., T. 1068–15 (copy).

[126] Lord Gower to Lord Anglesey, 15 Aug. 1828, P.R.O.N.I., D.O.D., 619/x/124.

[127] Lord Anglesey to Lord Gower, 17 Aug. 1828, P.R.O.N.I., T. 1068–15 (copy).

[128] Lord Anglesey to Lord Gower, 17 Sept. 1828, P.R.O.N.I., T. 1068–15 (copy).

[129] Lord Gower to Lord Anglesey, 31 Aug. 1828, P.R.O.N.I., D.O.D., 619/x/132.

mind at rest as to this exercise of your responsibility. The catholics will be disappointed and clamorous, but have no reason to despair.[130]

Gower advised Anglesey not to go in detail into his reasons for having to turn down the catholic bishops' application, since the bishops were as well aware as Gower himself of the circumstances of the case. Gower commented, just as Anglesey had earlier complained, that the whole situation was unfair, for the house of commons voted funds to the lord lieutenant but refused to let him spend them in the way he wished.[131]

4

Although the Kildare Place Society won the battle of 1828, with the formation of the whig cabinet of November 1830, it became clear that they would lose the campaign. The events of 1830–31 hinged largely upon the action of five men. The first of these, Daniel O'Connell, is notable by his absence from the field of educational controversy. But O'Connell did not need to be active in this regard, since it was his carrying of catholic emancipation in 1829 that had made inevitable the creation of a national system of education along lines acceptable to the Roman Catholics. In a sense, the educational activities of the other four men were really postscripts to O'Connell's achievement. The second man was Henry William Paget, first marquis of Anglesey, of whose educational concerns we have already had some indication. Anglesey was sympathetic to catholic claims and had favoured catholic emancipation. He did not get along with Wellington and had been recalled as lord lieutenant in January 1829, but was reappointed in 1830 by Lord Grey.[132]

Theoretically subordinate to Anglesey was Edward Stanley (usually referred to as Lord Stanley), later earl of Derby, the Irish chief secretary. Stanley was young and hard and refused to be put under Anglesey's thumb. Indeed, in 1831, Stanley was promoted to the cabinet, and when Anglesey asked to be admitted also he was refused. Hence, Stanley's political influence in Westminster greatly exceeded Anglesey's. Stanley's

[130] Lord Gower to Lord Anglesey, 1 Sept. 1828, P.R.O.N.I., D.O.D., 619/x/133.
[131] Lord Gower to Lord Anglesey, 11 Sept. 1828, P.R.O.N.I., D.O.D., 619/x/135.
[132] See *D.N.B.*, art, Henry William Paget.

record in Ireland was a mixed one. He conducted a small war against Daniel O'Connell in which he included a personal challenge to a duel, public prosecution, and coercion acts as weapons of attack. On the other hand, Stanley carried, in 1833, the church temporalities bill, a measure that reduced the number of established church sees from twenty-two to twelve and used the money saved to augment impoverished benefices. Moreover, a tax was laid on benefices of £200 annual income, to be applied in lieu of church rates. Also to Stanley's credit was the institution of the Irish board of works. Cool and arrogant, Stanley was willing to use the power of the government in any way he felt necessary to solve what he considered to be Ireland's problems.[133]

The fourth major figure was Earl Grey, the prime minister. Final approval of any scheme of Irish education rested with Grey. The most important aspects of Grey's conduct for our interest are, first, that he was occupied almost completely with the reform bill, and, second, that in general he favoured a hard line on Ireland; when he left office in 1834 the specific issue was a cabinet disagreement on renewal of the 1833 coercion act, a renewal that he strongly favoured.[134] Fifth, Thomas Wyse should be mentioned. A catholic, Wyse had been educated at Trinity College, Dublin. He was very active in the Catholic Association, and later, in 1830, became M.P. for Tipperary, a seat he subsequently lost for daring to disagree publicly with O'Connell. After the Catholic Association disbanded Wyse became something of an educational gadfly, eventually becoming known in the house as 'The member for education'.[135] In addition to these five major figures, bishops Doyle, Murray, and the other catholic prelates, Lord Cloncurry and Anthony Blake played significant parts in the planning and the negotiations of 1830 and 1831.

[133] See *D.N.B.*, art, Edward G. Stanley; Wilbur D. Jones, *Lord Derby and victorian conservatism* (Oxford, 1956); Thomas E. Kebbel, *Life of the earl of Derby, K.G.* (London, 2nd ed., 1893); Robert B. McDowell, 'The Irish executive in the nineteenth century', *Irish Historical Studies*, ix (Mar. 1955), pp 266–7; George Saintsbury, *The earl of Derby* (London, 1892).

[134] See *D.N.B.* art, Charles Grey; G. M. Trevelyan, *Lord Grey of the reform bill* (London, 2nd ed., 1929).

[135] See *D.N.B.*, art, Thomas Wyse; James J. Auchmuty, *Sir Thomas Wyse, 1791–1862: the life and career of an educator and diplomat* (London, 1939).

The first move on education after the creation of the whig administration of November 1830, seems to have come not from within the government, but from Thomas Wyse. Wyse prepared a draft education bill, probably sometime during the last half of 1830. He gave notice in the latter part of November of bringing a motion on the subject of Irish education before the house immediately after the Christmas recess. Wyse was optimistic. 'I have every confidence,' he wrote Bishop Doyle, 'that the new administration, liberal and energetic to a degree we could scarcely have hoped for a few years—I might even say a few weeks—since, will direct their immediate attention to the urgent wants of education.'[136] It is claimed that Wyse had 'many interviews with Stanley, the Irish chief secretary', and that he conducted 'a lengthy inquiry throughout the length and breadth of Ireland'.[137] In any event, on 9 December 1830, Wyse submitted a detailed plan for national education to the government in the form of the heads of an education bill.

The plan deserves scrutiny, especially in view of the claims (by Thomas Wyse himself, by Winifrede Wyse, and by J. J. Auchmuty) that Wyse was the mastermind behind the creation of the national system of education. Wyse postulated that a national system of education should be applicable to all of the nation, and that in catholic Ireland the Kildare Place Society could never be national. Hence, another system was necessary. Elementary schools, Wyse said, should be established in each parish, but this should not be compulsory, and the parish should have the right to refuse to support a school. The schools should be built, maintained, and managed jointly by the people and by the government. Parishes, if they wanted schools, should be empowered to assess themselves for the establishment and support of the schools. The government was to require at least one third of the building and outfitting costs to come from the parish. Catholics and protestants were to be educated together. Religious instruction was to be given on a separate day by the respective pastors of the children. A teachers' school was to be

---

[136] Thomas Wyse to James Doyle, 30 Nov. 1830, quoted in Winifrede M. Wyse, *Notes on education reform in Ireland during the first half of the 19th century, compiled from the speeches, letters, etc., contained in the unpublished memoirs of the Rt Hon. Sir Thomas Wyse, K.C.B.* (Waterford, 1901), p. 15.

[137] Auchmuty, p. 152. The statement is not documented.

created and teachers hired from among its graduates. A board of national education should be created, Wyse stated, composed of protestants and catholics, clerical and lay members. The board was to be entrusted with the allocation of the national grants and with the publication of books and with other necessary educational activities. Wyse then went on to describe a plan of provincial colleges to educate the middle classes and the opening of Trinity College, Dublin, to catholics, or, alternatively, the founding of another university.[138] In the face of the grandiose claims made for it, the most obvious point to be made about Wyse's plan is that it offers little or nothing new concerning the elementary education of the common people. His heads of a bill was merely a rehash of generally accepted educational ideas, without the admirable clarity and specificity that characterized the report of the 1828 select committee on education in Ireland.

The other important point to be made regarding Wyse's plan is that Lord Stanley seems to have paid no attention to it, at least not in late 1830, nor in the first half of 1831. Stanley's views on the education grant were surprisingly faint-hearted. He would have preferred to tinker with the allocation of the existing grants rather than create a new educational system, but as the catholics' anti-Kildare Place Society petitions continued to roll in, he realized that he had to do something. He was unwilling, however, to accept the method espoused by Anglesey, of creating a system along the lines of the 1828 report: 'I own, however,' he wrote the prime minister, 'I cannot agree with him, in wishing to throw the whole education of the catholics, supported by the state, into the hands of the priesthood.'[139] What he apparently proposed instead was to create an education fund, distinct from the Kildare Place fund, the Kildare fund to be gradually extinguished. Some indication of how the catholics would have fared under that system is found in Richard Sheil's estimate that about £9,000 annually would be set aside for catholic schools.[140]

Anglesey, who favoured the 1828 solution, set about under-

---

[138] Head of education bill reproduced in W. Wyse, pp 21–5.

[139] Lord Stanley to Lord Grey, 9 Mar. 1831, N.L.I., MS 8400 (photostat of original in Durham University Library).

[140] Richard Sheil to James Doyle, 25 Feb. 1831, reproduced in Fitzpatrick, ii, 270.

cutting Stanley's position, a difficult task in view of Stanley's presence in the cabinet and his own exclusion. Stanley, he felt, was 'a little tainted upon the subject'.[141] He wrote Lord Grey: 'I wish Stanley did not hang *a little* too much to their Kildare Place Society's system, and I also hope that whatever money is granted, it may be peremptorily laid down that the schools shall be carried on upon a system that would not force the catholic clergy to forbid upon the principle *of their faith*, the children of that creed from attending the schools.'[142] Anglesey also cut into Stanley's position by having an alternate plan prepared, as indicated in the following letter to Lord Grey:

I send you the papers upon education, that I promised. It was drawn up by Blake after a long discussion that I had with the chancellor, Lord Cloncurry, and him.

Up to page 11, it is historical. It then points out the matter of expending the grant made to the Kildare Place Society and points out a change. Should that change take place, namely to discontinue the 4th and 5th objects, and to leave the savings which would arise therefrom, at the disposal of the lord lieutenant, it would be advisable that from the fund, he should grant aid to such schools only, as would through the medium of the pastors of the protestants and Roman Catholic religions of the parish jointly apply for that aid upon the full understanding that the said schools should be conducted upon the principle laid down by the committee.

I cannot help thinking that if a conference were now to take place between the prelates of the two religions, a general system of education might be agreed upon. And that a selection of the scriptures might be made that would be palatable to both. But if that failed, that they might be brought to consent to a selection of moral books for general use, setting apart certain hours or days for religious instruction by their respective pastors.[143]

[141] Lord Anglesey to Lord Holland, 20 Apr. 1831, P.R.O.N.I., T. 1068-7 (copy).

[142] Lord Anglesey to Lord Grey, 31 Mar. 1831, N.L.I., n. 4036/p. 3707, microfilm of original in Durham University Library.

[143] Lord Anglesey to Lord Grey, 21 Mar. 1831, P.R.O.N.I., T. 1068-4 (copy).

The mention of Blake is important, for, of the men near the centre of power on the education issue, he was the closest to being invisible. He did, however, have considerable influence. Although technically the treasury remembrancer, he was really the government's official catholic. He was on very close terms with Lord Anglesey. He had been one of the education

This plan does not seem to have taken with the prime minister, for Anglesey had to write Grey again in July saying, 'I must soon get your thoughts to education.'[144] Serious revision of the Blake plan must have been necessary, as Anglesey referred in a letter to Lord Holland to a scheme that he himself was preparing.[145] Anglesey became discouraged, fearing that the Kildare Place Society would once again outmanœuvre him.[146]

During the summer of 1831 Stanley was converted to something approximating Anglesey's views, although it is impossible to tell exactly when this conversion took place. Lord Cloncurry, a proponent of the 1828 proposals, gave the following background in his memoirs:

> Mr Stanley was then a member of the cabinet, and so, in reality a sort of viceroy over the lord lieutenant and he was, at first, much disinclined to the measure. It was indeed the subject of an anxious discussion the very night before he left Dublin to attend parliament that session. There dined together on that occasion, *en petit comiteé*, Lord Anglesey, Lord Plunket, Mr Stanley, Mr A. R. Blake, and myself, and when we parted, at two o'clock in the morning, it did not seem that the united arguments of that party had produced any effect upon the chief secretary . . . I presume, nevertheless, that the seed did not fall upon stony ground, as it was but a few weeks afterward, the plan was brought by Mr Stanley himself.[147]

Since that session of parliament began on 14 June 1831, the meeting must have taken place in early June 1831. The meeting probably had some effect, for in early July Stanley wrote Lord

[144] Lord Anglesey to Lord Grey, 1 July 1831, P.R.O.N.I., T. 1068–8 (copy).

[145] Lord Anglesey to Lord Holland, 4 July 1831, P.R.O.N.I., T. 1068–5 (copy).

[146] Lord Anglesey to Lord Plunkett, 10 July 1831, P.R.O.N.I., T. 1068–3 (copy).

[147] Valentine Cloncurry, *Personal recollections of the life and times, with extracts from the correspondence of Valentine Lord Cloncurry* (Dublin, 2nd ed., 1850), p. 326.

---

inquiry commissioners of 1824–7. Richard P. J. Battersberry claims, but fails to document the statement, that the essential source of both Wyse's and Stanley's plan of education was Blake's work. Battersberry further states that the official education documents of 1831 and of later years were prepared by Blake. Battersberry, *Sir Thomas Wyse*, 1791–1862, *an advocate of a 'mixed education' policy over Ireland* (Dublin, 1939), p. 28.

Anglesey, following a conversation with him on the subject, stating that 'I still adhere to the propriety of appointing fairly-chosen education commissioners, who shall apply parliamentary grants in aid of local funds, upon fixed principles, and under certain restrictions, and till their appointment I am afraid we must place in your hands the distribution of what I consider an experimental grant'.[148]

Apparently, Stanley and Grey had worked out a plan for a two-stage educational operation. The first stage was to be the uniting of the grants for the Kildare Place Society and for the Association for Discountenancing Vice into one main fund for the purpose of education, this fund to be at the disposition of the lord lieutenant.[149] The second stage would be the creation of a set of commissioners to allocate money on some as yet undefined principle. The mention of a single fund, principles, restrictions, and local aid suggests that Stanley had modified considerably the earlier plan to set up a fund parallel to the Kildare Place fund, and to gradually extinguish the Kildare grant. But he had come only half way to the solution that Anglesey desired, namely that embodied in the 1828 select committee's report. Anglesey wrote to Stanley: 'your change in the mode of disposing of the education grant does not go far enough. I feel more strongly every hour the absolute necessity of an early settlement of these matters [education and the poor law] and as Ireland can have no repose until they are settled you shall have none until you have accomplished them.'[150]

Sometime during the summer Thomas Wyse re-entered the stage. During February 1831, he had busied himself by drawing up a series of queries about a plan of national education which he sent to the catholic prelates, to several members of parliament, and to distinguished members of the presbyterian communion. The answers received were, he reported, with few exceptions perfectly consonant with his own views.[151] In a letter to his

[148] Lord Stanley to Lord Anglesey, 6 July 1831, quoted in *Report from the select committee appointed to inquire into the progress and operation of the new plan of education in Ireland*, p. 452, H.C. 1837 (485), ix.

[149] Lord Grey to Lord Anglesey, 5 July 1831, P.R.O.N.I., T. 1068–30 (copy).

[150] Lord Anglesey to Lord Stanley, 15 July 1831, P.R.O.N.I., T. 1068–16 (copy).

[151] W. Wyse, pp 25–6.

brother of 2 August 1831, he wrote, 'I had a conference today with Stanley, and he promises to lay the whole before Lord Grey, with my observation and though there be difficulties— and I am conscious of many—I have great hopes'.[152] On the fifteenth of August 1831, he again wrote his brother about education: 'Last night Stanley told me in most positive terms, little or no opposition would be made by government to my plan, and begged me to send him the heads of my bill to look over; he asked explanations, made objections to parts which I fully answered. He says we almost perfectly agree; this was a great triumph, knowing as you do how opposed he was a little time ago.'[153] Whether it was Wyse or someone else who converted Stanley to the more radical education views remains unclear. In any event Wyse, together with Thomas Spring-Rice and More O'Ferral, were given leave on the ninth of August 1831, to bring in a bill to establish a national system of education.[154] At the end of August, however, Wyse had to cancel his plans and redraft the bill, 'owing to the extraordinary blundering on the part of his friend'.[155]

Meanwhile, Stanley was active and on the ninth of September 1831, was ready with his own educational prescription. The occasion for the introduction of the plan was the voting of supply for Irish education. Spring-Rice, then secretary to the treasury, moved that £30,000 be granted for enabling the lord lieutenant to assist the education of the Irish people. Spring-Rice added that the mode of its expenditure fell more properly within the department of the chief secretary, and, accordingly, he turned the floor over to him. Stanley began by defining the question under debate as not one of how much to spend annually on Irish education, but how the sum was to be granted so as best to serve the general welfare. He mentioned the reports of 1812, 1824, 1825, 1828 and 1830 (the latter on the condition of the Irish poor generally), and then launched into a long history of the grant to the Kildare Place Society and the reasons why it was no longer suitable as the major recipient of government education funds in Ireland. Stanley proposed that £30,000, the

[152] Quoted ibid., p. 26.
[153] Quoted ibid., pp 26–7.
[154] *Journals of the house of commons*, lxxxvi, pt 11, p. 737.
[155] W. Wyse, p. 27.

amount voted in the previous year to the Kildare Place Society and the Association for Discountenancing Vice, be placed at the lord lieutenant's disposal. A board was to be created, partly catholic, partly protestant, to oversee the direction of the schools. The general principle upon which the schools were to be conducted was of one or more days a week to be spent in separate religious instruction, the remainder in common literary instruction. He did not go into much greater detail. After quite a long, but insignificant, debate, the motion was agreed to.[156]

'The plans outlined in Stanley's proposals,' according to Auchmuty, 'were taken verbatim, and without any form of acknowledgement whatsoever from the draft suggestions that Wyse had handed over to the Irish secretary.'[157] This is non-sense. The ideas Stanley presented (and for that matter, the educational views that Wyse held) were by 1831 part of the conventional vocabulary of any official or politician thinking about Irish education. Further, Stanley's statement cannot by any stretch of the imagination be called a 'verbatim' reading of the heads of Wyse's bill, since Stanley did not go into the particulars of proposed arrangements, details covered in Wyse's bill.[158] Most important, during the debate Stanley stated that, 'with regard to the business of education, they proposed to follow the course recommended by the committee which sat last session, and of which his right hon. friend near him was chairman.'[159] In all probability, he was referring to the select committee on the state of the poor in Ireland, of which Spring-Rice had been chairman. This suggestion makes sense because Spring-Rice was almost certainly near Stanley on the front bench when Stanley made his speech; and Spring-Rice's committee was the only one that had met during the previous session

[156] *Hansard 3*, vi, 1249–305.

[157] Auchmuty, p. 153.

[158] This point holds true only if Wyse's December 1830 head of bill and Wyse's August 1831 head of bill were the same, or at least similar, in content. Unfortunately, no copy of the August 1831 head of bill was preserved. One writer states that the head of bill examined by Stanley in August 1831 was the same as forwarded to the government in December 1831 (William J. Bradley, 'Sir Thomas Wyse—Irish pioneer in education reform', unpublished Ph.D. thesis, University of Dublin, 1947, pp 87–8).

[159] *Hansard 3*, vi, 1258.

that had had any reference to Irish education. Significantly, that committee, in addition to reaffirming the instructions of the 1828 select committee, had ordered the 1828 committee's report to be reprinted.[160] Clearly, then, Lord Stanley was not parroting the educational prescriptions of the member for Tipperary, but was converting the ideas of the Irish educational consensus into the Irish national system of education.

Once the general suggestions for the national system had been approved, the hard task of making the suggestions a reality was at hand. 'We must lose no time in naming our commissioners for our new board of education,' Stanley wrote Anglesey in mid-October. He continued:

> This will be a task of some delicacy. I propose, however, if you approve, to make them a board of seven of whom three to be established church, two catholics and two protestant dissenters; this will, I think, be a fair distribution. The names which have occurred to me are Dr Whately and Dr Sadleir (if they will accept) to whom we must add some liberal layman of the Church of England; for the catholics, Dr Murray and some layman. For the dissenters only one has occurred to me; I believe Mr Holmes, the barrister, if he will take the office would be unexceptionable; I am afraid [name deleted] would not join as he disapproves the plan . . .
>
> I am drawing up instructions which shall be sent to you forthwith before I take any steps.[161]

Anglesey replied almost immediately:[162]

> The names that have occurred to me (and I place them as I prefer them) are
>
>
>
> *Protestants*
> Duke of Leinster – 1
> Archbishop of Dublin – 2
> Dr Sadleir – 3
> Dr Radcliffe
> Dr Sands
> [illegible]
>
>

[160] *Report from the select committee appointed to take into consideration the state of the poorer classes in Ireland*, p. 50.

[161] Lord Stanley to Lord Anglesey, 20 Oct. 1831, quoted in *Report from the select committee appointed to inquire into the progress and operation of the new plan of education in Ireland*, pp 449–50.

[162] Lord Anglesey to Lord Stanley, 24 Oct. 1831, P.R.O.N.I., T. 1068–17 (copy).

Dissenters
Rev. Montgomery – 2
Barrister Holmes – 1
Rev. J. Armstrong
Catholics
Archbishop of Dublin – 1
Dr Colter, Maynooth – 2
Sir A. Laughlin

Anglesey urged that the duke of Leinster be appointed president. He argued first that the duke would be good as he was constantly resident in Ireland and then, inconsistently, that although it was probable that the duke would not very often attend, his name would be very useful and would at once stop any sectarian jealousy.[163] Significantly, in view of later developments, Anglesey realized, and perhaps intended, that Richard Whately, newly appointed archbishop of Dublin, would act as the invisible president of the board, with Leinster only bearing the title.[164] The board as finally constituted comprised seven members. Three were Anglican: the duke of Leinster as president, Archbishop Whately, and Dr Sadleir. Two were presbyterians: Reverend James Carlile and Mr Robert Holmes. And two were catholic: Archbishop Murray and A. R. Blake.

Before these appointments could be made final, however, guidelines for the operation of the commissioners had to be drawn up. These guidelines were contained in Lord Stanley's well-known 'instructions', written in the form of a letter to the duke of Leinster. Three questions surround these instructions. First, why were they contained in a letter rather than in a statute? It is possible that Stanley was afraid of creating an educational monster and wished to keep things on the basis of an experiment. He could back out of an experiment much more easily than he could get a law repealed. A more probable explanation is that the pressure of practical politics made a statute impossible. Grey had written Anglesey in mid-August implying

[163] Lord Anglesey to Lord Stanley, 28 Oct. 1831, P.R.O.N.I., T. 1068–17 (copy); Lord Anglesey to Lord Stanley, 2 Nov. 1831, P.R.O.N.I., T. 1068–17 (copy).

[164] Lord Anglesey to Lord Stanley, 2 Nov. 1831. 'It is probable that the duke would not very often attend but his name would be very useful and at once stop any jealousy that might be between the 2 churches by naming Whately as president, altho' he w' usually officiate as such.'

that the impossibility of speeding any Irish education measure through parliament would tend to prevent the government from taking up such a measure.[165] Behind such an implication lay the volatility of the political scene during the reform bill crisis. Thomas Wyse introduced, with Stanley's approval,[166] his promised education bill on 29 September 1831,[167] but in the parliamentary snarl over the reform bill, it never received a second reading.

The second question is: 'when was Stanley's letter to Leinster written?' The various transcriptions of the letter all bear the date 'October 1831', and it is usually concluded that the letter was written sometime in late October of that year. A letter from Anglesey to Stanley of 2 November 1831, however, implies that the letter was probably completed only in early November and then backdated to October. It appears that Stanley had sent the letter to Anglesey for final approval before sending it on to Leinster: 'The letter to the president of the education board appears to me to be unexceptionable and admirably adapted to its object', Anglesey replied.[168] It is possible that Anglesey received a copy only after Leinster received the original. Such a course would, however, be out of keeping with the almost obsequious deference with which Stanley treated Anglesey on the education issue, once the major matter of what to do with the Kildare Place Society had been settled, and, further, would have been in direct contravention of Anglesey's request to Stanley of 28 October 1831: 'Of course you will send me the instructions to the commissioners of education for approval, before it is promulgated for I cannot bear that anything should go out in my name without having considered it'.[169] Thus an

[165] Lord Grey to Lord Anglesey, 16 Aug. 1831, P.R.O.N.I., T. 1068–30 (copy).

[166] Bradley, p. 88; W. Wyse, p. 28.

[167] *Journals of the house of commons*, lxxxvi, pt. ii, p. 879; *A bill for the establishment and maintenance of parochial schools, and the advancement of the education of the people in Ireland*, H.C. 1831 (286), i.

[168] Lord Anglesey to Lord Stanley, 2 Nov. 1831, P.R.O.N.I., T. 1068–17 (copy).

[169] Lord Anglesey to Lord Stanley, 28 Oct. 1831, P.R.O.N.I., T. 1068–17 (copy). James Carlile before the house of lords committee in 1831 said that he thought the date of the letter was 31 Oct. 1831; quoted in *Royal commission of inquiry into primary education (Ireland)*, *report of the commissioners*, p. 22 [C 6], H.C. 1870, xxviii, pt i.

early November date seems to be most likely for the final draft of the letter.

The third, and by far the most perplexing question regarding the instructions is: what, precisely, did they say? The answer to this question is not as easy as it seems, because no original of the Stanley-to-Leinster letter of instructions remains and because there are two distinct versions of the letter in Parliamentary Papers. It appears that a first draft of the letter was drawn of which no transcriptions whatsoever remain. This draft was submitted to the commissioners before their appointment was confirmed and at their suggestion a number of alterations were made. The original draft imposed upon the commissioners the duty of seeing that children attended their respective places of worship. The duty was removed from the instructions upon the objections of at least Mr Carlile, and perhaps others from among the protestants, on the grounds that this would involve encouraging attendance at a place of which he might disapprove. The commissioners also forced Stanley to change the description of the plan from one of 'combined literary and separate religious education, each department altogether to exclude the other', to one of 'combined moral and literary, and separate religious instruction'. He was further required to add 'it is not designed to exclude from the list of books for the combined instruction, such portions of sacred history, or of religious or moral teaching, as may be approved of by the board'. Hence, even before it began, the system was changed from one that rigidly separated religious and literary instruction to one in which literary and moral instruction overlapped, and in which books of scripture extracts, as envisioned by the 1824–7 commissioners, could be introduced. The protestant ecclesiastical members made Stanley drop from his draft a provision to which Archbishop Murray and Mr Blake had assented, that the Roman Catholic edition of the New Testament should be supplied to catholic children by the board, and read at times of separate religious instruction.[170]

The first draft being lost, we must deal with the two transcriptions of the final draft sent to the duke of Leinster. 'Version A' was published in the *Dublin Gazette* of 8 December 1831, and was published in Parliamentary Papers of 1831–2, with the

[170] Ibid., pp 21–2; James Carlile to editor of *The Times*, 20 Aug. 1853.

attestation of the Irish Office, dated 23 February 1832.[171] The same version appears in the minutes of the commissioners of national education for 1 December 1831, and was also published by the 1837 select committee on the progress and operation of the Irish national system of education.[172] The Powis commissioners of 1870 found an 'original' of the letter—now missing—in the Irish Office, and reproduced it.[173] 'Version B' was published by the commissioners of national education during their early years,[174] but in 1841 the commissioners began printing 'Version A' of the letter.[175] The somewhat disingenuous explanation of why the commissioners' version of the letter had varied for so many years from the version published in the *Dublin Gazette* and in Parliamentary Papers was that 'some variations were made in the letter as it was passing through the office'.[176]

Both versions of the letter are set forth in the appendix, with comments on the major differences between the two versions. The points of agreement between them were more important, however, than the differences. On most points the wording of the versions was identical. Because Lord Stanley's instructions served as the written constitution of the national system, its major points deserve our notice. As they are mentioned it will become clear that Stanley did not produce any strikingly new ideas but merely brought forward ideas that had been minted, debated, and generally accepted in the course of the preceding five decades of Irish education discussion.

The first portion of Stanley's letter was chiefly given over to a historical review. Stanley summarized the work of the various commissioners and committees on Irish education that had met

[171] *Copy of a letter from the chief secretary for Ireland to the duke of Leinster, on the formation of a board of commissioners for education in Ireland*, H.C. 1831–2 (196), xxix.

[172] *Report from the select committee appointed to inquire into the progress and operation of the new plan of education in Ireland*, pp 579–81.

[173] *Royal commission of inquiry into primary education (Ireland), Report of the commissioners*, p. 22.

[174] See, for example, *Report of the commissioners of national education in Ireland, for the years 1834, 1835, and 1836* (Dublin, 1836), pp vii–xiii.

[175] *Eighth report of the commissioners of national education in Ireland, for the year 1841*, pp 6–8, H.C. 1842 [398], xxiii.

[176] *Royal commission of inquiry into primary education (Ireland), Report of the commissioners*, p. 26.

since the union. Second, he judged the Kildare Place Society to be an inappropriate recipient of the funds for the education of the Irish working classes. Third, he proposed that a board be created to superintend a system of national education. This board was to be composed of men of high personal character and to include individuals of high ecclesiastical rank. These church dignitaries were to be chosen from the several denominations. The board was to have complete control over schools erected or placed under its auspices. Fourth, Stanley stated that one of the main objects of the proposed system was to unite the children of different creeds in a common school. Hence, the board was to look with favour upon applications for aid made jointly by catholics and protestants. Fifth, Stanley laid down certain conditions that were to be satisfied before aid was granted to a school, such as local provision of a permanent salary for the master, of furniture and repairs, of books, and of one third of the building costs. Sixth, he proposed that the schools be kept open four or five days a week for moral and literary instruction, and that the remaining one or two days a week be set aside for religious education of the children by their respective clergy. Seventh, Stanley suggested that the commissioners assume complete control over school books and control over the funds voted annually by parliament, subject to certain limitations. Eighth, he propounded that the right to hire and fire teachers be given to local managers of schools, but that the right of removing any teacher be reserved to the commissioners should they feel such action necessary. Local managers were to be required to hire teachers who were to be trained at a model school to be operated under the board's auspices in Dublin. The commissioners of national education took these instructions as their marching orders, and attempted to arrange the national system in a manner consonant with Stanley's wishes.

Surveying the course of events leading to the founding of the national system, then, we have seen that the founding of the Irish national system of education can be accounted for only by reference to a unique pattern of Irish events. As background causes of Irish educational development we discussed the early and unusual tendency of the government to intervene in Irish education affairs, and also the striking willingness of the peasantry to support indigenous schools. The Roman Catholic prelates were brought to favour an undenominational system of state-provided education by the activities of the protestant proselytizing societies, and the government yielded to the prelates' demands. The lines which the national system assumed were determined by years of cumulative educational consensus, as articulated in a genealogy of official government reports on education. Individual personalities were important in shaping the events of 1830 and 1831, but everyone involved spoke in the vocabulary of the conventional educational wisdom. From the vantage point of the present century and within the perspective of Irish history, the creation of the Irish national system of education in 1831 seems a natural, indeed an almost inevitable, event.

IV

SOME BUREAUCRATIC
ARCHAEOLOGY, 1831–49

~~~~~~

I

ANY ATTEMPT TO UNCOVER the administrative outline of the
national system of education in its first twenty years is necessarily
a confusing job. During this period the bureaucracy grew from
a tiny collection of amateur educationists into an intricate
assemblage of professional administrators. At any given moment
during its first two decades the probabilities were that the system
was undergoing some kind of administrative expansion. But if
the job is a confusing one it is also a necessary one. Without an
understanding of the administrative configuration of the national
system of education, it is impossible to understand the system's
subsequent history, especially the twisting of the system by
religious groups. A detailed description of its administrative
arrangements is necessary to prevent our making erroneous
assumptions about the way the system operated; the system was
far different from twentieth-century civil bureaucracies, and
indeed was even atypical by nineteenth-century standards.
Aside from the necessity of understanding the system's administrative structure as a prerequisite for understanding the system's
history, the bureaucracy of the national system demands attention on its own account as an example of one of the methods by
which the government ran Irish affairs. Moreover, the arrangements for the national system are worth attention because the
system was created at a time in which the bureaucratic pattern

of the entire British civil service was beginning to undergo reform and expansion. The method of administering Irish national
education represented one of several alternative methods that
could be used to manage the array of government agencies that
were to emerge during the remainder of the nineteenth century.

In the discussion that follows three related points serve as a
ground base which sounds beneath the discussion of the individual units of the bureaucracy. The first of these is the idea that
the most accurate way to analyse a bureaucracy is to discover
who had the right to make a given decision. The bureaucracy of
the national system of education consisted, in the main, of a
series of specialized compartments distinguished by function
(i.e. inspectors, secretaries to the commissioners, etc.); but
these compartments also fitted into a hierarchy of authority
within the board.[1] The right to make certain decisions was given
to the functionaries of each compartment, but the right to make
major decisions was reserved to higher authorities, sometimes

[1] The terminology of education for nineteenth-century Ireland is confusing, especially concerning the 'board of education'. The commissioners who conducted the inquiry of 1806–12 were known as the 'commissioners of the board of education in Ireland'. The group of men formed in
1813 to oversee the endowed schools was given the title 'commissioners
of education', and were often referred to, up to 1830, as the 'board of
education'. These commissioners of endowed schools continued to exist
as a body after the national system was founded, but popular usage transferred the title 'board of education' from them to the new commissioners
of national education. The proper title for the new set of educational
overseers was 'the commissioners of national education in Ireland'.
(In their first report the commissioners went under the title of 'Commissioners appointed by the lord lieutenant to administer funds voted by
parliament for the education of the poor in Ireland' but thereafter used
the name of 'commissioners of national education in Ireland'.)

In the remainder of this book whenever the word 'commissioners' is
used it refers specifically to the body of men selected by the lord lieutenant
to oversee the national system. The term 'board' is used to refer to the
whole central establishment of the system of national education in Ireland,
including the commissioners, secretaries, inspectors, professors and clerks.
Except in quotations from contemporary sources, 'board of education' will
not be used to refer to the commissioners of national education in Ireland.

If all this is somewhat confusing, it is comforting to note that during the
1830s the chief secretary's office was often unable to remember the distinction between the commissioners of national education, and the commissioners of education, and often sent mail intended for the one group to the
other.

the commissioners of national education and occasionally the chief secretary or lord lieutenant. The second point involves the distinction between the formal and the informal aspects of bureaucracy. The formal aspects represent the theoretical line of authority and the theoretical delegation of the right to make decisions. The informal aspects involve the way decisions were made in spite of what the blueprints may have said. A third overriding point is that there was insufficient coordination between the central bureaucracy of the national system and the local managers of schools. Hence, a curious picture emerges of an educational system in which there was at once a high degree of administrative centralization and a large degree of local autonomy.

The prime minister and the parliament of the United Kingdom of Great Britain and Ireland formed, at least in theory, the very top links in the chain of authority under which the Irish national system of education operated. Parliament annually voted the funds for Irish national education and controlled the way these funds were spent. Parliament's control, however, was much more apparent than real, especially during the system's early years. The system was created not by an act of parliament, but by the instructions of an Irish chief secretary. No statutory limitations bound the commissioners of national education. Of course parliament could dictate the conditions under which the money it granted was spent, but in practice the house of commons could give little of its time to discussing Irish education. Further, the commons' rules of procedure made significant discussion of Irish education difficult. The Irish education estimates were presented by the government as a recommendation that a certain amount be granted for Irish education. A member disagreeing with some aspect of Irish educational policy could not propose to alter the details of the education vote, but could only move that the total amount of money voted be reduced by a small sum, and then talk about details. In later years, John Redmond in at least two instances moved that the Irish education estimates be reduced by £100 simply so that he would have a chance to discuss the national system in some detail.[2] Although theoretically at the top of the chain of com-

[2] Joseph D. Lynam ('Jacques' *pseud.*), *Irish education as it is and as it should be* (Dublin, 1906), p. 58.

mand, parliament actually had little influence on Irish national education during the early years of its development.

Much the same statement could be made about the prime minister. As head of the executive he was responsible for all administrative activities. In point of fact, prime ministers during the first half of the nineteenth century paid attention to Ireland only as it threatened England's peace. Only rarely were Irish educational matters forced upon the prime minister, as when the synod of Ulster harassed him during the 1830s with deputations about the national system's rules. Also, the prime minister sometimes received educational intelligence from outside the official channels of communication. For instance, Archbishop Whately felt free to write Grey when the latter was prime minister about problems the national system was having.[3]

Below parliament and the prime minister in the chain of authority was the home secretary. The lord lieutenant of Ireland was ostensibly subordinate to the home secretary. Actually, the home secretary did little, if anything, in Irish matters, and there is no instance in which the home secretary had any influence upon the affairs of the commissioners of national education in Ireland.

The lord lieutenant, in contrast to the prime minister and home secretary, had an immediate interest in Irish affairs and a direct concern with the conduct of the national system of education. The lord lieutenant was the queen's representative in Ireland and the head of the Irish executive. His powers respecting the conduct of education in Ireland were quite wide. Up to 1848 the commissioners of national education drew their money from the lord lieutenant's education fund. Parliament did not have time to shoulder direct financial control of the system, and this authority devolved upon him. Even in 1849 when the fund was removed from his control and began to come through the exchequer,[4] he maintained great power because of his position as head of the Irish executive. Appointment of the commissioners of national education were made by the lord lieutenant, thus giving him an indirect control over the commissioners' activities.

[3] Richard Whately to Lord Grey, 29 June 1832, N.L.I., MS 8401 (photostat of original in Durham University Library).
[4] Irish Free State, *Report of the department of education, the school year 1924–25, and the financial and administrative years 1924-25-26* (Dublin, 1926), p. 12.

A much more direct control existed in the implied regulation, recognized by both the lord lieutenant and the commissioners, that the commissioners would not change any major rule or procedure of the system without his approval. The lord lieutenant, therefore, was not merely a theoretical link in the chain of command, but also the possessor of real power over the conduct of education in Ireland. As we shall see, however, during the system's first two decades successive lord lieutenants chose to give increasing autonomy to the commissioners, and they came to conduct most of their business without official reference to anyone but themselves.

The chief secretary for Ireland was supposedly the lord lieutenant's assistant, but during most of the century was an equal partner with him and in practice was sometimes the lord lieutenant's superior. Although the chief secretary and the chief secretary's office exercised a great influence upon the conduct of Irish administration, the chief secretary rarely dealt with important educational matters during the national system's early years: policy matters were referred to the lord lieutenant. The chief secretary's resident assistant, the under-secretary, dealt with routine matters concerning the national system.

At the heart of the national system were the commissioners of national education. The commissioners are worth considerable attention since responsibility for the conduct of national education was their direct charge. Initially, it is important to note that the commissioners were amateurs in at least two senses of the word. They were amateurs in the sense that no member of the group was professionally involved in elementary education. This is not to say that they were not informed in educational matters. Of the original commissioners, Dr Sadleir was provost of Trinity College, James Carlile had done some part-time school teaching, Archbishop Whately had been a fellow of Oriel College, Oxford, and A. R. Blake had been one of the education inquiry commissioners of 1824–7. But none of them were named as commissioner of national education because of their educational achievement. Rather, they were appointed because they held important positions in church or state.

This meant that they were amateurs in a second sense: each man spent most of his life at his own profession and only spent time on national education as something of a hobby. In the true amateur tradition, the commissioners were unpaid. One wonders how Dr Sadleir, for example, found as much time as he did to spend upon his duties as a commissioner. In 1835, Sadleir held the following posts in Trinity College, Dublin, in addition to being one of the commissioners of national education: provost, senior fellow, librarian, senior dean, catechist, Regius professor of Greek, bursar, and Erasmus Smith professor of mathematics. In addition, he was chaplain to the lord lieutenant and an ecclesiastical commissioner for Ireland.[5] The duke of Leinster, although resident in Ireland, could spend little time at the commissioners' meetings since he was that rare phenomenon in Ireland, a conscientious landlord, and spent a great deal of time performing his civic duties. When he resigned as a commissioner in December 1840, it was because his duties as a poor law guardian and as a magistrate of petty sessions did not leave him enough time to attend the commissioners' meetings.[6] Anthony Blake served as treasury remembrancer. As a well-liked and amiable, informed and influential merchant, he was of great value as a commissioner. He seems to have been able to find time to attend most of the commissioners' meetings. James Carlile was a full-time presbyterian minister to Mary's Abbey congregation in Dublin, but he, like Blake, was able to spend considerable time on educational matters and soon became the paid resident commissioner, thus losing his amateur standing. Robert Holmes, as a queen's counsellor, was not often free for national education matters. Both the protestant and the Roman Catholic archbishops of Dublin, Doctors Whately and Murray, respectively, seem, in spite of the demands of their posts, to have been able to find a surprising amount of time for the affairs of national education.[7]

[5] *Dublin Evening Mail*, 11 Nov. 1835.   [6] M.C.N.E.I., 31 Dec. 1840.
[7] One contemporary rumour should be dealt with here: that the offer of the archbishopric to Whately was made contingent upon his supporting the national system of education, and upon his becoming a commissioner of national education. The rumour was plausible, for Whately took up his post at about the same time the system of national education was being created, but was untrue. Whately was offered the archbishopric on 14 September 1831 by Lord Grey (Lord Grey to Richard Whately, 14 September 1831, reproduced in E. Jane Whately, *Life and correspondence of Richard Whately, D.D., late archbishop of Dublin*, London, 1866, pp 97–8). In this letter no mention was made of education. As we know from the chron-

If some of the commissioners did give considerable time to national education, we should remember that their doing so was really an act of charity on their part and that there was nothing anyone could do to force any one of them to do his educational job if he preferred not to do it. In fairness to the commissioners, however, it should be remembered that unpaid boards were often used in the nineteenth century to bring together different sections of opinion in the management of a department, and that on the especially volatile issue of Irish education amateurs who could consolidate national opinion possessed an attribute no professional civil servant could have. The personal prestige of the commissioners, especially the archbishops, was certainly important during the system's early years, and no set of civil servants would have been likely to match it. Unpaid boards also had the virtue of being somewhat more independent in their thinking and action than were the professional bureaucrats and occasionally threw off the good manners of civil service protocol and publicly differed with the government.[8]

Religiously, the commissioners were assorted as follows:[9]

Years	Established church	Roman Catholic	Presby.	Total
1831–7	3	2	2	7
1838	4	3	2	9
1839	6	4	2	12
1840	6	4	2	12
1841–6	5	4	2	11
1847	6	5	2	13
1848	6	5	3	14
1849	6	4	3	13

[8] Robert B. McDowell, *The Irish administration, 1801–1914* (London and Toronto, 1964), p. 33.

[9] Derived from *Royal commission of inquiry into primary education (Ireland)*, vol. vii, *Returns furnished by the national board*, p. 5, para. 3 [C6–VI], H.C. 1870, xxviii, pt v. No distinction is made between presbyterian and unitarian. The table is taken from the situation as of 31 December of each year.

---

ology of events described in the last chapter, the September date preceded by several weeks the period in which Stanley and Anglesey began corresponding about the appointment of the commissioners of national education. A select committee on Irish education in 1837 spent considerable time on this point and the testimony and evidence of Lords Grey and Stanley clearly established that the rumour was untrue. *Report from the select committee appointed to inquire into the progress and operation of the new plan of education in Ireland*, pp 449–54, H.C. 1837 (485), ix.

In addition to the seven original commissioners, three commissioners were named in May 1838: Sir Patrick Bellew, Richard W. Greene, and J. P. Kennedy. The first was a Roman Catholic of no stature who attended the commissioners' meetings only occasionally, the second a member of the established church who was the Irish solicitor-general, and the third a member of the established church who was paymaster of the civil services in Ireland and who only remained a commissioner about six months before resigning. Rev. James Carlile resigned in 1838, and in December 1838 Rev. Dr Pooley Shuldham Henry, later president of Queen's College, Belfast, replaced him as the orthodox presbyterian among the commissioners. In June 1838 three more commissioners were named: Viscount Morpeth, the chief secretary for Ireland, an Anglican; Alexander MacDonnell, also an Anglican, and chief clerk in the chief secretary's office; and John R. Corballis, a Roman Catholic barrister. The duke of Leinster resigned in December 1840 and was replaced by his son, the marquis of Kildare in January of the next year. In January 1840, Lord Plunket, the Anglican lord chancellor of Ireland, became a commissioner. Unfortunately for the influence of the commissioners upon the Irish administration, Viscount Morpeth resigned as a commissioner in 1841 when he ceased to hold the office of chief secretary, and his example of the chief secretary's becoming a commissioner of national education was not followed by any of his successors. Lord Plunket too resigned in 1841. Three new commissioners were created in November 1847, one of them being the Roman Catholic undersecretary for Ireland, Sir T. N. Redington. The others were the Anglican Lord Chancellor Brady and the unitarian barrister Robert Andrews. The latter took the place of Robert Holmes, the commission's unitarian member, who resigned in the same year. In early February 1848, James Gibson, a presbyterian barrister, was named as the third presbyterian among the commissioners; Anthony Blake died in January 1849, and James O'Ferral, a Roman Catholic of gentlemanly pursuits, took his place. John Corballis, the other catholic lay commissioner, resigned in the same year.[10]

How well did this miscellaneous assortment of amateurs get along with each other? The answer seems to be, 'surprisingly

[10] Ibid., p. 5.

well', although it is hard to tell precisely how well, because the commissioners' minutes during their early years did not record dissent from majority decisions in any detail. Lord Anglesey played the mother hen to the commissioners during their first months, attended some of their meetings, and was most sanguine about the commissioners working well together.[11] He realized at once that Whately and Murray were the foundation stones of the structure. Fortunately for the commissioners' survival, he quite correctly observed that 'Whately and Murray seem to understand each other perfectly'.[12] One can only conjecture the reasons for the solidarity of the Murray–Whately axis, but it is clear that each believed in the principles of united literary instruction of protestant and catholic children, and that each was extremely careful of the other's sensitivities. Time and again in the commissioners' minutes, one finds Whately making certain no action was taken on potentially controversial points until Murray was allowed to approve or amend the proposed action. Murray himself had the patience and disposition of a saint.

Whately did not seem to get along as well with all the other commissioners. J. P. Kennedy, the Anglican paymaster of the civil services in Ireland who joined the commissioners in May 1838, resigned in the same year because of the unkindness he felt from Archbishop Whately and from A. R. Blake. His letter to Thomas Spring-Rice explaining his resignation reveals a good deal about the commissioners at work:

With the duke of Leinster and Archbishop Murray I would have gone on to the end of time. The provost seems to be a good easy man. Mr Holmes and Richard Greene are able to attend little, but quite well disposed, Sir Patrick Bellew unexceptionable, but the archbishop of Dublin and Mr Blake really make it quite impossible to continue . . . When I went to the board meeting it was clear that I was looked on totally as an intruder and meddler by the archbishop of Dublin . . . I could not submit to the position in which I found myself placed.[13]

[11] Lord Anglesey to Lord Holland, 2 Dec. 1831, P.R.O.N.I., T. 1068–17 (copy).

[12] Lord Anglesey to Lord Stanley, 1 Dec. 1831, P.R.O.N.I., T. 1068–17 (copy).

[13] J. P. Kennedy to Thomas Spring-Rice, 12 Dec. 1838, N.L.I., Monteagle Papers.

Whately, it is clear from the group's minutes, was the un-official president of the commissioners, just as Lord Anglesey had intended him to be. When the duke of Leinster was absent he almost invariably took the chair. When neither Whately nor Leinster was present, Murray usually succeeded to the chair, although this was open to some variation. During their first seven years, the commissioners' meetings seem to have been largely dominated by Whately, Murray, A. R. Blake and James Carlile, with Dr Sadleir being a constant attender. When Carlile retired as resident commissioner in 1838, his replacement, Alexander Macdonnell, formerly chief clerk of the chief secre-tary's office, quickly assumed the influence Carlile had aban-doned. The commissioners met weekly, usually on Thursdays, to transact ordinary business. They also held a number of special meetings, monthly at most, to deal with controversial topics. The following record of attendances at ordinary and special meetings of the commissioners during 1838 provides a good indication of the commissioners who were active and of those who were not so active during the early years:[14]

Commissioners	Ordinary meeting attendances	Special meeting attendances
Duke of Leinster	16	3
Archbishop Whately	23	3
Archbishop Murray	26	3
Dr Sadleir	41	4
R. W. Greene	11	1
J. P. Kennedy	18	2
A. R. Blake	40	3
Sir Patrick Bellew	4	1
Robert Holmes	15	0
Reverend James Carlile	34	2

Despite their efforts, the commissioners were soon buried under an avalanche of detail. Their response was to specialize within their body and to delegate some of their corporate power to individual members or small groups of members. By mid-century, the commissioners had resolved themselves into three sub-committees to handle certain routine matters. The earliest of these was called simply 'the sub-committee' and met to

[14] *Royal commission of inquiry into primary education (Ireland)*, vol. vii, *Returns furnished by the national board*, p. 7. Greene, Bellew and Henry began as commissioners in May of the year.

consider all applications to the commissioners for aid of any sort, plus minor disciplinary matters concerning violations of the commissioners' rules. The finance committee kept watch on the state of the commissioners' funds and controlled expenditure for categories not controlled by the sub-committee or by the third committee, the agricultural committee. The latter was created when the commissioners began seriously entering the field of agricultural education and was charged with overseeing business connected with the agricultural schools. Each of these committees met regularly, usually weekly. Their transactions were submitted each week to the commissioners as a whole for approval. In actual operation, the sub-committee system became a method of shifting the burden for details from the amateur commissioners to the professional civil servants, for at most of the various sub-committee meetings the only commissioner who actually appeared was the paid resident commissioner, with various of the higher civil servants 'in attendance'.[15]

In view of their elaborate procedures it is a bit disconcerting to recall that the commissioners as a body did not have the legal right to exist. They existed because the Irish executive approved of their behaviour and because parliament voted them money to spend each year. Their legal non-existence had two major implications for their situation. One aspect was that they were extraordinarily free from supervision. The commissioners were not a government department, they had no minister, and were responsible to parliament only to the extent of having to produce an annual report for parliament's benefit. They were responsible to the lord lieutenant, but he was not himself a member of their body. They were in no way responsible to local units of government and were not directly accountable to the voters. Thus, if they were legal phantoms, the commissioners were at least remarkably free ones.

The obverse side of the coin, however, meant that the commissioners had a hard time laying their case before the cabinet and parliament. Hence, in April 1839, we find the commissioners writing to the lord lieutenant suggesting, in view of the way their proceedings had been publicly misrepresented, that

[15] Ibid., pp 8–11; M.C.N.E.I., 1831–7, 1841–9, passim.

some members of the government be added to their number in order that the government might be acquainted with its activities.[16] A further and more worrisome disadvantage of the commissioners' anomalous position was that as an educational group they could be snuffed out at a moment's whim by the lord lieutenant or prime minister. Since the commissioners had been assembled by a whig government many tory Irishmen assumed that they would be disbanded the moment the whigs were removed from office. Peel's short administration of 1834–5 left the commissioners' enemies disappointed, and when Peel returned in 1841 the government gave no visible signs of intending to destroy the national system. With the tories countenancing their existence, it was clear that the commissioners were going to remain on the Irish scene for a long season. Nevertheless, their lack of legal status continued to gall the commissioners.

The redoubtable Thomas Wyse tried to come to their rescue. Upon his return to parliament in 1835, he brought in a 'bill for the establishment of a board of national education, and the advancement of elementary education in Ireland'.[17] The bill was essentially a restatement of his 1831 bill, but it did at least attempt to give legal sanction to the commissioners' existence. Wyse made an exceptionally long speech in asking leave to bring in the bill, it was read a first time, and proceeded no further.[18] He made a favourable impression upon the government, however, for the Melbourne administration appointed Wyse chairman of a select committee on the foundation schools in Ireland and upon the system of national education, a commission originally given in June 1835, and twice extended before the committee reported in 1838.[19] The report envisaged a system

---

[16] Commissioners of national education in Ireland to Viscount Elrington, 26 April 1839, reproduced in *Royal commission of inquiry into primary education (Ireland)*, vol. i, pt 1, *Report of the commissioners*, pp 88–9 [C 6], H.C. 1870, xxviii, pt i.

[17] *A bill for the establishment of a board of national education, and the advancement of elementary education in Ireland*, H.C. 1835 (285), ii.

[18] *Hansard* 3, xxvii, 199–234, 19 May 1835; James J. Auchmuty, *Sir Thomas Wyse, 1791–1862, the life and career of an educator and diplomat* (London, 1939), p. 163.

[19] Auchmuty, p. 164; T. W. Moody and J. C. Beckett, *Queen's Belfast, 1845–1949: the history of a university* (London, 1959), i, lvii–lviii.

of education covering all forms of schooling from elementary to collegiate level and was impressive both for its vision and for its impracticality. The relevant point is that the report strongly recommended that the new educational institutions it envisaged, and the board of national education it suggested be created, should be established by law, not by administrative fiat.[20]

In August 1844, the government finally gave in to the pressures of the educationist and to the prayers of the commissioners, and granted the commissioners a charter of incorporation. The government's motivation in granting the charter may have been partially defensive self-interest, for the charter limited the commissioners' range of action. In any event, the granting of the charter marks the point from which the commissioners were universally recognized as a permanent Irish institution. Under the charter, the commissioners of national education in Ireland were named a body corporate and granted perpetual succession. The commissioners were licensed to hold property not to exceed the yearly value of £40,000 and to manage and dispose of that property as necessary. Also, they were given the right to grant leases on their land and to erect as many schools in Ireland as they thought necessary. Vacancies in the succession were to be filled, as before, by the lord lieutenant.[21] The commissioners had obtained, at last, the right to exist.

In addition to establishing a legal purchase, the commissioners in their early years had to define and then defend their area of autonomy in financial affairs. Not surprisingly, the treasury was the chief enemy of the commissioners' financial freedom. Each year the board's civil servants drew up an estimate for the commissioners of how much money was required for the coming year. The commissioners submitted this estimate to the treasury which, after arguments with the commissioners, passed the estimate on to the government, from whence it was presented to the house of commons to be voted. In their first two decades the commissioners did not have a great deal of difficulty with the treasury's paring their estimates nor with

[20] *Report from the select committee on foundation schools and education in Ireland*, p. 80, H.C. 1837–8 (701), vii.

[21] *The twelfth report of the commissioners of national education in Ireland, for the year 1845*, pp 10–11 [711], H.C. 1846, xxii.

parliament bolting at the sight of the government's recommendations. The parliamentary grants from 1831 to 1849 were as follows:[22]

1831	£30,000	1840	£50,000
1832	37,500	1841	50,000
1833	25,000	1842	50,000
1834	20,000	1843	50,000
1835	35,000	1844	72,000
1836	50,153	1845	75,000
1837	50,000	1846	85,000
1838	50,000	1847	100,000
1839	50,000	1848	120,000
		1849	120,000

Admittedly the commissioners did not always have all the money they wanted; at times they were unable to grant aid to as many new schools as they would have liked[23] and on one occasion, they had to ask the stationery office to be allowed to postpone paying their bill because their funds were low.[24] In most years, though, they had nothing to complain of, for if in any year during which the grants made to schools pushed the commissioners' expenditures beyond the estimate they simply submitted a supplementary estimate[25] which was usually granted without much opposition. At one point the commissioners were so well-off financially that, while asking for £20,000, they still had more than £32,000 in the bank unspent from previous years. They were told thereafter to keep their bank balance under £5,000.[26]

Clearly, the commissioners' problem in financial matters was not the total amount of money available to them. Rather, the question was whether they would be allowed to spend the money as they pleased or forced to spend it as the treasury pleased. Operationally, the issue revolved around the question of how the commissioners' accounts were to be audited. On 8 April 1834, the commissioners of the treasury wrote Dublin

[22] *Royal commission of inquiry into primary education (Ireland)*, vol vii, *Returns furnished by the national board*, p. 490.
[23] M.C.N.E.I., 8 Oct. 1835; *Tenth report of the commissioners of national education in Ireland, for the year 1843*, p. 3 [569], H.C. 1844, xxx.
[24] M.C.N.E.I., 8 Dec. 1836.
[25] McDowell, p. 101.
[26] M.C.N.E.I., 14 Feb. 1835.

Castle, enclosing a letter from the commissioners of audit that raised this matter.[27] In their letter of 20 March 1834, to the treasury, the auditors asked their lordships' directions. They cited Lord Stanley's instructions in which it was stated that the commissioners of national education would invariably require as a condition of granting aid to schools that local funds be raised, and that these funds be sufficient to provide for school repairs, books and requisites, and to provide a certain amount for the teacher's salary and to cover at least one third of the building costs. The auditors wished to know if they should require satisfactory evidence from the commissioners of national education that these conditions had been met before sanctioning their accounts or whether the statement in Stanley's letter, that the commissioners should have 'absolute control over the funds which may be annually voted by parliament' freed them from such scrutiny. If the latter was the case, the auditor would be limited to checking the arithmetical correctness of the education accounts.[28] The Castle authorities told the commissioners of national education that the auditors probably would be correct in disallowing grants made when the requisite conditions had not been met and did solicit the commissioners' reaction to this conclusion.[29] The commissioners of national education reacted swiftly. Contending that the auditors' function was limited solely to checking their arithmetic, they sent a delegation to the lord lieutenant to press their point.[30] The commissioners won, and as will be seen later, in only a minority of the grants they made through the years did they comply with Lord Stanley's conditions.

In the financial arena the commissioners of national education won another major battle on the matter of school books. On 27 December 1833, the lords of the treasury informed the commissioners, through Dublin Castle, that the commissioners should use the stationery office for all their printing needs.[31]

[27] Lords of the treasury to E. Littleton, reproduced in M.C.N.E.I., 24 Apr. 1834.

[28] Reproduced in M.C.N.E.I., 24 Apr. 1834.

[29] E. Littleton to commissioners of national education in Ireland, 14 Apr. 1834, reproduced in M.C.N.E.I., 24 Apr. 1834.

[30] M.C.N.E.I., 12 May 1836.

[31] Lords of the treasury to E. Littleton, cited in M.C.N.E.I., 9 Jan. 1834.

The commissioners replied on 17 January 1834, that they had made arrangements with a Dublin firm of high reputation for the printing and binding of their books, and that they regarded these arrangements as the most advantageous ones for the promotion of education in Ireland. They refused to cancel these arrangements in favour of the stationery office, but did consent to place the orders for their office requisites with the stationery office.[32] When the treasury raised the issue again in 1836, the commissioners were even more obdurate than previously, for their dealings with the stationery office for requisites had convinced them that the stationery office was not qualified to have control over the printing and binding of national school books. They continued to contend that they could not do that part of their duty which involved editing and printing of books unless they were left in sole control of the funds voted by parliament for national education in Ireland.[33] Victorious, the commissioners continued to deal with whomever they pleased.[34]

The doctrine of absolute control over educational funds extended to the salary grants made to teachers by the commissioners. The commissioners never, however, gained control over financial matters relating to their own central establishment. Their clerks and secretaries were all civil servants and as such under the hand of the treasury. Any changes in salaries and all additions to staff had to be approved by the treasury. Further, any expediture related to the buildings and furnishings of the central establishment had to have prior treasury approval. The commissioners seem to have consented to this degree of treasury meddling as a necessary evil; the commissioners won in their early years control over money to be spent on educational matters and they could afford to allow the treasury to reign over purely administrative areas.

The commissioners also had to define their area of rights regarding the rules and regulations of the national system, which

[32] Commissioners of national education to E. Littleton, cited in M.C.N. E.I., 12 May 1836.

[33] M.C.N.E.I., 12 May 1836.

[34] Ironically, the commissioners of their own choice began placing large orders for printing of textbooks with the firm of Alexander Thom, one of the stationery office's largest sub-contractors.

is really to say concerning how Irish primary education was to be run. The danger of infringement in this area stemmed not from the treasury but from the lord lieutenant. Fortunately, the question never became as complicated as the question of financial control. One reason for the lack of conflict on this issue was the lord lieutenant had unquestionable sway over the commissioners if he wished to exercise it. Another was that the best interests of the lord lieutenant dictated that, whatever his potential powers might be, he should delegate all of the routine educational decisions to the commissioners. The informal statement of the relationship between the commissioners and the lord lieutenant was that the commissioners were vested with control of the national system, but that they should not change 'fundamental rules' without his approval. In practice, the commissioners submitted almost all rule changes to him, and they informed him before taking any action that might be controversial. During their first two decades, the commissioners were not imposed upon by the lord lieutenant. If anything, the opposite was true, for on controversial topics a deputation from the commissioners usually waited upon the lord lieutenant for the purpose of obtaining his explicit approval for their actions and the implicit promise of his support should opposition to one of their moves develop. In summary, then, it appears that during their first twenty years the commissioners of national education had all the autonomy they needed or wanted, and on occasion had even more freedom from official interference than they wished to have.

2

In order to understand the bureaucracy that grew up to support the commissioners, one must recognize that a primary characteristic of the national system of education in its early years was that it was constantly expanding:[35]

[35] *The thirty-first report of the commissioners of national education in Ireland, for the year 1864,* p. vi [3496], H.C. 1865, xix. The number 'on the rolls' refers to all children who attended at least once during the year and hence who were enrolled as students. It should not be confused with average daily attendance. No enumeration was made in 1834.

Year	No. of schools in operation	No. of children on rolls
1833	789	107,042
1835	1,106	145,521
1836	1,181	153,707
1837	1,300	166,929
1838	1,384	169,548
1839	1,581	192,971
1840	1,978	232,560
1841	2,337	281,849
1842	2,721	319,792
1843	2,912	355,320
1844	3,153	395,550
1845	3,426	432,844
1846	3,637	456,410
1847	3,825	402,632
1848	4,109	507,469
1849	4,321	480,623

This growth, it should be realized, did not all come from scratch. When the advantages of connection with the national system became apparent, former pay schools and schools previously associated with the protestant societies were united to the system; former hedge school masters and ex-teachers for voluntary educational societies entered the commissioners' payroll.

The commissioners needed a great deal of help to deal with their expanding system. One of their first efforts at administrative delegation was the appointment of one of their number, Rev James Carlile, as resident commissioner. Carlile's appointment to this post brought him £300 a year plus residence and a horse and carriage worth another £100 a year, and did not require him to relinquish his parish income.[36] In return for this handsome amount of money he took care of the routine work that the commissioners as a body had not time to do and oversaw the system generally. Carlile resigned in 1838 for reasons that have never been made clear. In the succeeding year he was replaced by Alexander Macdonnell, previously chief clerk of the secretary's office. Because Macdonnell had no outside source of income and because of the increase in the work and responsibility of the resident commissioner, Macdonnell received £1,000 a year from the beginning of his appointment.[37] Inevitably, not

[36] M.C.N.E.I., 10 Oct. 1833, 12 Nov. 1835.
[37] T. Elrington to Lord Morpeth, 26 May 1839, S.P.O., Chief Secretary's Office, Government Correspondence Books, vol. 72, pp 63–4.

only routine details but extraordinary powers flowed into the resident commissioner's hands. Since the resident commissioner was a member of each of the commissioners' three sub-committees, and since the other commissioners who were members of the respective sub-committees rarely attended, the power to make all sub-committee decisions was effectively the resident commissioner's. Further, in matters such as the rewriting of the rules and regulations, the resident commissioner, sometimes with the aid of another commissioner, was usually called upon to write the first draft of the new rules. The resident commissioner served as potentate over the commissioners' civil service staff and hence, in the commissioners' name, controlled almost all day-to-day correspondence. James Carlile indirectly controlled a great deal of the curriculum of the national schools, for he wrote a number of original textbooks published by the commissioners, as well as editing the *Scripture lessons*. On routine matters, the resident commissioner was, for all practical purposes, 'the commissioners', and in policy matters he was a man to be consulted with respect, for he was the lone professional among the band of amateurs.

One of the commissioners' first official acts was to appoint Thomas Kelly secretary to the commissioners at £500 per annum.[38] Kelly, an Anglican barrister, served until his resignation in November and retirement in December 1833. He was replaced by two men, Hamilton Dowdall, a Roman Catholic school inspector, and Maurice Cross, an Anglican, as joint secretaries. From 1838 onwards, one secretary was always a Roman Catholic, the other a protestant. Upon Dowdall's death in 1841 he was replaced by James Kelly, a catholic, who was previously joint manager of the inspection department.[39] The joint appointment of an Anglican and a Roman Catholic introduced a pattern of religious dualism in major appointments that gradually spread to most other important posts.[40] At this stage

[38] M.C.N.E.I., 1 Dec. 1831.

[39] *Royal commission of inquiry into primary education (Ireland)*, vol. i, pt i, *Report of the commissioners*, pp 26, 90; *Royal commission of inquiry into primary education (Ireland)*, vol. vii. *Returns furnished by the national board*, p. 8.

[40] At about the same time as the joint secretaries were appointed, the model school professors were appointed, one being protestant, the other Roman Catholic. The head inspectorships were split equally between the

in Irish history a roughly even division of appointments between catholics and protestants was real liberalism. (Even so it under-lined the actual disparity in power and influence between the two denominations, since the catholics were by far the more numerous.) The secretaries had considerable influence over the commissioners since they arranged the commissioners' agenda, called important matters to their attention, and took their minutes and transmitted their communications to managers, teachers, and civil servants. The secretaries, while not members of any of the commissioners' sub-committees, were almost al-ways 'in attendance', and were, with the resident commissioner, the ranking officials present.

Beneath the secretaries was the entire central establishment of the board, an organization over which the secretaries had direct charge. The central establishment came into being in January 1832, when the commissioners harkened to the secre-tary's plea that a clerk be hired to aid in performing the general business of the national system.[41] From this lone clerk the num-ber had grown to about forty-five members of the central establishment at mid-century.[42] Unfortunately, the number of clerks always seems to have lagged behind the increasing volume of work, and the clerks often had to work evenings and Satur-days, while the commissioners laboured to convince the treasury that they did indeed need still more central staff. Within their central establishment, the commissioners arranged their clerks into departments according to function. One department dealt with the inspectors and was by far the most important. Through this department application was made to the commissioners for aid and through it the work of the inspectors was coordinated. A second department was the correspondence department which handled all communications between the commissioners or higher civil servants and the school managers that did not arise from the inspection department. The financial department was under the direction of the accountant who was first ap-pointed in 1835. The fourth department dealt with books and

[41] M.C.N.E.I., 12 Jan. 1832.
[42] McDowell, p. 249.

two religions in 1846, the assistant professorships at the model school being split the same way in 1852, and the chief inspectorship similarly in 1859.

apparatus. Its main function was to serve as intermediary store-house between the printers of books and the individual schools. The last division, created in 1845, was the appointment of a clerk of works and staff to superintend the building and repairing of national schoolhouses.[43]

If we ask how efficient the central establishment was, the answer we receive will depend upon the standards adopted. A modern management consultant would have shuddered at the office's inefficiency, but that is hardly relevant. It appears that by nineteenth-century standards the establishment was quite efficiently managed. The establishment had the advantage of being a new office, and hence it was not saddled with the host of indolent sinecurists and aged retainers that most government departments had to carry. The commissioners were able to report for the benefit of the select committee of the house of commons on sinecure offices in the colonies, that they had no redundant offices and no superannuation allowances to pay.[44] Admittedly, the establishment was often far behind in its correspondence, but this was probably more a result of treasury parsimony in providing staff than of gross inefficiency in the office itself. If, in 1849, forty-five clerks were shouldering the clerical burden of a school system in which nearly 500,000 children were on the rolls, they without any doubt deserved their wages.

The inspectorial arm of the board operated from a base within the central establishment and reported to the commissioners through the secretaries and the resident commissioner. Not until April 1832, was the question of inspection brought to the commissioners' attention. It has been established that the national system's arrangements were derived directly from those of the Kildare group. Robert Holmes, who raised the issue of school

[43] [James J. Kavanagh], *Mixed education, the catholic case stated; or, principles, working, and results of the system of national education, with suggestions for the settlement of the education question, most respectfully dedicated to the catholic archbishops and bishops of Ireland* (London and Dublin, 1859), pp 282–4; *Royal commission of inquiry into primary education (Ireland)*, vol. VII, *Returns furnished by the national board*, p. 33; *Sixteenth report of the commissioners of national education in Ireland, for the year 1849*, vol. I, p. 5, [1231], H.C. 1850, xxv.

[44] Thomas Kelly to Viscount Morpeth, 23 Nov. 1837, S.P.O., Chief Secretary's Office, Registered Papers, 3731/1835.

inspection on 19 April 1832, sent to the Kildare Place Society for a copy of its instructions to inspectors. A comparison of the instructions to inspectors issued by the commissioners and the Kildare Place instructions reveals only three differences in the two codes: the government inspectors were ordered to make their visits as unexpected as possible, they were told to check on the use of the 'general lesson', *Scripture lessons* and *Sacred poetry*, and were also ordered to attend the model schools, none of these three being required of the Kildare inspectors.[45] The commissioners resolved in May 1832, to appoint four inspectors (sometimes referred to in the system's early years as 'superintendents'), at a salary of £250 a year each. Thirty-eight applications were received and from these fourteen men were chosen to appear before the commissioners for an oral examination. From these four were chosen, two protestants and two catholics. One man was assigned to each province.[46] Due to the large number of applications for aid that had to be investigated four temporary inspectors were voted in August 1833. In the case of these temporary inspectors, as well as in that of all regular inspectors, the commissioners spent a considerable amount of time in interviewing individually all of the better candidates (twelve in this case), before picking the four men for the posts. When an inspectorship fell vacant in 1836, the commissioners personally interviewed thirty-six candidates before choosing their man.[47]

No matter how carefully selected, eight men could not bear the ever-increasing load, and in 1838 a major reorganization of the inspectors took place. As early as 1834 the commissioners had presented the Irish government with a proposal to divide Ireland into school districts, each under an inspector. They

[45] Eustace Hayden, 'National school inspection and the Kildare Place Society—II', *Irish Ecclesiastical Record*, 5 ser, lxxxvii, (May 1957), pp 343–54. Also see Eustace Hayden, 'National school inspection and the Kildare Place Society', *Irish Ecclesiastical Record*, 5 ser, lxxxvii, (April 1957), pp 241–51. Since the above was written Hayden's (Eustas O'Heidan) excellent monograph, *National school inspection in Ireland: the beginnings* (Dublin, 1967) has become available.

[46] M.C.N.E.I., 3 May 1835, 14 June 1832; Michael Breathnach, 'The infancy of school inspection', *Irish School Weekly* (7 and 14 Nov. 1953), p. 488.

[47] M.C.N.E.I., 22 Aug. 1833, 29 Aug. 1833, 6 Oct. 1844.

made their wishes known again in their 1837 report in which they called for the division of the country into twenty-five districts, with a similar number of inspectors,[48] a division that became a reality in 1838. The districts were again recast, and raised to thirty in 1844, and to thirty-two later in the same year.[49] In order to keep the melange of inspectorial personnel under control, the commissioners created the office of head inspector in July 1845, with Thomas J. Robertson as the first incumbent.[50] The head inspector's job was to act as a roving eye for the commissioners, examining special cases and making general observations and suggestions upon all aspects of the educational system. The number of head inspectors was raised to four in 1846 and they were charged with over-seeing the administration of the inspectorial service. Simultaneously, the number of districts was raised to thirty-four. The thirty-four inspectors under the head inspectors had an average of slightly more than 117 schools under their respective charge, and the commissioners felt that not even the most diligent of the inspectors could handle such a large load. Hence, they resolved to introduce a number of sub-inspectors, chosen from the ranks of the most fit national school teachers, to aid the inspectors.[51] By mid-century, then, the inspectorial corps had grown to a sizable number, and a hierarchy of status and authority had developed within its ranks.

The inspectors did not spend all of their time on routine visits to schools. They were charged by the commissioners with investigating the new applications for aid from their districts. In the first few years of the system, more time seems to have been spent on this task than upon inspecting existing schools. Inspectors also spent a great deal of time investigating complaints. A typical case might involve a complaint to the commissioners by a Church of Ireland vicar that the children of his flock were being taught popish practices in the neighbourhood national school. Before answering the letter the commissioners would

---

[48] *Fourth report of the commissioners of national education in Ireland, for the year ending 31st March 1837*, pp 3–4, H.C. 1837–8 [110], xxviii.

[49] M.C.N.E.I., 20 Aug. 1844, 24 Oct. 1844, 26 Oct. 1844.

[50] M.C.N.E.I., 3 July 1845.

[51] *Thirteenth report of the commissioners of national education in Ireland, for the year 1846*, pp 9–10 [832], H.C. 1847, xvii.

send the inspector into the field to ascertain the facts and to draw any conclusions the evidence might demand. He was then to report confidentially to the commissioners so they could take action. As far as routine inspection visits were concerned, the inspectors' tasks were just what one would expect. The inspector was instructed to visit the schools on his district list in any order that he wished, but to endeavour to arrive at each without being expected. (It would be interesting to know how an inspector was supposed to be able to manage an unexpected visit in rural Ireland.) At each school he was to inspect the building and its state of repair and in the classroom to make certain that all the fundamental regulations of the commissioners were respected. Special attention was to be paid to the rule that religious instruction should not encroach upon the combined literary instruction. In the case of violation of any rule he was first to inform the conductors of the school and, if the practice was not rectified, he was to inform the commissioners. The inspector was to observe the teacher conducting the class and suggest any improvements that might occur to him. In all relations with the teachers, the inspector was specially admonished to treat them with kindness and respect and was especially warned against correcting a teacher's faults in the presence of his pupils.[52]

Another major off-shoot of the commissioners' central bureaucracy was the training department. The Kildare Place Society had conducted a model school in Dublin and Stanley's letter had mentioned the need for teacher training facilities. During the first half of 1832 the commissioners set about procuring premises for a male and female model school which opened in 1834. The training department was under the directorship of a Dr MacArthur who superintended a three-month course of training for teachers, most of whom were brought up to Dublin from the country. Between 1834 and 1838, roughly 300 teachers were trained.[53] The commissioners had far grander

[52] *Reports of the commissioners of national education in Ireland for the years 1834, 1835, and 1836* (Dublin, 1836), pp 128–31.

[53] Durham Dunlop, *A review of the administration of the board of national education in Ireland, from its establishment in 1831 to 1841; with suggestions for its improved administration* (London, Edinburgh, and Dublin, 1843), pp 13–16; Kavanagh, pp 291–2; M.C.N.E.I., 24 May 1832, 31 Jan. 1833, 16 May 1833.

designs than merely providing a three-month stop-gap system of teacher training. In the report for 1835 they outlined a plan for covering the country with model schools. They proposed the establishment of five professorships at their training institution in Dublin. These were to cover the art of teaching, of composition and English literature, of natural history in all its branches, of mathematics, and of mental philosophy, including the elements of logic and rhetoric. The central training institution was to provide a two-year course during which candidates could be instructed in all the branches of the professorships and practise teaching in the central school under the direction of the professor of teaching. Radiating around the country were to be thirty-two district model schools under the direction of teachers of superior attainment who would be specially paid for their services. All aspirants to the Dublin training establishment were to spend some time in a district model school before proceeding to the central training establishment.[54]

For a long time nothing came of these dreams. Lord Morpeth told the commissioners, in January 1837, that he approved of their plan generally and of their taking preparatory steps for establishing district model schools, but that he could not provide any money for the project in the present year.[55] Aside from the appointment in 1838 of professors McGauley and Sullivan as heads of the Dublin training establishment, matters languished. In mid-1845 the commissioners' attention was recalled to the subject by Anthony Blake, and the inspectors of each district were instructed to look for suitable sites for a model school in their respective districts.[56]

In April 1846, a special meeting of the commissioners was held at which the resident commissioner presented a plan for establishing model schools. The commissioners resolved on thirty-two schools, one for each district. The ground rent and all building expenses the commissioners proposed to assume themselves. In return, the schools would be vested in them, not

---

[54] *Reports from the commissioners of national education in Ireland for the years 1834, 1835, and 1836*, pp 15–23.

[55] Lord Morpeth to the commissioners of national education in Ireland, 2 Jan. 1837, S.P.O., Chief Secretary's Office, Country Letterbook, vol. 157, p. 64; M.C.N.E.I., 5 Jan. 1837.

[56] M.C.N.E.I., 1 Aug. 1845.

in local trustees. Each model school was to have an infant, a female, and a male school among its components, each division having a capacity of 100 students. Dormitory space was to be provided for three candidate teachers in the male school, and a residence was to be found for a female candidate in the neighbourhood. Candidate teachers were to be lodged and boarded at the commissioners' expense. Training was to take six months, thus allowing each model school to produce six trained male teachers and two trained female teachers each year. Following their work at the district model school, candidates were to teach for two years and after passing an examination on material that they were to study during their two years of teaching, then were to proceed to the central model school in Dublin. In order to fill the model schools with apt pupils on whom the candidates could practise, the most promising students in local national schools were to be admitted free to the district model schools where they would act as monitors and receive a small weekly wage.[57] The lord lieutenant approved the scheme and was willing to see money spent on the venture.[58] The first district model school was opened in 1848,[59] and eventually twenty-four more were added. The commissioners seemed, at mid-century, to be achieving their ends concerning teacher training. Parenthetically, it is important for the understanding of later events to note that the commissioners insisted that the control of the district model schools remain entirely in their own hands, rather than be shared with local patrons as in the case of ordinary national schools.

The commissioners began expressing concern about agricultural education almost as soon as they began worrying about teacher training. As an experiment they granted aid, in 1832, to two agricultural schools under local management. In the succeeding year the commissioners created a model farm and garden at Glasnevin for the purpose of instructing those in teacher training the principles of agricultural education as well as to educate a small number of pupils in agricultural techniques. During the 1840s, the commissioners took to establishing model agricultural schools, of which there were five in operation and

[57] M.C.N.E.I., 18 Apr. 1846.
[58] M.C.N.E.I., 14 May 1846.
[59] M.C.N.E.I., 5 Apr. 1849.

eleven under way in 1846.[60] Unlike the district model schools, all of which were under the commissioners' sole jurisdiction, most of the agricultural model schools were under local management: only four of the fourteen model agricultural schools in operation in 1849 were under the exclusive control of the commissioners.[61] The commissioners also created a special type of ordinary national school known as an 'ordinary agricultural school'. For all practical purposes, these were ordinary national schools with a small farm attached. In 1848 an agricultural inspector, Dr Kirkpatrick, was hired to oversee these schools. In 1849, Kirkpatrick had thirty-three ordinary agricultural schools under his charge.[62]

3

To turn from the organization that surrounded the commissioners at the centre of the national system to the local arrangements that supported each school is a difficult transition. There was no intermediate authority to act as a go-between between the central administration and the patrons of each individual school. The relationship between the central administration and the local patrons was a singularly fuzzy one despite the clarity of the printed rules. Moreover, the pattern of local management in which each school was embedded is very easy to outline theoretically but most difficult to describe in practice. Reading contemporary writers, one finds that one man decried the fact that the national system was really a system of educational anarchy in which each local patron did what he pleased, while another denounced the system as an educational dictatorship of the central government. Although both claims were wrong, the truth about the relationship of the central administration did not lie between them. The fact was that the local patrons and the central authorities did not simply split prerogatives between

[60] *Thirteenth report of the commissioners of national education in Ireland, for the year 1846*, p. 6.

[61] *Royal commission of inquiry into primary education (Ireland)*, vol. vii, *Returns furnished by the national board*, p. 500.

[62] Ibid., p. 500. On agricultural schools see also [Thomas Kirkpatrick], *Agricultural education in Ireland: its organization and efficiency with a reply to recent criticisms* (Dublin, 1858); M.C.N.E.I., 7 Jan. 1836, 29 Sept. 1836, 16 Dec. 1846, 20 Dec. 1847, 28 Aug. 1848.

themselves in a rational manner. Instead, each group seems to have lived on a plane of its own, largely oblivious to the other. Like blots of ink spreading over parallel sheets of glass, the commissioners and the local patrons superimposed their spheres of influence over one another, without making many significant contacts. In many ways this was a case of the spiritual and the temporal failing to understand each other, for most school patrons and managers were clergy and viewed the schools as a spiritual trust, while the central administration for its part looked upon the institutions as a national investment.

The commissioners are partially responsible for the confusion that clouded the managerial question, since almost from the very beginning of their tenure in office they began reneging on the conditions they had set for granting aid to schools. Lord Stanley's letter had stated that the government would look with particular favour upon applications coming jointly from clergy of protestant and catholic denominations, and in the case of applications made by persons of only one denomination the matter would be investigated before aid was granted. Yet, from the very start, the commissioners granted aid to anyone of good character without requiring inter-denominational religious cooperation. The result of this practice was that individual clergymen took to applying for aid for local schools which each then ran as part of his own clerical fief. Although the commissioners' rules effectively protected the religious consciences of all children enrolled in any school, the fact that the protestant vicar and the Roman Catholic priest were not forced to work together meant that it was very easy for a clergyman in charge of a school to forget that it was intended to be a community trust, not merely one of his specifically religious responsibilities.

The commissioners further undercut the idea of the school as a community responsibility by failing to enforce their own grant regulations. In their first code, dated 13 December 1831, they clearly stated that aid for a school building would be granted only in cases in which at least one third of the estimated expenses were locally contributed and a site provided by the local citizenry. Moreover, the code required that local sources provide for all repairs, for a permanent salary for the teacher, and for the purchase of books and requisites. The commissioners failed in many cases to enforce the local aid requirement, and, it will be recalled, they won in their battle with the treasury in 1834 an undoubted right to violate their own rules on the matter if they so desired.[63] Although the effect of the state paying for almost all expenses in certain schools may have been to strengthen central control, it also clearly served to destroy the grass root support and interest the local contribution would have provided, and to reduce further the concept of the school as a local civic institution.

In fairness to the commissioners we should note that Ireland lacked local government organizations from which the sort of school committee that would be necessary to raise the money, obtain the land, and manage yearly contributions to expenditures could emerge, especially if this were to be an inter-faith venture. Nevertheless it is tantalizing to think of the possible results if the commissioners had held to their requirements. Perhaps if they had insisted on the original requirements they would have forced the emergence of inter-faith civic organizations at the local level. In that case we would have a far more dramatic and revolutionary story to survey. More likely, though, the national school system would simply have foundered at the start.

When we turn to determining who actually ran the local school three terms appear which the commissioners never bothered to define: 'trustee', 'patron', and 'manager'. Trustee was usually used in legal sections of the code; the commissioners spoke of the title of the schools being vested in trustees. As often as not the trustees turned out to be a single person, as in the case of the landlord or clergyman who brought the school into

[63] It would be a mistake to conclude that the commissioners infringed their contribution rules in all cases. A tabulation of the amount spent on building grants and of the amount contributed locally reveals that, in 1847, a typical year, government building grants were £5,580, local aid to building being £2,819. The national ratio of government to local aid in many years was actually less than two to one. The total figures, however, hide the numerous cases in which little or no local aid was forthcoming. In 1851, the first year for which figures are available, a year in which the parliamentary grant was £134,560—the amount from local aid for teacher's salaries was £24,673. *Return of the amount voted each year by parliament for the purpose of national education in Ireland, from the commencement of the system to the year 1861; and of the amount of local contributions each year in aid of teachers' salaries, of the building, fitting and inclosing of schools . . .*, p.1, H.C. 1861 (532), xlviii.

being. The commissioners recognized a patron for each school, this usually being the man who first applied for aid. In the early years the trustees and the patrons were closely connected, being the same person in the case of a piece of individual philanthropy. In the case of a group effort, the man named patron was usually the leader of the group that had subscribed the money, this same group usually being named trustees. With the passage of time, a disjuncture developed. The trustees and their successors in office seem to have become mere legal entities with no practical influence on the school. The patronship of almost all of the Roman Catholic schools was transferred to the bishop of the diocese after the death of the original patron. The one important prerogative of the patron was to appoint, and dismiss if he wished, the school manager. The school manager, who hired and dismissed teachers, oversaw the general functioning of the school, and carried on all dealings with the commissioners and their representatives. In the case of schools under lay patronage, the patron usually chose the local vicar or priest to manage the school. A patron could, if he wished, name himself school manager, a possibility that was seized upon by many clerical patrons.

As time passed, the entire patron-manager system seems to have come more and more under the control of religious authorities, and by mid-century, the word 'manager' could usually be translated 'local clergyman'. In the Roman Catholic church, the patronship of the bishop meant that the local parish priest was appointed manager as part of his religious duties. In such a situation it is hardly surprising that the majority of managers took their educational marching orders not from the civil authorities but from their religious superiors.

The commissioners of national education and the local authorities had one face-to-face confrontation before mid-century and that on the question of the vesting of school titles. The commissioners were incorporated in 1844 and seem to have taken their new-found dignity a bit too seriously. The commissioners voted, on 13 November 1845, that they were to be the trustees of all national schools thereafter built with their aid. As a bribe to new applicants the commissioners undertook in schools of which they were trustees to pay all maintenance and repair expenses, costs which had previously fallen upon the local subscribers.[64] Despite the financial attractiveness of such an arrangement, the plan raised considerable opposition, especially among the Roman Catholic bishops. Although local managers still appointed and dismissed teachers and controlled the schools, the bishops saw the new form of vesting as an indication of a government conspiracy to usurp their educational prerogatives. As of the thirty-first of December 1849, only 441 schoolhouses were under the new form of tenure,[65] and probably no more than fifteen per cent of all the national schools were ever vested in the commissioners.[66] Eventually the bishops won. In 1861, applicants for government aid were given the choice of either vesting their school in the commissioners or in their own trustees. In 1866, the commissioners went one step further and allowed the managers of any school vested in the commissioners to have the school reconveyed to themselves by repaying the extra money received from the commissioners.[67]

Aside from this one direct clash the commissioners and the managers never faced each other on the question of who controlled the school. The manager's powers were quite extensive, since he was entrusted with the daily oversight of the local school. He had the right to hire whomever he pleased as a teacher, and to dismiss the teacher whenever he pleased, for any or no reason at all. The manager could, within certain broad limits, arrange the school's timetable as he pleased. The commissioners paid continual lip-service to the idea of managerial autonomy and in each of their successive codes reaffirmed the manager's rights. This should not blind us to the fact, however, that the commissioners controlled the educational process in the local school more than it would at first appear, certainly more than they would ever publicly admit. Granted, the commissioners had only a few official methods by which they could control local managers—such as the rarely exercised right to remove local managers and the unexercised power (abolished in 1851) to block teacher dismissals—but they were able to indirectly limit

[64] M.C.N.E.I., 13 Nov. 1845, 20 Nov. 1845.

[65] *The sixteenth report of the commissioners of national education in Ireland, for the year 1849*, i, 5.

[66] *Republic of Ireland, report of the council of education* [Pr. 2583], Dublin, 1954, p. 44.

[67] Graham Balfour, *The educational systems of Great Britain and Ireland* (Oxford, second ed. 1903), p. 88.

managerial autonomy without publicly admitting that this was their intention. For example, the rules and regulations of the commissioners of national education in Ireland were really lists of restrictions on managerial freedom, although no one chose to refer to them as such. In one sense, the job of the inspector was to see that local managers toed the commissioners' line on major educational issues. The greatest single control the commissioners had over the local managers was almost invisible: through their control over the school curriculum the commissioners determined much of what went on within each local school. The commissioners published a series of textbooks for use in the schools that was in its time probably the best text series produced in the English-speaking world. They did not require that this series be used in the schools, but they provided them for the schools at half-price, a powerful inducement to the series' adoption. Moreover, any other text or series of texts to be used in the schools during the hours of combined literary instruction had to receive the commissioners' sanction before they could be employed. Thus, local autonomy seemed to prevail. In actual fact the commissioners maintained considerable uniformity, if not a rigid discipline, throughout the system.

The teachers were the lowest rung on the system's organizational ladder. Although the system could not run without them, one would never have surmised this fact from observing the way they were treated. Teachers were hired and fired at the manager's whim. They had, until late in the century, no appeal rights in case of dismissal. They were not civil servants and were treated as day labourers rather than as educated men. Although under the thumb of the local manager, their salary came mostly from the central establishment. Until the last quarter of the nineteenth century they remained unrepresented, unappreciated cogs in the system.[68]

Finally, one should ask, 'what rights and prerogatives did the parents of the children have under the national system?' The

[68] An interesting commentary on the teachers' lack of security and also upon the absurdity of the regulations relating to local control of the schools is found in the commissioners' finding it necessary at one time to stop teachers from pooling their savings in order to be able to provide a school house over which they could themselves become patrons. As patrons they could then name a benign manager of their own choosing, and proceed to enjoy a lifetime tenure as teachers.

answer is 'almost none'. As we have seen earlier, the commissioners themselves were well insulated from any direct political pressure and were directly responsible only to the lord lieutenant. On the local level, the manager of the national school was not an elected official nor a representative of a local government body, but was dependent only upon the good will of his patron and upon the neutrality of the commissioners to remain at his post. When we recall that the local patron was often the bishop or sometimes the local cleric, and that the local priest or vicar was generally the school's manager, it becomes clear that the common peasant would have no voice at all in deciding how his children were to be taught. Ultimately, the only way a parent could express disapproval of the conduct of his local national school was to withdraw his child from education.[69]

[69] In addition to the major types of schools conducted by the commissioners that have been discussed in the text, four minor types of institutions should be briefly mentioned. The first of these was the small number of schools that the commissioners conducted in connection with the Irish jails. The commissioners provided only grants of books and the benefit of inspection for these schools. By the commissioners' own admission, the education in these schools was very inferior. Unlike the ordinary national schools, both children and adults were taught. In 1846 there were only six jail schools in operation. *Eighteenth report of the commissioners of national education in Ireland, for the year 1851*, p. 6 [1582], H.C. 1852–3, xlii.

The commissioners granted aid to a number of schools in connection with the workhouses. Of the 130 Irish poor law unions, ninety-nine had workhouse schools connected with them as of 31 December 1846. The workhouse schools were conducted in accordance with the commissioners rules, but the appointment of teachers and the management of the schools were in the hands of the local guardians. M.C.N.E.I., 23 Mar. 1847; *Thirteenth report of the commissioners of national education in Ireland, for the year 1846*, p. 5.

The commissioners also aided industrial schools, these being similar to the ordinary national schools, but requiring only two hours of literary work each day, the rest of the time of combined education being given over to industrial training. Although the number later grew considerably, industrial schools were not an important facet of the system before mid-century: in 1847 only five industrial schools were operating. *Fifteenth report of the commissioners of national education in Ireland, for the year 1848*, p. 9 [1066], 1849, xxiii.

The commissioners contributed to the support of evening schools as well, the aid being limited to salary and books. There were thirty-six such schools open in 1852. *Nineteenth report of the commissioners of national education in Ireland, for the year 1852*, p. 623 [1688], H.C. 1852–3, xliii, pt i.

The national system of education, then, was a sprawling structure with all types of odd wings, tunnels, and battlements. We have seen that its primary characteristic in its early years was growth. We have also noticed that the system itself was surprisingly isolated from parliamentary influences and free from most interference from the executive branch of the government. Within the system extreme centralization and a considerable degree of local autonomy existed simultaneously. *The Times* writer was correct when he said that the Irish national system of education was like York Minster: 'It is necessary to go around it, and view it from different points, to get an adequate conception of its magnitude'.[70]

[70] *The Times*, 24 June 1864.

V

SPINNING THE EDUCATIONAL
TOP 1831–49

∿∿∿∿∿∿∿∿∿∿∿∿∿∿∿∿∿∿∿∿∿∿∿

I

DESPITE THE SIZE AND sophistication of the national system's administrative structure, and in spite of the commissioners' insulation from popular control, the system was vulnerable to pressure exerted by any of the three major religious denominations. In its first two decades the system was spun by sectarian forces until its religious orientation was almost directly opposite to that originally intended by Lord Stanley: the system was intended to be non-denominational, but by mid-century it had become denominational. In order to understand how this transformation came about we must first survey the original regulations of the commissioners, then note what effects the actions of each of the three major denominations had upon these rules, and finally, examine the evidence that *de facto* denominationalism was the result.

The basic principle that underlay each of the national system's original religious regulations was that the schools were to be undenominational in character.[1] A number of approximate

[1] In this discussion of the original rules no citations will be made, except for direct quotations and for material found outside of the sources listed below. The material for the discussion is from Lord Stanley's Instructions and from the Rules and Regulations of the Commissioners of 1831. This material is found in the following volumes: *Copy of a letter from the chief secretary for Ireland to the duke of Leinster, on the formation of a board*

synonyms for the word 'undenominational' were used during the nineteenth century: 'general', 'united', 'combined', and 'mixed'. Two connotations were common to each of these words, one having to do with the student body of the schools, the other with their curriculum: first, that the system was to be undenominational in the sense that children of all faiths were to attend it. Emphatically, this did not imply that the schools were merely to be open to all denominations, but that in the schools a strong and positive effort was to be made to mix children of all faiths, with the hope that by learning to live together as children they would at least tolerate each other as adults. The second connotation was that when children of different faiths were in school together, no material peculiar to any one denomination was to be introduced. Great chunks of moral platitude were forced upon the children during the hours of combined instruction, but these homilies were of a sort upon which all denominations could agree. An important implication of the idea of curricular undenominationalism was that dogmatic religious, and literary, instruction were to be rigidly separated to prevent the former from encroaching upon the latter.

In order to ensure that local schools would contain a religiously mixed group of children, Lord Stanley stated in his instructions that the commissioners would look with 'peculiar favour' upon applications from protestant and catholic clergy, from protestant and catholic laymen, and from clergy of one denomination and parishioners of the other. In the case of applications proceeding from only one denomination, the commissioners, the instructions said, were to make special inquiry into the circumstances that led to the absence of names of clergy or parishioners of the other persuasion. The commissioners, in their first code of December 1831, followed Stanley's example and stated that they would look with peculiar favour upon mixed applications, but they did not include his proviso about investigating cases in which applications stemmed from only one denomination. In practice the commissioners did not require that applications be

---

of commissioners for education in Ireland, H.C. 1831-2 (196), xxix; *Royal commission of inquiry into primary education (Ireland)*, vol. i, pt ii: *Appendix to the report and also special report by royal commissioners on model schools (district and minor), the central training institution, etc., Dublin, and on agricultural schools*, pp 607-11 [C 6a], H.C. 1870, xxviii, pt ii.

made jointly by persons of different denominations. Their laxness on this point undercut the principle of combined education at its very root.

In contrast to their looseness on the application rule, the commissioners exercised with considerable rigidity their veto power over what could and what could not be taught during the hours of combined instruction. They required that combined literary and moral instruction take place on four or five days a week, for a minimum of four hours a day. During these hours anything that smacked of religious controversy was strictly excluded. Bible reading during these hours was not permitted, although the use of the commissioners' scripture extracts was allowed. Acts of piety, such as making the sign of the cross, were not permitted. The commissioners required that the following 'general lesson' be taught in all schools and that a printed copy of the lesson be hung in each school:

Christians should endeavour, as the Apostle Paul commands them, to 'live peaceably with all men' (Rom. cap. 12, v. 18) even with those of different religious persuasions.

Our Saviour, Christ, commanded his disciples 'to love one another'. He taught them to love even their enemies, to bless those that cursed them, and to pray for those that persecuted them. He himself prayed for his murderers.

Many men hold erroneous doctrines: we ought not to hate or persecute them. We ought to seek the truth, and to hold fast what we are convinced is the truth; but not to treat harshly those who are in error. Jesus Christ did not intend his religion to be forced on men by violent means. He would not allow his disciples to fight for him.

If any persons treat us unkindly, we must not do the same to them; Christ and all his Apostles have taught us not to return evil for evil. If we would obey Christ, we must do to others, not as they do to us, but as we should wish them to do to us.

Quarrelling with our neighbours and abusing them is not the way to convince them that we are in the right and they in the wrong. It is more likely to convince them that we have not a Christian spirit.

We ought to show ourselves followers of Christ, who, 'when he was reviled, reviled not again' (1 Pet. cap. 2, v. 23) by behaving gently and kindly to every one.[2]

[2] *Royal commission of inquiry into primary education (Ireland)*, vol. i, pt. ii: *Appendix to the report and also special report by the royal commissioners on model schools (district and minor), the central training institution, etc., Dublin, and on agricultural schools*, p. 607.

The rules relating to religious instruction were much more specific than the regulations for moral and literary education. The commissioners clearly wished to encourage separate religious instruction as part of their educational system and demanded that at least one day a week be set aside for it. In 1837 an official of the board dogmatically stated before a select committee on the plan of education in Ireland that even if the local authorities wished to dispense with religious instruction and give literary instruction on the day set aside for religious instruction the commissioners would not allow it; rather than permit literary instruction to be given on the day for religious instruction, the school should be vacant that day.[3] In practice, although two days were allowed for religious education one day was all local patrons chose to set aside.[4]

The managers of the schools were also expected, in addition to allowing the one day a week for religious instruction, to permit religious instruction to take place either before or after the ordinary instruction on days of combined education if the parents of the children so desired. The rules relating to how and where religious instruction was to take place seem to have been scrupulously fair to all denominations. Clergy of every faith of which there were children in the school had the right to provide religious instruction at the time set aside and had the liberty of assembling the children in the schoolroom for their religious instruction, or, if the clergyman preferred, at any other place of his choosing. The commissioners vested the right of approving or disapproving of books for religious instruction in the hands of those commissioners who belonged to the denomination for which the books were intended. The commissioners were judicious about Roman Catholic holy days, allowing the manager of any school the right to close the school for any reasonable amount of time during the year.[5] Because of the controversy that was to develop about the religious rules it is important to underline the fact that the religious rules applied equally to all schools that received any form of aid from the commissioners, whether this aid was for the building of schools

---

[3] *Report from the select committee appointed to inquire into the progress and operation of the new plan of education in Ireland*, p. 3, H.C. 1837 (485), ix.

[4] Ibid., p. 19.

[5] M.C.N.E.I., 17 July 1846.

that were vested in trustees, or merely annual grants in aid of teachers' salaries and requisites.

2

In slightly less than ten years after the inception of the system the presbyterians were able to bend many of the rules almost out of recognition.[6] To understand their reaction to the system and to understand their dealings with the commissioners, it is important to realize that in the early 1830s the synod of Ulster was dominated by illiberal men and by reactionary attitudes. The bigotry and rigidity of the synod during the 1830s was, unfortunately for the system of national education, closely tied to educational matters. The evangelical movement of the eighteenth and early nineteenth century had produced painful tensions in the synod of Ulster, for the evangelical (or 'orthodox') party attempted to reimpose subscription to the Westminster confession upon all candidates for the ministry, a practice which had died out during the eighteenth century. The evangelicals were headed by Rev. Dr Henry Cooke, a brilliant orator, a militant tory, and a natural demogogue. Opposed to Cooke's evangelical group was the new light (or 'arian') party headed by Rev. Dr Henry Montgomery, a much loved and intelligent gentleman whose dignified speeches were no match for the sledge-hammer attacks of Dr Cooke. The conflict came to a head in 1821 when a vacancy fell open in the classical department of the Belfast Academical Institution. The classical professorship was awarded to Rev. William Bruce, a man known to hold arian views. Cooke thereupon attacked the institution in the most violent terms, and in 1822 and 1823 he tried, unsuccessfully, to induce the synod to undertake an inquiry into the orthodoxy of the professors at the institution. While continuing to attack the institution, Cooke also tried, beginning in 1824, to have the synod re-enact the law of subscription. Cooke won a major victory at the synod's 1827 meeting when the synod voted 135 to 10 to require subscription to the shorter catechism. When the synod met the next year those who had not

[6] Presbyterian in this section refers to members of the synod of Ulster, unless otherwise noted. In July 1840 the synod of Ulster and secession synod joined to form the presbyterian church in Ireland. From that point on, 'presbyterian' refers to these united synods.

been present the preceding year were called upon to cast their votes for or against subscription. Again Cooke won. Eventually, in May 1830, the non-subscribing ministers withdrew to form the 'remonstrant synod of Ulster'. With their withdrawal, all checks on Cooke's power by liberal elements vanished, and the synod of Ulster entered the 1830s as the church truculent.[7]

The synod lost no time in expressing its complete disapproval of the national system of education. To begin with the presbyterians opposed the system because it was a whig creation and Cooke and his followers were die-hard tories. But the presbyterian objections were fundamentally religious and only superficially political. One of the basic reasons for rejecting the system was that it forced the presbyterian ministers to share the powers of educational decision with the commissioners of national education. Cooke denounced the 'board' because of 'the despotic power with which it is vested. It is vested with "complete control" over all teachers ... Further, the board is invested with the "entire control" over all school-books whether for literary or religious instruction ...'[8] Moreover, to the presbyterians' horror, the commissioners of national education were composed of men of all christian denominations, including Roman Catholics. Worse still, the presbyterians were a minority of the group of commissioners. Cooke decried the national system with theatrical alarm: 'Its first essential feature is a supreme despotic board. Three parts protestant establishment, two parts Roman Catholic, one part unitarian and one part Church of Scotland ...'[9]

The presbyterians were especially opposed to the commissioners' rules regarding the use of the Bible, which they felt were essentially anti-protestant and which they viewed as completely incompatible with presbyterian dogma. In speech after speech,

[7] John M. Barkley, *A short history of the presbyterian church in Ireland* (Belfast, 1959), pp 44–9; J. C. Beckett, 'Ulster protestantism,' in T. W. Moody and J. C. Beckett (ed.), *Ulster since 1800: a social survey* (London, 1957), pp 159–62; John Jamieson, *The history of the Royal Belfast Academical Institution, 1810–1960* (Belfast, 1959), pp 36–47; William T. Latimer, *A history of the Irish presbyterians* (Belfast, second ed., 1902), pp 427–44.

[8] Henry Cooke, *National education: a sermon, preached in the presbyterian church, May Street, Belfast, upon Sunday the 15th of January 1832* (Belfast, 1832), pp 28, 30.

[9] Ibid., p. 27.

pamphlet upon pamphlet, presbyterian zealots maintained that the Bible was barred from the schools, a statement as inflammatory as it was inaccurate. Even when the writers and speakers admitted that the Bible was not banned, but only forbidden during the hours of combined instruction, they were not pacified, for the presbyterians demanded that the Bible be allowed to be used at any hour of the school day that the teacher might wish. If possible, the presbyterians would have preferred a system in which the Bible was employed as one of the textbooks for ordinary reading instruction, as well as for a religious text.

Reinforcing the opposition to the limit on the use of the Bible was a much subtler and less vociferously expressed objection: the presbyterians did not accept the distinction between religious and literary learning that the commissioners' rules laid down. In their view, all education was at least partially religious education or it was not education; and all religious education, it might be added, began with Bible education. Great scorn was reserved for the *Scripture lessons* that the commissioners circulated for use during the hours of combined instruction. Mutilation of the Bible and interference with the integrity of the scriptures were laid to the commissioners' charge.

The presbyterians were extremely illiberal in their reactions to the national system's arrangements with Roman Catholics. The Cooke wing that dominated the synod of Ulster had strongly opposed catholic emancipation and was in principle against any concession to the Roman Catholics. To the more rabid presbyterians the placing of Roman Catholics upon the commission that controlled education was a work of the devil. More immediate, and hence even more objectionable to the presbyterians, were the arrangements for separate religious instruction, for under the commissioners' rules these arrangements implied that Roman Catholics had a right to educate their children in the catholic faith; the phrase used by presbyterians to denominate the separate days of religious instruction was 'the fifty-two popish holidays'. Since national school buildings could be used for such purposes this meant that both central government funds and local monies were being used to support indirectly the propagation of popery.

In the face of such an array of objections to the national system it seems almost facetious to ask, 'was there anything about the system of which the presbyterians approved?' The answer is that there was only one thing, and that was the government's money. Whatever its numerous faults, the system's promise of large-scale state aid to local schools was enough to keep the presbyterians from turning their back on the possibility of joining the national system. From 1832 to 1840 the synod of Ulster carried on an extremely skilful campaign of negotiation, agitation, and intimidation, eventually bringing the government to modify its religious rules so that the presbyterians could join the system without injury to their consciences.

The first round in this process took place in the meeting of the synod at Cookestown on 11 January 1832, in which the national system was strongly denounced. The synod's meeting was called especially to consider the national education question. Dr Cooke moved a series of ten resolutions, which the synod adopted, condemning the national system. The resolutions, which are too wordy to reproduce in their entirety, may be summarized as follows:

1 As christian ministers and elders the synod prayed divine blessing upon the crown.
2 Thanks were expressed for the countenance and support given the presbyterian church by the government.
3 The synod declared that it did not wish to embarrass the government, but felt compelled to approach the government upon the subject of national education.
4 It was the synod's 'deliberate opinion and decided conviction that in a christian country the Bible, unabridged and unmutilated, should form the basis of national education. . . .' Consequently, they could never 'accede to any system that in the least degree interferes with the unrestricted possession and use of the scriptures in our schools'.
5 They expressed their deep regret that a board of education had been created with complete control over schools and teachers receiving public aid, and over all school books, whether for literary or religious education.
6 They protested against the government's giving to one presbyterian member of the commissioners the control over books of religious instruction for children of that denomination.
7 They expressed 'peculiar disapprobation' of the part of the system that required members of the synod to encourage the religious teachers of erroneous doctrines to inculcate their beliefs.

8 For the reasons embodied in the preceding four resolutions, they concluded that the new system did not possess their confidence, and presbyterian ministers and laymen were 'earnestly entreated to keep themselves totally unconnected with it'.

9 If the government could not produce a satisfactory system, it was entreated to abstain from the field of education altogether.

10 The synod resolved to petition parliament.[10]

At this point James Carlile entered the picture. Throughout the subsequent proceedings he played a murky and uncertain role, but it appears that he served as an agent both for the commissioners and for the synod. Before his fellow commissioners he argued the synod's claims; and as one of the members of the synod of Ulster's education committee he pressed for that body to compromise with the commissioners. Since the nature of his activities was by necessity clandestine, we can only conjecture from the few times he was seen operating in public what he was attempting in private. It is reasonably certain that Carlile brought pressure upon the commissioners in the early months of 1832 to modify the national system so that it would be acceptable to the presbyterians. At his instigation the commissioners, with Lord Stanley's approval, issued an explanatory document sometime in the early months of 1832 in response to the synod's ten resolutions.[11]

In its original form (it was modified in 1833 when a subsequent code of rules and regulations appeared), the commissioners' document contained seven points.[12] They first explained that in giving control to individual commissioners over books used in the separate religious instruction of children of their respective denominations, the commissioners did not intend to claim any control over the use of the scriptures or over the standard works of the established, Roman Catholic, or presbyterian churches, but only over books composed by private

[10] The resolutions are set forth in full in *Royal commission of inquiry into primary education (Ireland)*, vol. i, pt i, *Report of the commissioners*, pp 47–8, [C 6], H.C. 1870, xxviii, pt i.

[11] Richard Batterberry, 'The synod of Ulster and the national board', *Irish Ecclesiastical Record*, 5 ser, lvi (Dec. 1940), p. 554.

[12] *Royal commission of inquiry into primary education (Ireland)*, vol. i, pt ii: *Appendix to the report and also special report by the royal commissioners on model schools (district and minor), the central training institution, etc., Dublin, and on agricultural schools*, pp 608–9.

authors that might be inflammatory and destructive of good feeling between religious denominations. In the second place the commissioners issued the assurance that they did not think it imperative for them to edit all books used in the schools receiving grants from them, and were willing to sanction other books that local managers might prefer. They did, however, require a list of the books used in each school to be forwarded for their approval. As evidence of their liberality they mentioned that they had frequently sanctioned the use of books both of the Kildare Place Society and of the Catholic Book Society. They emphasized that they did not make the use of any particular book or books imperative. Third, in order to further soften the charge of despotism imputed to them by the synod, the commissioners emphasized that the control over teachers of schools was vested primarily in local patrons and managers, and that the commissioners' power of fining and dismissing teachers was exercised only in cases in which patrons insisted on protecting or maintaining teachers who had violated the commissioners' rules or who were manifestly incompetent.

Fourth, the commissioners stated that a permanent submission to their regulations was required only in cases in which grants were made by them towards the erection of the schoolhouse. In cases in which they gave only annual grants for teachers' salaries and supplies they required submission to the regulations only for the time when the grants were made. Evidently, this section was a covert invitation to the synod to give the system an experimental whirl, and a reassurance that if the synod's schools were not built with government money, they could withdraw from connection with no trouble whatsoever.

Fifth, the commissioners tried to calm the presbyterian fears that the system was some sort of Roman Catholic conspiracy. By encouraging the pastors of different denominations to give religious instruction to the children of their respective faiths, the commissioners stated they were merely affording facility of access to the pupils out of school hours and were not themselves employing or remunerating the religious teachers. The commissioners emphasized that they took no cognizance of what denomination the children belonged to and that that question was to be determined by the parents and guardians of the children. Moreover, as their sixth point, the commissioners noted that they did not have anything to do with the setting of times for religious instruction, for this was a matter left to the local patrons. The commissioners' only duty was to see that at least one day a week was set apart for religious instruction. The choice of the site for religious teaching was left to the discretion of the local pastor of each group, he being free to use the school-room or any other place he preferred for religious education. Seventh, the commissioners stated that in the ordinary case they would not exercise control over the use of schoolrooms on Sunday, this control being left to the local manager. They added the proviso, however, that any use of the schools on Sunday that would raise the complaints of adverse parties would be prohibited. This statement was a trifle disingenuous for, in practice, the commissioners banned any religious meeting that was protested by a rival religious group, and for all practical purposes this meant that the use of the schoolhouses for Sunday services was banned.

The commissioners concluded with the pious statement that their explanation did not in any way alter Lord Stanley's original instructions. Technically it did not, but the explanation seems to have been intended as a broad hint to the presbyterians of what they could get away with under the new system. Carlile deserves credit for inducing the commissioners to draw up such a document, the more so because its language made it appear as if the explanation was merely an attempt to elaborate on Stanley's original instructions in response to general questioning rather than what it really was: an attempt to strike a bargain with the synod of Ulster.

The synod considered the commissioners' explanation when the synod met in Monaghan on 3 July 1832. The members agreed that while the explanation reduced some of the system's offensiveness, they were by no means satisfied. Special concern was expressed about the exclusion of the Bible from the schools during school hours. A committee was appointed to correspond with the government on behalf of the synod. The committee (of which Cooke was a member) was to tell his majesty's administration that the synod could not concur in the national system 'unless that, in the schools which our children shall attend, there may be liberty for all who choose it to read the Bible during the ordinary school-hours'. It was further moved that 'should the government concede this principle, which we conceive fundamental and indispensable, our moderator be directed to enter into a negotiation upon the other points involved in the synod's resolutions on this subject'.[13]

The committee seems to have partially disregarded the synod's instructions, for it presented Lord Stanley with seven propositions covering more than merely Bible reading, this in violation of the implied proviso that the Bible question should be resolved before other matters were raised. The committee presented the following demands to Lord Stanley on 1 September 1832:

I That his majesty's government recognize the right of all who choose it, to read the scriptures in the national schools in school hours.

II That no person superintending any school shall, in any case, prevent the exercise of this right when it is claimed by the children, their parents or guardians.

III That while the deputation recognize the duty of every government to provide the means of religious instruction, they conceive that all that can be expected in the circumstances of Ireland, of which the population is so widely divided in religious sentiment, is the privilege of free and uninterrupted access to the holy scriptures, in the divine origin of which all religious parties are agreed; and therefore, respectfully propose, and earnestly recommend to his majesty's government to abstain from all further interference with the religious instruction of children in the national schools; by which means every idea of compulsory reading of the Bible will be avoided on the one hand, and the fullest liberty of conscience will be conceded on the other.

IV That it is inconsistent with the principles of presbyterians to admit, in any degree, the exercise of such a power over books of religious instruction as has been vested in one of their body, a member of the board of education; and the deputation are, therefore, directed to require that the selection of books for the religious instruction of the children of the presbyterian people do remain, as heretofore, in the hands of ministers, subject merely to the control of the synod.

V That instead of having only one model school in Dublin, it be recommended to government, as a measure highly conducive to the interest of education in this country, to establish four provincial

[13] *Report from the select committee appointed to inquire into the progress and operation of the new plan of education in Ireland, p. 432.*

model schools, and four provincial committees, with four depots for books; and that all candidates for the office of schoolmaster shall be licensed by one of these committees appointed by government; and that no one shall be eligible to the charge of any national school until he shall have been examined and approved of by one of these committees.

VI The appointment and dismissal of schoolmasters shall be vested in the local patrons, whether individuals or committees.

VII That the choice of books for literary education be vested in the patrons or local committees, subject to the approval of government.[14]

The Dublin government refused to budge, however, and the synod attempted to by-pass it with a deputation to London in May of the following year. The deputation called upon Earl Grey, Lord John Russell, Thomas Spring-Rice, and E. Littleton. Three propositions were submitted:

I That persons of all denominations shall have the right, either jointly or separately, of applying to the board for aid.

II That patrons of schools, on making application for aid, shall fix the ordinary period of school-hours and shall have the right of setting apart such portion or portions of school-hours as they may deem sufficient for reading the holy scriptures.

III That all children, whose parents or guardians may so direct, shall daily read the holy scriptures during the time appointed by the patrons; but that no compulsion whatever be employed to induce others to read or remain during the reading.[15]

Besides possessing the admirable virtue of being briefer than the seven resolutions sent to Dublin Castle, the three demands were noticeably more conciliatory in tone than the preceding resolutions. The second of the three demands admitted the principle of allowing Bible reading only during certain portions of the school day and thus implicitly accepted its exclusion for the remainder of the day. The resolutions, however, were ambiguous on whether this Bible-reading time should be part of religious instruction or whether it should be part of ordinary instruction. The uncertainty would have disappeared had the 'school hours' been defined. It is also worth noting that although

[14] *Royal commission of inquiry into primary education (Ireland)*, vol. i, pt. i, *Report of the commissioners*, p. 48.
[15] Ibid., p. 48.

the synod was willing to forego forcing children to read the Bible if their parents did not approve, there is no mention of provisions for children who were not taking part to leave the classroom.

As a counterpoint to these official resolutions, Cooke and the moderator, John Brown, were in contact with Earl Grey. In a letter of 22 May 1833 Brown informed Grey of the synod's disapproval. 'They object,' Brown wrote, 'to that part of No. 3 in the printed regulations of the board by which they are required to give their children 52 holy days in the year.' The series of holy days, Brown claimed, was one of the chief means of demoralizing the south of Ireland and the presbyterians were anxious to prevent its being established in the north. Brown added that the synod objected 'to any *human control* over the Bible as required in No. 4—as also to any control over the books of religious instruction as required in said No. 2'. Rather testily, Brown stated in regard to the regulation that joint applications from different religious denominations would receive peculiar favour, that the presbyterians sought not favour but freedom.[16] Neither the official deputations nor the personal dealings made much of an impression upon the government and Lord Stanley wrote a chilling letter that damned the proposition that any child at any hour, in the midst of any other school activity, should be permitted to read the Bible, as a proposal so perfectly novel as to be unheard of. He refused to recommend to the government modifications of the system that would so entirely strike at the principle of the system.[17]

At the synod's June–July meeting in 1833, the ubiquitous Carlile kept the pot boiling by charging the deputation to London with misconduct. After a violent debate in which Carlile was charged with having frustrated the deputation's purposes, the deputation was given a vote of confidence.[18] Strangely, the synod then proceeded to appoint Carlile a member of a committee that, in a report of 2 July 1833, changed the three resolutions of May 1833, into four propositions that were subsequently

[16] John Brown to Lord Grey, 22 May 1833, N.L.I. 4038/p. 3709 (microfilm of original in Durham University Library).

[17] *Royal commission of inquiry into primary education (Ireland)*, vol. i, pt 1: *Report of the commissioners*, p. 49; *Royal commission of inquiry into primary education (Ireland)*, vol. vii, *Returns furnished by the national board*, p. 279 [C6-VII], H.C. 1870, xxviii, pt v.

[18] *Belfast Newsletter* 2 July 1833.

submitted to the government. The four propositions were prefaced by three resolutions that repeated the fact that the synod's opinion of the national system remained unchanged, that the synod felt anxious to obtain modifications in the system so as to be able to accept government aid, and that the synod was submitting the following resolutions to the government:

1stly. That the ministers and people of this church, without the necessary concurrence of the ministers or members of any other church, shall enjoy the right of applying to the board of education for aid to schools, by a statement of the constitution and regulations of the schools, accompanied with an engagement to adhere to them; but in this proposition recognizing the right of the board to consider the regulations, and to decide accordingly.

2ndly. That it shall be the right of all parents to require of patrons and managers of schools, to set apart for reading the holy scriptures a convenient and sufficient portion of the stated school hours, and to direct the master, or some other whom the parents may appoint and provide, to superintend the reading.

3rdly. That all children whose parents and guardians shall so direct, shall daily read the holy scriptures during the period appointed, but that no compulsion whatever be employed to induce others to read, or remain during the reading.

4thly. That every use of school-rooms be vested in the local patrons or committees, subject, in case of abuse, to the cognizance of the board.[19]

Proposition four was really a statement of existing rules or practices of the commissioners, as was the first half of proposition one. The second half added the new suggestion that applicants should be bound by their own rules, not the commissioners'. Propositions two and three suffered from the same ambiguity that characterized the propositions of May 1833. Because the synod did not define 'school hours', the second poposition did not make clear whether the term referred only to ordinary school hours or also included the hours of religious instruction. If the synod was demanding that the Bible be read during the ordinary school hours, it was asking that a basic principle of

[19] *Report of the commissioners of national education in Ireland, for the years 1834, 1835, and 1836* (Dublin, 1836), pp xvi–xvii; *Report from the select committee appointed to inquire into the progress and operation of the new plan of education in Ireland*, p. 434.

the national system be abandoned. On the other hand, it may merely have been asking that permission be given for the hours of religious instruction to occur any time during the day that the manager wished, rather than having to be at the beginning or the end of the day.

The situation was further muddied by an application being made in July 1833 on behalf of the Temple Meeting House School by Rev W. Love, patron of the school. At that school the children received the usual literary education from ten in the morning until two each day. From two to three o'clock those children whose parents permitted were taught in an Old and New Testament class. Children not permitted by their parents to attend the religious class were allowed to spend their time reading the Bible, or in the routine business of the school, or were allowed to retire if they wished. Saturdays were spent in religious education, presumably under the same rules that bound religious teaching during the week. The commissioners stated their opinion that the rules governing the Temple Meeting School agreed in principle with those by which the national schools were governed. They found the rules regarding religious instruction acceptable, 'provided that such children only as are directed by their parents to attend, be then allowed to continue in school, and that all others do then retire; and with respect to the exercise on Saturday, it also is compatible with their rules, provided that those children only shall attend upon that day whose parents direct that they shall join in reading or receiving instruction in the holy scripture'. They added, 'that it is the essence of their rules that religious instruction should be given only at the time specifically appointed for that purpose; and that children whose parents do not direct them to be present at it, should previously retire'.[20] This explanation of their religious rules is very important, for it clarified for the first time something hitherto only implied in the code of regulations: that in the national schools the manager was responsible for seeing that children whose parents did not require them to attend religious training should be excluded. In essence, the managers were

[20] *Report of the commissioners of national education in Ireland for the years 1834, 1835, and 1836,* pp xvii–xviii; T. Ó'Raifeartaigh, 'Mixed education and the synod of Ulster, 1831–40', *Irish Historical Studies,* ix, 287 (Mar. 1955).

required to prevent proselytizing of children under their care.

Meanwhile, the government was coming to a decision about the synod's four propositions. On 30 July 1833, Lord Grey wrote the synod agreeing to the synod's propositions:

I have read with great attention the four resolutions extracted from the minutes of the general synod of Ulster assembled in June and July 1833 and am happy to say that I see nothing in them which may not be agreed to as in perfect accordance with the general principles on which the new system is founded. I trust therefore that all objections being now removed, we may look forward to the full attainment of those benefits for which that system was introduced.[21]

On the basis of this letter the committee of the synod was prepared to recommend that presbyterian schools attach themselves to the national system. The committee, however, was not content to let a good thing be and therefore wrote to the commissioners on 24 August 1833, including a copy of their four resolutions, an extract of Earl Grey's reply, and in addition including a form of application as the basis on which the committee proposed to recommend the members of the synod apply for aid.[22] The idea of the synod demanding that it apply on its own application forms, rather than the commissioners', is notable, in addition to its presumptuousness, as a totally new demand, one never even tangentially mentioned in all of the synod's resolutions.

The commissioners replied—or at least appeared to reply— that they 'were of the opinion that these propositions do not contain anything inconsistent with the principles of the system of education committed to their charge, and his excellency the lord lieutenant having approved thereof, they will receive applications from the patrons of schools in conformity thereto and grant aid upon having such queries as they shall deem necessary to put satisfactorily answered'.[23] Actually, however, the commissioners' minute book makes it clear that this letter to the synod was not written in reply to the presbyterian committee's letter of 24 August 1833, but to the synod's four resolutions,

[21] M.C.N.E.I., 26 Aug. 1833.
[22] *Report from the select committee appointed to inquire into the progress and operation of the new plan of education in Ireland*, p. 448.
[23] M.C.N.E.I., 26 Aug. 1833.

which they had received, together with an extract of Grey's letter to the synod, in a letter from Lord Grey to Archbishop Whately dated 20 August 1833.[24] A letter from Thomas Kelly on behalf of the commissioners dated 6 September 1833 was the real reply to the 24 August letter, and in it Kelly stated that the commissioners wished to add to their minute of 26 August that all applications for aid made to them by members of the synod of Ulster would, like all other applications, be dealt with separately according to the circumstances of each. The synod interpreted this exchange to mean that presbyterian schools would be bound not by the commissioners' regulations, but solely by the rules of their own schools as set forth in public resolutions and applications for aid.[25]

On behalf of the education committee, the moderator of the synod of Ulster wrote the commissioners on 8 November 1833, stating the belief that the presbyterian schools in conjunction with the national system would be bound by the conditions of their own applications, rather than by the commissioners' rules and regulations. Significantly, despite the earlier fencing over the application form to be used, the moderator stated that he saw nothing objectionable in the query sheet the commissioners asked applicants for aid to complete.[26] The commissioners answered on 26 November through T. F. Kelly, directing special attention to the formula on the query sheet which applicants for aid were to sign. The commissioners said they agreed with the moderator that the formula thereon held applicants only to such rules and regulations for their schools as set forth by their answers, but the commissioners also emphasized that any application not compatible with their regulations could not be accepted.[27]

At this point an impasse had been reached, for, as the moderator's letter made clear, in several matters the synod's practices and the commissioners' rules were incompatible.[28] Admittedly, in applying for aid on the query sheet, the applicants only agreed that in conducting the school they would follow the regulations set forth in their own answers, but the committee of

[24] Ibid.

[25] *Report from the select committee appointed to inquire into the progress and operation of the new plan of education in Ireland*, pp 444, 448.

[26] Ibid., p. 443.   [27] Ibid., pp 444–5.   [28] Ibid., p. 443.

the synod must have been either extraordinarily naïve or exceptionally pigheaded to think that the commissioners would sanction aid to applicants whose own regulations did not coincide with the commissioners' regulations. Indeed, an examination of the query sheet indicates that a large number of questions simply asked whether the applicant would or would not enforce this or that rule of the system.[29]

In retrospect, the impasse and the confusion leading up to it was a result of the commissioners and the committee of the synod failing to interpret the commissioners' 'acceptance' of the synod's four propositions in the same way. The commissioners in accepting the propositions meant that applications based upon them would be seriously considered and would not be summarily rejected; they did not mean that such applications would necessarily be acceptable. The presbyterian committee on the other hand, assumed that all applications made on the basis of the four propositions were by definition acceptable, and that if the details of such applications clashed with the rules of the commissioners, the commissioners' rules would be ignored since the four propositions were first principles, and the commissioners' rules merely derivative details.

When the break in negotiations occurred, it came not on matters of principle, but on the details of the query sheet. The committee, which had previously approved the query sheet, now reversed itself. Two queries drew their fire. One of these was, 'Have the clergymen of the different denominations in the parish, or in the neighbourhood of the school been applied to in order to obtain their co-operation and their signature to this application?' The other was, 'Will access be given to clergymen of all denominations to visit the schools in the manner set forth in the regulations?'[30] (The regulation referred to was the stipulation, added to the code of October 1833, that 'It is expected that clergymen of all denominations even although they may not have signed the application to the board, shall have free admission to the school not to take part in the ordinary business, or to interrupt it, but as visitors, to observe how the school is

[29] *Report of the commissioners of national education in Ireland for the years 1834, 1835, and 1836*, pp 134–5.
[30] Ibid., pp 134–5.

conducted'.[31] These two queries touched the presbyterian committee at its most sensitive point and reawakened its anti-catholic zeal. The basic objection was that each of them implied a recognition of the educational function of the catholic clergy, a recognition which the presbyterian church could not accept. In 1832 Henry Cooke claimed before a select committee on Irish education that the presbyterians did not object to any rule that required schools to be open to all persons, but that they did object to a rule which suggested that the catholic priest in his clerical capacity had a right to visit any school.[32]

Although anti-catholicism lay at the base of the committee's decision to change its mind about answering the queries, it may be surmised that they were also deterred by the obvious determination of the commissioners to make them abide by the rules and regulations that applied to all other applicants. A letter of 18 February 1834 signalled the end of the negotiations. In that letter the committee informed the commissioners that their demands for answers to the queries rendered nugatory their previous acceptance of the four propositions. The chance of an early settlement between the synod and the commissioners was past, and Cooke's band settled down to the long process of grinding away the commissioners' resistance.

Significantly, it appears that the majority of presbyterian ministers did not approve of the way Cooke's forces had dealt with the government, but they were unable to do anything about it. When the synod met in Londonderry it was moved, on 27 June 1834, that it was the opinion of the synod that the ministers and people of the presbyterian church could, if they saw fit, make application for aid from the commissioners of national education, providing they adhered strictly to the synod's four propositions. Cooke rallied his forces behind a four-part amendment that skilfully shifted the ground back to the emotionally charged issues of Roman Catholicism and of Bible reading. The first portion of his amendment declared that the presbyterians in Ireland had heretofore enjoyed the free and

[31] *First report of the commissioners appointed by the lord lieutenant to administer the funds voted by parliament for the education of the poor of Ireland*, p. 5, H.C. 1834 [70], xl.

[32] *Report from the select committee appointed to inquire into the progress and operation of the new plan of education in Ireland*, p. 436.

unrestricted use of the holy scriptures and that their children had been accustomed until recently to learn to read with the sacred volume as their primer. Second, the amendment stated that the exclusion of the Bible from the national schools during ordinary school hours was in deference to the opinions of the Roman Catholic hierarchy. Third, Cooke pointed to the previous condemnation of the national system by the synod and added that the system remained unchanged and the synod's objections unmet. Fourth, the synod therefore renewed its exhortations to the faithful not to connect themselves with the system and resolved to continue using every means to bring about a change satisfactory to the synod. After a long debate a vote was taken and Cooke's forces won. The breakdown of the voting is important: fifty-six ministers and twenty-five elders voted for Cooke's amendment, and sixty-four ministers and twelve elders against it. Thus, Cooke was able to thwart the will of the majority of the synod's ministers by his control over the lay elements of the synod.[33]

It is worth turning aside briefly from the oriental debate which we have been following to ask, 'How many of the presbyterian clergy favoured the national system?' Since the vote on Cooke's amendment at the Londonderry meeting was clearly a vote either for or against the national system, the clerical vote on that occasion serves as one index of opinion. In their report for 1835 the commissioners of national education reported 180 signatures of presbyterian clergymen on the various applications for aid.[34] The report for 1836 indicated that the 180 signatures were those of roughly 100 individuals.[35] A tabulation of the managers of individual schools indicated, in 1836, that in Ulster forty presbyterian clergymen were in charge of national schools.[36]

After the synod met in Belfast in special session in December 1834, a number of presbyterian schools connected with the

[33] *Belfast Newsletter*, 1 July 1834; Latimer, p. 454; *Royal commission of inquiry into primary education (Ireland)*, vol. i, pt 1: *Report of the commissioners*, p. 61.

[34] *Second report of the commissioners of national education in Ireland, for the year ending 31st March 1835*, p. 3 [300], H.C. 1835, xxxv.

[35] *Third report of the commissioners of national education in Ireland, for the year ending 31st March 1836*, p. 38 [44], H.C. 1836, xxxvi.

[36] Ibid., p. 40.

national system were withdrawn in consequence of the synod's voting to create its own system of schools. In the presbyterian schools the Bible was to be read daily and the presbyterian catechism used. The schools were to be open to children of all denominations, but children of other faiths were not to be compelled to join in presbyterian religious exercises. Management of the schools was to be left in local hands and supervised by the session and presbytery. With the exception of the Bible-reading rules and the failure to mention rights of other denominations, the presbyterians were creating a system similar to the national system, but financed by voluntary contributions.[37]

The synod's mission-directors were appointed temporary directors of the presbyterian system, and a treasurer was chosen. In 1839 the synod had 127 schools, enrolling 6,590 pupils. As one might expect, the synod had a great deal of difficulty raising enough money to run the schools efficiently: The synod was able to raise enough to contribute only five pounds a year per teacher towards teachers' salaries.[38] The fact that the synod could not afford to run its own system of schools became increasingly obvious during the later 1830s and was one of the chief reasons the synod eventually reopened negotiations with the commissioners.

For the moment, however, the Cooke forces were strongly in control. At the Belfast meeting of the synod in June and July 1835, a resolution was passed with only one dissenting vote declaring 'that inasmuch as this synod had unanimously adopted a system of education for itself, and has repeatedly borne its testimony against the system of national education, and as its mind on this subject remains unchanged, it is not necessary to repeat the discussion of this question at the present meeting'.[39] Cooke had given notice at the Belfast synod that he would move at the synod's next meeting 'that for the purpose of advancing the interest of religion, and securing the peace of their body, none of them in future shall remain patron or correspondent for any school under the new board, or be in any way connected

---

[37] *Royal commission of inquiry into primary education (Ireland)*, vol. i, pt 1: *Report of the commissioners*, pp 63–4.

[38] Latimer, p. 454.

[39] *Royal commission of inquiry into primary education (Ireland)*, vol. i, pt 1: *Report of the commissioners*, p. 64.

with the system'.[40] The motion was moved at the 1 July 1836 meeting at Omagh and a special meeting was called to discuss it in Cookstown on 12 August 1836. Because of the press of business it was not dealt with until a meeting in Belfast on 15 September 1836, when it was passed.[41]

If the presbyterians' activities had been confined to passing resolutions and to building schools of their own no one would have had much cause for complaint. The more fanatical, however, indulged in a series of local intimidations and agitations. For instance, Rev. James Porter, a minister of the secession church in Drumlee, County Down, placed his school under the commissioners with the result that an armed mob expelled his teacher and assaulted Porter himself.[42] Thomas Kelly, secretary to the commissioners, testified that, in addition to the wrecking of the Drumlee school by the mob, the Dressage National School, County Tyrone, was burnt in January 1834, the Beltoney National School, County Tyrone, was burned in September 1835, and the Armalough National School, also in County Tyrone, was wrecked in November 1835. In addition, Kelly stated that although the schools had not been destroyed, they had had to be closed in the following towns because of mob intimidation: Laymere, Clinty, Galgorn, and Bridge-end in County Antrim, and Drummaway, in County Down. Further, the manager of the Corbolly National School, County Tyrone, was forced to close the school because of violence to the schoolmaster.[43]

Agitation of this sort, it should be emphasized, was not any part of the official policy of the synod of Ulster, but some of the blame for exciting acts of violence against local national schools must be ascribed to the intemperate language and manner of Dr Cooke. The Orange Order also bore responsibility. It decreed against the schools,[44] and in so doing guaranteed that an anti-education mob could be raised in most parts of Ulster on a moment's notice. As in any campaign of intimidation the threat of violence was more often present than actual violence.

---

[40] Ibid., p. 64.   [41] Ibid., p. 64.   [42] Latimer, p. 452.

[43] *Digest of the evidence before the committee of the houses of lords and commons in the year 1837 on the national system of education in Ireland* (London, 1838), p. 41.

[44] Latimer, p. 452.

Daniel Sharkey, a frightened school manager in Ballinahinch, wrote the following note to Thomas Kelly:

Sir:

I am glad to inform you that the B-hinch National School is doing well, but its success has given rise to hostility which threatens to be of a peace breaking kind. I enclose you an inflammatory placard published by the Revd Charles Boyd, the implacable enemy of n. education calling on the protestants, by whom he means the orangemen to assemble with a view of having the school *removed* or its prospects injured. A good deal of alarm prevails here that the schoolhouse will be attacked and the peace of the town endangered in a serious degree by the intended meeting. . . . The committee and other friends of the national school are very anxious, sir, to receive advice as to the best method of protecting the school from violence and preserving peace here on the day of the intended meeting. . . .

Daniel Sharkey

P.S. Our apprehensions of violence taking place are the more serious and better founded for the fact that the lives of many were alarmingly endangered at a former meeting against n. education (to which orangemen were summoned from six surrounding parishes). . . .[45]

In addition to direct violence, threats of violence, and mob agitation, the system's opponents could also resort to church politics to attack the system's supporters. Rev. Alexander Patterson, a minister of the Ulster synod in Ballymena, had for a short time conducted a school under the commissioners of national education. This, combined with the fact that he spoke and voted against Cooke's resolution condemning the national system at the 1834 meeting at Londonderry, brought his congregation down upon him. When he returned home from the Londonderry meeting his congregation passed a resolution against the national system, and after agitation headed by Rev. George McClelland (of whom more later), his salary was cut by the presbytery meeting from £100 a year to £50 a year. The presbytery also resolved that he should give up all connection with the commissioners and that he should vote against the national system at the next synod. Patterson replied that he had already given up connection with the national system, but he would not promise his vote on any issue since so doing would be a violation of the right of private conscience. Although

[45] Daniel Sharkey to Thomas Kelly, 21 Jan. 1836, S.P.O., Chief Secretary's Office, Registered Papers, 313/1836.

Patterson was no longer in connection with the national system and although he had become a strong supporter of the local branch of the Presbyterian Education Society, he was tried before the united presbyteries of Conor and Ballymena for disturbing the 'united harmony' of the faithful. He was publicly censured after the moderator of the presbytery cast the deciding vote against him. Patterson, however, did not surrender. He took his case to the annual meeting of the synod of Ulster, where the charge was overthrown by a vote of 133 to 42. Dr Cooke was able to block a move to have the agitators who had brought the trouble upon Patterson suspended from the synod for twelve months, and they escaped with a formal admonition.[46]

If there had been an award given for being the most fanatical of the anti-education agitators, Rev. George McClelland would easily have taken the honour. McClelland was a synod of Ulster minister at Ahoghill. The extremes to which he went suggest that his opposition to the system was founded as much on his own psychopathic personality as upon presbyterian theory. McClelland's best efforts were, of course, on his home ground. In his own district he felt no compunction, after having collected a mob of supporters, about taking possession of places of worship at the conclusion of Sunday services, whereupon he would lecture the assembled worshippers on the iniquity of the national system. Supported, it is claimed, by 5,000 followers, on one occasion he marched to every protestant national school in his district and after dismissing the children, smashed anything he considered offensive, painting crosses and the letter 'P' for 'popery', on the doors and windows before withdrawing.[47] Not inclined to keep his light under a bushel, McClelland made a tour through other parts of Ulster during the fall of 1834, leading mobs and seizing churches pretty much at will.[48] Eventually, it became clear to all but the most rabid orangemen that McClelland had overstepped the bounds of propriety. At the same meeting of the synod at which Rev. Mr Matterson's censure was reversed, McClelland was suspended from the pulpit, although he was later restored. The punishment would have

---

[46] *Belfast Newsletter*, 7 July 1835.   [47] Latimer, p. 453.
[48] For details of McClelland's agitation tour see the *Northern Whig*, 8, 15, 22, 25 Sept. 1834.

been much more severe had not McClelland been under Cooke's protection.[49]

One other agitator deserves brief mention, and he not for his violence nor for his effectiveness, but for his perverseness. Rev. William K. McKay of Portglenone was an Ulster synod minister and an associate of McClelland. Besides assisting McClelland's exercises in mob management, McKay produced a thirty-two stanza poem on the national education question, of which the following verses are highlights (McKay's Biblical footnotes are omitted):

> Shall presbyterians yield the palm,
> Won by the glorious victors
> Who conquer'd Rome but to embalm
> The truth taught by Scotia's doctors?
>
> . . . .
>
> If, then, protestors stop the light
> That through the school, as church's eye,
> Should send forth rays, both pure and bright,
> To show the paths to those that die.
>
> The people of the Lord shall mourn,
> Because of dim and thwarted vision;
> The fountain-pipe shall be up torn—
> The river of life held in derision!
>
> It's not the judgment of Belfast,
> That shall guide the church of God;
> The ruling-elders form the mast,
> Her sails to raise by Aaron's rod.
>
> And if they lift her standard blue,
> And make a patriotic stand;
> The ark of God shall still be free,
> For all the sons of Erin's land![50]

Inappropriately, McKay was rebuked by the synod in 1835, 'not for his iambics, but for aiding and abetting Mr McClelland'.[51]

---

[49] Latimer, p. 453.

[50] *Report from the select committee appointed to inquire into the progress and operation of the new plan of education in Ireland, pp* 605–6.

[51] Ibid., p. 606.

The commissioners made one concession to the synod in 1838. In their fourth report, dated 12 October 1837, the commissioners proposed to the lord lieutenant that the rule concerning religious instruction be modified. The intent of the proposed modification was to allow the managers of schools to set the time for religious instruction any time during the school day, not, as previously, only at the beginning or end of the day. If such a mid-day arrangement was made, it had to be publicly announced, in order that only those children of parents who wished them to be present would be in attendance.[52] The rule was adopted the succeeding year.[53] Although this rule change did not undercut the theoretical distinction between religious and literary instruction it did mean that in practice the national system had moved a step towards becoming very much like a denominational system of schools, for after 1838 national school managers, like the managers of private denominational schools, were able to give religious instruction whenever they pleased, provided public notice was given in advance.

Relations between the commissioners and the synod seem to have been bettered by the adoption of the new religious instruction rule, and also improved by the retirement in 1838 of James Carlile as resident commissioner. Carlile had made considerable efforts to bring the commissioners and the synod to an understanding, but it is clear that he and Cooke were at odds, especially after the passage of Cooke's amendments at Londonderry in 1834. Rev. Dr Henry, Carlile's replacement as the orthodox presbyterian among the commissioners, was the major power in the subsequent negotiations, and it was largely due to his efforts that the commissioners and the synod eventually came to terms.[54]

At the 1839 meeting of the synod, the directors of the synod's schools were ordered to make application to the government for

[52] *Fourth report of the commissioners of national education in Ireland, for the year ending 31st March 1837*, p. 6 [110], H.C., 1837–8, xxviii.

[53] *Fifth report of the commissioners of national education in Ireland, for the year ending 31st March 1838, p.* 5 [160], H.C., 1839, xvi.

[54] In July 1840, when the negotiations were complete, the synod moved a vote of thanks to Henry, stating, 'it was owing very much to him that these modifications have been obtained by which they were entitled to receive aid for their own schools from the national board without the compromise of any scriptural principle', *Belfast Newsletter,* 17 July 1840.

aid to their schools. Drs Cooke and Stewart and Rev. Mr Blackwood proceeded to London in August 1839 to press the presbyterian claims. They saw a number of cabinet members and were told that except through the medium of the national system, no money would be granted, but that the commissioners would be found anxious to receive a deputation from the synod. Thereupon Cooke opened a correspondence with Henry and, at Henry's advice, he resubmitted the 1833 resolutions to the commissioners.[55] Henry brought the subject to the attention of the lord lieutenant, Viscount Ebrington, who asked that a deputation from the synod wait upon him. On 24 January 1840, a conference of the presbyterian delegation and the commissioners of national education took place in the lord lieutenant's apartments in Dublin Castle. The synod's delegation consisted of Cooke, Stewart, Brown, Morgan, Kirkpatrick, Blackwood, and Gelston. The commissioners present were the duke of Leinster, Archbishop Whately, Dr Sadleir, and Messrs Blake, Corballis, and Macdonnell. Archbishop Murray was absent because of illness. In his preliminary remarks the lord lieutenant stated that the query sheet had been totally withdrawn, and that in the conference now being held, it was to be put entirely out of sight. Thus, at the very beginning of the conference, a major presbyterian objection was removed.

Ebrington, in clarifying the rules of the national system, emphasized that the system was one of equal right and was open equally to children of all persuasions, a position with which the presbyterians had never quarrelled. He also emphasized that managers could give religious instruction whenever they pleased during school hours, as long as such instruction was announced in advance and did not impede literary instruction. In this regard, Ebrington's further explanation is important, for he added the proviso that no children were required to attend religious instruction of a sort of which their parents or guardians disapproved. This represented a small, but very important, change in the interpretation of the rules, because previously it had been required that only children of parents who actively approved of the religious instruction could be present, thus

[55] J. L. Porter, *Life and times of Henry Cooke, D.D., LL.D.* (Belfast, 'People's edition', 1875); *Belfast Newsletter*, pp 309–11, 21 Feb. 1840.

implying a responsibility of excluding children of other faiths than that for which religious instruction was intended. Ebrington's interpretation of the rule placed the onus of removing a catholic child from presbyterian religious instruction on the child's parents. They had to actively disapprove of his being present before the child should be excluded. In response to the question of whether all the rules and regulations of the commissioners were binding on the synod's schools, the deputation was told that the only rules binding upon them were their own rules upon the basis of which they made application to the commissioners. When the deputation from the synod asked how they should then proceed to apply for aid, A. R. Blake suggested that they submit a test application at once.[56]

The school chosen was the Correen School, County Antrim, a school already built by presbyterian money, and hence one which would be classified as a 'non-vested' school. (Schools built with the commissioners' aid were required to be vested in local trustees who were legally responsible for the property.) Either the synod's deputation had received some intelligence that the commissioners were about to give in to them or the Correen application was drawn up on the spot, for the application is dated 24 January 1840, the very day of the meeting in the lord lieutenant's apartments. As Stewart, the patron, described the Correen School, it was open from 9.30 to 5.30 during the summer and from ten until three in the winter. In both summer and winter it was open six days a week. The school was open every day of the week to the adult public of all denominations, all of whom had the right to visit and observe the teaching, but no person of any sort was an *ex officio* visitor of the school. The books used were the Kildare Place texts. Religious instruction was so arranged as not to interfere with secular instruction; no child whose parents objected was required to take part in the religious instruction, and none was offered to children of parents who wished them to receive it elsewhere. By implication, the school was open to children of all faiths. Stewart asked for a grant of the commissioners' books and an additional grant of

[56] *Belfast Newsletter,* 21 Feb. 1840; *Dublin Evening Post,* 26 Jan. 1840; Ó'Raifeartaigh, in *Irish Historical Studies,* ix, 292–3; *Sixth report of the commissioners of national education in Ireland, for the year 1839,* p. 3, [246], H.C. 1840, xxviii.

eight pounds per annum.[57] The commissioners acceded to the request, and tactitly agreed to accept all applications that followed the Correen pattern. Almost immediately after the Correen application was accepted, sixty-two other synod applications were accepted, and but little later two hundred more.[58]

The adhesion of the synod of Ulster to the national system was a watershed in the system's history both because of the numerical strength the synod's schools brought to the system and because of the price the commissioners paid for these additional numbers. The mechanism whereby the synod's relationship to the system was legitimized bears attention. As mentioned previously, the commissioners had from their early years distinguished between vested and non-vested schools. The former were built with the commissioners' aid and were bound to the commissioners' rules in perpetuity, while the latter received only annual grants for books and teachers' salaries and were bound to the commissioners' rules only as long as they received the commissioners' money. No distinction, it is important to emphasize. was originally made in the rules which the two types of schools followed. In order to effect the adhesion of the synod's schools, the commissioners reinterpreted the status of non-vested schools, deciding that they were not under the same rules as vested schools. While the vested schools remained under the rules and regulations of the commissioners, the non-vested schools were only under the rules and regulations which they themselves drew up and upon the basis of which they applied for governmental aid. Thus, an anomalous situation arose, in which, technically at least, one type of school in the national system was not under the rules of the national system. Administrative chaos was prevented by the commissioners refusing to grant aid to non-vested schools whose rules did not approximate their own. In practice, a set of unwritten rules for non-vested schools emerged, and unless these were accepted the commissioners did not grant aid.

[57] *Copies of any applications made by clergymen of the synod of Ulster to the board of education in Ireland, for aid to schools connected with the synod, since the recent conference between the deputation from the synod and the board, in presence of the lord lieutenant of Ireland; and of any answers returned to such applications, or of any minutes made, or resolutions entered into by the board in relation thereto,* H.C. 1840 (110), xl; *Sixth report of the commissioners of national education in Ireland for the year 1839,* pp 3–4.

[58] Ó'Raifeartaigh, as above, p. 296.

These unwritten rules were the same as the written rules, except in the following very important regards: first, in non-vested schools the clergymen of faiths different from the manager's did not have the right to give religious instruction, although children of their denomination could repair to them during the hours devoted to religious instruction. Second, although all members of the public were allowed to visit non-vested schools whenever they wished, the clergymen and priests of the various faiths were to be admitted only as members of the public, not because of their religious office. Third, in non-vested schools it was not required that a separate day be set apart for religious instruction. Fourth, it was not necessary to exclude children of another faith from the religious instruction of the majority faith, but only necessary to allow them to go if they wished to leave.

These four differences represent major concessions by the commissioners to the synod of Ulster. When one adds to them the concessions that the query sheet was withdrawn and that religious instruction was allowed to take place at any time during the day, it is obvious that the synod of Ulster's campaign of violence, intimidation, and negotiation produced a considerable educational victory. Indeed, it is reasonable to ask, 'How did the non-vested schools differ from privately supported denominational schools?' The only significant differences were that a theoretical distinction between religious and secular education was maintained (but since even in a denominational school religious teaching cannot go on all the time, the same distinction was usually made in denominational schools in practice, if not admitted in theory), and that no child was to be forced to take part in any religious instruction as a condition of his being in school. Clearly, non-vested schools were merely 'denominational schools with a conscience clause'.

3

The actions of the members of the established church of Ireland, while contrasting in many respects to those of the presbyterians, served to reinforce the effects of the presbyterians' actions. The presbyterians' victory meant that the curriculum in non-vested schools would be effectively denominational. The anglicans refused to join the national system, and created a system of their own schools which drew large numbers of anglican children; they thereby guaranteed that the national system would be effectively denominational, at least in the south, in terms of the student body of each school since only Roman Catholic children would be left to fill the national schools. Thus, by abstaining from connection with the system the anglicans gave the system a further spin toward denominationalism, a trend that had been begun by the presbyterians joining the system.

The anglicans' reasons for disliking the system were similar to the presbyterians' reasons. Like the synod of Ulster, the anglican communion in Ireland was dominated by conservative elements and by evangelical enthusiasts. Overwhelmingly tory, the church was goaded into unthinking rage by whig ecclesiastical reforms. Catholic emancipation had been opposed by most of the established clergy, but emancipation had had little direct effect upon their position. In its wake, however, arose considerable agitation against the tithe system under which Roman Catholic peasants were forced to support the anglican clergy. Lord Stanley produced an act in 1832 that made the composition of tithes for money payment compulsory, but this did not solve the problem. As a further bow to the tithe agitation an Irish church temporalities act was passed in 1833, over vigorous anglican opposition. The act provided for the reduction of the anglican archbishoprics of Cashel and Tuam and for the union of ten less important bishoprics with their more important neighbours. The revenues of the remaining bishoprics were to be reduced. After a considerable struggle it was decided that the money thus saved would be used for clerical purposes and administered by ecclesiastical commissioners. Finally, a tithe act of 1838 converted the tithes into a fixed rent charge at seventy-five per cent of their nominal value.[59] Raging from the government's attack upon their privileges, the dignitaries of the established church were not inclined to miss any opportunity to

[59] J. C. Beckett, *The making of modern Ireland, 1603–1923* (London, 1966), pp 309–12, 318–19; Thomas J. Johnston, John L. Robinson and Robert W. Jackson, *A history of the Church of Ireland* (Dublin, 1953), pp 254–5; N. D. Emerson, 'The last phase of the establishment' in Walter A. Phillips (ed.), *History of the Church of Ireland from the earliest times to the present day*, iii (London, 1933), pp 295–308.

attack the whigs, and certainly were not willing quietly to tolerate any further invasion of their ecclesiastical rights.

The national system, being a whig creation, would have been roasted by the majority of church dignitaries whatever its structure. When the bishops perceived that it constituted a threat to their privileges they met it with pious fury. The clergy of the established church, like the presbyterians, disliked sharing control of educational institutions with anyone, be it the government or other denominations. The objections of the anglicans were, however, even stronger on this point than were those of the presbyterians, for a considerable segment of the clergy still maintained that it was the right of the established church to control any system of education the state might create. Even if the feeling had not run high that the national system denied the church's rightful role as patron of national education, and even if a majority of the clergy had granted the government's right to intervene in the education of other denominations, the opposition would have remained vigorous, for the system implied the power of the government to intervene in the education of anglican children as well as that of Roman Catholic and presbyterian children. The current of opposition was further quickened by a mistrust of the commissioners of national education as a group. The religious constitution of the commissioners was partially responsible; not only were catholics and presbyterians among the commissioners, but the anglican commissioners comprised only three of the original seven members. Indeed, some clergy held that among the commissioners only the archbishop of Dublin could really be considered a protestant.[60] And as time wore on, it became clear that even Whately, a whig and an Englishman, was not trusted.

The anglicans' theological objections to the national system were markedly similar to the early presbyterian objections. The majority of the clergy would not countenance the disjuncture between religious and literary education. With the presbyterians, the established clergy denounced the restriction of the Bible to hours of separate religious instruction. Like the presbyterians, the anglicans protested the commissioners' issuing of books of scripture extracts, and charged the commissioners with handling the Word of God deceitfully.

[60] *Dublin Evening Post*, 23 Nov. 1831.

Much of the anglican opposition to the national system was the result of a disease that infected nineteenth-century Irishmen of all the reformed faiths: a pathological fear of the Roman Catholic church. Thus, *The Christian Examiner and Church of Ireland Magazine*, a publication that fanned the orthodox anglican opposition to the national system, continually proclaimed that the entire system was a whiggish accommodation to the papists:

Lord Stanley's letter instructing the board made this evident, his language is express, and pointedly sets forth as a concession to the Roman Catholic church . . . An attempt has been made to mystify the public by stating that it is a concession to the prejudices of certain of our fellow-countrymen as such, and not to the *Church of Rome*.[61]

In addition to discountenancing the presence of Roman Catholics on the central board of commissioners, the anglicans refused to accept the right of Roman Catholic priests in the local area 'to make use of the schoolrooms for the purpose of teaching the peculiar dogmas, the superstitious rites, the intolerant sentiments, the blasphemous fables, the dangerous deceits, and, in a word, all the errors of popery'.[62] Indeed, irrespective of the question of priestly access to the schools, the anglicans felt that by allowing Roman Catholic pupils any form of religious training, much more by encouraging it, the system abetted the dissemination of religious error. The anglican opposition raised one point that was not often mentioned in presbyterian agitation, namely that the national system should be condemned because it interfered with the duty of proselytizing Roman Catholics:

We conceive the national system very objectionable as regards the protestants, but infinitely worse as it regards Roman Catholics . . . *The System as far as they are concerned is a conspiracy between its supporters and the Roman priests, to keep the light of God's word from ever shining upon a Roman Catholic child.* They see not the Bible in the schools; and out of the schools they only see as much of it as the priests will allow, which is avowedly NONE AT ALL.[63]

[61] 'Parliamentary evidence on national education in Ireland', *Christian Examiner and Church of Ireland Magazine*, 3 ser., ii (Nov. 1837), p. 883.

[62] Parliamentary evidence on national education in Ireland', *Christian Examiner and Church of Ireland Magazine*, 3 ser., iii (Jan. 1838), p. 52.

[63] 'Board of national education', *Christian Examiner and Church of Ireland Magazine*, 2 ser., iv (Oct. 1835), p. 686.

Archbishop Whately was the only anglican clergyman of importance to support the national system from its beginning. Whately's publicly expressed reasons for adhering to the system are interesting. In January 1832, in response to a memorial from the dean and chapter of St Patrick's, Dublin, he explained his position. As he understood the system, the government did not intend it to provide complete education in the sense of instructing children in all they should know, but to create a national measure, providing some degree of instruction for children throughout the nation, leaving the remainder, as it were, blank pages to be filled in by the clergy. Thus, Whately's major educational premise differed from that of most anglican clergymen, for he was willing to admit that education was in large part a national trust to be looked after by the government, rather than solely a religious trust to be controlled by the established church. Although he admitted that he was not sanguine about the success of the plan, Whately was anxious that it not fail through anglican opposition.[64]

In a subsequent letter to the same chapter, written in March 1832, after the chapter had restated its objections to the national system, he explained at great length that although the national system was open to a number of questions it was still the best system that under the present circumstances could be created in Ireland. Here again Whately was at odds with the majority of the church, for his entire course of reasoning was based on the assumption that realism was necessary in judging such matters, and that a realistic assessment of the Irish religious situation implied a recognition that Roman Catholics existed, and that any education solution had to be satisfactory to them as well as to the anglicans.[65]

It is difficult to know how many anglican clergymen followed Whately in approving the national system, but it is certain that in the system's first twenty years they were in the minority. In 1852, Bishop O'Brien of Ossory, a sturdy enemy of the national

---

[64] *Reply of his grace the archbishop of Dublin to the address of the clergy of the diocese of Dublin and Glandalough on the government plan for national education in Ireland; to which are added, the above-mentioned address, and the observations of some of the archbishops and bishops of the United Church of England and Ireland on the same subject* (London, 1832), pp 8–10.

[65] Ibid., pp 12–29.

system, estimated that at the very most, one quarter of the entire body of anglican clergy in Ireland had become proponents of the national system.[66] In one sense the established church could count it a blessing that there was substantial agreement on the national education question for it had other things to worry about during the trying times of the 1830s. During the 1840s support for the national system gradually increased, and, as we shall see later, during the 1850–70 period the communion split violently on the issue.

Whereas the presbyterian opponents of the national system relied upon negotiation with the Irish administration and with the commissioners of national education to get their way, the anglicans trusted their case to parliament. As our examination of the administrative structure of the national system showed, however, parliament actually had little to do with Irish education, control of which rested with the executive and with the commissioners. Hence, the anglican efforts were foredoomed to failure. During 1832 parliament was flooded by petitions against the national system from anglicans from all over Ireland and England. Of this mass of petitions, that of the majority of the anglican hierarchy most deserves quotation:

It is ... with unfeigned regret that they are constrained to express their deliberate and conscientious persuasion that the proposed plan of national education, instead of producing these salutary and much to be desired effects, would tend rather to embitter existing animosities by marking more distinctly the difference of creed in the public school, and by pointedly excluding, as a common source of instruction, that volume which authoritatively inculcates, under the most awful sanctions, universal charity, mutual forbearance, and the cultivation of peace and order ... They further state, that they do not affect to conceal their grief at beholding the clergy of the established church deprived of the trust committed to their hands by the legislature of superintending national education. ...

John George Armagh	John Elphin
Power Tuam	Robert Ossory
Nathanial Meath	Richard Waterford and Lismore
Charles Kildare	James Dromore

[66] *A speech delivered by the lord bishop of Ossory and Ferns, at the annual meeting of the Church Education Society for Ireland, held in the Rotunda, Dublin, on Thursday, April 15, 1852* (Dublin, 1852), p. 9.

George Kilmore	Richard Down and Connor
Robert P. Clogher	Thomas Leighlin and Ferns
Christopher Clonfert	William Raphoe
and Kilmacduagh	John Cloyne
James Killalla and Achonry	Samuel Cork and Ross[67]

In the commons the government was harassed on the subject, especially each year at estimates time, but to little effect. It was clear that the anglicans' hope of destroying or modifying the national system through political action would remain unfulfilled until the tories returned to power.

Outside of parliament mass meetings fanned the anglican agitation, and it was at these meetings that most of the public petitions to parliament were prepared. During the early 1830s the education agitation coincided with a general Orange agitation under the auspices of the earl of Roden. There is some evidence that landlords coerced their tenants into opposing the national system. For example, several landed proprietors of the parish Errigle Trough drew up a formal resolution declaring their disapproval of the national system and intimating, 'that none of our tenantry will receive encouragement from us who are opposed to schools founded on a religious basis'.[68]

A surprising amount of interest in the question of Irish national education was shown by members of the established church in England. A considerable number of petitions in 1832 were from England, and Exeter Hall in London was the site of mass meetings in opposition to the Irish system in 1832 and again in 1836. In the house of lords the bishop of Exeter joined the earl of Roden as one of the chief opponents of the national system.

In view of his later dealings with Irish education, William E. Gladstone's meddling with Irish national education in the 1830s is of considerable interest. Gladstone composed a series of six private memoranda on Irish education which he circulated, in 1832, to Archbishop Whately, Dean Murray (not to be confused with Murray the Roman Catholic archbishop of Dublin), Dr Elrington, Sergeant Jackson, and a bishop whose name is

---

[67] *Belfast Newsletter*, 16 Mar. 1832.
[68] *Digest of the evidence before the committees of the house of lords and commons, in the year 1837, on the national system of education in Ireland*, p. 41.

illegible.[69] He began his discussion with the major premise that the government of the country was christian. Second, he emphasized that the government was protestant as well as christian. In Ireland the protestant doctrine was embodied in the beliefs of the established church. All who became officers of the state were obliged to do nothing hostile to the established faith. No christian government, Gladstone stated, could adopt the principle of giving education to the people independent of religion. Further, the government, being a protestant government, could not give the people an education in opposition to the principle of the protestant establishment. Since the national system was neither protestant nor religious, it was declared lacking. Gladstone listed the following objections to the national system that he adjudged to have weight:

1 It involved no recognition of the word of God as the proper food of christian people.
2 It allowed the teaching of popery at public expense, or at least made it appear that way.
3 It allowed the popish priests to use the schoolhouse for separate religious instruction.
4 The government, under the plan, merely provided secular education and left religious training to the various clergy.
5 It did not recognize the duty of prayer in schools.

Gladstone then outlined his own plan for the creation of a system of 'united education embracing religion by means of scripture extracts'. His proposed system was to be administered by a board for which Roman Catholics, presbyterians, and anglicans would be eligible. The board would grant aid for building schools and for repairs, salaries, and school requisites. He suggested that two types of schools be created, one type to be under the exclusive control of the board and to be used only for combined education; the other type was to receive no building grant, but the local patrons were to do as they pleased subject only to their being a stipulated amount of time spent on religious education. He went on to argue that in schools under exclusive board control the schools should open and close with prayer and the scriptures be read daily during school hours. Attendance at neither one of these exercises was to be compul-

[69] British Museum, Add. MS. 44,727, Gladstone Papers, vol. 642, ff. 12–25.

sory. Those children, however, who did not attend the scripture reading were to be taught daily in a class that used the scripture extracts, attendance therein being compulsory. Gladstone's proposal for two types of national schools foreshadows the distinction which prevailed in Ireland after 1840. His description of what were to be known as 'non-vested' was close to being prophetic. Gladstone's sixth memorandum refers to Whately's criticism of some of his points, thus making it clear that the ranking protestant among the commissioners had studied the proposal in detail. This knowledge is as frustrating as it is fascinating, for, unfortunately, the loss of the minutes of commissioners of national education for 1838–41 makes it impossible to know how the commissioners came to consider and finally accept the idea of non-vested national schools being governed by a different set of rules than vested schools.

The only group of anglicans to make a set of public proposals for modification of the national system were the clergy of Derry and Raphoe. Upon the death of the bishop of Raphoe in 1834 the diocese was united to the diocese of Derry, and at the first combined meeting of the clergy of the two dioceses a number of the leading members raised the education question and accordingly signed a requisition to the bishop to formally convene a meeting of the clergy on the subject. A plan was proposed for using some of the bishop's visitation fees for education of the poor, but when the clergy assembled to discuss this it became clear that the amount was inadequate. The clergymen then turned to the possibility of joining the national system. In addition to the want of funds the clerics were driven to discuss the possibility because of their feeling that it was dangerous to have the government and the established church divided against each other on a matter of such importance. A large committee of the most influential of the clergy was appointed which, after two to three months of meetings, determined a number of changes that might be made in the national system so that the anglicans could conscientiously take part. The great majority of the clergy of the diocese approved the report and it was determined to present the propositions to the clergy of the nation in printed form. Preparatory to presenting the proposals publicly, the secretary of the committee wrote the bishop of Exeter, a man whose approval was necessary for any plan to be accepted among anglicans, and he endorsed the proposal.[70]

The address to the nation began by annunciating the evils that the national system had introduced and then listed three alternative courses of action. First, anglicans could sit down in 'despair and submission' refusing to connect themselves with the system, but leaving it undisturbed. Second, they could direct their efforts towards effecting the system's extinction. Third, they could attempt to procure its modification. Favouring the last course, the committee then discussed the necessary modifications. The underlying principle of any modification, it was postulated, should be 'that, to the children of such parents, whether Roman Catholic or protestant, as chose them to have scriptural instruction, free access to the word of God shall be prohibited at no hour or minute of the day'.[71] This principle implied that the practice of requiring religious instruction to be scheduled in advance at a particular period of the day would be abolished. Children whose parents did not approve were not required to participate, but it was not the intention of the clergy to allow children who did not participate in the scripture classes to leave the school building.[72] Effectively, this meant that Roman Catholic children would not be at liberty to receive religious instruction in their own faith.

Given our knowledge of the success of the presbyterians in negotiating with the commissioners, we might expect that proposals of this sort would have served as a basis for bargaining between the church and the commissioners. This was not to be, however, for the wrath of the rest of the nation's clergy fell upon the ministers of Derry and Raphoe. Their proposals were characterized as being in the 'language and sentiments, which we thought were held only by the opponents of scriptural education'.[73] Not only did the ideas not take hold with the rest of the anglican clergy in Ireland, but at a number of meetings of clergy

[70] *Digest of the evidence before the committee of the house of lords and commons, in the year 1837 on the national system of education in Ireland*, pp 123–31. The bishop of Exeter later withdrew his approval.

[71] *Dublin Evening Mail*, 5 Dec. 1836.

[72] *The Derry and Raphoe propositions, the Church Education Society, the national board schools compared, with remarks* (Dublin, 1849), pp 9–10.

[73] 'Derry and Raphoe address on national education', *Christian Examiner and Church of Ireland Magazine*, 3 ser., ii (Jan. 1837), p. 18.

of other dioceses resolutions were passed condemning the Derry and Raphoe proposals. A substantial minority of the diocese of Derry and Raphoe itself (forty of the 137 clergy of the diocese) protested against the proposals. The Derry and Raphoe committee petitioned parliament on the basis of its proposals, but nothing came of it. By 1838 the clergy of the diocese had returned to condemning the system in the terms used time and time again by all of the other opponents of national education.[74]

Rather than negotiate with the government the anglican clergy tried to create their own education system. This system, unlike the presbyterians', was substantially endowed in its early years and for a time was a considerable success. The Church Education Society was founded in 1839. The presidents were the lord primate and eleven bishops, the vice-presidents a collection of lay nobility and gentry and twenty-one deans and twenty-eight archdeacons.[75] Everyday business was conducted by a managing committee of lay and clerical members resident in Dublin. The backbone of the system was not, however, the central organization, but the diocesan education societies organized throughout the country. The national organization of the Church Education Society coordinated diocesan efforts and allocated money subscribed to the central organization. Schools connected with the society were open to children of all faiths and in them the reading of the holy scriptures in the authorized version was required for all. Only children of the established church, however, were required to learn the catechism and doctrines of that church.[76]

Financially, the society was well supported. Set forth below are the figures of total receipts of the central body of the Church Education Society. The income of diocesan education societies is not included in the figures. Since the ratio of diocesan to central income usually was between six and seven to one,[77] to gain an accurate idea of the total income of Church Education

[74] *Dublin Evening Mail*, 14 Nov. 1836, 29 Feb. 1837, 23 Mar. 1838; *Dublin Evening Post*, 9, 12 Dec. 1836.

[75] *Royal commission of inquiry into primary education (Ireland)*, vol. viii, *Miscellaneous papers and returns*, p. 30 [C 6–VII] H.C. 1870, xxviii, pt v.

[76] Ibid., pp 31–2.

[77] See financial statement, ibid., p. 33.

Society schools, the central body's figures should be multiplied by a factor of seven or eight:[78]

Year	Income of central organization of Church Education Society		
1839	£1,854	10s	1d
1840	2,606	10	0
1841	3,915	14	3
1842	2,977	7	5
1843	4,003	3	1½
1844	4,509	8	2½
1845	5,863	9	5
1846	5,042	11	5
1847	7,595	0	4
1848	4,510	5	9
1849	5,979	14	10

During the society's first decade the number of children on the rolls grew spectacularly. The following figures are from information provided by the society and must, of course, be treated with caution:[79]

Year end	Number of schools	Total on roll	Roman Catholics on roll	Non-Anglican protestants on roll
1839	825	43,627	10,868	N/A
1840	1,015	59,067	N/A	N/A
1841	1,219	69,043	20,451	N/A
1842	1,372	86,102	29,612	8,365
1843	1,729	102,528	33,115	13,899
1844	1,812	104,968	32,834	13,668
1845	1,811	100,755	30,057	12,691
1846	1,899	96,815	N/A	N/A
1847	1,859	116,968	44,638	14,697
1848	1,861	120,202	46,367	15,713
1849	1,868	111,877	37,857	15,562

If the figures are at all accurate the Church Education Society was operating a school system which was, in 1849, educating

[78] Ibid., p. 33.

[79] Table derived from *First annual report of the Church Education Society for Ireland* (Dublin, 1840), p. 10; *Second annual report . . .* (Dublin, 1841), p. 17; *Third annual report . . .* (Dublin, 1842), p. 17; *Fourth annual report . . .* (Dublin, 1843), pp 7–8; *Sixth annual report . . .* (Dublin, 1845), p. 7; *Seventh annual report . . .* (Dublin, 1846); p. 11; *Eighth annual report . . .* (Dublin, 1848), pp 14, 22; *Ninth annual report . . .* (Dublin, 1849), pp 11, 17; *Tenth annual report . . .* (Dublin, 1850), pp 11, 19.

almost one-fourth as many children as the national system. Although the schools of the Church Education Society contained a surprising number of Roman Catholic and dissenting children—51·6 per cent in 1848—the society's important effect upon the national system came through its education of large numbers of anglican children. If mixed education in the national system was to be a reality the parents of children of the protestant denominations had, especially in the south, to be convinced that the children should attend the national schools with their Roman Catholic neighbours. The Church Education Society undercut the mixed principle in the national schools by removing a large number of anglican and other protestant children to its own schools. Thus, in creating a denominational system of their own, the anglican clergy gave the allegedly non-denominational national system another spin in the direction of denominationalism.

For a brief time during the 1840s it looked as if the anglicans had guessed right, and that the government was about to replace the national system with denominational grants. That time was during Peel's early administration when the lord lieutenant, Earl De Grey (expressing the views of the archbishop of Armagh, Lord John George Beresford) urged Peel to give up the experiment in united education because the system was virtually for the benefit of the catholics only. De Grey favoured appointment of a commission to investigate the Irish education question, and, presumably, to recommend denominational grants. Lord Eliot, the chief secretary, argued against any change in the existing system, thus creating open disagreement within the cabinet. At the beginning Peel was prepared to abandon mixed education but he gradually came to favour the national system. In November 1842, the lord lieutenant was informed that the government would not countenance any inquiry into Irish education. One of Peel's reasons for supporting the national system was that any change in the system would certainly have produced three systems of denominational education, one for each of the major Irish faiths. Further, he was afraid that any change would cause controversy and disturb the religious peace of Ireland.[80]

[80] Kevin B. Nowlan, *The politics of repeal: a study in the relations between Great Britain and Ireland, 1841–50* (London and Toronto, 1965) pp 28–30.

With Peel's decision to back the national system the anglicans lost their last chance of either extinguishing the system or converting it into an avowedly denominational network. They did not understand this, however, and in 1845 the clergy of the established church began a major drive for a separate grant to the Church Education Society. Such a drive was an inevitable concomitant of the society's success in garnering large numbers of children for its schools: the more than 100,000 children on the rolls cost more than the pocketbook of the established church could bear without strain. On 31 May 1845, the lord primate presented Peel with a petition for a parliamentary grant to be made to schools in connection with the Church Education Society. The petition was the product of considerable agitation and was endorsed by the majority of the anglican bishops in Ireland, 1,700 of the anglican clergy, more than 1,600 of the nobility and gentry, and 60,000 of the people.[81] Peel firmly refused the possibility of a separate grant in a letter that affirmed the usefulness of mixed education in pacifying Ireland,[82] and although the correspondence continued briefly between the lord primate and the prime minister the government held firm.[83] In the years that followed, the majority of the anglican clergy continued to favour a separate grant to the Church Education Society. It was another two and a half decades before it became clear to the diehards among them that the government was not going to give in on the subject, and that they would eventually have to choose between joining the national system on the government's terms or watching the Church Education Society crack under financial strain.

The only dent that all the activities of the established church made upon the regulations of the national system was made in 1847. It will be remembered that the rules applying to vested schools were interpreted to require that the manager of a national school had to exclude all children from religious instruction unless their parents asked that they be present. This

[81] Lord John George Beresford to Sir Robert Peel, 31 May 1845, reproduced in *Report from the select committee of the house of lords appointed to inquire into the practical working of the system of national education in Ireland*, pp 1604–5, H.C. 1854 (525), xv, pt II.

[82] Sir Robert Peel to Lord John George Beresford, 9 June 1845, reproduced ibid., pp 1607–9.

[83] See ibid., pp 1610–13.

meant that catholics had to be excluded when protestant instruction began and protestants turned out when Roman
Catholic religious instruction was in progress. As noted earlier,
one of the anglican objections to the national system was that it
interfered with the anglican duty of proselytizing catholics.
Thus, in 1844, Archdeacon Stopford of Meath began badgering
the commissioners with a series of questions and hypothetical
applications for connection with the national system in which
the central issue was the rule concerning exclusion of children
from religious instruction. (It is hard to see why Stopford was
not, like the presbyterians, satisfied with applying for non-
vested status, a status that would have left him bound only by
the terms of his own application, and a status that in the case
of the presbyterians had already been interpreted as not requiring the exclusion of any children during religious instruction.) In any event, Stopford concentrated on changing the
printed rule that applied to vested schools, and in 1847 the
commissioners gave in and changed the rule under the guise of
interpreting its true meaning. As newly interpreted the rule
required that no compulsion could be employed by managers
to cause children of one faith to attend the religious instruction
of another, but mention of the necessity of their being excluded
was removed. Thus, the commissioners allowed one more safe-
guard against proselytizing to crumble, and in so doing caused
the system to become that much more like a denominational
one.[84]

Archdeacon Stopford's victory seems to have been a solo
achievement. Its effect was to reinforce the trend towards curricular denominationalism that the presbyterians had begun.
The effect of anglican agitation generally, though, was not to
modify the rules of the national system but rather to alter the
religious makeup of the typical national school class. By withdrawing large numbers of anglican children from the Church
Education Society schools the authorities of the established
church guaranteed that in the south of Ireland most of the

---

[84] Isaac Butt, *The liberty of teaching vindicated* (London and Dublin, 1865),
pp 120–3; Fergal McGrath, *Newman's university, idea and reality* (London,
1951), pp 32–3; M.C.N.E.I., 23 Sept., 4, 11, 18 Nov. 1847, 20 Jan. 1848;
*Sixteenth report of the commissioners of national education in Ireland for the year
1849*, pp 18–19 [1231], H.C. 1850, xxv.

national schools would be filled exclusively with Roman Catholic children. Thus, although anglican aloofness contrasted with the presbyterian shrewdness, the two denominations' activities were complementary, the presbyterians producing curricular denominationalism, the anglicans greatly reducing the possibility of mixing children of different faiths in a single classroom.

4

The Roman Catholic clergy, unlike the anglicans and presbyterians, did not immediately disapprove of the system. Benignly neutral towards it during most of the 1830s, and cautiously bewildered by it thereafter, the Roman Catholic clergy applied for government aid in great numbers and filled the national schools with droves of catholic children. Paradoxically, this was the one reaction towards the system that would most reinforce the actions of the other two denominations. This meant, outside of Ulster at least, that at the very time the protestants were holding aloof from the system, the national schools were being packed with Roman Catholic students, the result being that a great many schools were not mixed denominationally.

During the early 1830s, the majority of the Roman Catholic prelates and clergy seem to have been at least mildly approving of the national system, an attitude that is not at all surprising, since it had been created as a response to their demands. Three prelates in particular were strong supporters of the national system. One of these was William Crolly, bishop of Down and Connor and later archbishop of Armagh. Crolly stood as a bulwark of the system until his death in 1850.[85] The second was Daniel Murray, archbishop of Dublin and one of the commissioners of national education. The third was James Doyle, bishop of Kildare and Leighlin, who until his death in June 1834 exhorted his clergy to connect their schools with the system. The following excerpts from a circular letter to his clergy provide an indication of Doyle's feelings about national education:

[85] Michael E. Sadler, 'The history of the Irish system of elementary education', in Michael E. Sadler (ed.), *Special reports on educational subjects, 1896–7* (London, 1897), p. 231.

Carlow, December 26, 1831

You have been made acquainted, through advertisements in the public newspapers, with an outline of the plan or terms on which the funds placed by parliament at the disposal of the lord lieutenant, to promote the education of the children of the Irish people, will be dispensed.

These terms had been long sought for, by repeated applications to government, and by petitions to parliament, and have at length, with much difficulty, been obtained. They are not perhaps the very best which could be devised, but they are well suited to the especial circumstances of this distracted country. They provide for the religious instruction of children by their respective pastors, or persons appointed for that purpose by them, as often as those pastors can deem it necessary. This instruction shall be given on one or two days in the week, and may be given, as I hope it will, every day.

The school-house, to be built at the public expense, is to be secured to the public. This is all the commissioners require, and this is just, nay, it is necessary, in order to guard against individual rapacity.

The commissioners claim to have control over the books to be used in schools. This appears an assumption from which evil, as well as good, might follow. It is good, that useless or immoral books be utterly, and by authority, excluded. This precaution is idle in our regard, but it may not be so elsewhere, and 'law', says the apostle 'is placed not for the just man, but for the unjust'. It gives no trouble to the man who acts properly; it gives pain and brings punishment only to him who omits or transgresses his duty.

This assumption would produce evil if the commissioners sought to corrupt the education of the Irish people. We defy them to do so, even if they were so minded; but they are not. Their purpose is upright; their views are to promote education, religious as well as literary, and to preserve full and entire freedom of conscience. Should bad men succeed to the present commissioners, and attempt to corrupt the education of youth, we are not dumb dogs who know not how to bark; we can guard our flocks, and do so easily by the simple process of excluding the commissioners and their books and agents from our schools. We might, by doing so, forfeit the aid which they would, if the supposition were realized, be entitled to withhold, but in withholding it they would be answerable to parliament, to which we also would have access.

Some years past it would have been easy to combine education and have only one school-house in place of two: not so at present, and time only can effect that union which has hitherto been prevented at great sacrifice, and at great expense. I notice this, that you may be enabled, in your application or reply to the commissioners, to point out the true and very sufficient reason, why in these dioceses so well supplied with school-houses, few requisitions for aid to assist schools can, as yet, be made in that joint manner, by catholic and protestant clergymen, which the commissioners so justly recommend.

Having premised this much, I now beg you will, without unnecessary delay, apply to the commissioners before mentioned, for aid, whether to build or to furnish, or to support, as the case may warrant, each of your parochial schools.[86]

Throughout the nation catholic priests applied for connection of local schools with the national system. The commissioners' report for the year 1835 noted a total of 1,397 signatures of Roman Catholic clergymen on applications for aid,[87] these being the signatures of 941 individual members of the catholic clergy.[88]

The first crack in the wall of approval came in 1836 when the Christian Brothers withdrew their schools from connection with the national system. Originally the superior general, Edmund Rice, had decided not to connect his schools with the national system as he disapproved of its principles. But under considerable pressure from Archbishop Murray he consented to give the system a trial, and in 1833 and 1834 placed six of the Christian Brothers schools in connection with the commissioners. The experiment was an unhappy one because the commissioners' rules confining religious instruction to specific hours prevented the children from reciting prayers and doing devotional exercises throughout the day and also prevented the permanent display of crucifixes, statutes, and similar devotional articles. As a result, four of the six schools were withdrawn from association with the national system in 1836, and the others were disassociated thereafter.[89]

[86] Reproduced in *Royal commission of inquiry into primary education (Ireland)*, vol. i, pt i, *Report of the commissioners*, p. 70.

[87] *Reports of the commissioners of national education in Ireland, from the year 1834 to 1841, inclusive* (Dublin, 1842), p. 11.

[88] Ibid., p. 37.

[89] J. D. Fitzpatrick, *Edmund Rice, founder and first superior general of the brothers of the christian schools of Ireland (Christian Brothers)* (Dublin, 1945), pp 249–51, 312; Timothy J. Walsh, *Nano Nagle and the Presentation Sisters* (Dublin, 1959), p. 212.

As the temporary connection of the Christian Brothers schools with the system implied, the commissioners granted aid to monastic (and convent)

At this point, before considering the great catholic educational controversy of 1838–41, it is important to understand the intellectual equipment through which the Roman Catholic prelates dealt with the national system. From the 1850s onwards catholic writers have been embarrassed, in view of the church's position on mixed education, by the fact that the prelates took so heartily to the national system in its early days. This embarrassment is misplaced, for it is a result of projecting the views of the synod of Thurles of 1850 and of subsequent educational decrees back into a period to which they do not apply. The sophisticated arguments that were used after 1850 to condemn mixed education on the grounds of its producing an artificial disjuncture between the sacred and the profane were not part of the vocabulary of the Irish hierarchy in the 1820s and 1830s and probably would not have been understood at that time by most of its members. In the penurious days before the famine the Irish prelates could not afford the luxury of viewing mixed education as a theological abstraction, but rather they had to see it in terms of a practical necessity, as the only possible means of raising their people from illiteracy. Whereas after 1850 the alternative to mixed education was generally seen to be government grants for separate catholic education, the alternative to mixed education in the 1820s and 1830s was understood to be government support of proselytizing societies. Thus, when the catholic connection with the national system came under fire in the late 1830s, the connection was condemned only partially on theological grounds—and then very crudely—and in the main because of alleged abuses and failings of the system in practice. At that point in time even the Roman Catholic critics of the system were discussing the system within the same framework of assumptions and attitudes in which its proponents defended it, and these assumptions were primarily pragmatic and political rather than theoretical and theological.

---

schools provided they were operated under the same rules as other national schools. Since the commissioners refused to allow any minister or priest to be a teacher in a national school, the commissioners rationalized the granting of aid to such schools on the grounds that the teachers were actually laymen and women and not in orders. See *Royal commission of inquiry into primary education (Ireland)*, vol. i, pt 1, *Report of the commissioners*, p. 31.

The man responsible for raising catholic doubts about the national system was John MacHale who was translated from bishop of Killala to archbishop of Tuam in August 1834. Mac-Hale was an extraordinary man by any definition. He was a fervent nationalist, and one of the most scathing critics of British rule in Ireland. His nationalism was not without his rewards, for, according to one estimate, MacHale was by 1840 second only to Daniel O'Connell as the most popular man in Ireland.[90] MacHale's political programme included disestablishment of the anglican church, repeal of the union, tenant right, and the abolition of tithes. Noble as these ends were, MacHale had the unfortunate habit of pursuing them with little concern for the means he employed, and on the matter of education he was at his most fanatical and least scrupulous. MacHale had been suspicious of the national system from its start. On 8 March 1832, he had written his clergy from the Irish College in Rome:

Many thanks for your interesting communications regarding Ireland. Among the other topics you ask my opinion on the new plan of national education. It has one feature of some promise, that it has met with the disapprobation of some of the most rancorous foes of the religion of the people of Ireland.

Except in that negative merit, it is entitled to very little praise . . . It is a great mistake to imagine that because it is disliked by the abettors of the old proselytizing spirit, it should on that account alone be hailed by catholics . . . I will not dwell upon the dispro-portioned number of its catholic commissioners, where the vast majority of the poor to be educated is of that communion. I shall only advert to one condition which, if it be not a mistake, renders the system objectionable on principle. I mean that the books even for the religious department must be submitted to the choice or approval of the commissioners.

[90] Emmet Larkin, *The quarrel among the Roman Catholic hierarchy over the national system of education in Ireland, 1838–41* (Cambridge, Mass., 1965; originally published in *The Celtic Cross*, 1964), p. 142.

The standard lives of MacHale are Nuala Costello, *John MacHale, archbishop of Tuam* (Dublin, 1939), and Bernard O'Reilly, *John MacHale, archbishop of Tuam: his life, times and correspondence*, 2 vols (New York and Cincinnati, 1890).

See also F. Pius Devine, 'John MacHale, archbishop of Tuam', *Dublin Review*, cix (July, 1891), pp 27–40.

. . . Besides the one already mentioned there is another advantage in the new plan, that it is adopted by way of experiment, without having received, as yet, a legislative sanction. It is, on that account, the more necessary to expose its defects and watch its operation, lest, if it should silently gain ground, it should be as difficult to upset as the Kildare-Street Society . . .

To conclude, consult your bishop and him alone in the selection of books to be used in the schools and the hours set apart for religious instruction, and shall that selection not be approved by the board of education, the system ceases to be entitled to the confidence of the catholic people of Ireland.[91]

Despite all these misgivings, MacHale allowed the clergy under him to take government money under the regulations of the commissioners of national education, from the system's beginning until 1838, this without audible protest.

In late 1837, for reasons that his biographers do not make clear, MacHale changed his public attitude from sceptical neutrality to outright condemnation of the national system. Like Samson, MacHale attacked his enemies with the jawbone of an ass. He began contributing a series of open letters to Lord John Russell to the Dublin papers. These letters denounced various aspects of British policy in Ireland but focused increasingly upon education. Most of his criticism was about as far removed as possible from being a theological condemnation of the national system. For example, the main theme of a letter to Russell published in the *Dublin Evening Post*, on 1 January 1838, was that the commissioners stood convicted of not having allocated Connaught its share of available funds.

MacHale did not really reach top form until February 1838, when he attacked the government, the commissioners, and the policy which allowed an unnamed Roman Catholic member of the commissioners (Archbishop Murray) to veto the reading by catholic children of inflammatory books during the hours of religious instruction:

I take occasion to address your lordship thus briefly to remove a delusion under which many members of the legislature manifestly labour. They seem to be under the impression that it is competent for them, through the agency of boards of their selection, to assume

[91] *Freeman's Journal*, 9 May 1832.

and exercise complete control over the education—even the religious education—of the people . . . It is but right to acquaint your lordship that the catholic bishops alone have the right to regulate the choice of the books out of which the faithful are to draw the nutriment of piety and sound doctrine. It would be a lamentable day for Ireland that books of piety were regulated by the devotional taste of those alone to whom any government would wish to confine the spiritual care of the people . . . I beg leave, therefore, to assure Lord Stanley, and others who would wish to subject the catholic church to the influence of the ministers of the day, that to no authority on earth save the pope shall I submit the books from which the children of my diocese shall derive their religious instruction.[92]

This letter makes it appear that MacHale was as much concerned about the system's giving Archbishop Murray power over the religious books used in MacHale's archdiocese as he was about any danger to the faith of the catholic children. MacHale wrote further open letters to Russell dated 24 February, 8 March, 20 March, 10 May, and 4 August 1838. Coincident with his letter writing, MacHale organized clerical opinion in his archdiocese against the commissioners and eventually forced thirteen schools to sever connections with the national system.[93]

MacHale, assisted by Bishop O'Higgins of Ardagh, brought the matter to the attention of Rome, and on 2 May 1838 the pope ordered the Sacred Congregation of Propaganda to write both MacHale and Murray asking each for an account of the national system.[94] Meanwhile, battle lines were being drawn among the Irish bishops, and it became clear that MacHale commanded a strong ten-member minority of the twenty-six members of the Irish hierarchy.[95]

Before the two sides clashed, however, Archbishop Murray took on MacHale in a letter in the Dublin press. Murray directed the letter to MacHale rather than Russell or any other intermediary figure. Murray's literate and polished style was so

[92] *Dublin Evening Post*, 13 Feb. 1838.

[93] Larkin, p. 123; *Sixth report of the commissioners of national education in Ireland, for the year 1839*, pp 1–2.

[94] P. C. Barry, 'The holy see and the Irish national schools', *Irish Ecclesiastical Record*, 5 ser., xcii (Aug. 1959), p. 91.

[95] Larkin, p. 125.

different from MacHale's crudeness that one cannot help being surprised that they were both archbishops in the hierarchy of the same church. Murray pointed out to MacHale that Mac-Hale's own clergy had been among the system's most efficient supporters, and that the system had the concurrence of over 1,100 catholic clergymen and most of the bishops. He enclosed copies of two letters approving the system, one from Archbishop Crolly of Armagh, the other from Bishop Denvir of Down and Connor. Murray considered the objections to the system in some detail and concluded that it provided the most perfect freedom for catholic religious instruction and the most effective guards for tender consciences.[96] Much to the discomfiture of Rome, the exchange of letters in the public press continued, MacHale publishing two letters to Murray in November 1838, and Murray writing a reply in the same month.[97]

If Rome was embarrassed about the public brawling of the two archbishops, this did not mean that it would hurry its decision about the national system. Hence, when the Irish bishops met on 22 January 1838 for their annual general meeting, it was clear that they would have to do something about matters themselves. Three resolutions were passed. The first expressed a strong approval of the national system and declared that there was nothing in it injurious to faith or morals. The second approved highly of the conduct of the commissioners of national education, and expressed a hope that the parliamentary grant would be increased. The third expressed the determination of the prelates to watch most carefully lest any modification of the system be introduced that would be injurious to the catholic faith. Sixteen of the twenty-four prelates present voted for the resolutions.[98]

While the Irish hierarchy was affirming its approval of the national system, the Sacred Congregation of Propaganda was moving in the opposite direction. On 15 July the congregation answered the question 'whether, considering the nature and the form of the system of national education in Ireland, the participation of catholics therein could be tolerated' in the

---

[96] *Dublin Evening Post*, 23 Oct. 1838.
[97] *Dublin Evening Post*, 3, 10, 24 Nov. 1838.
[98] *Dublin Evening Post*, 5 Feb. 1839; Larkin, pp 128–130.

negative.[99] The condemnation was never promulgated by the pope, partially because of the delicacy of the whole issue, and more specifically because of a strong appeal to him by Archbishop Murray.[100] Each side was asked to send a deputy to Rome to argue the case, a process taking several months. When the Irish hierarchy met in February 1840 for its general meeting, matters were still unresolved. At that meeting, on 12 February 1840, a committee was appointed consisting of three prelates favouring the national system (Crolly, Kinsella, and Ryan) and three opposing it (MacHale, O'Higgins, and Keating) for the purpose of making arrangements concerning national education that would establish unanimity on the education question within the hierarchy. On 14 February a set of six demands drawn up by the committee was approved by the assembled bishops for transmittal to the lord lieutenant.

The first demand was that in every school for the mixed education of Roman Catholic and protestant children, a Roman Catholic bishop, parish priest, or curate should be patron of the school, with power to appoint and dismiss teachers. In the second place the bishops asked that no book or tract used for the moral or religious instruction of the Roman Catholic children be admitted into any national schools without the previous approbation of the four Roman Catholic archbishops. Third, the bishops asked that the Roman Catholic managers of mixed schools should have access to the schools at all times for the purpose of giving religious or moral instruction, and that every book used in a school for religious or moral instruction be approved by the Roman Catholic bishop of the diocese. Fourth, they asked that in the future the lord lieutenant select two lay catholic members for the board of commissioners from each of the four provinces and that one catholic bishop from each province be also appointed a commissioner. In the fifth place, the bishops asked that the lecturer appointed to instruct Roman Catholic candidates in the model schools in religion, morals and history, should be a Roman Catholic. Finally,

[99] Barry, p. 96. Larkin, p. 132, says the condemnation was of the scripture extracts, and, in contrast to Barry, makes no mention of its being a condemnation of the entire system.
[100] Barry, p. 97; Larkin, pp 132–3.

they asked that a model school be created in each of the four provinces.[101]

It is difficult to decide what this petition—to which, of course, the lord lieutenant refused to accede[102]—really meant. The phrase 'moral and religious' instruction was never defined, and was not one commonly used by the commissioners of national education. The commissioners drew a distinction between separate 'religious education' and combined 'moral and literary education', but never grouped 'moral' with 'religious'. Hence, it is hard to tell if the prelates were asking for control of all teaching that went on within the national schools, for control of only the religious teaching, or for control of the religious teaching plus some undefined portion of the combined instruction that was usually called 'moral and literary'. More fundamentally confusing is the question of whether or not this set of demands was meant to be a serious statement of what the hierarchy wanted. The instructions to the committee that drew up the resolutions indicated that they were to produce something on which all the prelates could agree; the demands, then, appear to be simply a statement of what MacHale's price would be for granting his approval to the system. This suggestion is reasonable in light of the fact that the majority was already satisfied with the system and persuasive if we assume that none of that majority would have refused to accept any of the baubles for which MacHale yearned.

MacHale somehow managed to ignore the fact that the 1840 resolutions were adopted, in the words of the petition to the lord lieutenant, 'for the purpose of receiving the unanimous co-operation of the Roman Catholic prelates in diffusing the advantages of national education'.[103] In his lenten pastoral for 1840 MacHale maintained that the February resolutions proved that the system was inconsistent with the maintenance of the catholic religion. Murray publicly refuted this interpretation, and another journalistic free-for-all began between the two.[104]

Finally, the Sacred Congregation, to whom the argument had been again referred, came to a decision at a meeting of 22

[101] *The Times*, 16 Aug. 1840; *Royal commission of inquiry into primary education (Ireland)*, vol. i, pt. 1, *Report of the commissioners*, pp 123–4.

[102] Ibid., p. 124.   [103] Ibid., p. 123.   [104] Larkin, p. 140.

December 1840. That decision was no decision, for the congregation resolved that no judgement should be passed on the matter and that the decision should be left to the conscience of the individual bishops.[105] The judgement was approved by the pope and transmitted to the four Irish archbishops in a document dated 16 January 1841:

Having, therefore, accurately weighed all the dangers, and all the advantages of the system, having heard the reasons of the contending parties—and having—above all, received the gratifying intelligence that for ten years since the introduction of this system of education, the catholic religion does not appear to have sustained any injury—the Sacred Congregation has, with the approbation of our Most Holy Father Pope Gregory the XVI, resolved that no judgement should be definitely pronounced in this matter, and that this kind of education should be left to the prudent discretion of each individual bishop . . . [In order] that, however, so momentous a question shall not be dismissed without suitable counsel and precautions, the Sacred Congregation has decided on giving the following admonitions—

1st. That all books which contain any noxious matter either against the canon or the purity of the sacred scriptures, or against the doctrine of the catholic church, or morality, ought to be removed from the schools . . .

2nd. That every effort is to be made that none but a catholic preceptor shall give religious, moral or historical lectures to the catholic schoolmasters in the model schools . . .

3rd. That it is much safer that literary instruction only should be given in mixed schools, that the fundamental articles, as they are called, and the articles in which all christians agree, should alone be taught there in common, reserving for separate instruction the tenets peculiar to each sect . . .

The Sacred Congregation desires that henceforward the bishops and other ecclesiastics should refrain from contending on this controversy in the newspapers, or other such publications . . .[106]

With the exception of the archdiocese of Tuam where MacHale laboured to create his own school system, the excitement of 1838–41 had very little direct impact on the

---

[105] Barry, p. 103; Larkin, p. 141.

[106] *Rescript of his holiness Pope Gregory XVI to the four archbishops of Ireland, in reply to the appeal to the holy see on the subject of the national system of education in Ireland* (Dublin, 1841).

national system.[107] Catholic children continued to increase on national school rolls throughout the 1840s. Catholic desires were never forced upon the commissioners, and no modifications were made to meet the demands of the catholic dissidents. We may surmise, however, that the catholic controversy had a considerable impact upon the action of the commissioners during the 1838–41 period. A question that might have been raised earlier when considering the commissioners' dealings with the presbyterians was intentionally postponed until this point: 'why, if the presbyterians were so short of money that they wished to join the national system, did the commissioners give in so easily to the extensive presbyterian demands, rather than hold firm until the presbyterians accepted the commissioners' terms?' The answer is that in early 1840, the commissioners were in a much weaker bargaining position than would at first appear. The fact that the number of children and number of schools in connection with the national system grew steadily during the 1830s disguised the fact that in 1839 and 1840 the system was in danger of complete collapse. It will be recalled that in 1839 the Church Education Society was founded to provide schooling for anglican children and such others as wished to attend. This development threatened the commissioners with the loss of most of their protestant adherents. If we realize that at the same time there was a strong possibility that the holy see would pronounce against the national system, thus robbing it of the majority of its Roman Catholic constituents, the weakness of the commissioners' position becomes clear. In such a position the commissioners, like politicians running for office, sought support any place they could find it. Since the presbyterians were at that time the only group willing to negotiate with them the commissioners had no choice but to deal with the presbyterians and to gain their backing no matter what the price. Thus, unwittingly, the activities of Archbishop MacHale and of the founders of the Church Education Society contributed to the presbyterian victory of 1840, and to the national system's becoming a network of denominational schools.

---

[107] The national system faced catholic opposition in the province of Tuam until MacHale's death in 1881, and his replacement by John Mac-Evilly who encouraged the government schools. Seamus Fenton, *It all happened* (Dublin, 1949), p. 188.

During the 1840s, the hierarchy maintained the attitude of watchfulness that Propaganda desired, and during the decade they found an increasing number of things about which to worry. As they became aware of the concessions made to the presbyterians the bishops at first were suspicious that they would provide openings for presbyterian proselytizing. Catholic suspicions were further aroused by the commissioners' decision, in 1845, to have all new schools vested in themselves, rather than in local patrons. The bishops strongly opposed these terms, but did not win full concession for another two decades. The commissioners' announcement during the late 1840s of plans to create model schools in each of the inspectorial districts created considerable apprehension, chiefly because the model schools were to be under the sole trusteeship and patronage of the commissioners. In addition, the modification of the religious rules in 1847 to accommodate Archdeacon Stopford seemed to the catholic prelates to open one more avenue for protestant proselytizing in the national schools. All the catholic apprehension on the above topics was to become tied to the controversy over the Queen's Colleges and thence to produce, after 1849, an aggressive and demanding attitude towards the national system.

5

Throughout most of the nineteenth century the government refused to admit that the Irish national school system was a denominational one in reality if not in law. We have already seen that the rules, or lack thereof, regulating non-vested schools gave the managers of such schools almost all the freedom possessed by managers of independent denominational schools. In this section it will be suggested that the national schools were *de facto* denominational institutions in terms of their personnel and in terms of their student body. It will become clear that the typical national school, whether vested or non-vested, was under the control of a manager of a single denomination, not of joint religious managers, that the teachers were almost inevitably of the same denomination as the manager, and that the children were preponderantly, and often solely, of the same faith as the manager and teachers. This situation held throughout the nineteenth century. Because of the availability of statistical data, the statistics cited will mostly be drawn from the second half of the century.

That the Irish national system of education turned into an effectively denominational one is partially the fault of the commissioners themselves. It will be remembered that Lord Stanley's instructions, and the original regulations of 1831, strongly encouraged joint applications by protestants and catholics for government aid, and stated that any applications stemming from one faith only would be investigated. In practice, the commissioners never made any attempt to enforce this rule. Thus, from the very beginning national schools were under the managership of persons of a single faith. Of the 4,795 schools in operation in 1852, only 175 were under joint managership.[108]

The denominational tone of the system was heightened by the fact that most managers were in holy orders. Some 3,418 of the 4,547 schools operating in 1850 were exclusively under clerical managers.[109] In 1900, 7,636 of the 8,684 national schools were under clerical managers.[110] Generally, the Roman Catholics tended to place greater reliance upon clerical managers than did the protestant denominations. The situation in 1867 was as follows:[111]

Denomination	% of schools under clerical managers	% of schools under lay managers
Roman Catholic	85%	15%
Established church	34%	66%
Presbyterian	62%	38%
Dissenters	61%	39%
National average	70%	30%

---

[108] *Eighteenth report of the commissioners of national education in Ireland, for the year 1851*, p. xlvii [1582], H.C. 1852–3, xlii.

[109] *Seventeenth report of the commissioners of national education in Ireland, for the year 1850*, vol. 1, p. i [1405], H.C. 1851, xxiv, pt i.

[110] *Sixty-seventh report of the commissioners of national education in Ireland, for the year 1900*, pp. 9, 12, 13 [Cd. 704], H.C. 1901, xxi.

[111] *Royal commission of inquiry into primary education (Ireland)*, vol. i, pt i, *Report of the commissioners*, p. 235.

It is hardly surprising that managers usually appointed only head teachers and assistant teachers of their own denomination to schools under their charge. The following table indicates the number of schools in which managers of one denomination appointed head or assistant teachers of another denomination. The figures are for the year 1867, when there were 6,349 schools in the national system:[112]

Provinces:	Anglican managers			R.C. managers			Presby. managers			Dissenting managers			Total
	R.C. teachers	Presby. teachers	Dissenting teachers	Anglican teachers	Presby. teachers	Dissenting teachers	Anglican teachers	R.C. teachers	Dissenting teachers	Anglican teachers	R.C. teachers	Presby. teachers	
Ulster	95	121	8	4	8	–	66	47	18	10	10	18	405
Munster	85	1	–	–	–	1	–	2	–	–	7	–	96
Leinster	63	4	–	–	–	–	1	1	–	–	–	–	69
Connaught	105	1	–	–	–	–	1	2	–	–	1	–	110
Total	348	127	8	4	8	1	68	52	18	10	18	18	680

Thus, only 10·7 per cent (680 of 6,349) of the national schools had, in 1867, a staffing arrangement that could be considered 'mixed'. As the table indicates, many of the instances in which a manager hired a head teacher or assistant of another denomination occurred when a protestant manager hired a teacher of a protestant denomination other than his own. If we exclude these cases and concentrate on the number of schools in which catholics hired protestant teachers and in which protestants hired catholic teachers, the total is only 6·8 per cent (431 of 6,349) of the total number of schools.

If much of the single denomination a character of school managerships, and consequently staffing, may be ascribed to the commissioners' failure to enforce their stated preferences for joint managerships, the fact that most schools contained children predominantly of one denomination was a result of forces

[112] Derived from *Royal commission of inquiry into primary education (Ireland)*, vol. vii, *Returns furnished by the national board*, p. 240 [C6–VI], H.C. 1870, xxviii, pt v.

beyond their control. The fact is that, except in Ulster, there simply were not enough protestants to make a significant degree of religious mixing among students possible. The census for 1861 may be taken as a reasonably representative indication of the way that the population was distributed throughout the century[113] as can be seen in the tabulation on the following pages. These data make it clear that throughout most of southern Ireland the achievement of a significant amount of religious mixing was not a realistic expectation. In many areas at best a few protestants were available for attendance at a national school, at worst none at all.

If anything, the census data will lead us to overestimate the number of protestant children available to attend national schools, for, outside of Ulster, the protestants tended to be middle class or better, and therefore unwilling to have their children schooled with the catholic peasant children who filled the national schools:

In Leinster, Munster, Connaught, protestants are principally to be found among the higher and middle classes; there are in general very few protestants of the class for which schools are intended, except in Dublin and in other cities or towns, where there are protestant schools supported by endowments, contributions from the clergy, collections after sermons etc. The mass of the poor, particularly in the rural districts, is composed of Roman Catholics; therefore, in these provinces, our schools are principally composed of them. In Ulster, the proportion of protestants to Roman Catholics in our schools approximates what it is in the mass of the population, but in the other provinces it does not and the reason is, that in Ulster there is an extensive poor protestant population, whereas in the other provinces that is not the case.[114]

The Church Education Society, while it flourished, further reduced the number of available protestants by providing a separate schooling for even the poorest members of the anglican faith.

The following table indicates the number of children of each

[113] Derived from, *Census of Ireland for the year 1861, report on religion and education*, pp 10–12 [3204–111], H.C. 1863, lix.

[114] Evidence of A. R. Blake, *Digest of evidence before the committees of the house of lords and commons in the year 1837, on the national system of education in Ireland*, p. 211.

CENSUS OF RELIGION, 1861

County, city or major town	Total no. of inhabitants	Anglican	% of total	R.C.	% of total	Presby.	% of total	Other	% of total
LEINSTER									
C. Carlow	57,137	6,229	10·9	50,539	88·4	106	·2	263	·5
T. Drogheda	14,740	1,031	7·0	13,342	90·5	207	1·4	160	1·1
Dublin City	254,808	49,251	19·4	196,549	77·2	4,875	1·9	4,133	1·5
Dublin Suburbs	50,485	17,668	35·0	29,639	58·7	1,724	3·4	1,454	2·9
C. Dublin	104,959	18,914	18·0	83,556	79·6	936	·9	1,453	1·5
C. Kildare	90,946	10,439	11·5	79,121	87·0	876	1·0	510	·5
Kilkenny City	14,174	1,242	8·8	12,769	90·1	97	·7	66	·4
C. Kilkenny	110,341	4,750	4·3	105,356	95·5	127	·1	108	·1
C. Kings	90,043	9,109	10·1	79,955	88·8	327	·4	652	·7
C. Longford	71,694	6,196	8·6	64,801	90·4	560	·8	137	·2
C. Louth	75,973	5,203	6·8	69,678	91·7	937	1·2	157	·3
C. Meath	110,373	6,492	5·9	103,327	93·6	428	·4	126	·1
C. Queen's	90,650	9,683	10·7	80,025	88·3	240	·3	702	·7
C. Westmeath	90,979	6,336	7·0	83,749	92·1	343	·4	551	·5
C. Wexford	143,954	12,759	8·9	130,103	90·4	287	·2	805	·7
C. Wicklow	86,479	15,285	17·7	70,044	81·0	285	·3	865	1·0
Leinster total	1,457,635	180,587	12·4	1,252,553	85·9	12,355	·9	12,140	·8
MUNSTER									
C. Clare	166,305	3,323	2·0	162,612	97·8	228	·1	142	·1
Cork City	80,121	10,632	13·3	67,148	83·8	881	1·1	1,460	1·8
C. Cork East	286,396	18,279	6·4	264,754	92·4	899	·3	2,464	·9
C. Cork West	178,301	14,543	8·2	162,140	90·9	219	·1	1,399	·8
C. Kerry	201,800	6,200	3·1	195,159	96·7	243	·1	198	·1
Limerick City	44,476	4,238	9·5	39,124	88·0	418	·9	696	·6
C. Limerick	172,801	5,648	3·3	166,604	96·4	148	·1	399	·2
C. Tipp. North	109,220	7,359	6·7	101,171	92·6	194	·2	496	·5
C. Tipp. South	139,886	5,441	3·9	133,710	95·6	304	·2	431	·3
Waterford City	23,293	1,989	8·5	20,429	87·7	234	1·0	639	2·8
C. Waterford	110,959	3,208	2·9	107,225	96·6	245	·2	281	·3

CENSUS OF RELIGION, 1861

County, city or major town	Total no. of inhabitants	Anglican	% of total	R.C.	% of total	Presby.	% of total	Other	% of total
ULSTER									
C. Antrim	247,564	45,275	18·3	61,369	24·8	131,687	53·2	9,233	3·7
C. Armagh	190,086	58,735	30·9	92,760	48·8	30,746	16·2	7,845	4·1
T. Belfast	120,777	29,832	24·7	41,237	31·4	42,229	35·0	7,482	6·2
Carrickfergus, C. of Town	9,422	1,821	19·3	1,046	11·1	5,582	59·2	973	10·4
C. Cavan	153,906	23,017	14·9	123,942	80·5	5,352	3·5	1,595	1·1
C. Donegal	237,395	29,943	12·6	178,182	75·1	26,215	11·0	3,055	1·3
C. Down	300,127	60,905	20·3	97,409	32·5	133,796	44·6	8,017	2·6
C. Fermanagh	105,763	40,608	38·4	59,751	56·5	1,909	1·8	3,500	3·3
C. Londonderry	184,209	31,218	16·9	83,402	45·3	64,602	35·1	4,987	2·7
C. Monaghan	126,482	17,721	14·0	92,799	73·4	15,149	12·0	813	·6
C. Tyrone	238,500	52,240	21·9	134,716	56·5	46,568	19·5	4,976	2·1
Ulster total	1,914,236	391,315	20·4	966,613	50·5	503,835	26·3	52,473	2·8
CONNAUGHT									
T. Galway	16,967	837	4·9	15,621	92·1	189	1·1	320	1·9
C. Galway	254,511	7,365	2·9	246,330	96·8	392	·2	424	·1
C. Leitrim	104,744	9,488	9·1	94,006	89·7	338	·3	912	·9
C. Mayo	254,796	6,739	2·6	246,583	96·8	961	·4	513	·1
C. Roscommon	157,272	5,728	3·6	151,047	96·1	277	·2	220	·1
C. Sligo	124,845	10,438	8·4	112,436	90·1	931	·7	1,040	·8
Connaught total	913,135	40,595	4·5	866,023	94·8	3,088	·3	3,429	·4
Ireland total	5,798,564	693,357	11·9	4,505,265	77·7	523,291	9·0	77,054	1·4

of the major denominations in the national schools at ten year intervals from 1860:[115]

Year	R.C. on roll	% of total	Anglicans on roll	% of total	Presby. on roll	% of total	Others on roll	% of total	Total on rolls
1860	455,582	83·11	30,863	5·63	59,086	10·78	2,607	·48	804,000
1870	807,330	80·82	74,237	7·44	110,189	10·02	7,243	·72	998,999
1880	855,057	79·0	102,218	9·4	115,629	10·7	10,116	·9	1,083,020
1890	799,797	77·2	111,467	10·7	110,666	10·6	15,178	1·5	1,037,102
1900	559,520	75·0	88,675	11·9	83,254	11·2	39,173	1·9	770,622

These figures should be compared with the statistics of religious distribution of the population in order to gain proper perspective:[116]

Census periods	R.C.s No.	% of pop.	Anglicans No.	% of pop.	Presbyterians No.	% of pop.	Others No.	% of pop.	Total population
1861	4,505,265	77·69	693,357	11·96	523,291	9·02	77,054	1·33	5,798,564
1871	4,150,867	76·69	667,998	12·34	497,648	9·20	95,868	1·77	5,412,377
1881	3,960,891	76·54	639,574	12·36	470,734	9·10	103,637	2·00	5,174,836
1891	3,547,307	75·40	600,103	12·75	444,974	9·46	114,366	3·09	4,704,750
1901	3,308,661	74·21	581,089	13·03	443,276	9·94	125,749	2·82	4,458,775

If the lack of protestants hindered mixing, the creation of

[115] Derived from, *Twenty-seventh report of the commissioners of national education in Ireland, for the year 1860*, pp 6, 8 [2873], H.C. 1861, xx; *Thirty-seventh report . . ., for the year 1870*, pp 9, 12, 13 [C 360], H.C. 1871, xxiii; *Forty-seventh report . . ., for the year 1880*, pp 3, 4, 5, 7 [C 2925], H.C. 1881, xxxiv; *Fifty-seventh Report . . ., for the year 1890*, pp 6, 9 [C 6411], H.C. 1890–91, xxix; *Sixty-seventh report . . ., for the year 1900*, p. 13 [Cd 704], H.C. 1901, xxl.

Working with the commissioners' statistics is a numerical nightmare. The commissioners often failed to define precisely what any figure given referred to, and, further, were rarely bothered with the niceties of maintaining the comparability of data from one year's report to the next, or, for that matter, within a single report. Whenever possible the muddle will be clarified in footnotes. For example, in the table of children by religious faith, the figures for 1860, 1870, and 1880 are for all children who appeared on the rolls for the national schools, even if only for a day. The figures for 1890 are for the number of children who made an attendance in the fortnight before the figures were collected. The figures for 1900 are for the average number on the rolls. Thus, if we use the 1860–1880 methodology as our base, the figures for 1890 understate the total number of children in each category, and the figures for 1900 understate the number even more.

It is hardly necessary to add that none of the figures of any sort given by the commissioners should be taken as definitive, but merely as indicative of the general state of the system.

[116] *Census of Ireland, 1901, pt. II, General report with illustrative maps, diagrams, tables, and appendix*, p. 50 [Cd 1190], H.C. 1902, cxxix.

non-vested schools reinforced the tendencies for the schools to be of a single denomination. Non-vested schools tended to attract only children of a single denomination, since the managers thereof were not required to allow their schools to be open for the religious teaching of minority groups. The only concession made to a child of a minority religion in a non-vested school was that he was allowed to absent himself from the religious teaching of the majority. The numbers of non-vested schools during the second half of the century were as follows:[117]

Year	Non-vested schools	Total no. of operational schools	% non-vested schools compared to total no. of schools
1850	3,076	4,547	68%
1860	4,073	5,632	72%
1870	5,019	6,806	74%
1880	5,681	7.590	75%
1890	5,545	8,298	67%
1900	5,762	8,684	66%

Although non-vested status in its post-1840 interpretation was the result of presbyterian pressures, the Roman Catholic clergy were swift to seize upon its advantages once they became apparent. In 1850, 2,310 of the 3,076 non-vested schools were under clerical managers. Of the 2,310 clerical managers, 1,746 were Roman Catholic priests or prelates.[118]

Another type of school, the monastic and convent school, further undercut the mixed principle, since such schools were run by catholic lay brothers and sisters and did not appeal to the parents of protestant children. Most monastic institutions followed the Christian Brothers' example and refused connection with the commissioners: even by the early 1890s there were only thirty-seven monastic schools associated with the national

[117] Derived from the *Seventeenth report of the commissioners of national education in Ireland, for the year 1850*, vol. i, p. 1 [1405], H.C. 1851, xxiv, pt i; *Twenty-seventh report . . ., for the year 1860*, pp 5, 11; *Thirty-seventh report . . ., for the year 1870*, pp 9, 12; *Forty-seventh report . . ., for the year 1880*, pp 3–5; *Fifty-seventh report . . ., for the year 1890* pp 5, 6; *Sixty-seventh report . . ., for the year 1900*, pp 9, 12, 13.

[118] *Appendix to the seventeenth report of the commissioners of national education in Ireland, for the year 1850*, p. 479.

school system.[119] The convent schools, on the other hand, joined the system with great alacrity. In the late 1850s, there were 112 convent schools in connection with the national commissioners, enrolling 44,116 girls. Only forty-one of the students were non-catholic. One hundred and three of the 112 schools were exclusively catholic.[120]

All of the factors that have been mentioned—the commissioners' willingness to accept separate applications, demographic factors, the creation of non-vested schools, and the existence of convent and monastic schools—meant that the national system could never be a mixed system in terms of having a religiously heterogeneous student body. The table that follows indicates the number of mixed schools in each province:[121]

Year	Ulster		Munster		Leinster		Connaught		Total		
	No. of mixed schools	% of total schools mixed	No. of mixed schools	% of total schools mixed	No. of mixed schools	% of total schools mixed	No. of mixed schools	% of total schools mixed	No. of schools	No of mixed schools	% of total schools mixed
1862	1,720	81·1	434	30·5	535	39·7	390	45·5	5,745	3,079	53·6
1870	2,047	82·6	672	40·5	693	46·7	513	48·6	6,806	3,925	58·8
1880	2,136	71·0	746	38·9	772	48·4	521	42·8	7,590	4,175	55·6
1890	1,937	62·8	673	32·9	735	43·2	521	36·4	8,298	3,866	46·7
1900	1,504	46·4	577	27·3	604	33·2	403	27·1	8,684	3,088	35·6

In reality the above statistics of mixed schools overstate the degree of mixing, because a school was counted as mixed if there

[119] *Return showing the number of monastic schools in Ireland under the national board of education, with the name of each; the number of children on the roll of each school; the number of children in average daily attendance at each; the number of teachers employed; and the names of the several religious orders to which they belong; and, copies of the form of application for the school to be taken under the board, and of the form in the quarterly returns certifying that the rules of the board have been duly observed*, pp 2–3, H.C. 1893–4 (243), lxviii.

[120] (James Kavanagh). *Mixed Education, the catholic case stated; or, principles, working, and results of the system of national education with suggestions for the settlement of the education question, most respectfully dedicated to the catholic archbishops and bishops of Ireland* (London and Dublin, 1859), p. 249.

[121] Derived from *Twenty-ninth report of the commissioners of national education in Ireland, for the year 1862*, pp xiv–xv [3235], H.C. 1863, xvii pt i; *Thirty-seventh report . . ., for the year 1870*, pp 9, 16; *Forty-seventh report . . ., for the year 1880* pp 3, 6, 10, 12; *Fifty-seventh report . . ., for the year 1890*, pp. 12–14; *Sixty-seventh report . . ., for the year 1900*, pp 12–16.

was even a solitary protestant in a catholic school, or *vice versa*. Following are statistics which indicate that in only a few of the 'mixed' schools was there any semblance of balance between the religious groups:[122]

Year	Pupils in mixed schools staffed exclusively by Roman Catholics				Pupils in mixed schools staffed exclusively by protestants				Pupils in mixed schools jointly staffed			
	# Roman Catholics	*% Roman Catholics*	*# Protestants*	*% Protestants*	*# Roman Catholics*	*% Roman Catholics*	*# Protestants*	*% Protestants*	*# Roman Catholics*	*% Roman Catholics*	*# Protestants*	*% Protestants*
1870	364,154	93·6	25,076	6·4	29,540	12·6	125,260	87·4	12,887	40·2	14,226	59·8
1880	377,677	94·0	24,011	6·0	25,183	16·4	127,868	83·6	10,580	47·0	11,923	53·0
1890	309,355	94·3	18,611	5·7	15,536	12·2	111,623	87·8	6,515	50·7	6,340	49·3
1900	176,613	94·6	10,024	5·4	6,581	9·4	63,270	90·6	3,843	63·0	2,260	37·0

By approximately mid-century, then, the national system had become a denominational system. Throughout the system, catholic children were taught in schools normally run by a catholic manager (usually the parish priest) and staffed solely by catholic teachers. Protestant children were taught in protestant schools managed by the local vicar or landlord and staffed solely by protestants. Butt described the situation in Dublin:

Walking down King's-Inn-street, the passenger may see, divided by a narrow line, two separate buildings, both bearing the inscription of 'national school'. On the one side of the line is a school under the management of the ladies of a convent; on the other is the school of a presbyterian church. Not a single protestant child attends the one—not a single Roman Catholic child the other.[123]

[122] Derived from the *Thirty-seventh report of the commissioners of national education in Ireland, for the year 1870*, pp 12–16; *Forty-seventh report . . ., for the year 1880*, pp 3, 4, 10; *Fifty-seventh report . . ., for the year 1890*, p. 12; *Sixty-seventh report . . ., for the year 1900*, pp 14–15.

The reader would do well to concentrate upon interpreting the percentages in the table and should use the enrollment numbers only as the most general indication of the number of children in mixed schools. The commissioners were at their most inscrutable in compiling these figures; they did not make clear to what the numbers referred. It is probable that the figures for 1900 refer to the number of children of each denomination on the rolls on 31 December 1900, those for 1890, 1880, and 1870 to the total number who at any time were upon the rolls of any national school.

[123] Butt, p. 7.

One is entitled to ask, 'How did the national system differ from a denominational system?' The only major differences were that in the national schools religious instruction was restricted to hours of the manager's choice which had to be announced in advance, that no child was compelled to remain during the religious instruction of children of faith other than his own, and that in vested schools (but not non-vested schools), clergy of all denominations had the right of access during hours of religious instruction. In practice, it may be argued, these restrictions had little effect because no reasonable school-manager could give religious instruction all the time anyway, and because the rules designed to protect minorities did not apply to the great number of schools in which no minorities were present. Granted, in a few areas truly undenominational education did exist, with joint managers, joint teachers, an evenly mixed student body, and with parson and priest of protestant and catholic faiths regularly providing religious instruction to their respective flocks. But such cases were the rare exception. In reality, the system was, in a fortunate phrase, 'undenominational in theory but denominational in practice'.[124] In one of the ironies of Irish history, the majority of anglican clergymen and of Roman Catholic prelates failed to perceive that *de facto* denominationalism reigned, and during the 1850s and 1860s agitated strenuously for a denominational system to replace the allegedly undenominational one.

[124] John Mescal, *Religion in the Irish system of education* (London and Dublin, 1957), p. 107.

VI

THE POLITICS OF THE CURRICULUM 1831–54

~~~~~~

I

WHILE GIRDING OURSELVES FOR more ecclesiastical and administrative intrigue, we should look briefly at the lowest rung of the national school bureaucracy, the national school classroom, to get an idea of what was going on there. In this chapter we will discuss very briefly the textbooks used in the national school classroom and then turn to the central issue of the religious controversy that arose around the scripture extracts. This controversy was a turning point in the history of the national system, for it led to the resignation of Archbishop Whately and then to a crippling reduction in the commissioners' ability to withstand ecclesiastical pressures. Once Whately had gone it was certain that the national system would not long continue to operate according to the instructions of 1831. Hence, in viewing the scripture extracts crisis we are actually watching the prologue to a revolution in the administration of the Irish national system of education.

Turning first for a glance at the average national school classroom, we find that it was far from palatial. The Powis Report of 1870 judged nearly nine per cent of the non-vested schools to be insufficiently lighted and ten per cent to be improperly ventilated. Even in 1868, six per cent of the vested national schools had earthen floors, the figure for non-vested

225

schools being almost twenty-three per cent. Such floors were especially cold in winter and, given the large numbers of bare-foot children, contributed to the irregularity of attendance, especially of the younger children.[1] The average national school consisted of only one or two rooms. The figures below, for the year 1867, indicate that average daily attendance was rarely more than seventy-five and often a good deal less:[2]

Average daily attendance of school	% of national schools
15 and under	·448%
16 to 20	2·555%
21 to 25	8·164%
26 to 30	15·151%
31 to 35	14·769%
36 to 40	11·566%
41 to 50	17·607%
51 to 75	20·345%
76 to 100	5·277%
101 to 150	2·207%
151 to 200	·477%
201 to 300	·199%
above 300	·016%
no information	1·261%

In a typical national school, row upon row of children sat at long communal desks facing the teacher. Eighteen inches per pupil was commonly allowed; thus a desk of ten and a half feet in length normally accommodated seven pupils. A row desk of this sort and the seat were estimated to take up only slightly more than two feet in width.[3]

Within this environment the teacher was expected to teach children of all ages and attainments. In the typical national school, one would observe one or two classes standing up to receive instruction from the teacher and a monitor, all the rest sitting, some for advanced work in writing or arithmetic, but the great majority, especially the younger children, being idle. Since most teachers spent their time teaching class after class in this manner, the majority of the pupils spent the day doing nothing. In the typical school, secular instruction took four and

[1] *Royal commission of inquiry into primary education (Ireland)*, vol. i, pt i, *Report of the commissioners*, p. 229 [C 6], H.C. 1870, xxviii, pt i.

[2] Ibid., pp 268–9.

[3] Patrick W. Joyce, *A handbook of school management and methods of teaching* (Dublin, 1863), pp 1–5.

a half or five hours a day, beginning usually at ten o'clock and
concluding around two thirty or three o'clock.[4] Rote teaching
was not widely practised in the national schools. Teachers, after
a talk or a reading lesson, usually questioned the children on
the contents and attempted to elicit some indication of understanding on the child's part. Questions by children were encouraged and teachers were expected to be prepared to deal
with questions arising from any of their lessons.[5] Discipline was
maintained in the classroom by the threat of corporal punishment, as well as by more humane methods. In one exceptional
case it was necessary for the authorities to exhume the body of a
child who had died following a beating in the Shinrone National
School in order to determine whether or not the beating was
responsible for his death.[6]

Surrounded by children of all ages and attainments, about
half the national school teachers could at least be grateful that
they had only boys or only girls under their charge, not both. A
return of 1843 indicated that 1,944 of 4,088 national school
classrooms (as distinct from entire schools) were used exclusively
by either boys or girls.[7] At century's end single-sex schools comprised roughly half the total number of national schools: in 1900
there were 1,973 male schools, 2,244 female and infant schools,
and 4,464 coeducational schools.[8]

The one thing that almost all national school teachers had in
common was the series of textbooks published by the commissioners of national education. Although the use of the books
was not compulsory, they were almost universally used anyway.[9]

[4] Ibid., pp 15, 37–41.

[5] Ibid., pp 91–3; [James Kavanagh], *Mixed education, the catholic case
stated; or principles, working, and results of the system of national education, with
suggestions for the settlement of the education question, most respectfully dedicated
to the catholic archbishops and bishops of Ireland* (Dublin, 1859), pp 41–2.

[6] The cause of death was ruled to be an inflammation of the brain of
long standing. *Saunder's*, 11, 12, 14 May 1855.

[7] *Fourteenth report of the commissioners of national education in Ireland, for the
year 1847*, p. 206 [981], H.C. 1847–8, xxix.

[8] *Sixty-seventh report of the commissioners of national education in Ireland, for the
year 1900*, p. 23 [Cd 704], H.C. 1901, xxi. Three schools did not report.

[9] James Godkin, *Education in Ireland; its history, institutions, system, statistics and progress, from the earliest times to the present* (London and Dublin, 1862),
p. 93; *Royal commission of inquiry into primary education (Ireland)*, vol. i, pt I,
Report of the commissioners, p. 39.

It might be argued that compulsion was implied by the commissioners' regulations, for the commissioners did require that if any book other than one published or sanctioned by them was employed, permission must be obtained from them for its use. In practice they were careful in exercising their veto right over school books, and there was no significant objection on religious or other grounds to their actions. (In 1831 and 1832, before they could publish their own books, the commissioners sanctioned the use of the books of the Kildare Place Society and those of the Catholic Book Society, the latter being slightly altered with the consent of the publishers.)[10] The commissioners scrupulously honoured the regulation allowing the manager of any school to refuse to use the commissioners' books, and in one case went so far as to allow a manager who did not like their *Third book of lessons*, but who did not feel like naming a substitute book, simply to stop conducting a third class in his school, since this was his preference.[11]

Granted, the commissioners' books were used in almost all national schools during the hours of combined instruction, but we must look further than the commissioners' rules for the explanation of this fact. One major reason why the commissioners' books were employed was that they were cheap. The original instructions were that they should supply books to the national schools at half price. It soon became clear that merely cutting the price would not drive out the books already in use, and the commissioners sought permission to grant a stock of their books without charge to each national school. Permission was granted in October 1833.[12] The free stock was renewed at the end of every four years and, after 1848, every three years, the value granted varying according to the average daily attendance of the school. The free stock, it should be noted, was not sufficiently large to suffice for the wants of the entire school,[13] but it was an effective carrot for the introduction of the commissioners' books, and so successful that in 1863 the commissioners were

[10] M.C.N.E.I., 26 Jan. 1832; *Royal commission of inquiry into primary education (Ireland)*, vol. i, pt i, *Report of the commissioners*, p. 38.

[11] M.C.N.E.I., 14 Mar. 1856.

[12] *Report from the select committee appointed to inquire into the progress and operation of the new plan of education in Ireland*, p. 10, H.C. 1837 (485), ix.

[13] *Twenty-first report of the commissioners of national education in Ireland, for the year 1854*, pp 45–57 [1950], H.C. 1854–5, xxiii, pt. i.

able to do away altogether with the triennial grant of free stock.[14]

When managers bought school books they found that the commissioners set the prices of them at attractively low levels. The prices below are those charged in 1846 for the most popular of the commissioners' books:[15]

Short title	Price to national schools		Price to poor schools not in connection		Price to public	
	s.	d.	s.	d.	s.	d.
First book of lessons	0	0 1/2	0	1	0	2
Second book of lessons	0	2	0	4	0	7
Sequel to second book	0	3	0	6	0	9
Third book of lessons	0	4	0	8	1	2
Fourth book of lessons	0	5	0	10	1	4

The other lure of the commissioners' books was that they were very good; indeed, during their first three decades they probably were the best set of school books produced in the British Isles. One witness before the 1837 select committee, a man familiar with the books used by the voluntary societies in England, testified:

I think they are far superior to any school-books I ever saw, and I have sent down some specimens of them to the towns with which I am connected in the north; and it has been so generally the persuasion of everyone, that I know one schoolmaster of an extensive national school who at his own expense has sent up and bought a set of them.[16]

The best testimonials to the books' quality were the requests for books that came to the commissioners for their works. The commissioners supplied books to schools of more than a dozen countries, in addition to Scotland and England. The commissioners appointed a London agent for their books in January 1836, and an Edinburgh agent in May 1836.[17] Business boomed, especially in London. A most significant testimonial to the books' high quality came from the English committee of council on education.

[14] M.C.N.E.I., 18 Sep. 1863.

[15] *Thirteenth report of the commissioners of national education in Ireland, for the year 1846* pp 47–50.

[16] *Digest of the evidence before the committees of the houses of lords and commons in the year 1837 on the national system of education in Ireland* (London, 1838), p. 29.

[17] M.C.N.E.I., 14 Jan. 1836, 12 May 1836.

Dealings between the Irish commissioners and the English committee began in January 1842, when James Kay (later Kay-Shuttleworth), secretary of the committee of council on education, requested, on behalf of the secretary of state for the colonies, a set of national school texts for the information of the governor of Trinidad.[18] In December 1847, Kay-Shuttleworth wrote requesting the terms upon which the commissioners would sell Irish national school books to the English committee of council on education. The commissioners replied that they would provide them at fifteen per cent over cost with these provisos: that the minimum order be 5000 copies in sheets, or 1000 copies bound, that the scale of prices be uniform and not drop as increasing quantities were bought, that the freight be paid by the English, and that prices be subject to change if supply prices changed.[19] An agreement was struck, and in 1848 the commissioners' sales to the committee of council on education averaged about £300 per month.[20] The commissioners also agreed to supply with books English workhouse schools and poor schools, including those schools associated with the various societies, on the same terms as to the committee of council.[21]

During the 1850s the commissioners exported almost as many books as they kept at home. In 1851 the commissioners sold nearly 300,000 books to Irish schools and gave away almost 100,000 more. In the same year about 100,000 books were sold in the English market. According to a conservative estimate, about 300,000 Irish national school books were sold to English buyers in 1859. The same source estimates that nearly one million Irish school books were being used in England in that year.[22] In 1861 the royal commission on popular education in England was forced to admit, despite their disapproval of the Irish national school text, that they were the most popular and widely used set of books in England.[23]

The most important of the books were, of course, the basic

---

[18] M.C.N.E.I., 13 Jan. 1842.   [19] M.C.N.E.I., 16 Dec. 1847.

[20] *Fifteenth report of the commissioners of national education in Ireland, for the year 1848*, p. 6 [1066], H.C. 1849, xxiii.

[21] M.C.N.E.I., 21 Dec. 1848, 1 Nov. 1849.

[22] J. M. Goldstrom, 'Richard Whately and political economy in school books,' *Irish Historical Studies*, xv, pp 136–7 (Sept. 1966).

[23] Quoted in *Royal commission of inquiry into primary education (Ireland)*, vol. i. pt i: *Report of the commissioners*, p. 117.

reading series.[24] These books formed a logical, integrated sequence of instruction, taking the child from elementary literacy

[24] Most of the commissioners' works, from 1831 to 1870, are listed below by short title, with the author's name and date of introduction given whenever it is known. Books still in use in 1870 are denoted by 'ff' following the date of introduction (*Royal commission of inquiry into primary education (Ireland)*, vol. vii, *Returns furnished by the national board*, pp 209–10 [C 6–VI], H.C. 1870, xxviii, pt v.

Title	Chief author	Years used
First Book of Lessons	James Carlile	1831–65
First Book of Lessons, 2 parts	William McCreedy	1865–7
First Book of Lessons, 1 volume	William McCreedy	1867 ff
Second Book of Lessons	James Carlile	1831–65
Second Book of Lessons	William McCreedy	1865–7
Second Book of Lessons	William McCreedy	1867 ff
Sequel to Second Book of Lessons	Richard Whately	1844–65
Third Book of Lessons	William McDermott	1835–46
Third Book of Lessons revised by	Richard Whately	1846–66
Third Book of Lessons	William McCreedy	1866–7
Third Book of Lessons	William McCreedy	1867 ff
Fourth Book of Lessons	James Carlile	1835–67
Fourth Book of Lessons	William McCreedy	1867 ff
Supplement to the Fourth Book	Richard Whately	1846–??
Fifth Book of Lessons	James Carlile and Alex. McArthur	1835 ff
Reading Book for Girls' Schools	James Carlile	1838 ff
Biographical Sketches of British Poets	Maurice Cross	1849 ff
Selection from the British Poets, 2 volumes	Maurice Cross	1849 ff
Introduction to the Art of Reading	Spaulding	1837 ff (for teachers)
English Grammar	Alex. McArthur	1836 ff
Key to Exercise in English Grammar	Alex. McArthur	1838 ff
First Book of Arithmetic	Alex. McArthur	1836 ff
Arithmetic in Theory and Practice	John Gregory	1835 ff
Key to above	James McGauley	1835 ff
Bookkeeping	James Carlile	1839 ff
Epitome of Geography	James Carlile	1844 ff
Elements of Geometry	Clairant	1836 ff
Treatise on Mensuration	John Gregory	1836 ff
Lectures on Natural Philosophy	James McCauley	1842–60 (after 1860 published in three volumes)

to fairly sophisticated lessons in geography, science, and literature. The *First book of lessons* was a small volume intended to
make the child familiar with the forms of the letters and thence
to teach him how to read words of one syllable and then how to
form and understand short written sentences. The modern
reader is apt to be struck by two things about the material in
the books. The first of these is that the sentences through which
the children learned to read were yeasty, interesting, but often
lacking in taste: 'Snap bit a rat; its leg bled; it is in a trap;
do not let it slip.'[25] Second, one is struck by the fact that these
sentences, although arranged in a paragraph were often merely
a series of *non sequiturs*, with no story to give continuity. The
following was typical: 'The beef is quite raw; will you roast it?
A flail is used to part the grain from the straw.'[26]

From the first book the children progressed to the *Second book
of lessons*, an all-purpose primer, which continued reading and
spelling practice, while introducing lessons on a variety of
subjects. The book contained the fundamentals of geographic
knowledge, some material on English grammar and upon
natural history, as well as a good deal of biblical history and
general moralizing. Because the jump from the *Second book of
lessons* to the *Third* was too great for most children, two sequels
to the second book were written. (Confusingly, the first to be
written was generally known as 'Sequel no. 2', the second to
appear as 'Sequel no. 1.') The purpose of each of these books
was to communicate factual knowledge to the children, and
each was edited upon the assumption that children using the
book would have already acquired basic reading skills. 'Sequel
no. 2' covered such diverse topics as the discovery of America,

Scripture Lessons, two Old		
Testament, two New Testament	James Carlile	1837 ff
Sacred Poetry	James Carlile	1837 ff
Agricultural Class-book	William Hickey	1848–67
Agricultural Class-book	Th. Baldwin	1867 ff
Farm Account Book	Th. Baldwin	1850 ff
Needlework Book	Mrs Campbell	1838 ff

[25] *First book of lessons for the use of schools* (Dublin, 1836), p. 11. Throughout the text of this chapter a short title for the books will be given. The
complete reference will be given in the footnotes.
[26] Ibid., p. 28.

the natural geography of the world, and the zoology of birds and quadrupeds. The work was essentially an attempt to fill in the child's knowledge of the world in logical, assimilable chunks. 'Sequel no. 1' was equally diverse but a trifle less advanced in content. The *Third* and *Fourth* books of lessons were constructed on the same plan as the preceding books and carried the instruction in each area to succeedingly higher levels. By the time the student finished the *Fifth book of lessons* he was able to read most books in the English language.

The detractors of the national system often asserted that the instruction given was solely elementary in character and that the system should bear the charge of having smothered the high attainments of the hedge schools. If we forget for the moment the question of how accurate these estimates of hedge school excellence may be, the charge has a certain plausibility. The commissioners' reports made it clear that the majority of children were engaged in studying the lower textbooks. In 1865 the distribution of children according to proficiency was as follows:[27]

Book	I Book	II Book	II Book Sequels	III Book	IV and higher Books	Total
Numbers:	282,196	182,088	70,240	93,893	46,739	675,156
Percentage:	41·80	26·97	10·40	13·91	6·92	100·00

The figures, however, mask the fact that the national schools gave an opportunity for education into what would presently be known as the 'intermediate' level. Although the majority of children stayed on for only two or three years, the fact remains that a number of national schools provided the opportunity for education into early adolescence. An examination of the science texts, for example, reveals that the children were given the chance to learn physics and chemistry on a level roughly equivalent to that taught in intermediate schools of the present day:

In estimating the volume of a gas, it is necessary to take its hygrometric state into account. For, if it contains moisture, the pressure . . . it exerts is made up of its own, and that of the vapour of water.[28]

---

[27] *Thirty-second report of the commissioners of national education in Ireland, for the year 1865*, p. 13 [3713], H.C. 1866, xxix.

[28] *Natural philosophy for the use of teachers and schools: electricity—galvanism—magnetism—electro-magnetism—heat—the steam-engine*, (Dublin, 1860), p. 126.

A series of science books filled with such explanations was hardly designed for elementary school children. Likewise, the grammar text was on a level that certainly would not be employed today below the intermediate level. The books of selection from the British poets and the biography of those poets were close to being on the level of adult literature. The following passage from the *Fifth book of lessons* indicates that those who progressed to this stage were dealing with material far above the juvenile level:

The bones form, as it were, the foundation of the body; and, besides being a basis or groundwork for the soft parts, are intended to enclose and support some organs which are of the first importance in the animal frame.

The skull or cranium, which contains the brain, is fixed at the top of the vertebral column, or bones of the back; in the centre of those bones is a hollow space destined for the reception of the spinal marrow, a substance which is a prolongation of the brain, and resembles it a good deal in nature and function.[29]

Granted that the majority of children did not attain much more than functional literacy in the Irish national schools, it is nevertheless true that, until 1872, nothing prevented the teachers from taking their best pupils on to intermediate instruction if both the teacher and the pupil were capable of working at that level. Moreover, the commissioners cooperated with those desiring advanced schooling by providing suitable texts for advanced study at cheap rates. The critics of the national schools are correct, however, in one respect: the national schools did not make any provision for the attainment of the polite and prestigious classical and modern foreign languages. Thus, the commissioners banished from the countryside the incessant misquoters of Latin tags and French epigrams. In defining the curriculum the commissioners were, if not utilitarian, certainly practical-minded. Given the pupils for whom they had actually to determine the curriculum, they preferred to encourage elementary chemistry and physics rather than Latin and Greek.

But if the commissioners emphasized science and mathematics, they did not go so far as to introduce much useful work into the curriculum. With the exception of the small number of

[29] *Fifth Book of Lessons for the use of the Irish national schools* (Dublin, 1835), p. 216.

agricultural schools and industrial schools, and of the girls' needlework classes, the national schools' curriculum was notable for its irrelevance to everyday Irish life. According to one contemporary observer the education had:

no direct bearing on the future career of the pupils. They are trained to exercise their memory, to be passive recipients of knowledge, to be quiet, submissive, and obedient and occasionally to sing the national anthem ... We anticipate the reply to such a statement: that Marlborough Street and Glasnevin are perfect models. Yes, perfect models; and so probably are the War Office and the Horse Guards, yet both failed, when they attempted to travel from theory to practice.[30]

The closest things to instruction relevant to the Irish economy was the *Agricultural class book* which attempted in simple language to teach how to best manage a small farm and kitchen garden. The book covered everything from crop rotation to field drainage to proper diet for farm labourers and was an admirable collection of popularized agricultural theory. But without practical work in a school garden the book remained just that: a statement of theory that was interesting to read, but whose suggestions were not apt to be brought into practice.[31]

One of the most important things to realize about the Irish national school textbooks is that they were not godless or 'secular' in the modern sense of the word. Actually, they were crammed full of moralizing and religiosity, and differed from denominational texts only in their religious content being neutral as between Christian denominations. James Carlile, the author of most of the first series of basic reading books, testified that he modelled the books upon those of the Catholic Book Society intermixing, however, a much larger amount of secular information than the catholic books contained.[32] Each of the textbooks was approved by each of the commissioners before being added to the commissioners' list. Of all the books, the *First book of lessons* was the least saturated in religion, probably

[30] *Daily Express*, 8 Oct. 1856.

[31] *Agricultural class book; or, how best to cultivate a small farm and garden: together with hints on domestic economy* (Dublin, 1848), passim.

[32] *Report from the select committee of the house of lords appointed to inquire into the practical working of the system of national education in Ireland*, p. 5, H.C., 1854 (525), xv, pt i.

because the children had not at that stage developed a vocabulary sufficient to deal with much religious reading. Even so, it contained such paragraphs as:

God loves us, and sent his Son to save us. The word of God tells us to love him. If we are bad, God will not love us, and we will not go to him, when we go from this world.[33]

The *Second book of lessons* included a great deal of biblical history and basic theology. In its second lesson the children learned:

God made man. He gave him ears to hear, eyes to see, a nose to smell, a mouth to taste and speak, hands to feel and work, and legs and feet to walk. He gave him sense to teach him right from wrong, and a soul that cannot die. *My dear child, thus are we made; then how ought we to love and serve the great God!*[34]

Also included was a paraphrase of the creation story and lessons on Adam and Eve, Cain and Abel, the flood, the tower of Babel and other Old Testament lore. The sequels and the *Third book of lessons* dripped religion from every page, but it was only in the *Fourth book* that the exercises came to centre almost entirely on New Testament religion. In that work the birth and work of Christ were covered, and there was a three page chapter on 'The Christian salvation':

Salvation means deliverance from something that is feared or suffered, and it is therefore a term of very general application; but in reference to our spiritual condition it means delivery from those evils with which we are afflicted in consequence of our departure from God.

It implies deliverances from *ignorance*—not ignorance of human science, but from ignorance of God, the first and the last, the greatest and the wisest, the holiest and the best of beings, the maker of all things, the centre of all perfection, the fountain of all happiness ...

Salvation implies deliverance from *guilt*. The law denounced a penalty against those who break it. That penalty is exclusion from heaven, and the deprivation of God's favour, and consignment to the place of misery.

But from this penalty there is deliverance provided. Christ has expatiated guilt. He has 'made reconciliation for iniquity'. He has

[33] *First book of lessons for the use of schools*, p. 20.
[34] *Second book of lessons for the use of the Irish national schools* (Dublin, 1837), pp 4–5

purchased eternal life. And 'to those who are in him there is now no condemnation.' Their sins are forgiven. They are at 'peace with God'. And there is nothing to prevent him from pouring out upon them the riches of his mercy, and making them happy for ever.[35]

Examples of this sort could be multiplied by the hundred. The crucial point is that the books were sufficiently religious to be adaptable to denominational purposes while being sufficiently neutral dogmatically to offend almost no one. Granted, the Roman Catholic prelates made a minor stir about the books at Thurles, and the presbyterians complained in 1868 about eight passages in national school books (the most sectarian of which was 'Her beads while she numbered her baby still slumbered'),[36] but neither group agitated seriously on the question, largely because there was not that much about which to be dissatisfied. The religious quality of the books, despite their dogmatic neutrality, gave the teachers of every national school in Ireland an opportunity to mix religious instruction with literary instruction; and when a presbyterian, Roman Catholic, or anglican teacher gave religious instruction of this kind it is altogether unlikely that the instruction was apt to be unfavourable to his own denomination. Thus, the books published by the commissioners of national education guaranteed that the commissioners' stated goal of separating denominational religious training from literary teaching would never be attained.

In addition to teaching religious belief, the national school texts also taught elementary lessons in social behaviour. In the *First book of lessons* were such sentences as 'You must not vaunt or boast of your skill', 'A good boy will not tell a lie', and 'When we are on the road, or in the street, we should take care that no

[35] *Fourth book of lessons for the use of the Irish national schools* (Dublin, 1935), pp 205–206.

[36] *Return showing the cost of last revision of the school books published by the commissioners of national education in Ireland; and time occupied in said revision; copies of any statement or memorial on the subject of these revised books presented to the lord lieutenant or the commissioners of education by the elementary education committee of the general assembly of the presbyterian church in Ireland; of any letter or protest of any member or members of the national board regarding said books; and, of the final resolution of the commissioners with respect to them*, pp 2–3, H.C. 1867–8 (363), liii.

harm comes to us'.[37] Concern for parents was the theme of a lesson in the *Second book of lessons*:

> When storks grow old, their young ones bring them food, and try all their art to make them eat. When dew falls, they spread their wings to keep them dry and warm. If a man or dog comes near, they take them on their backs, and bear them to a safe place. *Should not boys and girls do like these good storks, and be kind to those who gave them birth?*[38]

'Sequel no. 2' tied godliness to acceptable social behaviour in a panegyric of the virtues of education:

> First, then, you were taught to come to school with clean hands, face and hair; because dirt spoils and dishonours these comely bodies which God has given us, and makes them more liable to disease.
>
> Next, you were taught habit of order—to put away your things, your hats, or cloaks, or bonnets in their proper places; to be civil and respectful in your behaviour towards your teachers, and gentle to each other; to be silent during lessons; and to conform to all the other rules of your school.[39]

One of the greatest sins that can be imputed to the editors of the commissioners' books is that the books contained reference to Ireland as a geographical entity but as little else. This is understandable, given the government's fear of anything that might stimulate Irish nationalism, but it was hardly education-ally justifiable for Irish children to go through school without ever hearing of the history and culture of their own country.

Corresponding to the omission of lessons on Ireland was an omission, in most of the works of general instruction, of material on modern history; indeed, it would have been very easy for a child to have finished his schooling with the impression that nothing worth noting had taken place in the world after about 50 A.D. In the *Fifth book of lessons* the years from 1500 to 1800 were covered in six pages without any mention of the reforma-tion, and from 1800 to the date of publication in nine pages, many of which were spent dwelling upon the freeing of the slaves. Given the controversial nature of Irish history and also

[37] *First book of lessons for the use of schools*, pp 29, 32–3.
[38] *Second book of lessons for the use of the Irish national schools*, pp 6–7.
[39] *Sequel to the second book of lessons for the use of schools* (Dublin, 1846), pp 7–8.

the volatility of attitudes regarding the reformation and subsequent religious history, it may be that the commissioners made the right decision in choosing to avoid controversy; if they had tried to deal with the reformation and with such Irish events as the union and catholic emancipation, their books might well have been ripped to shreds by controversialists.

It would be easy for a modern reader to view the national school texts as quaint and laughable. Given the context of their time, however, and given the audience for which they were prepared, the books must be judged as successful productions. They provided the peasant child with a ladder of learning through which he could obtain not only literacy but could gain considerable proficiency in literary and scientific areas as well. The works were admirably adapted to the Irish religious and social political situation for they avoided unnecessary controversial matter while meeting the demands of Irishmen of all denominations for books upon which a christian education could be formed. Moreover, the books were good enough to be, for a time, the most popular set of school books used in England.

Ironically, the virtues of their books rained more trouble upon the commissioners' heads than did any of the books' vices. The works were so successful in England that they threatened to damage seriously the sales of commercial textbook publishers. In December 1849, Longman and Company and John Murray wrote Lord John Russell protesting against the publication of school books by the commissioners of national education in Ireland.[40] After two more letters Russell was stirred to action and questioned the commissioners on the matter. The commissioners vigorously defended themselves, but to no avail; a treasury minute of November 1852 withdrew from them the privilege of publishing their own books. Thereafter the commissioners' books for public sale were printed by private publishers who were chosen by open bidding. The commissioners maintained the privilege of providing books to the national schools at reduced prices, but anyone else, either in Ireland or abroad, had to buy them directly from the private publishers at full price. In itself, the clipping of the commissioners' wings

[40] For the correspondence on the subject, see the *Appendix to the seventeenth report of the commissioners of national education in Ireland, for the year 1850* [1405–11], H.C. 1851, xxiv, pt i.

in the matter of school books was not very important, for they maintained complete control of the books and curricula of their own school system. The treasury ruling was, however, the start of a series of treasury restrictions upon the commissioners that was eventually to make the system of national education in Ireland a fief of the lords of the treasury.

2

The commissioners were not content with including a good deal of non-dogmatic religious material in their literary school books but also produced three avowedly religious works. In so doing they were courting disaster. Each of these works was intended to be religiously non-controversial in that each contained only material upon which all christian denominations could agree and each was approved by every one of the commissioners before being published. The three works, in order of ascending importance, were *Sacred poetry*, *Lessons on the truth of Christianity*, and *Scripture lessons*, the last being a series of four individual volumes. *Sacred poetry* appeared in 1837 and was compiled by James Carlile. The material in it, while not rampantly sectarian, was more apt to be familiar to the protestant than to the catholic child, although a number of the psalms were taken from the Douay version of the Bible. The book provided sixty-seven pages of unabashed uplift. The preface noted that sacred truths in poetic form, when committed to memory, softened a man's manners, refined his tastes, and gave him a taste for pleasures of a higher order and of a purer kind than he might otherwise be tempted to seek. 'With the view of providing for the peasantry of Ireland these benefits, the commissioners of national education have made the following selection of sacred poetry, adapted to the understanding of children: and they earnestly recommend to the conductors and teachers of the Irish national schools that their pupils may be taught to commit them to memory.'[41] Two examples of the poetry are excerpted below, the first because it was typical of the collection, the second because it was noticeably inappropriate in a collection of poems for the pre-famine peasant child:

[41] *Sacred Poetry adapted to the understanding of children and youth for the use of schools* (Dublin, 1845), p. iv.

'A General Hymn of Praise'

How glorious is our heavenly king,
    Who reigns above the sky!
How shall a child presume to sing
    His dreadful majesty?

How great his power is, none can tell,
    Nor think how large his grace;
Not men below, nor saints that dwell
    On high before his face.

Not angels that stand round the Lord
    Can search his sacred will;
But they perform his heavenly word,
    And sing his praises still.

Then let me join this holy train,
    And my first offerings bring;
The eternal God will not disdain
    To hear an infant sing.

My heart resolves, my tongue obeys,
    And angels shall rejoice
To hear their mighty maker's praise
    Sound from a feeble voice.[42]

'Praise for Mercies Spiritual and Temporal'

Whene'er I take my walks abroad,
    How many poor I see!
What shall I render to my God
    For all his gifts to me.

Not more than others I deserve,
    Yet God hath given me more:
For I have food while others starve,
    Or beg from door to door.

[42] Ibid., pp 6–7.

How many children in the street
  Half naked I behold:
While I am clothed from head to feet,
  And covered from the cold.

While some poor people scarce can tell
  Where they may lay their head:
I have a home wherein to dwell,
  And rest upon my bed.

While others early learn to swear,
  And curse, and lie, and steal;
Lord, I am taught thy name to fear,
  And do thy holy will.

Are they thy favours, day by day,
  To me above the rest?
Then let me love thee more than they,
  And strive to serve thee best.[43]

The commissioners first published *Lessons on the truth of Christianity* in 1838. The book was intended as a sequel to the fourth reader. Actually, it was a modified edition of Archbishop Whately's *Introductory lessons on Christian evidences*, published in England. When Whately submitted the original work for the commissioners' approval, Archbishop Murray refused to sanction Whately's first two chapters, where children were given evidence by which they themselves were to judge whether Christianity or paganism should be adopted. Thereupon Rev. James Carlile set about editing the work, removing the first two chapters and various objectionable phrases. The work in its edited form received Dr Murray's approval. *Lessons on the truth of Christianity* was published by the commissioners. In addition, in 1843, the Parker edition of *Introductory lessons on Christian evidences* was placed upon the list of books sanctioned for use in national schools but not published by the commissioners.[44]

Lessons on the truth of Christianity consisted of 141 pages arranged

[43] Ibid., pp 9–10.
[44] M.C.N.E.I., 14 Dec. 1843; *Report from the select committee of the house of lords appointed to inquire into the practical working of the system of national education in Ireland*, pp 135, 259, 295–6; *Royal commission of inquiry into primary education (Ireland)*, vol. i, pt 1, *Report of the commissioners*, pp 43, 128.

in eighteen chapters. In the first chapter Whately extolled the virtue of the Christian faith, and, in a phrase clearly aimed at pacifying Dr Murray, explained the book's purpose: 'Although it is not to be expected that a child should be able to weigh the proofs of the Christian religion, although in his childhood, he must depend upon his parents, or on those religious teachers under whom his parents place him, for religious instruction, yet it is important, both for his own sake and for the sake of those he lives with, that he should be made early acquainted with some better reasons for being a Christian, than that his parents were so before him'.[45] The central theme of the first third of the book was that the general history of the world, especially after the introduction of Christianity, was a series of proofs that Christ was sent by God to heal the moral diseases of man. In the second and third chapters of the book Whately set down the changes brought into the world by the introduction of Christianity and then detailed the obstacles to the general spread of that religion. Whately next pointed to the evidence of ancient books, of prophecies, of miracles (three chapters), of wonders and signs, all of which pointed to the truth of the Christian religion. After summarizing these evidences in history he turned to internal evidences of the truth of Christianity, such as the character of the Gospel itself. Following three chapters of internal evidences he turned to arguing that the Christian religion was true because of the good effects of Christianity. He concluded with two chapters given over to answering possible objections, and with two final chapters on, inexplicably, the modern Jews.

The work in the form published by the commissioners was not, it is important to note, of a sectarian nature. Throughout, Whately avoided the question of which type of Christianity was best and simply argued the case for an undefined general Christianity. The work was objectionable to many Irish critics primarily because it recognized the possibility of doubts, and this in a country in which such questions were not generally raised. To the modern observer a more reasonable argument against the use of the book in the schools would have been that it was deadly dull. Far from being controversial or polemical,

[45] *Lessons on the truth of Christianity, being an appendix to the fourth book of lessons for the use of the schools* (Dublin, 1846), p. 5.

it was a bland, reasonably well-written, compilation of everyday theology. The main danger to children from the work seems to have been that it would be very likely to kill any interest they might have had in further theological study.

The origins of the *Scripture lessons* antedate the founding of the national system. It will be recalled that the commissioners of 1806–12 in outlining their plan of education had suggested that a volume of extracts from the scriptures should be compiled for use in schools. The educational inquiry commissioners of 1824–7 had tried in vain to produce such a volume. Even before the commissioners of national education began to meet officially Rev. James Carlile had called on all the proposed commissioners to ascertain whether or not they would be favourably disposed to the compilation of a book of extracts. Archbishop Murray was not only willing but anxious for such a compilation, but laid down three stipulations: first, that it should not be extracted solely from the authorized version. He wished the work to be drawn either from both the catholic and the protestant versions of the scriptures or to be translated directly from the original. Second, he did not wish the compilation to be in the form of chapters and verses, but of ordinary school lessons. Third, he demanded that notes be added, not notes of a theological order, but explaining history, chronology, geography and other matters related to the scripture lesson. Carlile readily agreed to these stipulations. Archbishop Whately, it appears, had some difficulties on the subject, chiefly because he was worried that the national system's opponents would charge that the extracts were the only religious instruction the commissioners intended to give in their schools and that even these lessons were imperfect and mutilated. Carlile put Whately at ease on this point, and, because no existing book filled Dr Murray's stipulations, Carlile set about writing the lessons himself. He began with a lesson from Genesis, had it set in type and laid before the commissioners, all of whom approved it. From thence he continued throughout the series, giving each proposed section to each of the commissioners, and if they made no objection within a fortnight's time, they were understood to have approved the lesson.[46] Carlile received some help in trans-

[46] *Report from the select committee of the house of lords appointed to inquire into the practical working of the system of national education in Ireland*, pp 4–5.

lating and drafting from an unremembered Dublin clergyman, and, in the section on the Acts of the Apostles and the Gospel of Luke, from Dr Arnold of Rugby.[47]

In their final form the extracts comprised four volumes. The first volume began with creation. The book was arranged along narrative lines, incorporating relevant portions of scripture to illuminate the narrative. Thus, after the compilation on creation, portions from the Psalms dealing with creation were introduced. After the material on the deluge were inserted extracts from the New Testament dealing with that event. In many respects the work was simply an edition of the Bible with the confusion removed. As Archbishop Murray wished, the individual narrative passages were arranged as school lessons, without division into chapter and verse. At the end of each section was a list of vocabulary words and a set of questions on the lesson. The following questions, from the list following the Cain and Abel story, are typical:

> Who was Adam's first son?
> Tell me the name of the second.
> What did Cain offer to the Lord?
> What was Abel's offering?
> Which of the offerings did God accept?
> What effect did this produce on Cain?
> What did Cain do?
> How was Cain to be punished?
> What does the Apostle John say concerning the
> history of Cain and Abel?[48]

The first book of extracts ended with the Israelite bondage in Egypt. It was later divided into two separate volumes.

The first of the New Testament lessons contained the whole of the Gospel of Luke, in addition to related passages from other parts of scripture. The questions listed below are selected as the most controversial in the entire volume, being chosen from among those centering on Christ's death and resurrection:

[47] *Royal commission of inquiry into primary education (Ireland)*, vol. i, pt 1, *Report of the commissioners*, p. 40.

[48] *Scripture lessons, adapted to the use of the schools: no. 1, Old Testament* (Dublin, 1832), p. 20.

What prophecy was fulfilled by his [Christ's] crucifixion with malefactors?

What was the superscription over him and in what languages was it?

What testimony did one malefactor give in Christ's favour?

What does the word 'paradise' mean?

What extraordinary appearances occurred during the crucifixion?

On what day of the week was the sepulchre first visited, and by whom?

What was the 'power from on high'?[49]

The second book of New Testament lessons continued the story using material chiefly from the Acts of the Apostles, concluding with Paul's suffering and last letter before his death.

It is difficult to determine how many children actually read the scripture books. Thomas Kelly testified before the select committee of 1837 that the books were read in 839 of the 1,051 schools.[50] A return of 1843 indicated that of the 2,614 schools answering, the *Scripture lessons* were read in 1,308.[51] Unfortunately, it is impossible to obtain any indication of how the use of the books varied from one denomination to another. It would be tempting to assume that the extracts were used in a greater proportion of protestant than of Roman Catholic schools, but at least during the early years this does not seem to have been true. It will be recalled that during the 1830s the protestant objectors to the national system fiercely denounced the mutilating of the scriptures. In all probability even those protestants who joined the system remained sceptical of the extracts. Hence, it is not safe to assume that the *Scripture lessons* were used in the protestant managed national schools in any greater degree than in catholic managed national schools. There is some testimony that during the

[49] *Scripture lessons, New Testament, no. 1, for the use of the Irish national schools* (Dublin, 1834), pp 132–3, 144–5.

[50] *Report from the select committee appointed to inquire into the progress and operation of the new plan of education in Ireland*, p. 190, H.C. 1837 [485], ix. Convent schools were not included in the statistics.

[51] M.C.N.E.I., 10 Aug. 1843.

1830s Roman Catholic schools employed the extracts in large numbers.[52]

It was much easier for the commissioners of national education to draw up the scripture extracts and other religious publications for general instruction than it was for them to define how they were to be used. Until 1838, there was no rule regarding their use, but managers of schools possessed the undoubted right to choose not to use the religious books if they so preferred. In the prefaces to the *Scripture lessons* the commissioners stated that they recommended very strongly that the lessons be used in the schools but made it clear that they would not in any way compel their use, leaving it to the merits of the books to secure their adoption. Like the other school books, the commissioners sold the religious books at attractively low prices: the first edition of the *Scripture lessons* was offered to schools at 2¼d. a book, and to the public at 6d.[53] During the early 1830s it appears that inspectors checked on the use of the *Lessons* in the schools and at times were somewhat heavy-handed in recommending their use. In 1838, the Roman Catholic manager of the Shan-ballymore National School complained about the behaviour of an inspector on this subject, and on 31 August 1838, the commissioners issued a stiff warning to the inspector, with a copy to all the other inspectors. In this edict the commissioners laid down the rule that inspectors were to confine themselves to tabulating the number reading the *Scripture lessons* and to refrain from giving any suggestions, either verbal or written, on their use.[54]

In 1839 the commissioners finally framed a regulation concerning the religious books published for use during the hours of common instruction. In the report for 1839, drawn up by A. R. Blake,[55] the commissioners affirmed:

We by no means insist on having the scripture extracts published by our authority, read in any of the national schools, nor would we

---

[52] *Report from the select committee of the house of lords appointed to inquire into the practical working of the system of national education in Ireland*, p. 190.

[53] M.C.N.E.I., 1 Nov. 1832.

[54] *Sixth report of the commissioners of national education in Ireland, for the year 1839*, p. 9 [246], H.C. 1840, xxviii.

[55] *Report from the select committee of the house of lords, appointed to inquire into the practical working of the system of national education in Ireland*, p. 10.

allow them to be read during the time of secular or literary instruction in any school attended by any children whose parents or guardians objected to them. In such case, we should prohibit the use of them, except at the times of religious instruction, when the persons giving it might use them or not, as they should think proper.[56]

Blake also drafted the rule on the subject that was added to the rules and regulations as the 'eighth rule', which was first printed in the code of 1843.[57] Strangely, the rule as printed was not the same rule described in the 1839 report:

The commissioners do not insist on the scripture lessons being read in any of the national schools, nor do they allow them to be read during the time of secular or literary instruction, in any school attended by children whose parents or guardians object to their being read. In such case, the commissioners, prohibit the use of them, except at the times of religious instruction, when the persons giving it may use these lessons or not, as they think proper.[58]

As described in the 1839 report, the rule probably meant that if even a single child in a class objected to the use of the extracts, they were to be banished from the classroom during the hours of literary instruction. The rule, as published in 1843, implied that a large number of parents would have to object before the books would be banished to the hours of religious instruction.

Blake wrought further confusion by a ruling he made in 1840 that was taken by some of the commissioners as a precedent for future actions. The case was that of N. L. Tottenham, a protestant patron, who had complained on 27 August 1840 that an inspector had ruled that the *Scripture lessons* and *Sacred poetry* could not be used during the hours of secular instruction because of the objections of several parents agitated by the local parish priest. The only commissioners present when the answer was given were Whately, Corballis, and Blake, with Blake

[56] *Sixth report of the commissioners of national education in Ireland, for the year 1839*, p. 5.
[57] *Royal commission of inquiry into primary education (Ireland)*, vol. i, pt i, *Report of the commissioners*, p. 128.
[58] *Tenth report of the commissioners of national education in Ireland, for the year 1843*, p. 10 [569], H.C. 1844, xxx.

drawing up the answer.[59] The answer, dated 7 September 1840, confused things considerably:

In reply, we are directed to state that the commissioners do not insist on having the 'Scripture Extracts', or 'Sacred Poetry' read by any children whose parents or guardians object to them; nor can they sanction any compulsion for the purpose. But the patrons of any school who think proper, may have them read on the opening, or immediately before the closing of the school, provided no children shall be required then to attend against the will of their parents or guardians.[60]

The letter appears to sanction a third type of instruction in national schools, in addition to combined literary and moral teaching and separate religious instruction: combined religious instruction at which no children were required to be present whose parents disapproved. Archbishop Whately testified before the lords' committee of 1854 that he believed such an additional rule was sanctioned by the commissioners, and that it comprehended the *Scripture lessons*, the *Sacred poetry* and the *Lessons on the truth of Christianity*.[61]

Because no issue of any importance arose during the 1840s to force the definition of this issue, the commissioners and their subordinates went in various directions, each secure in his own interpretation of the rule. Maurice Cross, one of the secretaries, believed that the rule was to be interpreted literally and that the objections of the parents of a single child would bring the extracts' exclusion during the hours of religious instruction. On a number of occasions when questioned on the issue by clergymen of the established church he gave the literal interpretation.[62] Master Murphy, one of the catholic commissioners, believed that this was Archbishop Murray's interpretation, as well as his

[59] *Report from the select committee of the house of lords, appointed to inquire into the practical working of the system of national education in Ireland*, p. 15; *Royal commission of inquiry into primary education (Ireland)*, vol. i, pt 1: *Report of the commissioners*, pp 128–9.

[60] *Copies of correspondence of education commissioners (Ireland), relative to school books, with Mr Tottenham, in 1840, etc.*, p. 2, H.C. 1852–3 (972), xciv; M.C.N.E.I., 5 Sept. 1840; *Royal commission of inquiry into primary education (Ireland)*, vol. i, pt 1: *Report of the commissioners*, p. 129.

[61] *Report of the select committee of the house of lords, appointed to inquire into the practical working of the system of national education in Ireland*, p. 141.

[62] Ibid., pp 9–10.

own, although there is some reason to believe he was misin-formed.[63] Macdonnell, the long-time resident commissioner, also interpreted the rule literally, as did Holmes, one of the original commissioners.[64] Archbishop Whately, on the other hand, did not accept the exclusionist interpretation of the rule.[65]

To add one more element of confusion to the picture, it should be noted that the position of the *Scripture lessons* and other religious books in relation to the model schools was as unclear as their position in the ordinary national schools. Because the model schools did not have local patrons (the commissioners themselves were the patrons), there was no chance of the *Scripture lessons* being excluded by a local patron. Since the model schools, by definition, required the use of the commis-sioners' works, the implication was that the children therein would be required to read the religious works as well as the other books intended for combined instruction. In one case, however, that of a child in the Central Model School in Marlborough Street whose parents objected to the *Scripture lessons*, a student was allowed to withdraw while the extracts and related books were being read.[66]

The important point to be made about the uncertainty sur-rounding the rules on the *Scripture lessons* and associated religious works is that the ambiguity of interpretation left the com-missioners vulnerable to attack from without and susceptible to a split within their own ranks. In the early 1850s this ambiguity was the cause of a crippling fissure in the commissioners' ranks, and of a humiliating surrender to the desires of the Roman Catholic bishops.

3

At this point we must step back and review the catholic prelates' attitude toward the extracts and then observe the hardening

[63] Ibid., pp 164–7.

[64] *Royal commission of inquiry into primary education (Ireland)*, vol. i, pt 1: *Report of the commissioners*, pp 138–9.

[65] *Report from the select committee of the house of lords appointed to inquire into the practical working of the system of national education in Ireland*, p. 141.

[66] Ibid., p. 40.

of their attitude during the 'forties and 'fifties. The extracts had been forwarded to Rome during the 1838–41 controversy, but the Papal Rescript left the matter of the *Scripture lessons* up to the discretion of the individual bishops. Increasingly during the 1840s the prelates' attitude towards the entire national system became one of scepticism. This was partly the fault of the commissioners, as they gave the bishops a good deal about which they could be sceptical. For instance, the bishops were violently opposed to the rule, introduced in the mid-1840s, which required that all schools towards whose construction the commissioners gave aid must be vested in the commissioners rath r than in local trustees. During the 1840s they were further a nated by the commissioners' plans for a national network of m chools, each of which would be under the direct control com- missioners, with no provision being made for local n hips. Suspicion of the commissioners and their system led by the framing of the Stopford rule in 1847, do h the necessity of protestant managers excluding ca from protestant religious instruction.

Further, during the same decade the prelat raised by a series of issues only indirectly rel education; by 1850, they were in a sufficiently lash out at the national system itself. The first of measures to pique the bishops was the charitai passed in 1844. The act replaced the board of quests, a forty-member body created under the p parliament and an almost exclusively protestant thirteen-member board of whom three were *ex off* Of the ten seats reserved for active members, five to Roman Catholics. Although the act appeared siderable improvement over previous measures, the failed to discuss the matter with the clergy of eithe result of this oversight was that, following an agitat by Archbishop MacHale and Daniel O'Connell, was condemned by a goodly number of the Ro bishops. The bone of contention was the prov devise of real property for charitable or reli within three months of the death of the benefact The measure was viewed by MacHale as an a catholic church, and he attempted to have it

Rome. Although he failed in this venture, he was supported by
the majority of the hierarchy in his clamour against the charitable bequests board. For a time it seemed as if no catholic
bishops would join the new board, but eventually Archbishops
Crolly and Murray and Bishop Denvir agreed to serve as
members.[67]

The mistrust engendered by the charitable bequests act was
reinforced by the controversy over higher education for Roman
Catholics. Peel made the important decision to separate the
problem of catholic priestly education from that of university
education for the catholic laity. Maynooth College, founded in
1795 by the Irish parliament, received only the inadequate sum
of £9,000 annually from the government. In 1841 the catholic
bishops petitioned Peel for an increase in the grant, a request
which he turned down then and also when it was renewed
in 1842. Peel changed his mind in 1844, however, and the
following year his Maynooth act raised the annual grant to
£26,360 and provided £30,000 in a single grant for building
purposes.[68]

This measure might have brought the hierarchy to an increased trust of the government had it not seemed to the bishops
that Peel chose to combine this bit of sugar with some very bitter
medicine. During the summer of 1845, an act was passed providing for the establishment of provincial colleges. In some
ways it appears that Peel intended to replicate the national
system on the university level; the colleges were non-sectarian
institutions open to students of all denominations and for-
swearing instruction in dogmatic religion. As in the national
schools, clergy of the various denominations were allowed to
make provision for the personal counsel and religious instruction
of students of their own denomination. John MacHale was in
the vanguard of attack against the 'Godless colleges'. The
majority of the hierarchy sided with MacHale, while the
minority, under Archbishop Murray, favoured accepting the
government order provided that certain conditions were met. In

---

[67] J. C. Beckett, *The making of modern Ireland, 1603–1923* (London 1966),
pp 328–9; Kevin B. Nowlan, *The politics of repeal: a study in the relations between Great Britain and Ireland, 1841–50* (London and Toronto, 1965), pp
66–8.

[68] Nowlan, pp 30–1, 63, 80–2.

May 1845, the bishops petitioned that a 'fair proportion' of the colleges' staffs be catholics approved of by their bishops and that the instruction of catholics in history, logic, moral philosophy, geology, and anatomy should be given only by catholic professors. MacHale and his seventeen followers among the hierarchy were not satisfied with these demands and in September 1845, issued a protest stating that the provincial colleges would be dangerous to the faith and morals of Roman Catholics. The government was not prepared to compromise and went ahead with its plan. Meanwhile, the matter was referred to Rome, from whence came, in 1847 and 1848, rescripts condemning the colleges.[69]

As if there were not worry enough within the catholic hierarchy about the government's policy towards the church, Lord John Russell raised, in 1848, the possibility of the government in some way endowing the catholic clergy. As Russell envisaged the plan, the catholic clergy were to be paid and parish churches maintained by an Irish land and house tax. The catholic bishops would have none of the scheme since it raised the sinister threat of state control and, at their October 1848 meeting, they pronounced against it.[70] Thus, by 1850, the hierarchy seems to have had every reason for being in a state of collective paranoia. During the previous decade the government had touched so many sensitive nerves that the prelates were extremely wary of government activity of any sort. Like baited animals, they were ready to snap at anything that moved, whatever its intent.

Although government activities bear chief responsibility for producing this increasing waspishness amid the hierarchy, constitutional changes within the hierarchy also warrant notice. The split within the hierarchy on national education between 1830 and 1841 may be viewed partly as a split between generations. The older generation consisted of men such as Murray and Crolly who were willing to work with the government and who took a fairly trusting view of the government's intentions. The younger group, a minority at that time, was led by men of MacHale's disposition who were thoroughly sceptical of any

[69] Beckett, pp 330–1; T. W. Moody and J. C. Beckett, *Queen's Belfast, 1845–1949: the history of a university* (London, 1959), i, 1–39; Nowlan, pp 83–9, 175, 226.
[70] Nowlan, pp 224–6.

253

gh in a minority in the later 1830s,
uring the next decade added weight
scale. The young guard gained con-
famine which, if nothing else, was a
the catholic church. Prior to the
a poor bargaining position relative
was responsible for ever-increasing
peasants. The famine dramatically
educing the church's financial load
s.[72]

ively against the old guard with the
of Armagh in April 1849. Crolly was
vho provisionally assumed the see in
consecrated in February 1850. Cullen
enteen years in Rome as the agent of
had become thoroughly Romanized.
suspicious, persistent and industrious
his tenure he worked to discipline the
nto line with Rome, as represented by
the difficult trick of being strongly
ing effectively anti-nationalist as well.
vernment found relations with the
est, and at their worst almost un-

ue and the trend towards truculence
ne together in August 1850, at the
d was convened, with Cullen in the
upon the colleges. Although it was
ing MacHale for two and a half years,
es in 1841 to block a condemnation of
his fact should not lead us to think that

rrel among the Roman Catholic hierarchy over the
Ireland, 1838–41 (Cambridge, Mass., 1965,
Celtic Cross, 1964), p. 143.
ch and state in Ireland in the nineteenth cen-
(Sept. 1962), p. 303.
orough treat ent of the church in the age of
orman, *The catholic church and Ireland in the age of
don, 1965).
among the Roman Catholic hierarchy over the national
land, 1838–41, p. 142.

he was a proponent of mixed education. Indeed, as the synod of Thurles and later developments were to prove, he was opposed to it from principle. Whether or not that principle was his own or that of Rome is immaterial; it is known that Pius IX, who succeeded Gregory XVI in June 1846, had much stronger ideas on mixed education than did his predecessor.[75] Whether Cullen's opposition to mixed education was part of his own theological kit or part of his Roman baggage, the outcome was the same, for the synod of Thurles, under Cullen's hand, declared strongly against mixed education. Besides performing the duty for which the synod had been summoned, namely the condemnation of the Queen's Colleges, the bishops passed sixteen articles referring directly to the national schools. The first of these marks an important watershed in the hierarchy's thinking:

ARTICLE I. The prudent course of proceeding which the holy see has followed in regard to the system of national education, on which it refrained from pronouncing definitively, we think we should also follow. However, we deem it to be part of our duty to declare that the separate education of catholic youth is, in every way, to be preferred to it. We have seen, with satisfaction, the British government latterly give, in England, aid towards education of catholic children separately, and according to the standard of catholic religion. A right thus admitted we claim to participate in for ourselves. For, if it be just and expedient that the catholics of Britain be aided out of the public treasury in the separate education of their youth, there is no reason why the faithful catholics of Ireland should not be treated in the same manner.[76]

Articles II and III repeated the cautions of the papal rescript of 1841 on national education. Article IV declared that the rule requiring schoolhouses whose construction was aided by government money to be vested in the commissioners was objectionable and Article V forbade catholic trustees of schoolhouses built before the rule went into effect to transfer the title of their schools to the commissioners. The sixth and seventh articles were as follows:

[75] Peader MacSuibhne, *Paul Cullen and his contemporaries, with their letters from 1820–1902* (Naas, 1961), i, 17.

[76] The decrees of the synod of Thurles on national education are reproduced in Kavanagh, pp 412–15.

ARTICLE VI. We deem it dangerous for catholic children to attend schools conducted by protestants alone; and, it is, therefore, necessary for their safe education, that, in every school frequented by them there should be, at least, one catholic schoolmaster or schoolmistress in attendance. In schools where the majority of the male or female pupils is catholic, it behoves that the head master or mistress would be a catholic. We command that only catholics who are approved by the ordinary be placed at the head of these schools.

ARTICLE VII. It is proper that, whether in common schools or in normal schools to which catholics resort, the books used, even for secular instruction, should be approved by the ordinary. The bishops alone are to be regarded as the judges of the books used for the religious instruction of catholic youth.[77]

The next article stated that in every school frequented by catholics the schoolmaster should be bound to see that no catholic be present at any religious exercise conducted by a protestant minister. In the ninth article the prelates declared that no protestant professor of history in any training school was to be allowed to teach history to catholic schoolmasters. The remaining articles on national education had to do with the duties of parish priests and arranged for the publication of the decrees.

The decrees mark a turning point in the relationship of the hierarchy to the national system. Besides the obvious point that a new hard line was taken, it is important to note that the hierarchy had come to think of the national system within an entirely different framework than previously. Whereas in 1838–41 discussion of national education had hinged upon the question of whether or not the national system was dangerous in practice to the faith, the first article of the Thurles decrees declared that denominational education was preferable to the national system, without in any way referring to the actual working of the system. The Thurles decrees represented a shift from the previous mode of judging the system as it worked in practice to a judgement of the national system upon theological grounds, specifically upon the theological question of mixed education as an abstract idea. Another noteworthy point about the decrees is that they indicated a substantial increase in self-confidence among the bishops. The best index of this fact is that the bishops in their first article clearly implied that the only

[77] Ibid., p. 414.

alternative to the national system which they believed the government would dare to suggest would be a denominational plan under which the catholics would share equally with other denominations. To the older generation of bishops the alternative to undenominational education had been government support of protestant societies. The catholic bishops in their first article, then, were acting upon the knowledge that they were sufficiently powerful to prevent the government from giving money to aid protestant education without giving similar aid to catholic schools.

Significantly, the decrees also indicate that the hierarchy did not perceive that the system was, in practice, already very close to being a denominational system. It is hard to understand why this should have been, except that by 1850 the hierarchy was in such an irritable mood, that it could not see anything the government provided for what it was; if the government provided it, the hierarchy felt that it had to be bad. One of the more interesting aspects of the synod's work was the attention the bishops paid to English precedents. Although the prelates cannot be expected to have realized it at the time, the English system to which they so glowingly referred was at that time less advanced than the Irish system of national education. Ireland had given up depending upon state-aided voluntary societies for educating the nation's youth in 1831 when Stanley introduced a state system of schools. England, in contrast, did not even begin to aid voluntary societies until 1833 and did not begin to create a network of state schools until 1870. In pointing to the English system, the prelates were really admiring a system less advanced than their own and one destined to be largely replaced by a system of state schools during the following half century.

Despite their yearning for a denominational system, it is important to note that the bishops did not openly condemn the national system, or suggest that children should be withdrawn from it. Rather, the prelates began doing what the presbyterians had done so successfully in the 1830s: demanding specific modifications in the constitution of the system. This represents another turning point in catholic dealings with the national system and is in sharp contrast to the reluctance of the hierarchy from 1831–49 to make specific demands upon the government. As we shall see later, once the bishops began to haggle about

details of the system they showed themselves to be every bit as
skilled bargainers as the members of the presbyterian education
committee had been.

4

The catholic hierarchy, then, was spoiling for a fight about
national education. The commissioners gave them the opportunity and on an issue on which the commissioners themselves
were in the most vulnerable of positions, namely upon the question of the use of the *Scripture lessons*. The battle concerned, in the
first instance, the use of the books in the model schools, but later
spread to the question of the 'eighth rule' concerning the use of
the extracts in ordinary national schools. When the Newry
Model School opened in 1849, the resident commissioner,
Alexander Macdonnell, ruled, on the advice of Edward Butler,
the head inspector of that district, that the *Introductory lessons on
Christian evidence* and the *Scripture lessons* were not to be introduced. The reasons for this ruling were the opposition of the
Roman Catholics, and especially of Bishop Blake to their use in
his diocese, and Macdonnell's belief that there was no rule or
principle of the system that required them to be introduced.
Upon hearing of similar catholic objections from James
Kavanagh, head inspector for the Clonmel district, Macdonnell
made a similar ruling in the case of Clonmel Model School
which opened in June 1849. Maurice Cross, secretary to the
commissioners, called these rulings to the attention of the commissioners and those present agreed to the rulings. Archbishop
Whately, it should be underlined, was not present at that
meeting.[78]

Subsequent events were influenced by three occurrences. The
first two merely complicated the situation; the third brought
matters to a boil. First, in January 1851, the commissioners'
attention was called by Cross to the eighth rule on the use of
Scripture lessons in ordinary national schools, and the rule was

[78] *Report from the select committee of the house of lords, appointed to inquire into
the practical working of the system of national education in Ireland*, pp 237–8. Although Macdonnell's evidence on this point does not mention the book,
later events made it clear that the *Lessons on the truth of Christianity* were also
banned.

amended so that it mentioned not only the *Scripture lessons* but also the *Lessons on the truth of Christianity* and the *Sacred poetry*.[79] This guaranteed that when the controversy that was to develop over the use of the scripture books in the model schools spread to the issue of the scripture books in the ordinary national schools, there would be considerable fuel for controversy. Second, on 26 February 1852, Archbishop Murray died, thus robbing the commissioners of their last important advocate within the hierarchy. Things augured even less well for the commissioners when Paul Cullen was transferred from Armagh to Dublin in May 1852. Third, in July 1852, Archbishop Whately decided to visit Clonmel Model School to check on its progress. He was conducted on the tour by James Kavanagh,[80] the head inspector of the district, and found, much to his anger, that the *Scripture lessons* and the *Lessons on the truth of Christianity* were not used. Whately at once sent off an indignant memorandum to his fellow commissioners, calling their attention to the fact that the works were being excluded. 'It appears to me most important', he stated, 'that in all the schools of which we are patrons, viz. the model schools, all our books should be read. The inference naturally to be drawn from this not being done is, either that we are insincere in recommending books, which we prove by our conduct we do not think well of, or else that we suffer this or that person to usurp our power and dictate to us.'[81] He followed this with another memorandum in which he answered possible arguments against his opinions.[82]

Parenthetically, it should be underscored that Whately was neither attempting to make the use of the *Scripture lessons* or of the *Lessons on the truth of Christianity* compulsory in ordinary national schools nor demanding that any child in a model school be required to remain during their use if his parents objected. In reply to a protestant clergyman he wrote:

Lately, one of the Roman Catholic bishops urged the board to withdraw from their list, that is, prohibit, one of the books it had sanctioned, and some of the commissioners were at first disposed to

[79] M.C.N.E.I., 2 Jan. 1851.   [80] Kavanagh, p. 27.
[81] 'First memorandum', 1 July 1852, reproduced in *Copies of correspondence of education commissioners (Ireland) relative to school books with Mr Tottenham, in 1840, etc.*, pp 2–3.
[82] 'Second memorandum', undated, reproduced ibid., pp 3–4.

comply; but I declared that if such a step were taken, which would be both unfair and unwise, I should feel bound to withdraw from the board.

So I should also if it were decided to make the use of any book compulsory on children, whose parents think it, however erroneously, at variance with their religion. Never, while I am a commissioner, shall any patron be precluded from introducing into a school any book once sanctioned by us, and on the strength of which sanction, he, perhaps, was induced to establish the school; and never, while I am a commissioner, shall the scripture extracts or the tract on evidences be forced on any children whose parents object on religious grounds.[83]

If we ask the next logical question, 'Why was Whately so enamoured with the scripture books?', the answer is disquieting:

The great instrument of conversion . . . is the diffusion of scriptural education. Archbishop Murray and I agreed in desiring large portions of the Bible to be read in our national schools; but we agreed in this because we disagreed as to its probable results.

He believed that they would be favourable to Romanism. I believed that they would be favourable to protestantism; and I feel confident that I was right. For twenty years large extracts from the New Testament have been read in the majority of national schools, far more diligently than that book is read in ordinary protestant places of education.

. . . .

Though the priest may still, perhaps, denounce the Bible collectively, as a book dangerous to the laity, he cannot safely object to the scripture extracts, which are read to children with the sanction of the prelates of his own church . . . But those extracts contain so much that is inconsistent with the whole spirit of Romanism, that it is difficult to suppose that a person well acquainted with them can be a thorough-going Roman Catholic . . .

Such, I believe to be the process by which the minds of a large portion of the Roman Catholic have been prepared, and are now prepared, for the reception of protestant doctrines. The education supplied by the national board is gradually undermining the vast fabric of the Irish Roman Catholic church.

. . . .

What I fear is a measure which, thought not avowedly sectarian, may be so practically. I fear that a grant may be offered to any patron who will provide such secular education as the government

[83] *Dublin Evening Post*, 16 Mar. 1852.

shall approve, leaving him to furnish such religious education as he may himself approve ... I believe, as I said the other day, that mixed education is gradually enlightening the mass of people, and that, if we give it up, we give up the only hope of weaning the Irish from the abuses of popery. But I cannot venture openly to profess this opinion. I cannot openly support the education board as an instrument of conversion. I have to fight its battle with one hand, and that my best, tied behind me.[84]

The juxtaposition of the two preceding quotations provides some interesting insights into Whately's mentality at this time. In the first place it appears that he was quite out of touch with what was actually going on in the national schools. Whately seems to have believed that mixed education was actually taking place, when, demonstrably, it was not occurring to any significant degree. In this regard he seems, like the Roman Catholic prelates at Thurles, to have been dealing with mixed education as an abstract theory, rather than as a practical arrangement that either worked or did not work in Ireland. Since both Whately and the Roman prelates, and especially Archbishop Cullen, seem to have viewed mixed education in abstract terms and to have largely ignored the realities of the national system, their clash when it occurred was bound to be all the more brutal for the intellectual inflexibility of their positions. A second noteworthy point is the faith Whately maintained in the power of the scripture extracts to undermine Romanism. This faith was close to being magical in nature, for it is hard to see in practice how the extracts, when taught by a catholic teacher to catholic children, as was the usual case, could undermine their faith. In such a situation, Dr Murray's idea that they would aid the propagation of catholicism was probably the correct judgment. Nevertheless, the intensity of Whately's faith in the extracts' efficacy is more important for matters at hand than the accuracy or inaccuracy of his views, for it was his faith in the *Scripture lessons* that meant he would fight to the last ditch to save them, and abandon the national system if the system abandoned the extracts. Third, there was an obvious

[84] The quotation is from Nassau Senior's entries, in his daily journal, on conversations with Whately. Quoted in E. Jane Whately, *Life and correspondence of Richard Whately, D.D., late archbishop of Dublin* (London, 1866), i, 243–6.

contradiction between Whately's protestant liberalism which decreed that no child should ever be forced to participate in any religious exercise against his parent's will, and his anti-catholicism which led him to desire the conversion of the papists through the national school system. Whately, in 1852, was a volatile, dogmatic, liberal, confusing, unrealistic man, one who could explode in any of several directions depending on what might detonate his feelings.

A special meeting of the commissioners was called on 16 July 1852 to discuss the issue raised by Whately but decisions were postponed in order to allow the secretaries to communicate with the head inspectors on the practices followed in all of the model schools.[85] Head inspector McCreedy reported that in both the schools under his charge the *Scripture lessons* were read daily by all children but that objections had led to the *Lessons on the truth of Christianity* being read only by the protestant children.[86] The head inspector of the Galway area reported that the scripture extracts were used in the Trim District Model School under his charge, chiefly at the time for separate religious instruction. In that school the *Lessons on the truth of Christianity* had never been introduced.[87] The reply from the third head inspector was evasive, stating that in 'some' of the district model schools the scripture extracts were used by all in attendance during combined instruction.[88] James Kavanagh, another head inspector, answered with two detailed letters which were also somewhat evasive. In the Dunmanway Model School he reported that scripture extracts were used by all children as a daily part of their secular education, with the approval of the Roman Catholic bishop of the diocese. He emphasized the Roman Catholic objections to the *Lessons on the truth of Christianity* but failed to state explicitly whether or not the books were used.[89]

[85] M.C.N.E.I., 16 July 1852.

[86] W. McCreedy to secretaries of national education, 3 Aug. 1852 reproduced in *Copies of Correspondence of education commissioners (Ireland) relative to school books with Mr Tottenham, in 1840, etc.,* p. 6.

[87] Edward Butler to secretaries of national education, 31 July 1852, reproduced ibid., pp 6–7.

[88] James Patten to secretaries of national education, 31 July 1852, reproduced ibid., p. 7.

[89] J. W. Kavanagh to secretaries of national education, 31 July 1953 [2], reproduced ibid., pp 7–9.

In the Clonmel School, Kavanagh reported, the Roman Catholic clergy would not permit any of the commissioners' religi~ works to be read at any time by catholic children. Th~ tants in the school read the Authorized version f~ daily during separate religious instruction ar ~ tracts were deemed unnecessary by the~

To Archbishop Whately's min~ factory and he responded b~ Whately argued that th~ widespread object~ reading sho~l would be merely bec~ that book th~ should be pre relevantly but s~ he had noted the to the schoolmaste masters and inspec minded, when there denomination is recog directions as to what a parents or guardians that may say (and so indeed m place themselves under his must not claim any direct co

A special meeting of the co consider the subject, but before to produce yet another positio 'delicacy' Whately felt he shou commissioners' meeting, (a practice quent occasion when the religious bo reiterated his feelings on the matter, a of educational policy should be decided in special session by the commissioners, and head inspectors or other functionari~

90 J. W. Kavanagh to secretaries of national educ. reproduced ibid., pp 9–10.
91 Third memorandum, undated, reproduced ibid.,
92 'Fourth memorandum,' 11 Nov. 1852, reproduced 1

meeting on the twelfth of November, the commissioners were unable to come to a decision.[93] Another special meeting was called early in December. Twelve commissioners were present at the meeting, Whately of course being absent. Thomas N. Redington introduced a resolution which effectively extended rule eight to cover the model schools as well as the ordinary national schools. That rule stated the commissioners did not insist on the *Scripture lessons*, the book of *Sacred poetry* nor the *Lessons on the truth of Christianity* being read in the national school. 'The commissioners', in the words of Redington's resolution, 'having fully considered the memorandums now brought before them, decline to direct that the above books shall be introduced generally into all the district model schools, or to other schools under the exclusive control of the board'.[94] The resolution passed without recorded dissent.

If Archbishop Whately had possessed the good grace to keep still and accept the commissioners' decision, the subject probably would have been dropped with the extension of the eighth rule to the model schools. The archbishop, however, chose to make a fuss and as a result, rule eight itself was eventually modified. Upon receiving a copy of the commissioners' minutes of 3 December 1852, Whately wrote the commissioners, tartly stating that he did not think it was asking too much that the commissioners should express themselves without ambiguity, and solemnly declaring that he was quite unable to discern the meaning of their decision with any confidence. This was a canard since, although the minute of 3 December 1852 was not a full exposition of the new principle, its meaning, when read in conjunction with the existing eighth rule, was unmistakable: that if the parents of children in the model schools objected to the use of the religious books during the hours when children of all faiths were required to be taught together, the books were not to be used during those hours.[95] Whately maintained that

[93] M.C.N.E.I., 12 Nov. 1852.

[94] M.C.N.E.I., 3 Dec. 1852; *Copies of correspondence of education commissioners (Ireland) relative to school books, with Mr Tottenham, in 1840*, p. 11.

[95] At this point, it is important to note, the commissioners still had not defined, nor did they realize that they needed to define, what constituted a parental objection. Some commissioners and board officials thought the objection of one parent was sufficient, others thought that a number of objections had to be made before the books would be removed.

the commissioners' vote was meaningless since in no ordinary national school was the use of any book required; local patrons had the right to use any school book they wished, subject to the commissioners' approval. Quite correctly, he argued that any book not required to be used by a patron was excluded since only the patron could bring about any book's introduction. Whately then argued, quite inexcusably given his knowledge of the national system's rules, that the commissioners' minute of 3 December in which they paraphrased the eighth rule as saying 'that they do not insist' on the *Scripture lessons* and other religious books being read, to mean, in the case of the model schools of which the commissioners were patrons, that they excluded the books.[96]

In response to this display of illogical hair-splitting, the commissioners called another special meeting. The meeting was originally scheduled for mid-December, but it was postponed to January, 1853, so that Redington could be present.[97] When they did meet, the commissioners did not consider the eighth rule itself, but voted favourably upon the resolution of Lord Chancellor Blackburne that 'whenever a district model school shall be opened, the commissioners will themselves decide and declare by a formal resolution whether any, and which of the books recommended by them to be used, shall be used therein or not'.[98]

Soon after the passing of this resolution the Gormanstown Model School was ready to be opened. Lord Chancellor Blackburne gave notice of a motion that all three of the commissioners' religious books should be read in the school, but that if the parent of any child objected to having the books, or any one of them, read by his child, the child should be excused from

[96] 'Fifth Memorandum', in *Copies of correspondence of education commissioners (Ireland) relative to school books with Mr Tottenham, in 1840, etc.*, pp 11–12.
[97] M.C.N.E.I., 10, 17 Dec. 1852.
[98] *Copies of correspondence of education commissioners (Ireland) relative to school books, with Mr Tottenham, in 1840, etc.*, p. 12; M.C.N.E.I., 14 Jan. 1853. Also see evidence of F. Blackburne in *Report from the select committee of the house of lords, appointed to inquire into the practical working of the system of national education in Ireland*, p. 115.

At the end of 1852, however, the commissioners were unaware of the confusion in their ranks on the issue, since the question had never caught the attention of the entire group.

attending while they were read. At that point, James O'Ferrall, a Roman Catholic commissioner, objected that this would be a violation of the eighth rule, his interpretation of that rule being that after even a single parental objection the books, not the child, were to be excluded. Thereupon, Blackburne investigated rule eight and was informed that the usual practice was not to exclude the books when objection was made but to exclude the child. Blackburne pressed on with his intention to introduce his motion. Archbishop Cullen heard of the motion, and in mid-March 1853, wrote Lord St Germans, the lord lieutenant, objecting that Blackburne's motion exempting the child, but not excluding the book, was an unacceptable innovation in the system. Simultaneously, Master Murphy, a Roman Catholic commissioner, sent the lord lieutenant amendments to Blackburne's motion, which stated that no teacher should be obliged to teach any book of which he disapproved. Although Archbishop Whately held aloof from attending the commissioners' meetings, he still pulled strings in the background. Both Whately and Blackburne, at different times, saw the lord lieutenant, and the three of them concurred that Blackburne should add a clause to his motion that whenever an objection was made, the objection was to have the effect of obliging the master of the school to appropriate a peculiar portion of the day, either immediately before or immediately after the school hours for the teaching of the religious books. Whately was in contact with Blackburne by letter and Blackburne faithfully added Whately's words on the subject onto his own motion.[99] Thus on 24 March 1853 Blackburne gave notice of a motion requiring that at the Gormanstown Model School the *Scripture lessons*, *Sacred poetry*, and *Lessons on the truth of Christianity* be used with the proviso, 'that they are not to be read by any children whose parents or guardians object to their being read by them—And that those books shall be read before the beginning or after the close of the more secular instruction or both'.[100]

Blackburne's motion was due to be considered on the first of April, but at the lord lieutenant's request, Blackburne, Murphy, and Sir John Young waited on the lord lieutenant at the Castle.

[99] *Report from the select committee of the house of lords, appointed to inquire into the practical working of the system of national education in Ireland*, pp 116–18.
[100] M.C.N.E.I., 24 Mar. 1853.

Murphy, who appeared to Blackburne to be speaking by authority of the Roman Catholic clergy, stated that the clergy of his communion relied upon the literal interpretation of the eighth rule, by which the exclusion of a religious book could be effected by the exercise of the veto by the parents of a single child. Murphy especially objected to the use of the *Lessons on the truth of Christianity* in the national schools. Because of the unsettled state of opinion and because parliament was beginning to inquire about the proceedings, Blackburne's motion was postponed until 29 April.[101] Murphy wrote Blackburne a letter on 2 April referring to a meeting of the commissioners on 1 April in which Maurice Cross had brought to notice two documents bearing out Blackburne's interpretation of the rule. Murphy further admitted error in acknowledging that before the first of April he had not known that there were two editions of Whately's evidences, the one published and sanctioned by the commissioners as *Lessons on the truth of Christianity*, and the other published by Parker's and only sanctioned by the commissioners under the title *Introductory lessons on Christian evidences*. Murphy stated that he had never seen the former book before the preceding day and found it 'free from any objection I have ever heard urged against the book, except one, to which I did not consider it necessary to advert on last Thursday'.[102] Soon thereafter Murphy gave notice for an amendment to Blackburne's motion that would have excluded both editions of Whately's book from the list of books approved for use in the national schools.[103]

Matters almost came to a head in late April. When the commissioners met on the twenty-ninth, Blackburne moved his two resolutions concerning the Gormanstown Model School. After considerable discussion Blackburne withdrew his motion in favour of a series of amendments proposed by Greene. Greene's amendments declared that the commissioners did not insist

[101] M.C.N.E.I., 1 Apr. 1853; *Report from the select committee of the house of lords, appointed to inquire into the practical working of the system of national education in Ireland*, p. 119.

[102] Quoted ibid., pp 119–20. The two documents Cross brought to the commissioners, attention were the letter to Mr Tottenham in 1840, and an obscure minute of September 1848, stating that patrons had the power to cause the religious books to be read.

[103] Ibid., p. 120.

upon the *Scripture lessons*, the *Lessons on the truth of Christianity*, or the *Sacred poetry* being used in any of the national schools, neither did they allow them to be read as part of the ordinary school business in any school attended by children whose parents objected to the book being read by their children. Ordinary school business was defined as time during which all children of all denominations are required to attend. In the case of parental objection the amendment provided that the use of the books be prohibited except at times set apart for the purpose, either before or after the ordinary school business. Such reading was to be limited by three conditions: first, that no child whose parents objected was to be required, directly or indirectly, to be present; second, that public notification of the time set apart be given in the school time table, and that the teacher verbally announce the beginning of the instruction as well; third, that sufficient ordinary school time be allotted each day so that those children who did not attend the reading of the religious books might still receive sufficient literary education. Greene's amendments were essentially a compromise between the view that the objection of one parent should result in the total banishment of the commissioners' religious books to the hours of separate religious instruction, and the view that the child of an objecting parent should simply be allowed to withdraw. Under Greene's amendments, the objection of a single child would have banished the books from the hours of combined instruction in which all children were present, but would not have limited them to the hours of separate religious instruction. Thus, he proposed that a third type of education be offered, in addition to compulsory combined literary instruction, and to separate religious instruction, namely, combined religious instruction at which attendance was optional.

After these amendments had been accepted as replacing Blackburne's original resolutions, James O'Ferrall moved three amendments, one merely verbal, the other two substantive. One of these was that no child should be allowed to be present at the reading of the books mentioned unless his parent or guardian had signified his assent to the teacher or patron. In addition, he moved an amendment which would have allowed any teacher in a model or ordinary national school who conscientiously objected to the use of the books to refuse to participate in their use. In such a case, someone approved by the parents was to be appointed to fill the teacher's place during the time such books were employed. After all this, J. J. Murphy moved that the *Lessons in the truth of Christianity* be omitted from Greene's earlier resolution, implying, if unclearly, that the book no longer be sanctioned by the commissioners. At this point, the commissioners decided to call it a day and went home with nothing decided.[104]

On the sixth of May, Murphy moved a further amendment the first of which was that the *Introductory lessons on Christian evidences* be dropped from the list of books not published but sanctioned by the commissioners.[105] The commissioners came to no final decision at this meeting nor at their meeting on 12 May 1853.[106]

Before the commissioners could meet again Archbishop Cullen put on a show of strength that left no doubt as to his opinions, or to his willingness to coerce the commissioners if necessary. Cullen's pastoral on the vigil of pentecost had warned his flock against the commissioners' three works,[107] but it was only in a pastoral to his bishops of 6 June 1853, that he openly stated his position:

All books to be used in the public schools should be free from all contagion of error and those which are destined for religious instruction should be approved of by your legitimate pastors. There are two little works which have been sometimes though rarely used by catholic children which we now wish to see banished from their hands. The first is a little treatise on the *Evidence of Christianity* composed by a protestant dignitary who has lately distinguished himself by his unprovoked attack on our conventional institutions under the hypocritical pretence of protesting personal liberty. We need scarcely state that this treatise coming from the pen of such an author is protestant in its principles and tendencies and that it is not fit for the instruction of catholic children in the important question of the truth of their religion. The other work is entitled *Scripture lessons*. It contains most difficult passages from the New and Old Testament and there are questions proposed at the end of each chapter which would open the way to the teaching of false doctrines and which the unlearned and unwary might wrest to their own destruction. This little work appears to have been compiled for the purpose of giving a

[104] M.C.N.E.I., 29 Apr. 1853. [105] M.C.N.E.I., 6 May 1853.
[106] M.C.N.E.I., 12 May 1853. [107] MacSuibhne, iii, 367.

united religious instruction to catholic and non-catholic children in the same class; we reprobate such a project; doubtless if the teacher were a catholic he would endeavour to give a catholic interpretation to the texts of scripture submitted to him, and catholic answers to the questions proposed; but a protestant or presbyterian would act in the same way, and under them a catholic child would not be safe. Separate religious instruction, as it was laid down by the statesman who first introduced the national system into Ireland, is the only protection for catholics. It is contrary to the spirit and practice of our holy church to sanction united religious instruction, or to sanction any instruction on matters connected with religion given to catholics by persons who themselves reject the teachings of the catholic church . . . The injunction we now give you to remove the two little works just mentioned from the hands of your children will be the more easily carried into effect, as the rules of the national board do not at all require the use of them.[108]

One immediate result of the pastoral was that a large number of the parents of children in the model school in Dublin notified the teachers that they objected to the use of the books in that institution.[109]

Thus, when the commissioners met on 17 June 1853, they were under considerable external pressure, as well as rent by internal dissension. Eleven commissioners were at the meeting, with Whately, Greene, Lord Kildare, and Lord Bellew absent. Both of Master Murphy's most recent amendments to Greene's resolutions were passed. The first of these, removing the *Lessons on the truth of Christianity* from the list of books published by the commissioners, passed by a vote of seven to four. The second, removing the *Introductory lessons on Christian evidences*, the Parker edition, from the list of works not published but sanctioned by the commissioners, passed by a vote of ten to one. The only man

---

[108] Quoted in *Report from the select committee of the house of lords, appointed to inquire into the practical working of the system of national education in Ireland*, pp 80–81. Portions are also quoted in MacSuibhne, iii, 368–9, from whom the dating of the pastoral is taken.

In passing, the pastoral bears additional notice because Cullen did not mention the desire for a separate denominational system as defined in the synod of Thurles' decrees, but rather seemed to yearn for Lord Stanley's system in its pure form. This attitude passed quickly and he was soon demanding a denominational system once again.

[109] *Report from the select committee of the house of lords, appointed to inquire into the practical working of the system of national education in Ireland*, p. 80.

to hold firm against both amendments was Francis Blackburne. After that, Greene's resolution was passed by a vote of seven to four with Murphy, Denvir, Meyler, and Redington (all catholics) opposed. The catholic commissioners voted against Greene's resolution, even though they favoured withdrawal of the two books, since they objected to the principle of allowing the *Scripture lessons* and *Sacred poetry* to continue to be used outside of the hours of separate religious instruction after a parent had objected to them.[110] Francis Blackburne, who had introduced the resolutions to require the use of the commissioners' religious books in the Gormanstown Model School, had the unhappy sight of seeing his resolution lead to the withdrawal of Whately's books from the approved list of books for combined instruction in the national schools; Whately, who had begun the entire affair by complaining that the religious books were not used in the Clonmel Model School, was forced to watch in self-imposed exile while the commissioners excluded his books.

The actions of the commissioners on 17 June were only the expression of opinions and still had to be translated into formal regulations. Before this could be done Whately tried to stem the tide by writing the lord lieutenant threatening, politely, to resign if the proposed changes were ratified.[111] The lord lieutenant was not paralysed with fear, and he allowed the commissioners to hammer their opinions into rules. The new eighth rule stated that the commissioners did not insist on the *Scripture lessons* or book of *Sacred poetry* being read in any of the national schools; neither did they allow them to be read as part of the ordinary school business (during which all children of all denominations were required to attend), in any school attended by children whose parents or guardians objected to the children using them. In such a case, the commissioners allowed their use either before or after the ordinary school business but only under the conditions that no child whose parents objected could be present, that the time for their use was to be announced in advance by methods specified by the commissioners, and that

[110] *Copies of correspondence of education commissioners (Ireland) relative to school books, with Mr Tottenham, in 1840, etc.*, pp 14–15; M.C.N.E.I., 8 July 1853.
[111] Richard Whately to Earl St Germans, 5 July 1853, reproduced in E. Jane Whately, ii, 268–72.

sufficient time be left in the day for the ordinary education of those children who did not participate.[112]

A month later, the commissioners expanded their statement of the rules with an explanation intended for publication in their annual report for the year 1852. The explanation made it clear that the *Lessons on the truth of Christianity* and *Introductory lessons on Christian evidence* were no longer on the list of books approved for combined instruction, but could still be used during the time set apart for separate religious instruction. In a very unclear statement the commissioners also implied that when any objection forced the limitation of the *Sacred poetry* and scripture extracts to before and after the combined hours when all children had to attend, that this was not really the same as limiting them to the hours of separate religious instruction.[113]

One wonders, however, if they really thought that this administrative hermaphrodite—combined religious instruction before or after school hours with attendance limited to those whose parents approved—differed in practice from separate religious instruction. What they had really said was that in protestant schools protestant children could use the books before or after school and that local vicars could salve their consciences with the theoretical statement that the scriptures were being used during combined school hours in schools under their patronage. Of course if he wished, the protestant patron could designate the first or last hour as separate religious instruction and read the scripture extracts and *Sacred poetry*, there being only one difference, besides that of nomenclature, between such arrangements and the non-compulsory-united-religious-instruction approach: if the pastor called the time used for reading the *Scripture lessons* and *Sacred poetry* 'religious instruction', he was bound to allow

---

[112] *Copies of correspondence of education commissioners (Ireland) relative to school books with Mr Tottenham, in 1840, etc., pp* 16–17; *Copy of a resolution lately adopted by the board of national education in Ireland, excluding the use of certain books for the schools under their management,* pp 1–2, H.C. 1852–3 (826), xciv; M.C.N.E.I., 8 July 1853.

[113] M.C.N.E.I., 5 Aug. 1853. The new rule and its exposition are found in the *Nineteenth report of the commissioners of national education in Ireland, for the year 1852,* pp xxix–xxx, [1688] H.C. 1852–3, xliii, pt i, and in *Royal commission of inquiry into primary education (Ireland),* vol. i, pt i: *Report of the commissioners,* p. 127.

the catholic children in his school to receive catholic religious instruction, whereas if he maintained that it was non-compulsory combined instruction, his only duty was to allow the catholic children to withdraw. In the case of the catholics the semantic juggling was immaterial, for they won their point, namely that no children in ordinary national schools should be required to read any of the commissioners' religious books and that for Roman Catholic children in protestant schools the arrangements for their withdrawal should be as convenient as possible. Subsequent rulings by the commissioners made it clear that the new rule was to apply to model schools as well as to ordinary national schools.[114]

True to his word, Whately resigned. Greene and Blackburne left with him. Not content to leave gracefully, Whately repeated his threat to resign, then resigned, then caused his carping letter of resignation to be made public.[115] The commissioners severed the archbishop's relationship with the system with an expression of 'their deep regret that his grace had used language, which, as the document is now made a public one, they are compelled to pronounce to be unjustifiable and unbecoming'.[116]

The importance of the great commotion over the commissioners' religious books should not, for all its pettiness and complexity, be underestimated. The immediate effects were to remove Whately's books of evidences from the commissioners' lists and to alter the rules regarding the use of the *Scripture lessons* and *Sacred poetry* to suit the Roman Catholics. The ultimate effect was to break the commissioners' administrative spine, for when Whately left the last strong proponent of the mixed system was lost. The manner of his leaving discredited his viewpoint in the eyes of the remaining commissioners and guaranteed that no one of stature would take it up. The course of events produced a great Roman Catholic victory, a victory which encouraged the prelates to be increasingly aggressive in their demands. With Murray dead and Whately no longer among the commissioners,

[114] M.C.N.E.I., 15 July 1853, 15 Dec. 1854.

[115] Richard Whately to Earl St Germans, 21 July 1853, 24 July 1853, 26 July 1853, reproduced in E. Jane Whately, ii, 272–81.

[116] *Copies of correspondence of education commissioners (Ireland) relative to school books, with Mr Tottenham in 1840, etc.*, p. 20; M.C.N.E.I., 12 Aug. 1853.

the commissioners were much easier to push around, not only for the catholic prelates but for others as well, most notably the treasury. The softening-up process continued for the two and a half decades after this extracts affair, and by 1870 the commissioners were easy prey for almost anyone who wished to bully them.

VII

OVER THE HILL AND INTO THE WOODS, 1850–70

~~~~~~

I

DESPITE THE SHRAPNEL OF CONTROVERSY flying past the commissioners, the system under their charge operated from day to day as if nothing were amiss. This even though the commissioners as a corporate body grew weaker, and Roman Catholic pressure grew stronger throughout the 1850s and 1860s. The number of schools and scholars in the system during the years 1850 to 1870 were as follows:[1]

---

[1] Compiled from *Royal commission of inquiry into primary education (Ireland)*, vol. vii, *Returns furnished by the national board* p. 490 [C 6 vi], H.C., 1870, xxviii, pt v; *Thirty-fifth report of the commissioners of national education in Ireland, for the year 1868*, p. 8 [4193], H.C. 1868–9, xxi; *Thirty-seventh report . . . for the year 1870*, p. 7 [C 360], H.C. 1871, xxiii; *Thirty-ninth report . . . for the year 1872*, p. 9 [C 805], H.C. 1873, xxv.

The large increase in children on the rolls between 1856 and 1857 was a result of the commissioners switching their statistical signals. Through 1856 the number of children on the rolls was computed as of a specific date in the year. From 1857 onwards the number was calculated on the basis of the total number of children who appeared upon the rolls of any national school at any time during the school year, even if the name was later removed from the roll because of withdrawal or transfer to another school.

275

Year	No. of schools in operation	No. of children on rolls	Average daily attendance
1850	4,547	511,239	N/A
1851	4,704	520,401	N/A
1852	4,875	544,604	282,575
1853	5,023	550,631	271,364
1854	5,178	551,110	267,099
1855	5,124	535,905	252,488
1856	5,245	560,134	254,011
1857	5,337	776,473	268,397
1858	5,408	803,610	266,091
1859	5,496	806,510	269,203
1860	5,632	804,000	262,823
1861	5,830	803,364	284,726
1862	6,010	812,527	284,912
1863	6,163	840,569	296,986
1864	6,263	870,401	315,108
1865	6,372	922,084	321,209
1866	6,453	910,819	316,225
1867	6,349	913,198	321,683
1868	6,586	967,563	354,853
1869	6,707	991,335	358,560
1870	6,806	998,999	359,199

Parliament continued to support the system with reasonable generosity.[2]

Year	Parliamentary grant		
1850	£125,000	0s	0d
1851	134,500	0	0
1852	164,577	0	0
1853	182,073	0	0
1854	193,040	0	0
1855	215,200	0	0
1856	227,641	0	0
1857	223,530	0	0
1858	249,443	19	7
1859	272,489	0	0
1860	294,040	16	2
1861	311,216	10	6
1862	317,635	0	0
1863	332,646	0	0
1864	339,944	0	0

[2] Compiled from *Royal commission of inquiry into primary education (Ireland)*, vol. vii: *Returns furnished by the national board*, p. 490; *Thirty-fifth report of he commissioners of national education in Ireland, for the year 1868*, p. 32; *Thirty-sixth report . . . for the year 1869*, p. 38 [C 120], H.C. 1870, xxiii; *Thirty-seventh report . . . for the year 1870*, p. 38.

Year	Parliamentary grant		
1865	£345,036	o	o
1866	357,836	o	o
1867	357,836	o	o
1868	301,700	o	o
1869	380,000	o	o
1870	394,209	7	11

With the death of Archbishop Murray and the resignation of
Archbishop Whately, the commissioners were bereft of men of
national stature. The catholic hierarchy was conspicuous for the
unimportance of the men by whom it was represented. The
Roman Catholic Bishop of Down and Connor, Cornelius Denvir, served from 1853 until 1858, when, according to some reports, pressure was brought upon him forcing his retirement.[3]
After Denvir resigned the only Roman Catholic ecclesiastic
among the commissioners was Dean Meyler of Dublin who became a commissioner in 1851 and remained active until his
death in 1863. With Meyler's death, no bishop or dean could
be found to take his place. Just as no catholic ecclesiastic
came forward to take Murray's place, so no bishop of the
established church filled the vacuum left by Whately's sever-
ance. Dr Higgins, bishop of Limerick and later of Derry and
Raphoe, took Whately's chair in late 1853, but neither his
personality nor his ecclesiastical position was a satisfactory
substitute for Whately's. Hence, the commissioners who
prior to 1850 had been dominated by the archbishops of
Dublin of the Roman Catholic and of the protestant faiths,
had become, by 1854, a group governed by laymen. This
meant that the collective strength of the commissioners was
greatly weakened, for, before the death of Murray and the
disappearance of Whately, the commissioners possessed strong
advocates within the inner councils of the two largest
Irish churches. The loss of Archbishop Murray was doubly
unfortunate since the time had passed when a catholic layman
with anything at stake could openly oppose or defy the
hierarchy.

The lay commissioners were not impressive individuals. J. J.
Murphy (1851–63) was a Roman Catholic master in chancery
whose court schedule hindered the performance of his education

[3] *Daily Express,* 1 Nov. 1864.

duties.[4] The anglican Mountifort Longfield (from 1853) was a queen's counsellor and eventually a judge who managed to attend fifteen to twenty meetings in most years. Thomas O'Hagan (from 1858) was a universally respected catholic barrister, but his practice and his chairmanship of County Dublin cut into the time he could spend on education. Among the Roman catholic laymen were the earl of Dunraven (from 1861), the Right Honourable Henry Monahan, chief justice of the common pleas (from 1861), and the Right Honourable D. R. Pigot, lord chief baron of the exchequer (from 1861), none of whom made more than ten appearances annually except in the rarest of years. In contrast, Laurence Waldron, Roman Catholic M.P. (from 1861), John O'Hagan, Roman Catholic barrister and nationalist poet (from 1861), and John Lentaigne, Inspector-general of prisons (from 1861), attended very regularly, Lentaigne making forty-one attendances in 1862. The most important new addition to the anglican commissioners during the years 1850–70 was James Lawson, solicitor general in Ireland and later attorney-general (from 1861); the marquis of Kildare and the Right Honourable M. Brady continued to serve as anglican members throughout the period. In 1864 and 1865 three commissioners were named to replace those who had resigned or died, two of whom, Thomas Preston, magistrate and deputy lieutenant, and J. D. Fitzgerald, judge of court of queen's bench, were catholics, the other of whom, J. W. Murland, was a liberal presbyterian barrister. Of this group of three (all of whom were still serving in 1870), only Murland regularly made more than twenty attendances during the year. Provost John H. Jellett, Rev. Charles Morell, and the Right Honourable Mr Justice Morris were appointed in 1868, and were still serving in 1870.[5] Preoccupied with their own affairs, the commissioners were easy prey for organized pressure groups.

With a few exceptions the board's administrative apparatus

[4] The dates in parenthesis represent the years each man served as commissioner. No terminal date is given for men still serving in 1870 (e.g., 'from 1858').

[5] [James W. Kavanagh], *Mixed education, The catholic case stated* . . . (London and Dublin, 1859), pp 259–80; *Royal commission of inquiry into primary education (Ireland)*, vol. vii *Returns furnished by the national board*, pp 5–7; *Thirty-seventh report of the commissioners of national education in Ireland, for the year 1870*, [C 360], H.C. 1871, xxiii.

was organized along the same lines during the years 1850–67 as it had been previously. One of the major exceptions was the inspection department which was organized in the mid-1850s. In September 1854, the commissioners decided to divide their district inspectors into three classes and after discussion it was decided that the grades and salary ranges would be as follows: sub-inspector, beginning salary £200 per annum, rising to £250 per annum; second class district inspector, beginning salary £275 per annum, rising to £305 per annum; first class district inspector, beginning salary £320 per annum, rising to £370 per annum. Men in each of these grades were expected to pay their travelling expenses out of their salaries. The total number of district inspectors was raised to fifty, six of whom were sub-inspectors and twelve of whom were first class district inspectors. Of the twelve first class district inspectors, it was stipulated that six were to be of various protestant denominations, six to be Roman Catholics.[6] Even though the 1854 reorganization added six new men to the inspectorial staff, the average number of schools allotted to each inspector still exceeded one hundred, a number precluding adequate inspection.[7]

Moreover, the inspectoral staff was woefully inadequate for efficient handling of paperwork. In January 1855, there was more than a full year's arrears of inspectoral business in the central establishment, including approximately 11,000 reports by inspectors on schools visited by them which had yet to be read and dealt with. Whole rooms were filled with bales of unread reports and some of the commissioners suggested that they be burned as the fastest means of dealing with them. In January 1855, Maurice Cross, the senior secretary, became alarmed by the treasury's holding inquiries into all civil service departments, and ordered the head inspectors to put the department in order. Aided by a temporarily augmented staff, the head inspectors worked off the arrears. The treasury was then called in and subsequently made a favourable report upon the

[6] M.C.N.E.I., 22 Sept. 1854, 20 Oct. 1854; *Twenty-first report of the commissioners of national education in Ireland, for the Year 1854*, p. 19 [1950.], H.C. 1854–5, xxiii, pt i.

[7] *Twenty-first report of the commissioners of national education in Ireland, for the year 1854*, p. 19.

administration of the department.[8] At the commissioners' suggestion,[9] the head inspectors produced a plan for the reorganization of the inspection department of the central establishment.

The plan, which was agreeable to five of the head inspectors, the sixth disagreeing only on details, entailed further rationalization of the department's arrangements. As approved by the commissioners, head inspector McCreedy was placed in charge of the office with the duties of reading all letters, analysing reports, and submitting views to secretary Kelly for the commissioners' attention.[10] McCreedy was subsequently given the title of chief of inspection, an office which, like almost every other major appointment, eventually became a dual office, shared by one catholic and one protestant. Apparently the remaining five head inspectors had not realized that McCreedy's position in the central establishment would not be a temporary one nor that he would come to be their superior. In May 1856, they wrote the commissioners, remonstrating upon McCreedy's exalted state and upon the peremptory manner in which they were being treated.[11] The commissioners responded by inviting anyone who was dissatisfied to resign, or, if he chose not to resign, to be ready for instant dismissal the moment he again dared to express such opinions.[12] This whipped the troops back into line, and the department functioned reasonably effectively thereafter. By 1870 the number of inspectors had grown to six head inspectors and sixty district inspectors, in addition to the two chiefs of inspection. In a mildly humanitarian move the commissioners retitled the sub-inspectors as 'third class inspectors', this being 'more gratifying to them and there was no objection to giving them the name'.[13]

In addition to the reorganization of the inspectoral staff, the duties of the two secretaries to the commissioners were re-

[8] Kavanagh, pp 282–3.   [9] M.C.N.E.I., 2 Mar. 1855.

[10] M.C.N.E.I., 20 Apr. 1855.

[11] 'Joint letter of remonstrance of all the head inspectors, dated 31st May 1856, against the direction of the inspection department', reproduced in Kavanagh, pp 424–7.

[12] 'Order of commissioners of national education, 6 June 1856', quoted in Kavanagh, p. 428.

[13] Robert B. McDowell, *The Irish administration, 1801–1914* (London and Toronto, 1964), p. 250.

allocated between the incumbents. This rearrangement was necessitated by the changes in the inspection department, since James Kelly, the junior secretary, had previously acted as head of the inspection staff, a position assumed by William McCreedy as chief of inspection. On the basis of a memorandum prepared in mid-1855 by Alexander Macdonnell, the resident commissioner, Kelly's duties were re-defined as consisting of attendance upon the agricultural committee, of serving as secretary to the weekly meetings on inspectoral matters, as acting as secretary to the finance committee, and of maintaining discipline in the commissioners' central office.[14] By implication, attendance upon the commissioners was to be left to the senior secretary, Maurice Cross. The only other administrative change of note that took place between 1850 and 1870 was the transfer, at the suggestion of the treasury, of the board's architectural department to the board of works.[15]

The administrative structure of the central establishment was, in 1868, constructed along the following lines:[16]

Position	Name	Religion of incumbents	Salary paid per annum
Resident commissioner	A. Macdonnell	Est. Church	£1,000, plus residence
Secretary	James Kelly	Rom. Cath.	750
	W. Newell	Est. Church	650
Accountant	J. Claridge	Est. Church	600
Chiefs of inspection and of statistical department	P. J. Keenan	Rom. Cath.	600
	W. A. Hunter	Presby.	600
Senior first class clerk in charge of correspondence department	C. Robertson	Est. Church	450
Assistant accountant	W. Gordon	Rom. Cath.	400
Storekeeper	A. Todd	Presby.	290

[14] M.C.N.E.I., 6 July 1855.
[15] M.C.N.E.I., 19 August 1856.
[16] Compiled from *Royal commission of inquiry into primary education (Ireland)*, vol. vii, *Returns furnished by the national board*, pp 6, 8, 33.

Accounts department:
  2 first class clerks: 1 Est. Church, 1 Rom. Cath.   315–400
  5 second class clerks: 4 Rom. Cath., 1 Presby.   180–270
  2 third class clerks: 1 Est. Church, 1 Rom. Cath.   120

Inspection and statistical department:
  4 first class clerks: 1 Est. Church, 1 Rom. Cath.
                       1 Presby., 1 undetermined   315–400
  12 second class clerks: 5 Est. Church, 6 Rom. Cath.
                       1 Presby.   190–280
  17 third class clerks: 3 Est. Church, 13 Rom. Cath.,
                       1 Presby.   90–170

Correspondence department:
  1 first class clerk: Est. Church   400
  1 second class clerk: Rom. Cath.   250

Storekeeper's department: 280
  2 second class clerks: 1 Rom. Cath., 1 Est. Church   280
  2 third class clerks: 2 Rom. Cath.   110–170

The above table is useful because it confirms that the internal administration of the board had taken on the lines of the classic bureaucratic model. This involved increasing specialization by function and implied a rational salary structure that cut across departments and guaranteed that men shouldering similar loads of responsibility received roughly equal salaries. The religious implications also bear note. Of the fifty-seven individuals covered by the table, twenty-three were protestant, thirty-three Roman Catholic, and one undetermined. If, however, we consider only the men who were in charge of departments, plus the two secretaries and the resident commissioners, we find that six were protestant, two catholic.

During the 1850s the commissioners' relations with the Irish administration changed slightly, one aspect of this change being that the lord lieutenant and chief secretary came to interfere more often than previously in educational affairs. In September 1854, the lord lieutenant, Edward Granville, earl of St Germans, suggested that the commissioners' rules be revised, with a view 'to making them perfectly clear'. He also made a considerable number of specific suggestions, with the result that the commissioners were forced to rewrite their regulations.[17] In the new code the old informal agreement that the commissioners would

[17] M.C.N.E.I., 26 Sept. 1854.

not undertake to revise any fundamental rule of the system without the lord lieutenant's approval was stated explicitly and thus became a formal principal of the system. It would be a mistake to over-read this set of events, but in retrospect they can be seen as the beginning of the Irish administration's encroachment upon the commissioners' autonomy.

Another small bit of freedom was taken from the commissioners by the activities of the civil service commissioners. In 1854, the famous Northcote-Trevelyan report on the civil service appeared, the fundamental principles of which were that promotion in the public service should be upon merit, entry should be by competitive examination, and, in order that staff might be shifted easily from one department to another, first appointments in all departments should be upon an uniform basis. In May 1855, the civil service commission, consisting of three commissioners, was established, and was charged with the duty of holding qualifying examinations for government positions. Each department, however, retained the power of selecting from among those qualified.[18] Arrangements were made almost at once in at least ten of the Irish departments to hold such examinations, the national education branch being one of them.[19] Not only did the examinations somewhat reduce the commissioners' freedom to hire whomever they pleased, but they also forced them to restyle their hiring procedures for major appointments, most notably the inspectorships. Whereas the national education commissioners had previously chosen their inspectors through individual interviews, after 1860 they filled vacancies by having a committee select the best candidates according to their credentials and then allowed only these candidates selected to take the examination. Inspectors were then hired from those who did best upon the examination.[20]

Besides somewhat restricting the commissioners' freedom of contract, and forcing them to rearrange their hiring procedures, the civil service commissioners directly influenced the commissioners by making suggestions about hiring policy. For example, the civil service commission led the commissioners of

---

[18] P. J. Meghen, *A short history of the public service in Ireland* (Dublin, 1962), pp 19–20.

[19] *Packet*, 26 June 1856.   [20] See M.C.N.E.I., 31 Aug. 1860.

national education to raise the maximum age for candidates for the sub-inspectorships from thirty-eight to forty-three, simply by suggesting that this might be a wise policy.[21] Though clearly the civil service commissioners were not a coercive threat to the autonomy of the education commissioners, they were one of a number of groups nagging at the commissioners and meddling in their affairs.

Although the full force of treasury control of Irish education did not fall until the 1870s, there were hints during the 'fifties and 'sixties of what was to happen later. For example, the lords of the treasury were largely responsible for the limitation upon the commissioners' freedom to publish textbooks, for it was their recommendation to which Lord John Russell acceded in the Longman's affair. Also, it was the treasury's investigation of all administrative departments that indirectly led to the shake-up in the inspection department in the mid-1850s. The incident of the inspectoral arrears illustrated how frightened the board's staff was of incurring treasury censure. On strictly financial matters the treasury became increasingly sticky. The commissioners were able to beat off a treasury move in 1869 to have all teachers' salaries come under treasury sanction rather than the commissioners',[22] but it was clear by 1870 that the lords of the treasury were antagonistic to the commissioners, and that the commissioners would not be able to withstand them forever.

In summary, then, the purely administrative developments that took place between 1850 and 1870 were neither dramatic nor surprising. The number of schools and school children continued to grow, and parliamentary money continued to increase. Nevertheless, within this shell of numerical and financial security there huddled an undistinguished body of commissioners. The group consisted almost entirely of laymen, who were often too busy to attend meetings, and who boasted almost no power within the major churches. In such a situation day to day control of national education fell increasingly into the hands of the resident commissioner and the professional civil servants. Even these professionals seem to have become somewhat slack in their standards, or so the inspectoral arrears

[21] M.C.N.E.I., 28 Mar. 1862.
[22] M.C.N.E.I., 13 Apr. 1869, 11 May 1869.

crisis would lead one to believe. Various groups and persons such as the treasury, the civil service commissioners, and the lord lieutenant and the chief secretary nibbled steadily at the commissioners' privileges. Although their enemies did not realize it, the commissioners were becoming too weak to put up much of a fight about anything.

2

Fortunately for the commissioners, they faced at least one opponent weaker than themselves, the clergy of the established church. The church at mid-century was manifestly a sick organization. The sickness was partly, but not crucially, a matter of numbers, the Irish religious census of 1834 showed 852,064 anglicans (including methodists) and the census of 1861 only 698,357. Nevertheless, due to the huge post-famine decline of the whole population, the adherents of the established church had advanced from 10·7 per cent of the population in 1834 to 11·9 per cent in 1861.[23] The problem was also in part financial, for, although the income of the clergy and bishops was estimated at the considerable sum of approximately £393,000 a year in 1863, this was roughly £250,000 less than they had received in 1834.[24] Politics, too, contributed to the problem, for the church was clearly losing its influence within the government and upon the country. Most debilitating of all, however, was the unspoken realization of the inevitability of church disestablishment. In 1843, Mr Ward, a member for Sheffield, had urged the transfer of some of the established church's endowment to the Roman Catholic church, and in 1849 the question was again raised when a committee to investigate the state of the church was moved unsuccessfully. With the advancing power and influence of Paul Cullen, first as Roman Catholic archbishop of Armagh and then of Dublin, it became clear that the catholics would not forever tolerate the church established. The issue smouldered into the mid-1860s, and with the conversion of

[23] N. D. Emerson, 'The last phase of the establishment', in Walter A. Phillips (ed.), *History of the Church of Ireland from the earliest times to the present day*, vol. iii: *The modern church* (London, 1933), pp 314–15.

[24] Alfred T. Lee, *Facts respecting the present state of the Church in Ireland* (London and Belfast, third ed., 1865), pp 14, 16.

Gladstone in 1865 the cause of disestablishment was all but won, although this was not obvious at the time.[25]

If the clergy and hierarchy of the established church had stood together in the face of declining numbers, slipping income, and the threat of disestablishment, they might still have been able to negotiate effectively with the government. Unfortunately, many of the clerics agreed only in detesting each other. Nowhere was the illness of divisiveness seen more clearly than upon the elementary education issue, upon which the split was as deep as had occurred on the same issue within the Roman Catholic church. In the 1830s, the clergy had divided for or against the national system, with the great majority opposing the system. The founding of the Church Education Society increased the polarity of opinion within the church's ranks for it provided an alternative to the national system and meant that each anglican clergyman had to make an explicit choice between the Church Education Society and the national system of education. Unlike the Roman Catholic prelates who fought about the education in the public press, the clergy of the church of Ireland flailed each other through the more elegant medium of the pamphlet. Unfortunately for historical neatness the pamphlet war did not, like the catholic scrapping, fall into a small period of time, but extended from the mid-1840s to the late 1860s. Without this span of time two stages of the war may be discerned. The first extended from 1831 to the lord primate's declaration of 1860 countenancing association with the national schools in cases where financially necessary. This first phase was nasty and bitter, but there were reasonable men on each side of the issue. After 1860, the battle was largely between the diehards who denounced the system in increasingly fanatical terms and the majority of the clergy who were gradually coming to realize that it was impossible for them to support a school system of their own and who accepted the national system as the only alternative to a poorly educated laity.

According to one estimate the opposing line-ups were as follows in 1848:[26]

---

[25] Emerson, pp 313–16.

[26] *Pros and cons, being a digest and impartial analysis of all the principal reasons that have been given, and arguments used for and against the national board of education; with brief remarks by 'Clericus Armachanus'* (Dublin, 1848), p. 5.

National Board advocates	*Church Education Society* advocates
Archbishop of Dublin	The Lord Primate
Dean of Ferns	Bishop of Cashel
Dean of Achonry	Bishop of Ossory
Archdeacon of Meath	Bishop of Down
Rev. Dr Elrington	Vicar-General of Armagh
Rev. Dr Martin	Rev. C. K. Irwin
Vicar-General of Kildare	Dr Trench
Rev. Dr Carlisle	Rev. J. F. Lloyd
Rev. Henry Woodward	Rev. R. H. Ryland
Rev. Thomas Woodward	Rev. J. Corvon
Rev. D. Bagot	Rev. James Disney
Rev. J. M. Hiffernan	Rev. Alexander Ross
Rev. Robert King	Rev. Dr O'Sullivan
Dr. Taylor	

The names included consist of the most important, or at least most vocal, of the opposing factions. As indicated in an earlier chapter, the Church Education Society advocates were in control at mid-century, boasting roughly three quarters of the clergy and the larger proportion of the hierarchy.

The arguments for the Church Education Society were simply restatements of the arguments against the national system, for the former became for many the incarnation of all the virtues the national system lacked. Thus, the national system continued to be attacked for its restrictions on the use of the scriptures, for its mutilation of the Bible, for its limitation of religious activities and for its refusal to recognize the educational rights demanded by the established clergy. The Church Education Society was lauded because it allowed the free use of the Bible, was under the control of the anglican clergy, and did not split religious education from literary training.

The arguments in favour of joining the national system were more original and more worthy of attention. One set of arguments contested the validity of the claim that the established clergy had the duty of educating the poor. T. S. Townsend, the lord lieutenant's chaplain, was the chief critic of this interpretation of anglican responsibility and repudiated it as a violation of the right of conscience and as a danger to religious toleration.[27]

[27] T. S. Townsend, *The policy of a separate grant for education in Ireland, considered; with some remarks on the ninth annual meeting of the Church Education Society, held in Dublin on the 12th April, 1849 at the Rotunda* (Dublin, 1849), p. 4.

Others protested that the Church Education Society's system was itself a violation of church doctrines for it made the reading of scripture compulsory, something nowhere prescribed by the church, while it made the use of the catechism optional which the church everywhere enforced upon all.[28] One of the most important arguments for the national system was that the opponents completely misunderstood its rules and that the clergy could attach themselves to the national schools without violating their priestly oaths.[29] Ultimately, however, the most telling argument was one of expediency: the national system offered a great deal of money for the support of schools, money which the increasingly hard-pressed anglican clergy could not afford to ignore. This argument appeared as early as the middle 1840s, and usually took the form that the opposition to the national system had been a noble thing, but that in cases in which a Church Education Society could not be formed or could not be adequately financed, the local vicar should apply to the commissioners of national education for aid.[30]

The financial argument was recognized by the adherents of the Church Education Society as well as by those who joined the national system. By the mid-1840s, the officials of the society had realized that they could not continue to operate, at least not at an efficient level, without government aid. As noted earlier, they applied, unsuccessfully, for a 'separate grant' of their own in 1845 but were firmly turned down by Sir Robert Peel. Throughout the 1850s, petition upon petition for a separate grant was presented to parliament from local branches of the Church Education Society, but little or no notice was taken of them. In the face of government inertia, the more moderate Church Education Society supporters wavered, and by the late 1850s it was clear that the majority against the national

[28] *Letters on national education in Ireland, containing suggestions with a view of obtaining the co-operation of the clergy of the established church with the incorporated national board* (Dublin, 1846), p. 4.

[29] Charles R. Elrington, *A few suggestions addressed to the clergy upon the present state of the question respecting national education in Ireland* (Dublin, second ed., 1847), passim.

[30] J. C. Martin, *A defence of the Irish clergy and a view of the past and present duty with respect to the system of national education in Ireland* (Dublin, 1844), passim.

system was declining.[31] The central society's income reached a plateau in the 1850s. It was £5,139 in 1850, rose considerably above £6,000 in 1851 and 1855 but remained between £5,000 and £6,000 for the other years of the decade.[32] The number of children ceased growing and the whole structure seemed to waver. In 1851 the society had 1,885 schools, enrolling 103,878 children,[33] but a decline set in and in 1855 there were 1,827 schools, with 90,572 children on their books.[34] By the late 1850s it was obvious that the Church Education Society was in trouble. 'It is not possible to disguise the fact,' one newspaper reported, 'that the Church Education Society occupies a position it is not able to fill, and proposes itself to a work it is wholly incompetent to perform.'[35]

In January 1860, the presidents of the Church Education Society petitioned Edward Cardwell, the chief secretary, to modify the national education commissioners' rules so that the society schools could be connected with the system. A meeting on the matter took place between Cardwell and Hamilton Verschoyle, one of the society's honorary secretaries. Cardwell clung to the principles that religious and secular instruction should be separate and that no child should be forced to receive religious instruction to which his parents objected. In reply, the presidents of the Church Education Society agreed with the principle respecting the right of parental authority but argued that there was no violation thereof in their schools, since parents were fully aware that the scriptures were read each day and since no one compelled the children to attend the society's schools. The society's dignitaries followed this extraordinary argument by suggesting that in any area in which there

[31] William Anderson, *The opposition to the national system of education, considered in its effects upon the established church in Ireland, with remarks upon a pamphlet recently published* (Belfast, 1858), p. 3.

[32] *Royal commission of inquiry into primary education (Ireland)*, vol. viii: *Miscellaneous papers and returns*, p. 33 (C 6–VII), H.C. 1870, xxviii, pt v.

These sums appear very small if contrasted to parliamentary votes to the national system. For example, the vote in 1855 was £215,200.

[33] *Thirteenth annual report of the Church Education Society for Ireland* (Dublin, 1853), pp 10–18.

[34] *Sixteenth annual report of the Church Education Society for Ireland* (Dublin, 1856), pp 10, 19.

[35] *Daily Mercury*, 22 Dec. 1859.

was not a set of national schools, the claims of the Church Education Society school in that area should remain in abeyance until a national school was founded in the neighbourhood and thereafter the society school should also receive aid.[36] Needless to say, the government was not impressed, and Cardwell decisively punctured the Church Education Society's balloon.[37]

The break in the anglican deadlock came in early 1860 when the lord primate, John George Beresford, a president of the Church Education Society, addressed a circular to the patrons of schools in connection with the Clogher Diocesan Church Education Society. The circular, dated 21 February 1860, was a reluctant surrender to reality:

The society's schools, it is evident, must continue to be dependent for their support on their own resources. A considerable number of them, I am happy to say, are adequately provided for, are in an efficient state, and are diffusing the benefits of good education in their respective bodies . . .

It is to be regretted, however, that many of the schools are in a condition far from satisfactory. Several of them are quite inefficient, owing to the want of adequate funds; the salaries are not large enough to secure the services of properly qualified teachers; and the supply of books and other school requisites falls very short of what is called for.

It is for the patrons of these impoverished and inefficient schools to judge whether, by renewed efforts, they can raise them from their depressed conditions. . . . But if all expectation of increasing the funds of these schools be at an end . . . it appears that it would be advisable to seek for aid from the commissioners of national education, rather than allow the children of our communion to grow up in a state of ignorance, or expose them to the danger which would arise from their resorting for secular education to national schools under the management and influence of patrons who are hostile to our church.[38]

[36] Hamilton Verschoyle to Earl Cardwell, 10 Jan. 1860, N.L.I., Larcom Papers (copy).

[37] Earl Cardwell to Hamilton Verschoyle, 7 Feb. 1860, N.L.I., Larcom Papers (copy).

[38] Quoted in James Godkin, *Education in Ireland; its history, institutions, system, statistics and progress, from the earliest times to the present* (London and Dublin, 1862), pp 103–104; also quoted in John Garrett, *Education in Ireland; comparison of the advice given in two addresses, recently issued by his*

Beresford, it is important to note, was not abandoning the Church Education Society; indeed, he reaffirmed his faith in its educational principles. What he was doing was suggesting that the Church Education Society was a luxury that should be supported if the local parish could afford it, but that if it could not, the local patrons should adhere to the national system rather than suffer their children to receive an inadequate education.

The lord primate's views were adopted by certain of the vice-presidents of the Church Education Society, by the lord chancellor, by the dean of Emly, and by Rev. Hamilton Verschoyle, senior honorary secretary of the Church Education Society.[39] But a great storm broke about these men, with the defence of the Church Education Society falling into fanatical hands. Beresford was publicly compared to Judas Iscariot.[40] Bishop O'Brien of Ossory led the anti-Beresford forces. O'Brien raised the cry of 'No Surrender' and was supported by perhaps two thirds of the anglican clergy.[41]

While denouncing Beresford and his followers, the Church Education Society militants continued to press for government money. Unfortunately for them, their understanding of the situation was marred by two major misperceptions. The first of these was that they failed to realize that once the Beresford group had broken ranks the chances for gaining money on the society's terms were reduced to almost zero. Beresford's circular was an explicit statement of the weakness of the society's position and a guarantee to the government that if the government stood firm it would eventually win the field. Second, the Church Education Society advocates failed to understand that money is a medium of exchange and that in return for government money they would have to bend to meet some of the government's requirements. Failing to realize the weakness of their position and unwilling to compromise, the society's supporters had little hope of coming to an agreement with the commissioners of national education.

---

[39] Godkin, p. 106. [40] Emerson, p. 311.
[41] *Dublin Evening Post*, 10 Apr. 1860.

---

grace the lord primate of all Ireland and the lord bishop of Ossory, Ferns and Leighlin, embodying an address to the archbishops, bishops and clergy of the Church of Ireland (London and Dublin, 1860), pp 12–14.

The commissioners themselves undercut the Church Education Society's position by an attempt to seduce the society's schools away from their parent organization. This was done by the introduction of a special set of regulations regarding recognition of schools with very small enrolments (meaning protestant schools). According to regulations introduced in June 1860, schools with an attendance below fifteen, but conducted on the principles of the national system, were entitled to inspection and the books and requisites and their teachers became eligible for training and their time in service counted for salary and allowances should their school ever be granted full recognition by the commissioners. Schools with an average attendance of between fifteen and nineteen received, in addition to the above benefits, an award of salary equal to two thirds of a probationary teacher's salary. The benefits to schools with an average attendance of twenty to twenty-four included the full salary of a probationary teacher, for a school of twenty-five to twenty-nine a salary as high as that of a teacher of the first division of the third class, and so on until a school with an average attendance of over thirty-five was awarded aid up to the amount of a teacher's salary.[42]

Bishop Robert Knox of Down and Connor exemplified the lack of realism of those who wished to obtain government concessions when he forwarded a petition from the clergy and laity of his diocese to the lord lieutenant, Lord Carlisle, in February 1862. The petition stated the signers' willingness to adopt the practice of non-compulsion in religious instruction as embodied in the rule of the national system that stated that no child should be compelled to receive or to be present at any religious instruction to which his parents objected. Other portions of the petition made it clear that by 'religious instruction' the petitioners meant doctrinal teaching, but that they did not include Bible reading in 'religious instruction'. Since only anglican children were required to attend anglican catechism in Church Education Society schools, the petitioners were making no concession whatsoever. They also submitted that they had no intention to use the scriptures during the hours of general instruction for denominational or controversial purposes, and they asked for an interpretation of the religious rule allowing the manager or

[42] M.C.N.E.I., 8 June 1860.

teacher to make references to the word of God as appropriate
during the hours of combined teaching. Were such an interpretation given, they would be glad to connect themselves with
the national system.[43] In other words, they promised to take the
commissioners' money if the commissioners would provide it
on the petition's terms.

Since at this date the national schools were well out of any
danger of numerical extinction, it is hard to conceive of a proposal that would be less attractive to the commissioners. They
replied that they could not sanction any change in the rule regarding scripture reading as it was one of the fundamental
regulations of the system.[44] Bishop Knox rejoined that the petitioners had not asked for any change in the rule regarding
scripture reading but had merely asked for permission to refer
to the word of God during the hours of combined instruction
whenever the lesson demanded.[45] The commissioners again said
'No'.[46] Besides the petitioners' attempt to bargain from weakness, the entire negotiations smacked of the absurd, for the petitioners were asking for a right in theory which, through the
scripture material included in the commissioners' reading books,
was already allowed in practice. Had Bishop Knox and his
followers looked at the actual operation of the national schools
instead of concentrating on the theology of the system's rules
they would have seen that they could have joined the system
without any injury to their consciences.

If the government and the commissioners needed any additional indication that it would be best for them to hold their
ground, they received it in the 1866 declarations of a large
number of the clergy of the established church in favour of
united education in preference to a denominational system.
Without pledging themselves to an approval of the national

---

[43] *Copy of a memorial lately presented to the lord lieutenant of Ireland by the lord
bishop of Down, Connor and Dromore, on behalf of certain clergy and laity of his
diocese, on the subject of national education in Ireland; of the statement read by the
bishop on presenting such memorial; and, of any correspondence which has since taken
place between the lord lieutenant and the bishop on the subject*, pp 1–3, H.C. 1862
(347), xliii.

[44] Ibid., p. 4; M.C.N.E.I., 14 Mar. 1862.

[45] *Copy of a memorial lately presented to the lord lieutenant of Ireland by the lord
bishop of Down, Connor and Dromore . . .* pp. 4–5.

[46] Ibid., p. 5; M.C.N.E.I., 11 Apr. 1862.

system in all respects, the signers stated their agreement with the rule which protected scholars from interference with their religious principles and which thus enabled members of different denominations to receive the benefits of a good education in harmony and peace. The declaration was signed by the lord primate, five bishops, 733 clergymen and almost 2,000 distinguished anglican laymen.[47] Meanwhile, the Church Education Society stumbled downhill. The annual receipts by the central headquarters of the Church Education Society declined from £5,829 in 1860 to £4,423 in 1866.[48] The society had 1,523 schools and 69,608 scholars in 1863,[49] and was down to 1,202 schools and 52,166 pupils on the rolls in 1870.[50] Thus, it was only a matter of time before the clergy of the Church of Ireland joined the national system upon the commissioners' terms.

3

Whatever satisfaction holding the whip-hand over the anglican clergy may have brought the commissioners, they were in no position to gloat, for the commissioners were themselves increasingly under the guns of the Roman Catholic hierarchy. As shown earlier, the hierarchy after 1850, and especially after 1852, was a much sterner, much more aggressive body of men than it had previously been. On the other hand, especially after 1854, the commissioners were increasingly wont to grant modifications in their system as the necessary price for peace. Consequent upon the departure of Whately and his followers, a committee of the house of lords was appointed to investigate the national system but was unable to agree upon any recommendations. The lords' committee did produce some action, however, for it moved the lord lieutenant, the earl of St Germans, to suggest to the commissioners that they revise their rules with a

---

[47] *Declaration in favour of united secular education in Ireland by members of the United Church of England and Ireland, with the List of Signatures* (Dublin, 1866), pp iv, 5–6; *The Times*, 1 Apr. 1866.

[48] *Royal commission of inquiry into primary education (Ireland)*, vol. viii; *Miscellaneous papers and returns,* p. 33.

[49] *Twenty-fourth report of the Church Education Society for Ireland* (Dublin, 1864), p. 12.

[50] *Thirty-first annual report of the Church Education Society for Ireland* (Dublin, 1871), p. 8.

view to making them perfectly clear and explicit. In his memorandum dated 26 September 1854, the lord lieutenant made
twenty-six specific suggestions about education regulations.
These suggestions represent the first time the Irish administration had intervened to any significant degree in the affairs of
the commissioners of national education.

In his very first point the lord lieutenant made it clear that he
not only expected the rules to be revised but that he demanded
that all alterations, omissions, and additions be submitted to
him for his approval. His second point was obviously raised because of catholic scruples concerning religious training. It provided that all religious instruction in the national schools,
whether denominational or general, except that found in the
national school texts, should be given at a separate hour to be
publicly designated on the timetable. On the other hand, St
Germans took the protestant viewpoint in asking that it be explicitly stated that the patron or manager of a school was not
bound to exclude children from the religious instruction of
another faith if the children's parents did not themselves explicitly object to their attending. He also asked the commissioners to make formal the established policy of excluding religious
rites and the exhibition of religious emblems during ordinary
school hours. Another of the lord lieutenant's suggestions
was that non-vested schools should be permitted to be used as
Sunday schools, but not as places of worship, provided that
nothing took place in them leading to contention. The lord
lieutenant's eighth suggestion bowed toward Archbishop
Whately, although too late to placate that prelate: no book of
a religious character having once been unanimously adopted by
the commissioners should be withdrawn or essentially altered
without the lord lieutenant's approval. Neither, he added, was
any fundamental rule to be changed without his sanction. In
his tenth point, he attempted to mollify the more extreme protestants by stating that since many persons objected to the form
of the Ten Commandments used in the national schools, their
use should not be obligatory. Significantly, the lord lieutenant
wished to lay to rest the catholic grievance concerning the vesting of schools and proposed that patrons should have the option
of vesting schools in trustees or in the commissioners but that
repair expenses would be borne by the government only in the

latter case. In the succeeding recommendation St Germans suggested that the commissioners be empowered to grant up to five pounds a year for the repair of convent schools and of schools vested in trustees. The lord lieutenant also dealt with desirable increases in local contributions, additions to the inspectoral staff, and an increase in the number of training establishments.[51]

The commissioners appointed a six man committee to consider the lord lieutenant's proposals, a committee consisting of two presbyterians (Dr Henry and James Gibson), two anglicans (M. Longfield and A. Macdonnell), one unitarian (R. Andrews) and only one Roman Catholic (James O'Ferrall).[52] Their revision of the rules was approved by the whole body of commissioners and sanctioned by the lord lieutenant in mid-1855. Several points should be noted about the substance and the process of this revision. First, as indicated previously, the impetus for the change came from the lord lieutenant. In contrast to his predecessors, St Germans was not content merely to allow the system to develop as it might. Previous lord lieutenants had of course possessed veto power over the commissioners' actions, but had never initiated innovations in the system's structure. Although it would be a mistake to read too much into this single occurrence, embedded as it was in the specific events of the scripture extracts crisis, it does serve as a symbol of increasing unwillingness on the part of the government to allow the commissioners single-handedly to determine the destiny of the national school system, and does serve to alert us to the possibility of increased government intervention in succeeding years.

Second, the revised code of 1855 marks a significant stage in the administrative evolution of the national system, for in it the commissioners explicitly defined the boundaries of their system and codified a number of informal procedures that had been regular practice but had never been set down in writing. Thus, for the first time they stated the 'fundamental principle' of the national system: 'The object of the system of national education

[51] M.C.N.E.I., 26 Sept. 1854; *Royal commission of inquiry into primary education (Ireland)*, vol. i, pt 1. *Report of the commissioners*, pp 146–9 [C 6], H.C. 1870, xxviii, pt i.

[52] M.C.N.E.I., 26 Sept. 1854; *Royal commission of inquiry into primary education (Ireland)*, vol. i, pt 1; *Report of the commissioners*, p. 148.

is to afford *combined* literary and moral, and *separate* religious instruction, to children of all persuasions, as far as possible, upon the fundamental principle, that no attempt shall be made to interfere with the peculiar religious tenents of any description of Christian pupils.'[53] Thereafter, the commissioners described the duties of patrons and of managers, defined the various types of schools under their jurisdiction, and delineated specific operating rules.

Third, the commissioners accepted the lord lieutenant's suggestions, but with certain notable exceptions. They refused to accept his proposal that vested schools could be vested either in local trustees or in the commissioners themselves, and they refused to adopt that which would grant up to five pounds a year for the repair of convent schools and schools vested in trustees. They took no notice of the suggestion that local contribution rules be more strictly enforced.

Fourth, the commissioners added a few wrinkles of their own, one of which was offensive to all religious groups: that 'no clergymen of any denomination, or (except in the case of convent schools) member of any religious order, can be recognized as the teacher of a national school'.[54] Needless to say the ruling incensed the Roman Catholic hierarchy, for it withdrew support from the, admittedly few, monastic schools in connection with the system. The rule did not even possess the virtue of pleasing the protestants, for it appeared to them to be a blatant case of favouritism to the catholics, since it definitely excluded protestant clergy from teaching in the national schools, while making explicit provision for catholic nuns to do so.

Fifth, the entire rules revision was almost perfectly designed to enrage the Roman hierarchy. By publicly affirming policies that had previously been understood, but unmentioned, the commissioners rubbed salt in old wounds. For instance, the rules separating religious instruction from literary instruction had always been interpreted to mean that making the sign of the cross during school hours was prohibited and to imply that religious statuary and emblems could not be displayed during literary hours. By putting these interpretations into print the

[53] *Royal commission of inquiry into primary education (Ireland)*, vol i, pt 1: *Report of the commissioners*, p. 150.
[54] Ibid., p. 151.

commissioners and the government were almost begging to be damned by the hierarchy. The explicit affirmation of the 'Stop-ford rule' which absolved the manager or teacher from the duty of excluding children from religious instruction of denominations other than the children's own, was especially galling to the catholic bishops.

The holy lightning of the catholic clergy fell upon the commissioners with considerable accuracy and with telling effect. Their fulminations were both general and specific. The former consisted of condemnations of state impertinence in intervening at all in educational matters. The *Tablet* ran a series of articles in 1855 centring on the question, 'Has the state the right to educate?' The lead article in the series contained the declaration that the state can have no right to educate except it derives its right from God, and that God had given the right to educate the child to the head of the family and not to the head of the state. State education, as evidenced in the cases of France and Germany, leads to the ruin of the state.[55] A subsequent article made it clear that any Irish parent who was not a heathen was expected to choose church education over state education for his children, but liberally allowed that, 'if catholic parents prefer to be serfs and bondsmen of the state, it is a matter for their own choice'.[56] Much the same question was discussed somewhat more than a decade later in the pages of Archbishop Cullen's *Irish Ecclesiastical Record*. In an article entitled, 'The right to educate: to whom does it belong?' the answer 'the parents' was repeated. The article used the argument for parental rights to aver that the state had no rights over education and that its sole responsibility was to aid those to whom the right of education was entrusted to carry out their task. Not surprisingly, the church was mentioned as the rightful guardian of education, for the parent in having his child baptized accepted the church as divinely appointed guardian of the truth, and the church, once having admitted a child into the company of the faithful, incurred the duty to oversee his instruction. In other words, the government should supply money to the church for education and otherwise keep its hands off.[57]

[55] *Tablet*, 16 June 1855.   [56] *Tablet*, 23 June 1855.
[57] 'The right to educate: to whom does it belong?' *Irish Ecclesiastical Record*, iii, 281–4 (Mar. 1867), passim.

Specific complaints and condemnations brought better results than generalized damning of the state's meddling in the
schools. In 1856 the entire hierarchy condemned, in a general
pastoral to the catholics of Ireland, the prohibition of making
the sign of the cross during combined school hours and in a
similar pastoral the following year repeated their declaration
that nothing but a separate education for catholics would ever
satisfy the catholic conscience.[58] The prelates of the province
of Tuam urged their constituents to use every constitutional
means to press for a separate education for catholics.[59]

Real enthusiasm and accuracy in scoring the commissioners
did not come, however, until the prelates were joined in their
attacks by a layman, James W. Kavanagh, formerly an officer
of the board. Kavanagh had had a checkered career with the
commissioners before becoming one of their chief adversaries.
He was appointed an assistant teacher in a national school at
age fifteen, and three years later, in 1837, a full teacher. His
name is first found upon the commissioners' minute book for
February 1841, when he was appointed master of the male
model school in Dublin. About a year later he came to the
commissioners' attention for having been caught by the police
while climbing the wall at Glasnevin in an attempt to gain
access to the training establishment, an act for which he was
severely reprimanded. Kavanagh also incurred the commissioners' censure by publishing an arithmetic book on the title
page of which he placed, contrary to the commissioners' explicit instructions, the information that he was head master of
the male model school. Kavanagh did not get along very well
with his colleagues at the model school and was reported by
Professor McGauley for insubordination. As a result of that incident the commissioners expressed their disapproval of both
Kavanagh's and McGauley's behaviour. Despite all this, Kavanagh seems to have done his job satisfactorily, and in November 1844 he was promoted to inspector. While an inspector, he
was reprimanded for using an 'unofficial and intemperate tone'
in dealing with a manager and also for leaving his district without permission. Nevertheless, he was raised to head inspector in

[58] Kavanagh, p. 379.
[59] 'Address of the provincial synod of Tuam', 16 Aug. 1858, quoted in
Freeman's Journal, 25 Aug. 1858.

1846. At that post he was reprimanded for making a disgraceful scene at a meeting of a board of poor law guardians and was also severely reprimanded for writing a letter to the lord lieutenant about the workhouse schools. He incurred censure in 1856 for being the chief author of the head inspector's remonstrance against the conduct of Mr McGreedy. In the following year Kavanagh violated the commissioners' rules for officers of the board by reading a paper before the British Association on the subject of education, the paper being offensive to the commissioners as well as being unsanctioned. Kavanagh defended himself in a somewhat discourteous manner and was depressed to the rank of a first-class district inspector, with a reduction in salary from £520 to £260 per annum. His protests being of no avail, Kavanagh resigned in February 1858.[60]

If Kavanagh had simply resigned and sought another means of livelihood his case would not be worth our attention, except as an example of administrative friction. Kavanagh, however, set to work to bring the national system down with him. He worked furiously in the months after his resignation, and in March 1859, anonymously published a book entitled *Mixed education: the catholic case stated, etc.* This volume contained nearly 450 tightly packed pages of data upon the faults of the Irish national system of education. It was filled with considerable misinformation as well as with a good deal of useful material, but the accuracy or inaccuracy of Kavanagh's case was less important than the effect the book was to have. Overnight it

---

[60] *Copies of report of the committee of the national board of education in Ireland, appointed on the 11th day of September 1857, to inquire into the conduct of J. Kavanagh, Esq., head inspector of national schools, etc.*, passim, H.C. 1857–8, (386), xlvi; *A copy of all correspondence from the 1st day of July 1857 to the present date, which passed between the commissioners of national education in Ireland and Mr James Kavanagh, etc.*, passim, H.C. 1859 (sess. 1. 254), xxi, pt ii; Kavanagh, pp 428–31; Peader MacSuibhne, *Paul Cullen and his contemporaries, with their letters from 1820–1902* (Naas, 1961), ii, 270–71, 275; M.C.N.E.I., 27 Feb. 1841, 10, 14, 17 Feb. 1842, 16 Feb., 13 Apr., 1843, 10, 18, 24 Oct. 1844, 7 Nov. 1844, 21 Aug. 1851, 27 Aug. 1852, 27 Jan., 21 Feb. 1854, 28 Dec. 1855, 11, 23 Sept., 30 Oct., 27 Nov., 1857; 'Statement of proceeding in the education board, Marlboro St. in reference to James W. Kavanagh, head inspector, most respectfully submitted to his excellency the earl of Carlisle, K.G., lord lieutenant and general governor of Ireland', 6 Feb. 1858, S.P.O., Chief Secretary's Office, Official Papers, Unregistered (Miscellaneous) Papers, 9/1858.

became the educational source-book of the catholic hierarchy. It was dedicated to the Roman Catholic archbishops and bishops of Ireland and was read and corrected by a number of bishops before it appeared in print. Public testimonials to the book's value were received from at least thirteen of the bishops.[61] Kavanagh was rewarded by the hierarchy by being installed, in 1860, in the chair of mathematics in the catholic university.[67] Even Cullen, who was originally sceptical of Kavanagh's project, came to value the book for its information, even if he did not take Kavanagh into his palace as his resident educational counsellor.[63] One paper sulked 'no man can henceforth be considered a good catholic who does not worship Mr James Kavanagh.'[64]

The hierarchy met in Dublin in early August 1859, to deal with a number of educational questions, national education being among them. The bishops had two courses open to them regarding national education. One of these, counselled by Archbishop MacHale, was to condemn the national schools and withdraw catholic children from them. The other, advocated by Archbishop Leahy of Cashel, was to tolerate the national system while pressing for its modification or its replacement

[61] *Dublin Evening Mail*, 13 Apr. 1859.

[62] MacSuibhne, ii, 276.

[63] E. R. Norman, *The catholic church and Ireland in the age of rebellion, 1859–1873* (London, 1965), pp 57–8.

[64] *Packet*, 13 Aug. 1859, quoted in Norman, p. 58.

In passing, two questions should be raised about Kavanagh. First, in view of his misbehaviour while in office, how did he manage not only to be kept on but to gain promotion as well? It would seem highly likely that Kavanagh had somebody's strong backing all the way along, but the source and nature of that backing remains unknown.

Second, how much influence did Kavanagh actually have on Cullen? In 1925 P. J. Quigley wrote in the *Irish Ecclesiastical Record* that Cullen was casting about for an authority on national education to help him deal with the subject and that he took Kavanagh to his bosom as his ally and guide (quoted in MacSuibhne, ii, 272–4). Attractive as this suggestion is, MacSuibhne was unable to find any evidence for it while compiling his extensive collection of Cullen's correspondence (MacSuibhne, ii, 274–5). A letter from Cullen to Kavanagh dated 25 July 1859 (reproduced in MacSuibhne, ii, 290–1) indicates that Cullen did not see a copy of *The catholic case stated etc.*, until after it was published, a fact which implies that there was no great intimacy between the two men.

by a denominational system.[65] Even Leahy's plan, it is important to note, assumed a course of activism against the commissioners of national education. Leahy's view predominated and it
was he who drew up the memorial that was forwarded to chief
secretary Cardwell dated 5 August 1859, over the signatures of
twenty-eight archbishops and bishops.[66] The prelates decried
the 'systematic refusal to recognize their legitimate authority
to direct and superintend the education of their flocks',[67] and
the failure of the commissioners and government to consult
them concerning the nomination of commissioners, the framing
and recinding of rules, the appointment of inspectors and the
selection of books. The bishops especially resented the national
system's administrative arrangements because the catholics had
little influence upon the system's management, although they
formed the great mass of the people. The bishops' petition continued:

They, therefore, respectfully but earnestly request such a participation in educational grants for the separate instruction of catholic
children as the numbers and fidelity of the catholic people, as well
as their contributions to sustain the burdens of the state, amply
entitle them.[68]

Although the letter to Cardwell was relatively mild, it was
soon followed by a general pastoral by the prelates to the catholic people of Ireland that was both specific and vigorous. The
pastoral declared that in order to ensure that schools for catholic youth be safe for tender consciences they should be subordinate to the respective bishops. In the schools, the prelates stated,
no books should be used for secular instruction to which the
local bishop might object, the appointment and dismissal of
teachers should be under the ordinary's control, and the arrangements for religious instruction should also be under his charge.
These principles, the bishops believed, could be realized only
in a system of education exclusively tailored for Roman Catholics. The prelates pointed to the English grants to denominational societies as a model to be emulated. Thereafter, the

[65] Norman, pp 57, 62.   [66] Ibid., p. 63.
[67] *Copy of the memorial of the Roman Catholic prelates relative to national education
in Ireland and of the reply thereto of the chief secretary for Ireland, dated 28th
November 1859*, p. 1, H.C. 1860 (26), liii.
[68] Ibid., p. 2.

bishops dealt with specific grievances. They deplored the constitution of the board of commissioners, which, besides consisting of
persons of several denominations, was protestant-dominated.
Moreover, the commissioners as a body were unacceptable because their power derived exclusively from the state even though
it extended to matters vitally affecting religion. The prelates
protested the education of catholic teachers in the model
schools, especially because they were often taught history and
philosophy by protestant teachers. The bishops denounced the
exclusion from the schools of the sign of the cross and of
catholic devotional images. Significantly, the prelates complained about the character of several of the school books, a
complaint previously unvoiced. Administratively, the hierarchy
objected to the arrangements whereby schools attended only
by catholic children were liable to inspection by protestant
officers of the board. They also protested the Stopford rule
which allowed children of one faith to be present at the religious instruction of another faith.[69] The pastoral caused a considerable stir both in England and in Ireland and became
'the blueprint for a decade of agitation' by the Roman
church.[70]

Although Cardwell responded to the bishops' letter by refusing to budge,[71] the prelates were not through attacking. The
prelates' flag received fresh adherents in December 1859, when,
without the hierarchy's prodding, eleven catholic M.P.s
signed a series of resolutions upholding the prelates' demands.[72]
The bishops themselves aimed a mighty salvo at Cardwell in
March 1860, when they produced a document containing fifty-
three points, each argued at some length. The document was
authored by Cardinal Cullen and signed by most of the prelates, with MacHale's name being chief among those absent.[73]
Essentially, the paper was an elaboration of the pastoral of the
preceding year, directed specifically at the government, rather

[69] *Freeman's Journal*, 19 Aug. 1859.
[70] Norman, p. 63.
[71] Edward Cardwell to Paul Cullen, 28 Nov. 1859, reproduced in, *Copy
of the memorial of the Roman Catholic prelates relative to national education in
Ireland and of the reply thereto of the chief secretary for Ireland, dated 28th November 1859*, pp 2–4.
[72] Norman, pp 70–1.
[73] Ibid., p. 71.

than aimed indirectly at it through the faithful.[74] In a letter of
10 August 1860 nineteen members of parliament backed the
bishops' demands.[75]

Cardwell finally buckled under all this pressure and agreed
in December 1859 to restructure the board of commissioners so
that it would include ten catholics and ten protestants.[76] This
arrangement continued throughout the remainder of the century. Actually, the catholics gained much more than numerical
equality among the commissioners, for the catholics usually
were able to act as a unit while the protestant commissioners
often split among themselves. Thus, Cardwell gave the Roman
Catholics a working majority among the commissioners. A
further, if less complete, victory for the catholic prelates was
gained in 1861 when the commissioners, under the prodding of
Master Murphy, decided that thenceforth all schools towards
which building grants were made could be vested either in the
commissioners or in trustees selected by the applicants and approved by the commissioners.[77]

Concessions of this sort were not to buy the prelates' silence;
one of their chief grievances, the model schools, remained especially rankling. The four district model schools that were
opened in 1849 could not have opened at a less propitious moment. Besides their unattractiveness to the hierarchy because
of the absence of arrangements for local patrons, they were
sufficiently similar to the Queen's colleges to be merged in the
ecclesiastical mind with those allegedly pernicious institutions.
Individual prelates damned the schools, Bishop Foran and
Archbishop Cullen condemning the Waterford model school
even before its erection. Bishop Murray blocked the attempt to
found a model school in Wexford, and the prelates of the
province of Tuam fought the creation of the model school in

[74] Roman Catholic prelates to Edward Cardwell, 18 Mar. 1860, reproduced in *Further correspondence relative to national education in Ireland (presented in continuation of parliamentary paper no. 26 of the present session)*,
passim, H.C., 1860 [206], liii.

[75] *Copy of a letter on the subject of national education in Ireland, addressed to the
chief secretary in the month of July last by certain members of parliament*, H.C.
1861 (212), xlviii. Despite the title of the parliamentary paper, the letter
was actually dated 10 Aug. 1860.

[76] Norman, p. 73.

[77] M.C.N.E.I., 27 June 1861, 5, 12 July 1861, 9 Aug. 1861.

Sligo.[78] The March 1860 letter of the bishops to the chief secretary censured the model schools as intrinsically anti-catholic and especially dangerous to the faith because they assumed the character of religiously mixed boarding institutions.[79] Once again the government yielded to catholic pressures, and in 1861 the chief secretary promised the house of commons that no more model schools would be erected without reference to the house.[80] But the existing model schools continued in operation, much to the bishops' fury. Therefore, in 1863 they resolved that no priest was to send any person to be trained in any model school, and that no teacher who was trained in a model school after the ban took effect was to be employed by any priest or by his consent in any national school. In addition, catholic priests were instructed to withdraw all catholic children attending the model schools.[81] The ban had an immediate effect. Of the 9,700 scholars in model schools in 1864, only 3,626 were Roman Catholics. In the model school in Sligo, it was reported that not a single Roman Catholic child was either in attendance or on the roll.[82]

For all that, the twenty-six district model schools (plus two in Dublin) remained, and in 1866 the Roman Catholic bishops again attacked, repeating the 1863 declaration condemning and banning the schools. As a direct result of this new assault the chief secretary, C. S. Fortescue, addressed the commissioners on the subject of the model schools.[83] In a letter dated 19 June 1866, Fortescue pointed out that the entire model school system turned out only about 400 teachers annually, whereas the number of new teachers required each year was about 900. The government, Fortescue admitted, viewed this situation with a good deal of concern, but in view of the expressions of the Roman Catholic community the government was not prepared to undertake the extension of the model school system. Rather,

---

[78] Kavanagh, p. 378.

[79] *Further correspondence relative to national education in Ireland (presented in continuation of parliamentary paper no. 26 of the present session)*, p. 14.

[80] Graham Balfour, *The educational systems of Great Britain and Ireland* (Oxford, second ed., 1903), p. 90.

[81] *Freeman's Journal*, 16 Sept. 1863.

[82] *Hansard 3*, clxxv, 1764, 14 June 1864.

[83] Anthony M. Gallagher, *Education in Ireland* (Washington, D.C., 1948), p. 80.

the government would prefer to stimulate private enterprise in this matter. He then propounded a plan for the establishment of model schools under local management, each school of this sort to accommodate at least fifteen resident trainees and at least 150 pupils. These schools, like ordinary national schools, would either be vested or non-vested, depending upon whether or not the government aided their construction, and were to be governed by rules similar to the rules for vested and non-vested ordinary national schools.[84] Clearly, Fortescue was suggesting to the commissioners that the model school system be so modified as to silence its catholic critics. The commissioners expressed their general approval of the plan without binding themselves to any particular detail.[85]

As the government and the commissioners bent more and more in the catholic wind, most presbyterians and some anglicans became concerned. Thus, in late 1859, the Ulster National Education Association was formed to uphold the principles of the national system and to resist attempts to encroach upon those principles by the Church of Rome. Significantly, the association was supported not only by such pivotal presbyterian leaders as Dr Cooke, but by a number of the anglican clergy as well, notably the bishop of Down and Connor and Dromore, and the dean of Dromore.[86] Throughout the 1860s the association, in combination with the education committee of the synod of Ulster, protested against the successive concessions to the catholics, but to no avail.

In November 1863, the national education commissioners passed, over the objections of the presbyterian members, a new and seemingly innocuous rule: 'In the case of a few very large and highly efficient schools, the commissioners are prepared to appoint young persons of great merit to act as first-class monitors, with a rate of salary somewhat higher than that of paid monitors of the above grades', the 'above grades' referring to normal pay scales for monitors.[87] Although apparently a neutral statement, the new rule represented another major concession to the Roman Catholic prelates, for, in 1862, the commissioners had secured the cooperation of some of the

[84] M.C.N.E.I., 26 June 1866.   [85] M.C.N.E.I., 30 June 1866.
[86] *Daily Express*, 12 Jan. 1860; *Saunder's*, 26 Dec. 1859.
[87] M.C.N.E.I., 21 Nov. 1863.

better convent schools in training pupil-teachers. These pupil-teachers were given the rank of first-class monitors when serving in the larger and more efficient convent schools.[88] Thus, the new rule was really an effort to provide extra money for convent-trained pupil-teachers. Moreover, the practice of allowing the convents to train teachers was itself a major departure from the commissioners' stated policy of providing facilities for teacher training in their own model schools. In reality, the new rule provided a special type of increased grant for the convent schools, while simultaneously undercutting the model school system.

In framing this rule the commissioners put themselves in the dubious position of providing money to aid the prelates' boycott of the model schools. Both the education committee of the general assembly of the presbyterian church and the representative of the Ulster National Education Association lodged vigorous protests.[89] Sir Robert Peel, the chief secretary, was sufficiently disturbed by the commissioners' proceedings to remind them that they had no power to alter any fundamental rule without the express permission of the lord lieutenant. The commissioners replied with a remarkably disrespectful letter, telling Peel that they were fully aware that they were not to change any fundamental rule, but denying that any fundamental rule change had been made. Patronizingly, they defined the fundamental rules as those protecting children from interference with religious opinions, as those entitling pastors to give religious instruction in vested schools, as those regulating and confirming the right of patrons, and as those defining the rights of the managers and the public. They argued that nothing in the nature of any increase in salary or nothing concerning an expenditure of money could be considered to be a change in a fundamental rule.[90] With bureaucratic indirectness, the commissioners suggested

[88] Balfour, p. 93.

[89] M.C.N.E.I., 22 Jan. 1864, 29 Jan. 1864; *Royal commission of inquiry into primary education (Ireland)*. vol. vii; *Returns furnished by the national board*, p. 16.

[90] M.C.N.E.I., 5 Feb. 1864; *Copy of any correspondence between the chief secretary for Ireland, and the chief commissioner of national education in Ireland, relative to the recent alterations in the rules of the board*, pp 1–2, H.C. 1864, (181), xlvi; *Royal commission of inquiry into primary education (Ireland)*, vol. vii; *Returns furnished by the national board*, p. 16.

that Peel mind his own business; surprisingly, Peel chose to accept this rebuff and dropped the matter, although the Irish protestant M.P.s pursued the matter in the commons for a time.[91]

More victories were to be won by the catholic prelates. In 1866, the commissioners surrendered almost completely on the vesting of schools questions and allowed the title to schools vested in the commissioners to be transferred to local trustees if the trustees would repay the commissioners for repair and maintenance money the commissioners had spent on the schools.[92]

During the same year the manager of the Wexford Convent School elicited a concession from the commissioners. The manager asked permission to take a class into a room adjoining the main school room for the purpose of giving religious instruction at the same time that secular instruction was continuing in the main classroom. Without any doubt this arrangement violated the original intention of Lord Stanley and of the earlier groups of commissioners to keep denomination a religious instruction distinct in time from literary instruction. Nevertheless, the resident commissioner, Alexander Macdonnell, argued that there was nothing in the rules or in the spirit of the national system to bar such a procedure, providing that the arrangement did not impede secular instruction, that secular instruction was carried on in the main classroom for those who did not take religious instruction, and that the teacher did not permit any child to leave the secular instruction who was of a different faith from the person giving the religious instruction. With minor dissent, the procedure was approved and the wall between religious and secular instruction crumbled just that much further.[93]

The marquis of Kildare moved for the abolition of the Stopford rule in May 1866, in a resolution stating that no pupil registered as a protestant of any denomination was to be permitted to remain in attendance during the time of religious instruction given by a Roman Catholic and that no child registered as a catholic was to remain attending during the hours of

[91] *Hansard 3*, clxxv, 1761–99, 14 June 1864; clxxvi, 1762–5, 23 June 1864.

[92] Balfour, p. 88.

[93] M.C.N.E.I., 27 June 1865; *Royal commission of inquiry into primary education (Ireland)*, vol. i, pt 1: *Report of the commissioners*, p. 185.

protestant religious instruction. This was precisely what the catholic prelates had demanded. The commissioners passed a reworded version of their resolution with the three presbyterian commissioners protesting. The proposed rule was submitted to the lord lieutenant, and in June 1866, C. S. Fortescue, the chief secretary, reported that approval would be forthcoming if a proviso were added to the rule that in case any parent or guardian should express a desire for his child to receive any particular sort of religious instruction, this request should be granted, irrespective of the parent's own religious profession. The commissioners accepted the proviso with the reservation that if the proviso should undercut the effective enforcement of the rule, they should feel bound to press for the proviso's repeal. The rule was subsequently amplified to make it clear that children of one protestant denomination could be present at the religious instruction of another protestant denomination without any special request being necessary.[94]

The catholic prelates' aggressiveness was reinforced, rather than extinguished, by their being rewarded with a concession almost every time they attacked the commissioners of national education. Since their complaints regularly produced results, the prelates passed another set of resolutions on education at their October 1867 meeting. These resolutions repeated the demands of 1863 and stated that mixed education was intrinsically unsound and at variance with the catholic religion and dangerous to the bishops' flocks. No change in the constitution of the body of commissioners could compensate for its inherent defects nor neutralize its injurious effects. The condemnation of the model schools pealed forth once again along with a variety of other complaints.[95] Once more the prelates' noise-making

[94] *Copy of all minutes and proceedings, from the 1st day of May 1866 to the present time, relating to changes of rules or of practice as to religious instruction,* etc., pp 2–5, H.C. 1872 (416), xlvi; *Copy of any new or altered rule on the subject of religious teaching made in May 1866 by the commissioners of national edvcation (Ireland) with the names of the commissioners present when the same was adopted, and the protests, if any,* pp 1–2, H.C. 1866 (407), lv; M.C.N.E.I., 8, 15 May, 22 June, 3 July, 1866, 2, 9 Mar. 1869; *Royal commission of inquiry into primary education (Ireland),* vol. vii, *Returns furnished by the national board,* pp 17–18.

[95] Paul Cullen, *Pastoral letter of his eminence Cardinal Cullen, catholic archbishop of Dublin, etc., for the festival of St Patrick* (Dublin, 1867), pp 21–23.

brought results. In 1868 a parliamentary circular was sent to each of the Irish bishops asking their opinion upon the national system and asking what modifications they desired.[96] In the same year the government appointed a royal commission to investigate the national school system and to make recommendations for reform. With the appointment of this commission it appeared that the prelates had won.

4

The royal commission on primary education in Ireland, commonly known as the 'Powis commission', met in 1869 and 1870 and produced eight volumes of evidence and conclusions. The commission under the chairmanship of Lord Powis consisted of fourteen members. Seven members were Roman Catholics and seven protestants; of the protestant members, two were presbyterian, the rest anglican.[97] The royal commissioners first met in mid-February 1868. Their original warrant had to be extended in February 1869, and at that time the chief secretary, Chichester Fortescue, urged them to complete their efforts by the first of January 1870.[98] The royal commissioners did not meet this deadline because of printing delays and because of the national commissioners' slowness in completing their returns.[99] Their last meetings were not held until May 1870. The report was an impressive document chiefly because of the extensive investigations made under the commission's aegis. Ten assistant commissioners surveyed the existing state of Irish education, and considerable search was made for material bearing on the historical development of the system. In order to produce nine heavy volumes within a two-year period, the royal commissioners quickly built up their own bureaucracy. Two full-time secretaries were hired to manage the accounts, to oversee the ten

[96] Anna-Magdalena Schroder, *Das religionsproblem in der Irisch-Englischen schulpolitik* (Charlottenburg, 1935), p. 83.

[97] Balfour, p. 97; *Report on elementary education adopted by the general assembly of the presbyterian church in Ireland at its meeting in Dublin in June 1871, etc.* (Belfast, 1871), p. 3.

[98] C. Fortescue to Bruce, 20 Feb. 1869, S.P.O.I., Chief Secretary's Office, Registered Papers, 12782/1873 (copy).

[99] D. B. Dunne to J. H. Burke, 11 Dec. 1869, S.O.P.I., Chief Secretary's Office, Registered Papers, 12782/1873.

assistant commissioners, and to serve as draftsmen for the final report. Just like any other arm of the English civil service, the commission had to fight continual skirmishes with the treasury in order to obtain adequate funds. If the treasury had had its way, the royal commissioners would not have hired any assistant commissioners, for their lordships thought that the royal commission should simply hire national education inspectors to do the work in their spare time, at a small fee.[100]

The royal commissioners' methods of compiling their historical sketch and their final report were not above reproach. They asked Lord Powis and Messrs Cowie and Stokes to prepare, with the aid of the two secretaries, the historical sketch that would commence the report.[101] Cowie and Stokes were both English school inspectors and Stokes was the sometime secretary of the Roman Catholic Poor School Committee in Great Britain. While the historical sketch was being prepared, the royal commissioners turned to a discussion of basic educational issues. Their practice was for a specific topic or set of topics to be scheduled for a given meeting and for each commissioner to come to the meeting with his conclusions on the subjects written out. After discussion a final recommendation was arrived at, and one of the members present was appointed to draw up a precis of the different views present and the reasons for which they were either accepted or rejected. After all the topics were discussed, provisional recommendations were to stand for final consideration and inclusion in the report.[102]

It soon became clear that the royal commissioners were not sympathetic to the national system as it then existed, and that they desired to limit the national commissioners' powers, while increasing those of the denominational groups. The only consistent dissent from these tendencies came from Gibson and Wilson, both of whom were presbyterians. Thus, only Gibson opposed the resolutions proposed by Cowie (Wilson being absent), that in all national schools any suitable reading book be allowed without any preface from the commissioners, that

[100] Treasury letter, 25 Apr. 1868, S.P.O.I., Chief Secretary's Office, Registered Papers, 12782/1873.
[101] 'Minutes of Royal Commission on Primary Education, 1868–70', 25 Feb. 1869, P.R.O.I., 1a–50–36.
[102] Ibid.

examinations be constructed so as to leave managers free to use any book they wished, and that the national commissioners should refrain in the future from publishing or preparing school-books.[103] Wilson tried to be Horatio at the bridge when the royal commissioners resolved that, like the English board, the Irish national education commissioners should make no rule change without laying the change before parliament for at least one month before its enactment. Wilson tried to meet this attempt to curtail the autonomy of those running the system by an amendment proposing that a board of paid commissioners be created, responsible to the crown. He was the only one in favour of it.[104] And so it went, each succeeding resolution making it more and more certain that the final report would recommend drastically curtailing the commissioners' powers. Of all the resolutions, the one that was eventually to have the most influence upon Irish education was Lord Powis's recommendation that it would be desirable to introduce an element of payment by results into the national teachers' salary scales. Gibson was absent and only Dr Wilson opposed the resolution.[105]

When the historical sketch was presented it too was kicked about like a football, Gibson and Wilson being the chief attackers. The royal commissioners marched through the sketch paragraph by paragraph, voting and amending as if they were dealing with matters of future recommendations rather than of past facts. Most often the split was denominational, the presbyterians against all the rest. For example, on the motion to add to the sketch, 'Mr Carlile states his objections in the following words, "I objected myself to being called upon on my responsibility as a member of the commissioners to see the children attending places of worship in which tenets might be inculcated which I did not approve"', Wilson and Gibson were in opposition, together with one other royal commissioner.[106]

Throughout the proceedings, Gibson and Wilson tried to have material that reflected badly upon either the commissioners or the presbyterians expunged, and to have material unfavourable to the Roman Catholics added. Other commissioners pushed for the addition of material unfavourable to the

103 Ibid., 27 February 1869.   104 Ibid., 28 May 1861.
105 Ibid., 1 June 1869.   106 Ibid., 24 Sept. 1869.

commissioners and favourable to the catholics. Although it is vaguely amusing to witness historical writing by committee, the final sketch, it is clear, must be treated with a certain amount of caution, especially in its interpretive sections.

The same committee—Powis, Cowie, and Stokes—that drew up the historical sketch also drew up the recommendations for the final report of the royal commissioners. The three submitted their recommendations to the other royal commissioners for approval or amendment in the same manner as they had the historical sketch. On only one occasion was there a close vote. On that occasion Stokes moved an amendment, 'That the rule or practice of the board which now prohibits managers from employing the members of religious bodies as teachers in vested schools should be repealed', and was met with a five to five tie. The chairman broke the tie by voting 'no'.[107] In its final form, the report presented 129 conclusions and resolutions.[108] The first was chilling: 'That the progress of the children in the national schools of Ireland is very much less than it ought to be. That in Church Education Society schools, non-national convent schools, and Christian Brothers' schools, the result is not very different.'[109]

The second recommendation contained the main prescription for Ireland's educational ills, namely the introduction of payment by results as an element in computing a teacher's salary. The sixteenth recommendation suggested another basic change in Irish educational policy by introducing the idea of compulsory attendance in townlands of all children of school age who were not actually at work. The Powis commissioners were disturbed by the relatively small amounts contributed to education from local sources and their twenty-second proposition advised that the grants made by the commissioners of national education should bear a fixed proportion to the amount locally contributed to education (the desirable amount of local aid was specified later in the report as one third of the commissioners' grant). The royal commissioners made the important suggestion that in default of voluntary local payments or of

[107] Ibid., 11 May 1870.
[108] *Royal commission of inquiry into primary education (Ireland)*, vol. i, pt 1; *Report of the commissioners*, pp 522–534.
[109] Ibid., p. 522.

adequate school fees, the requisite local contribution should be raised by local rates.

In their thirty-seventh to fortieth resolutions the Powis commissioners stated that in all schools any set of schoolbooks should be allowed, without preference being given to the commissioners' books, that the examinations of teachers and children should be conducted so as to leave the schools free to use any books they wished, and that the national commissioners should refrain in the future from publishing or preparing any school books. Significantly, managers of schools were still to be barred from using books to which the commissioners objected. The forty-fourth through forty-seventh clauses expressed the desirability of a new set of religious rules for areas in which there were at least two schools, one of protestant, the other of catholic management. If the schools in such an area had been established for three years and if each had had an average attendance of at least twenty-five children, then each of the schools should be allowed to become a denominational school subject to no religious regulations whatsoever, save that no child of any of the protestant denominations should be permitted to join in catholic religious instruction, nor any catholic children in protestant instruction. In such schools, the religious minority was to have the right to retire when religious instruction was being given and was to be provided with proper shelter during that instruction. The royal commissioners were really suggesting that in any area where there was a large enough number of protestants to make a significant amount of religious mixing a possibility, denominational schooling should be permitted so that such mixing did not take place.

Recommendations seventy-one to seventy-six also implied major changes in the fundamental rules of the system, namely that the distinction between convent schools and ordinary national schools should cease, that the teachers in convent schools should be examined and classed like other teachers, and also that the Christian Brothers should be examined and classed like all other teachers and admitted to the full benefits of the national system. The royal commissioners desired that the rule forbidding aid to monks be repealed. Recommendation 104 struck at the district model schools, recommending in one short sentence that they be gradually abolished. Recommendations 120 and 121 stated that the course of education in national schools ought not to be extended to secondary or intermediate subjects but that masters should be freely allowed to teach as extra branches of instruction any subjects in which they had qualified themselves. The final recommendation of the report parroted the provision of the English revised code of 1869 that no alteration to be made in any rule should be effective until the alteration had laid for one month before both houses of parliament.

It was obvious that if the Powis commissioners' suggestions were accepted, the national system would be completely transformed. The report was the logical conclusion of a series of complementary developments during the 1850–70 period, the the most important of which were the increasing weakness of the national commissioners and the increasing aggressiveness of the Roman Catholic prelates. After the Powis report appeared in 1870 there could be little doubt that the days of lip-service to Lord Stanley's ideas were over and that a new era was about to begin. The precise character of the new age would be determined by how closely the government followed the Powis guide-lines.

VIII

TWENTY HEARTS BEATING
AS NONE, 1871-1900

~~~~~~

I

MUCH TO THE FRUSTRATION of those who favoured the
immediate and wholesale adoption of the Powis commission's
recommendations, the commission's proposals were implemented
piecemeal and slowly. This was not the result of an attempt on
the part of the commissioners of national education to hold the
field against those wishing to restructure their system; rather,
it was a result of the political situation in England. Gladstone
intended to bring in legislation based upon the Powis report
but found this to be impossible. England, in 1870, was exper-
iencing a wave of anti-catholic feeling, an emotion associated
with the disestablishment of the Anglican church in Ireland and
with attempts in Westminster to repeal the ecclesiastical titles
act. At such a time the implementation of the Powis recommendations could only appear as truckling to the wishes of the Roman
Catholic hierarchy and hence was not politically feasible. The
catholics remained active, bombarding parliament and select
national leaders with petitions and letters urging the implementation of the Powis recommendations. Under this pressure Gladstone assured Cullen that the government did intend to act upon
the suggestions, preferably after the passage in the 1872 session of the Scotch education act. Gladstone, however, left office
in early 1874 having done little to modify the national system[1]

[1] Edward R. Norman, *The catholic church and Ireland in the age of rebellion,
1859-1873* (London, 1965), pp 440-4.

One important suggestion of the Powis commission was quicky acted upon and that was the recommendation that a portion of each teacher's salary should depend upon the marks the children under his charge received at regular examinations to be held under the charge of the inspectors. Payment by results had been introduced into England in 1862, and in 1866 the government had suggested to the commissioners of national education that the scheme be adopted in Ireland. At the request of the Powis commission, Patrick Keenan, then a chief of inspection, and later resident commissioner, drew up such a scheme for its consideration. On the basis of that scheme the commission recommended that all children in Irish national schools be examined annually by an inspector in reading, writing, and arithmetic, and that a fixed sum be paid for each child who passed in each subject, providing the child had made a given number of attendances during the year preceding the examination.[2]

The commissioners of national education seem to have swallowed this educational medicine without hesitation. There was no official debate among them on whether or not the policy should be introduced, but only a discussion as to what was the best means of effecting the policy. Two schemes for payment by results were submitted and, not surprisingly, Patrick Keenan's plan was the one selected. The commissioners, however, refused to condone a number of extra features with which Keenan studded his basic plan. With only one dissenting vote they passed a resolution that 'Mr Keenan's plan be adopted so far as it makes the payment to the teacher beyond his fixed salary, to depend upon the amount of information acquired by his pupils, and the number who have acquired such information', but they did not sanction his recommendation that the new system of payment be tied to local education rates, pensions for teachers, and changes in the regulations concerning local management.[3] It should be noted that under the Irish plan, unlike its English prototype, the teacher was not dependent solely upon results of the fees for his income, for he was paid a basic salary irrespective of results. Thus, at least some of the insecurity surrounding the English school teacher was removed, while, hopefully,

[2] *Vice-regal committee of inquiry into primary education (Ireland), 1913; Final report of the committee*, p. 3 [Cd 7235], H.C. 1914, xxviii.

[3] M.C.N.E.I., 28 Feb. 1871.

provision was made for incentives for increased educational production. The commissioners adopted Keenan's plan a fortnight after it was formally presented.[4] When Alexander Macdonnell resigned in early 1872 as resident commissioner, Keenan was named to succeed him and thus had charge of bringing his own plan into action.[5]

One of the implications of the results-fees system was that the treasury would gain increasing control over Irish education, for each aspect of the grant arrangements had to receive treasury approval. Through 1874 the treasury allowed the entire amount of the results-fees earned by the teachers to be paid to the teachers irrespective of any question of local contribution.[6] One of the treasury's complaints about the Irish national system, however, was that its cost fell almost entirely upon the central government. Payment by results appeared to their lordships to be an ideal opportunity to teach the Irish that education was a local responsibility. Hence, the National School Teachers (Ireland) Act, 1875 included a complicated mechanism for stimulating local contributions to the system of national education. Boards of guardians were given the choice of becoming either 'contributory' or 'non-contributory' unions. In the former unions, one third of the amount of results-fees earned by the teachers was to be raised by a rate to be struck by the guardians, the rest to be paid from the imperial exchequer. If the union refused to strike a rate, and thus was classified as non-contributory, one third of the amount of results-fees earned by the teacher was paid from imperial funds. In the treasury vocabulary, the result-fees above the guaranteed one-third were 'contingent results fees'. The act was a dismal failure for, of the 163 poor law unions in Ireland, only seventy-three were ever at any time contributory. In 1897 there were only twenty-five contributory unions.[7]

The teachers, who under the act's rules lost most of the results-fees they had earned, objected strenuously. The treasury, realizing its mistake, pulled back a bit in 1876 and allowed one half of the contingent results-fees earned by the teacher to be

---

[4] M.C.N.E.I., 14 Mar. 1871.   [5] M.C.N.E.I., 2 Jan. 1872.
[6] *Hansard 3*, cclxxxix, 990, 20 June 1884.
[7] Graham Balfour, *The educational systems of Great Britain and Ireland* (Oxford, second ed., 1903), p. 100.

paid by the central government, provided that at least three shillings and four pence per child per annum for the average annual number of children in attendance be raised.[8] That is, they granted the same amount (two thirds of the total earned by the teacher) to non-contributory as well as to contributory unions. In 1880 the rule was further relaxed. Whereas it had previously been required that in non-contributory unions at least one half of the contingent results-fees had to be raised locally if imperial money was to be granted, from 1880 onwards the central government matched whatever amount local sources could raise in non-contributory unions, even if this fell below the level of fifty per cent of contingent results-fees.[9] The government back-pedalled further in 1890 when the Local Taxation (Customs and Excise) Act was passed, under which £78,000 was paid annually to the commissioners of national education in Ireland. This money was distributed, proportionate to average attendance, to contributory unions in relief of local rates and in non-contributory unions as an addition to the local contributions to schools. This aid to local contributions was significant, for it meant that in 1890 only fourteen schools failed to receive the full amount of earned results-fees.[10] In 1892, the requirement of local contributions was totally abolished,[11] although contributory unions could continue to operate as educational rating authorities if they so desired.

The refusal of the majority of Irish communities to sanction local rates in aid of education is surprising, especially in view of the striking willingness to sacrifice for education which the Irish peasant showed in the eighteenth and early nineteenth century, and also in view of the enthusiasm with which the average Irishman sent his children to the national schools. In partial explanation, however, we must grant the Irishman his humanity, for one can hardly expect anyone to be pleased with the idea of paying local education rates when educational benefits have previously been paid by the central government. Since it was the teachers, not the parents of the school children who suffered when a local union chose not to be contributory,

[8] M.C.N.E.I., 3 Oct. 1876; *Hansard 3*, cclxxxix, 990.

[9] Ibid.   [10] Balfour, p. 101.

[11] Irish Free State, *Report of the department of education, the school year 1924– 25, and the financial and administrative years 1924–25–26* (Dublin, 1926), p. 17.

there was little incentive for parents to push for contributory status. Any desire local rate payers may have had to strike education rates was offset by the growing belief that Ireland was grievously overtaxed relative to its actual wealth. This popular belief was subsequently confirmed by the Childers' report of 1896 on the financial relations between Great Britain and Ireland: the report revealed that Ireland was being taxed beyond her proportionate share by £2,750,000 a year.[12]

In partial explanation we should also note that the control of the national schools had never been a civic concern. On the local level the schools were almost completely under the control of ecclesiastical authorities. By refusing to take on the burden of rating for educational purposes, the local guardians were indirectly affirming that the management and financial support of the local national school was the concern of the parish priest or vicar and not of the local citizenry. Even if the local citizenry had wished to take an active hand in managing primary education, they lacked suitable institutions of local government. Surely it was unrealistic and inappropriate to ask boards constituted to look after the poor to deal with educational matters, yet this was all that was available. A full system of popularly elected local governments was not introduced into Ireland until 1898, and then too fully and suddenly, and with too little preparation.

Although the idea of paying teachers according to the results of their students in examinations has been discredited, certain advantages of the system as it worked in Ireland must be mentioned. In May 1885, a number of the Roman Catholic prelates presented a memorial to the lord lieutenant in favour of retention of the results system. They declared that the results system had brought three major blessings to Ireland. First, it had acted as a powerful stimulus to the industry of teachers, had secured their more equal attention to the several classes of their schools, and had led to the adoption of better methods of teaching as well as to a more considerate treatment of the pupils. Second, it produced a livelier interest upon the part of managers in the work of the teachers and pupils in their charge. Third, the prelates gave the system credit for steadily raising the number

[12] F. S. L. Lyons, *The Irish parliamentary party, 1890–1910* (London, 1951), p. 69.

and regularity of attendances in the Irish national schools.[13] Although we may seriously question the accuracy of the first two observations, it appears that the prelates had a plausible case in stating that the system of payment by results did increase the regularity of attendance in the schools. (The rising enrollment figures are all the more impressive when one remembers that the population was steadily decreasing.)[14]

Year	Total no. making any attendance during the year	No. attending in fortnight before enumeration	Average daily attendance	No. of operating schools
1870	950,999	N/A	359,199	6,806
1871	972,906	N/A	363,850	6,914
1872	960,434	N/A	355,821	7,050
1873	974,696	N/A	373,371	7,160
1874	1,006,511	N/A	395,390	7,257
1875	1,011,799	N/A	389,961	7,267
1876	1,032,215	596,427	416,586	7,334
1877	1,023,617	595,655	418,063	7,370
1878	1,036,742	632,282	437,252	7,433
1879	1,031,995	559,081	435,054	7,522
1880	1,083,298	671,877	468,557	7,590
1881	1,066,259	674,290	453,567	7,648
1882	1,083,298	678,970	469,192	7,705
1883	1,081,136	666,115	467,704	7,752
1884	1,087,079	696,130	492,928	7,832
1885	1,075,604	712,512	502,454	7,934

[13] *Copy of a memorial presented to the lord lieutenant by certain catholic bishops upon the subject of elementary education, and which was alluded to by the chief secretary in introducing a bill upon the subject,* p. 1, H.C. 1884–5 (229), lxi.

[14] Compiled from: *Thirty-seventh report of the commissioners of national education in Ireland, for the year 1870,* p. 9 [C 360], H.C. 1871, xxiii; *Thirty-eighth report . . . for the year 1871,* p. 9 [C 599], H.C. 1872, xxiii; *Thirty-ninth report . . . for the year 1872,* p. 9 [C 805], H.C. 1873, xxv; *Fortieth report . . . for the year 1873,* p. 5 [C. 965], H.C. 1874, xix; *forty-first report . . . for the year 1874,* p. 5 [C 1228], H.C. 1875 xxv; *Forty-second report . . . for the year 1875,* pp 3–4 [C 1503], H.C. 1876, xxiv; *Forty-third report . . . for the year 1876,* p. 3 [C 1757], H.C., 1877, xxxi; *Forty-fourth report . . . for the year 1877,* p. 3 [C 2031], H.C. 1878, xxix; *Forty-fifth report . . . for the year 1878,* pp 3–4 [C 2312], H.C. 1878–9, xxiv; *Forty-sixth report . . . for the year 1879,* pp 3–4 [C 2592], H.C. 1880, xxiii; *Forty-seventh report . . . for the year 1880,* pp 3–4 [C 2925], H.C. 1881, xxxiv; *Forty-eighth report . . . for the year 1881,* pp 3–4 [C 3243], H.C. 1882, xxiv; *Forty-ninth report . . . for the year 1882,* p. 3 [C 3651], H.C. 1883, xxvi; *Fiftieth report . . . for the year 1883,* pp 3–4 [C 4053], H.C. 1884, xxv; *Fifty-first report . . . for the year 1884,* pp 3–4 [C 4458], H.C. 1884–5, xxiv; *Fifty-second report . . . for the year 1885,* pp 3–4 [C 4800], H.C. 1886, xxvii.

On the other hand, there can be no doubt that the system of payment by results considerably restricted the freedom of the individual teacher and thus narrowed the range of teaching in the average national school. Because a good deal of the teachers' wages depended upon the results examinations, unhealthy cramming often dominated the classroom. Educational journals blossomed with advertisements for review cards, sample tests, and assorted devices guaranteed to raise the students' grades on the results examinations and thus to raise the teachers' salaries. A district inspector and two model school head masters got into serious difficulty with the commissioners for providing a set of arithmetic review cards which duplicated the supposedly confidential packs of test cards placed in the hands of inspectors.[15]

Nevertheless, the national school curriculum did not change nearly as much as one might expect during the results era. A basic programme of instruction to be taught during school hours was defined for each class, including obligatory subjects and two optional subjects (bookkeeping and vocal music). After school hours a wide range of extra subjects could be taught to earn fees. The obligatory programme included the basic subjects of reading, writing, spelling, grammar, geography, and arithmetic for each class, plus agricultural theory for fourth to sixth class boys in rural schools and needlework for girls in all schools.[16] Prior to the results era considerable freedom for optional subjects was permitted, a freedom continued under the results system. The commissioners encouraged achievement in a number of extra subjects and their report for 1875 listed twenty-one extra subjects for which they would pay grants, including the following: geometry, algebra, trigonometry, navigation, magnetism and electricity, physical geography, geology, botany, Latin, Greek, French, sewing machine, cookery, poultry management.[17] In 1898, drawing was taught in about 2,000 schools, algebra in 1,400, geometry in 900, sewing machine and advanced dressmaking in over

[15] M.C.N.E.I., 20 June 1882.
[16] Republic of Ireland, *Report of the council of education* [Pr. 2583.], (Dublin, 1954), p. 54.
[17] *Forty-second report of the commissioners of national education in Ireland, for the year 1875*, p. 26.

450. Latin was taught in twenty-seven schools and Greek in three.[18]

It will be recalled that prior to the results era the great majority of children spent their time upon basic subjects, a situation which continued after the results system was introduced. Although it is impossible to obtain precisely comparable figures for the varying levels of proficiency in the national schools from before and during the results era, the following figures are close enough to being comparable to indicate that the introduction of payment by results may well have induced teachers to push their students on higher levels of schooling than they had previously done.[19]

Percentage distribution of students by books, 1865:

Book I	Book II	Sequel to Book II	Book III	Book IV and higher
41·80%	26·97	10·40	13·91	6·92

Percentage distribution of children examined by class, 1875:

Infants and Class I	Class II	Class III	Class IV and above
40·4%	19·6	16·8	23·2

Percentage distribution of children examined by class, 1898:

Infants and Class I	Class II	Class III	Class IV and above
37·6%	14·4	13·7	34·3

In one respect it can be argued that after the Powis report there was greater curricular freedom in the national schools than previously and that was in the matter of textbooks. Although the Powis report's recommendation that the commissioners of national education stop editing school books was not heeded, the commissioners adopted the report's suggestion that greater freedom be allowed school managers in the choice of books. By 1900 the commissioners had sanctioned the use of thirty-nine different sets of readers, comprising 294 volumes.[20]

[18] *Republic of Ireland, report of the council of education* [Pr. 2583], pp 54–6.

[19] Derived from, *Thirty-second report of the commissioners of national education in Ireland, for the year 1865*, p. 13 [3713], H.C. 1866, xxix; *Forty-second report . . . for the year 1875*, p. 24; *Sixty-fifth report . . . for the year 1898–99*, p. 33, [C 9446], H.C. 1899, xxiv.

[20] *Sixty-sixth report of the commissioners of national education in Ireland, for the year 1899–1900*, p. 40 [Cd 285], H.C. 1900, xxiii.

In retrospect, the policy of payments by results was most distasteful because it implied that the educational process, the children receiving education, and the teaching providing that education, could all be measured by examinations and governed in terms of money. The policy was symptomatic of a set of values coming to pervade the civil service of the British Isles and also of a swing in the balance of power within the civil service. Year by year the civil service was becoming a more rational, more efficient, more bureaucratic set of organizations. Increasingly, efficiency was measured in monetary terms. Given this trend, it was inevitable that the treasury would come to have considerable power over all branches of the civil service and that the treasury would often become the final arbiter on priorities and policy. Thus, the power of the treasury was increasing at the very time that primary education in Ireland was coming to be evaluated and discussed in terms of money. Inevitably, the treasury's power in educational matters grew, until in some matters the commissioners of national education became, for all practical purposes, merely advisory to the treasury.

Before examining the specific ways in which the treasury attacked the commissioners' autonomy, it is important to establish that the problem of the relation of the commissioners of national education to the treasury was not one of total amounts of money available for education, but rather of how the amount would be spent and of who would decide how it would be spent. Throughout most of the 1870–1900 period the parliamentary grant to education rose annually (customs and excise grants are included in the totals):[21]

[21] Compiled from: *Thirty-seventh report of the commissioners of national education in Ireland, for the year 1870*, p. 38; *Thirty-eighth report . . . for the year 1871*, p. 37; *Thirty-ninth report . . . for the year 1872*, p. 50; *Fortieth report . . . for the year 1873*, p. 30; *Forty-first report . . . for the year 1874*, p. 37; *Forty-second report . . . for the year 1875*, p. 31; *Forty-third report . . . for the year 1876*, p. 26; *Forty-fourth report . . . for the year 1877*, p. 28; *Forty-fifth report . . . for the year 1878*, p. 26; *Forty-sixth report . . . for the year 1879*, p. 26; *Forty-seventh report . . . for the year 1880*, p. 29; *Forty-eighth report . . . for the year 1881*, p. 31; *Forty-ninth report . . . for the year 1882*, p. 30; *Fiftieth report . . . for the year 1883*, p. 36; *Fifty-first report . . . for the year 1884*, p. 32; *Fifty-second report . . . for the year 1885*, p. 34; *Fifty-third report . . . for the year 1886*,

1870	£394,209	7s	11d
1871	408,388	11	9
1872	516,081	0	0
1873	542,222	0	0
1874	565,646	0	0
1875	639,368	0	0
1876	645,949	0	0
1877	645,236	0	0
1878	659,837	0	0
1879	681,829	0	0
1880	722,366	0	0
1881	729,868	0	0
1882	730,461	0	0
1883	726,339	0	0
1884	756,027	0	0
1885	814,003	0	0
1886	851,973	0	0
1887	874,051	0	0
1888	898,525	0	0
1889	731,473	15	7
1890	734,467	5	1
1891	866,539	0	0
1892	1,071,301	0	0
1893	1,069,969	0	0
1894	1,099,792	0	0
1895	1,206,088	0	0
1896	1,266,187	0	0
1897	1,276,559	17	1
1898	1,304,734	0	0
1899	1,149,692	8	5
1900	1,145,721	8	0

p, 34 [C 5082], H.C. 1887, xxxi; *Fifty-fourth report . . . for the year 1887*, p. 34 [C 5406], H.C. 1888, xl; *Fifty-fifth report . . . for the year 1888*, p. 51 [C 5738], H.C. 1889, xxxi; *Fifty-sixth report . . . for the year 1889*, p. 28 [C 6074], H.C. 1890, xxx; *Fifty-seventh report . . . for the year 1890*, p. 36 [C 6411], H.C. 1890–91, xxix; *Fifty-eighth report . . . for the year 1891*, p. 44 [C 6788], H.C. 1892, xxx; *Fifty-ninth report . . . for the year 1892*, p. 45 [C 7124], H.C. 1893–4, xxvii; *Sixtieth report . . . for the year 1893*, p. 52 [C 7457], H.C. 1894, xxx, part ii; *Sixty-first report . . . for the year 1894*, p. 48 [C 7796], H.C. 1895, xxix; *Sixty-second report . . . for the year 1895*, p. 71 [C 8142], H.C. 1896, xxviii; *Sixty-third report . . . for the year 1896–97*, p. 52 (C 8600), H.C. 1897, xxviii; *Sixty-fourth report . . . for the year 1897–98*, p. 54 [C 9038], H.C. 1898, xxvii; *Sixty-fifth report . . . for the year 1898–99*, p. 54 [C 9446], H.C. 1899, xxiv; *Sixty-sixth report . . . for the year 1899–1900*, p. 25 [Cd 285], H.C., 1900, xxiii; *Sixty-seventh report . . . for the year 1900*, p. 28 [Cd 704], H.C. 1901, xxi.

Within this context of increasing grants, the treasury blocked the commissioners in a number of niggling ways, the cumulative effect of which was seriously to hamstring their operation. For example, in 1872, the treasury refused to sanction a grant of £18,000 in the supplementary estimates which the commissioners wished to use to improve the conditions of the teachers.[22] Each year at estimates time the treasury became a little more difficult. In 1874, the treasury entered into a prolonged negotiation with the commissioners of national education about the propriety of their estimates for the coming year. Among other things, their lordships objected to the commissioners' policy of granting aid to local applicants who were willing to construct residences for the local national school teachers, the local contributor paying one third of the cost of such residence. Playing their familiar tune, their lordships demanded greater local contributions and suggested that a minimum of fifty per cent of the costs be raised locally.[23] In the succeeding year the treasury meddled in educational business by mentioning that it was important for model school fees to be increased, since the schools were attended by a better class of child than was the average national school.[24]

In the following year their lordships told the commissioners that they could not believe that a special agricultural inspector was necessary, that the methods of financial control in the departments under the control of the commissioners of national education seemed inadequate, and that one of the two secretaries to the commissioners was unnecessary.[25] The treasury letter concerning the inadequacy of the commissioners' financial arrangements was especially biting. Their lordships wrote the chief secretary, for the lord lieutenant's benefit, that 'some of the correspondence which has recently passed on subjects connected with the administration of the vote for national education in Ireland, has suggested to my lords grave doubts as to whether the arrangements now subsisting are such as to secure a satisfactory financial control over the expenditure in that department'.[26] Specifically, the treasury complained that

[22] M.C.N.E.I., 12 Mar. 1872. [23] M.C.N.E.I., 18 Aug. 1874.
[24] M.C.N.E.I., 14 Dec. 1875. [25] M.C.N.E.I., 16 Apr. 876, 3 Oct. 1876.
[26] William Law to Sir Michael Wicks-Beach, 15 Apr. 1876, S.P.O.I., Chief Secretary's Office, Registered Papers, 1869/1877.

in the preceding year the commissioners had granted an amount in retiring allowance for teachers in excess of the authorized amount without due warning to the treasury, that the commissioners did not inform the treasury that they would exceed the estimate for monitorial salaries by £8,000 until December of the previous year, and that the commissioners were irresponsible in not following any fixed schedule of fees for model schools. As a solution, their lordships suggested that one officer of high and independent rank be appointed by the commissioners to keep their financial house in order.

Little came of these specific suggestions, but this is not as important as the fact that the treasury felt free to enter into decisions that were previously the province of the commissioners, and that their lordships felt no compunction about involving themselves in decisions that were effectively ones of educational policy. Admittedly, in any set of educational situations the line between financial policy and educational policy is a difficult one to draw. Nevertheless, it is clear that the treasury was becoming accepted as a partner not only in purely financial decisions, but also in matters, such as school fees and results fees, that had considerable influence on the way the national schools carried out their educational task. One area of educational policy in which the treasury was concerned was that of school size. The treasury was scandalized by the small size of the average Irish school and by the apparently unnecessary multiplication of schools in Ireland, and pressed for fewer and larger schools. Their lordships included the following table in a letter bewailing the needless multiplication of schools in Ireland.[27]

	England and Wales	Scotland	Ireland
Estimated pop. 30 June 1875	23,944,459	3,495,214	5,309,494
Estimated no. of children of school age	4,788,892	699,043	1,061,899
No. of schools inspected in G.B. and no. of nat'l schools in Ireland	14,140	2,900	7,267

[27] M.C.N.E.I., 8 May 1877.

	England and Wales	Scotland	Ireland
No. scholars in average daily attendance	1,911,558	322,974	389,961
Total population per school	1,693	1,205	731
No. scholars in average daily attendance	135	111	53

Their lordships seemed unable to realize that Ireland was neither England nor Scotland, and that the religious situation in Ireland and the educational precedents established prior to the 1870s made larger schools impossible.

In 1878 the treasury forced a significant educational change by pressing the commissioners into omitting £62,000 from their estimates for results—fees for some of the extra subjects, on the grounds that the scheme of intermediate education provided for these subjects and that it was no longer necessary for the commissioners to encourage them.[28] In January 1881, the treasury interfered with the freedom of contract of national school managers by refusing to allow, on any terms whatsoever, the return to service of teachers who had received a gratuity upon their retirement.[29] The commissioners spinelessly accepted the treasury's ruling in this matter, a motion that a letter be written to the treasury saying that the commissioners 'cannot admit that the sanction of the treasury is necessary to such appointment', being lost by a vote of four to three.[30] In June 1882, their lordships set a record of niggardliness by informing the commissioners that the expense of burying students who died while in training should not fall upon public funds.[31]

It will be recalled that in the first ten years of the national system's operation the commissioners won the right to violate their own rules. They established that the treasury and its hand-maiden, the auditor general's office, did not have the right to question the wisdom of any expenditure made by the commissioners within the limits set by parliament, and that the auditor general's office was restricted solely to certifying the

[28] M.C.N.E.I., 22 Jan. 1878.
[29] M.C.N.E.I., 11 Jan. 1881.
[30] M.C.N.E.I., 1 Feb. 1881.   [31] M.C.N.E.I., 6 June 1882.

arithmetical correctness of the commissioners' accounts. In 1883 that freedom was lost. In January 1883, the treasury wrote the commissioners of national education averring that the commissioners were bound by their own rules, not only their own financial rules, but their educational rules as well. According to the treasury, the comptroller and auditor general were entitled to be satisfied that all money voted by parliament for any governmental service was expended in strict accordance with the rules applicable to that service. In their lordships' eyes the rules governing a service could be embodied in legislative statutes or in departmental regulations. Each was binding upon the department and could be altered only by the authority which framed the statutes or regulations; a department could violate neither regulation nor statute. If any department chose to alter its own regulations, even if it had the power to do so, such change, if it occurred during the interval between one parliamentary vote and another, was required to be laid before parliament at the time of the next vote for its approval.[32] The implications for the commissioners of national education were that their freedom of action was to be radically restricted and that the right to violate their own printed rules in exceptional circumstances was abrogated. The commissioners voted to comply with the treasury directive.[33] By so doing they admitted that the treasury was their master.

Until 1887 the commissioners of national education had a good deal of latitude as to how much money they could spend each year upon building and improvement for national schools. In any year in which their building expenses exceeded the estimates, they simply presented a supplementary estimate to cover the expense.[34] This the treasury could not tolerate. A very strongly worded treasury minute of 8 December 1887 noted that the amounts of building grants were growing annually, and that the commissioners would probably exceed by £10,000 the estimate of that year. Their lordships could not 'believe that it was ever the intention of the government to place in the hands of the national education commissioners authority to incur unlimited obligations to be defrayed from the exchequer. As has already been stated, they exercise their power under no statu-

[32] M.C.N.E.I., 23 Jan. 1883.   [33] M.C.N.E.I., 23 Jan. 1883.
[34] Robert B. McDowell, *The Irish administration, 1801-1914* (London and Toronto, 1964), p. 101.

tory authority . . . [Thus], it is in the power of the treasury to place a limit to the amount up to which grants may be made, or at least to the amounts which may be paid in any one year.'[35] Their lordships specified that no more building grants were to be made until the question was settled. To curb the spendthrift tendencies of the national education commissioners, the treasury proposed, and the government eventually sanctioned, that the amount to be spent on building grants was to be specified in the estimates for each year, and that once the amount had been settled the commissioners were to consider it binding. In order to guarantee that the commissioners did not overspend, the board of works was to keep the commissioners informed from time to time of the progress of expenditure and liability under the grants. Regarding the actual sums of money to be spent, the treasury suggested that £40,000 a year be provided for building grants for each of the next three years. Needless to say, the commissioners were horrified by this minute, the more so because they were simultaneously informed by the board of works that the £40,000 for the year 1888 was already completely committed through liabilities which the commissioners had previously incurred. The commissioners protested, quite justifiably, that this ruling meant that no new building grants whatsoever could be made in 1888–9, inasmuch as the ordinary advances to contractors of the works could not be paid until some time in the year 1889–90. This, they explained, implied a complete paralysis of a major arm of the national system of education. 'Since the institution of the national system, fifty-seven years ago, nothing so serious or momentous has happened,' they declared.[36] The treasury relented somewhat, allowing the commissioners to spend £30,000 for the coming year over the previous commitments.[37] Nevertheless, the treasury had clearly established the principle that the expenditures for educational building grants were limited and were under treasury control.

In point of fact the treasury's victory was a singularly harmful one for the Irish schools. While enjoining the commissioners to economy, the treasury refused to let them apply the money saved in one year to expenses incurred in the successive year. Out of fear of calling the treasury's wrath down upon themselves, the

[35] M.C.N.E.I., 20 Dec. 1887.   [36] M.C.N.E.I., 10 Apr. 1888.
[37] M.C.N.E.I., 8 May 1888.

commissioners tended to underspend. Hence in the first three years of the policy, more than £10,000 of the £120,000 budgeted lapsed,[38] money that certainly could have been useful in improving the quality of Irish schoolhouses. Worse yet, the treasury's method of accounting precluded accurate planning on the part of the commissioners. The building grants were counted as spent not as of the year granted, but as of the time that payment was actually made to the contractors. Because there was inevitably a delay of an uncertain amount of time between the approval of any project and the payment for its completion, it was almost impossible for the commissioners to know which of their projects would be completed within any given year, and thus accountable in that year's budget, and which would remain until the next year to be ascribed to that year's budget.[39] All this uncertainty caused the commissioners to spend cautiously, thereby keeping well within the authorization; the treasury's refusal to allow them to use one year's savings in the next year meant that the Irish national schools were annually robbed of part of their building vote.

After watching the commissioners surrender on issue after issue to the lords of the treasury, it is reasonable to conclude that as a body they were either unconcerned with the questions of who was to have direction of the system of national education, or were almost totally without political weight. In contrast to their predecessors of the 1830–50 period, the commissioners were, with certain exceptions, mostly men of relative unimportance. Moreover, no one could accuse them of making up for their unimportance by their fearlessness. The change in quality of the men chosen as commissioners meant a consequent reduction in the influence and authority of the commissioners of national education as a corporate body.[40]

[38] M.C.N.E.I., 12 June 1890.

[39] M.C.N.E.I., 4 Feb. 1896.

[40] The commissioners of national education from 1870 to 1900 are listed below, with their years of service given.

Men appointed before 1870: Dr P. S. Henry, 1838–81; Alexander Macdonnell (resident commissioner), 1839–72; marquis of Kildare (later duke of Leinster), 1841–87; Rt Hon. M. Brady, 1847–71; James Gibson, 1848–80; Montifort Longfield, 1853–83; Hon. Thomas O'Hagan, 1858–85; earl of Dunraven, 1861–71; attorney general James Lawson, 1861–87; John Lentaigne, inspector general of prisons, 1861–86; Rt Hon.

A certain amount of admirable indignation against the treasury's educational imperialism did boil over in 1896, at least on

---

Henry Monahan, 1861–78; Hon. Justice John O'Hagan, 1861–90; Lord Chief Baron D. R. Pigot, 1861–73; Lawrence Waldron, M.P., 1861–75; Rt Hon. J. D. Fitzgerald, 1864–89; Thomas Preston, 1864–73; James W. Murland, 1865–90; Provost John H. Jellett, 1868–88; Rev. Charles Morell, 1868–87; Rt Hon. Mr Justice Morris, 1868– (see below).

Commissioners completing their term between 1870 and 1900: Most Rev. Marcus Beresford, protestant archbishop of Armagh, 1871–85; Rt Hon. Sir P. J. Keenan, resident commissioner, 1871–94; Rt Hon. Viscount Monck, 1871–94; J. A. Dease, 1873–74; Sir Dominic J. Corrigan, 1874–80; Hon. Jenico Preston (Viscount Gormanstown), 1874–85; Sir Robert Kane, 1875–90; Rt Hon. W. H. F. Cogan, 1880–94; Rev. Hugh Hanna, 1880–92; David Ross, 1881–87; Rt Hon. Lord Justice Fitzgibbon, 1884–96; Rt Hon. Lord Justice Naish, 1885–90; W. H. Newell, 1886–99); Rt Hon. C. T. Redington, 1886–99 (resident commissioner, 1894–9) Sir John W. Stubbs, 1887–97; Rev. J. W. Whigham, 1887–90; Henry Doyle, 1891–2; John E. Sheridan, 1892–5; Most Rev. Lord Plunket, protestant archbishop of Dublin, 1895–7.

Commissioners still serving in 1900, with date of their appointment: Rt Hon. Lord Morris and Killanin, 1868; Edmund G. Dease, 1880; Sir Malcolm J. Inglis, 1887; G. F. Fitzgerald, S.F.T.C.D., 1888; Sir Percy R. Grace, 1888; James Morell, 1888; Sir H. Bellingham, 1890; Rev. Henry Evans, 1890; Lord Chief Baron Christopher Palles, 1890; Sir R. Blennerhassett, 1891; Rt Hon Judge James Johnston Shaw, 1891; Rev. H. B. Wilson, 1892; Stanley Harrington, J.P., 1895; W. R. J. Molloy, J.P., 1895; Most Rev. W. J. Walsh, Roman Catholic archbishop of Dublin, 1895; Edward Dowden, 1896; Rt Rev. Mervyn Archdall, bishop of Killaloe, 1897; Rev. John H. Bernard, 1897; Rt Hon. Mr Justice Gibson, 1899; W. J. M. Starkie, resident commissioner, 1899.

Sources: *Return giving the names, appointment and attendances, 1890–1900, of the commissioners of national education in Ireland*, pp 1–2, H.C., 1901 (305), lvii; *Royal commission of inquiry into primary education (Ireland)*, vol. vii: *Returns furnished by the national board*, pp 5–6 [C6–VI], H.C. 1870, xxviii; pt v; *Thirty-seventh report of the commissioners of national education in Ireland, for the year 1870*, p. 52; *Thirty-eighth report . . . for the year 1871*, pp 33, 48, *Thirty-ninth report . . . for the year 1872*, p. 62; *Fortieth report . . . for the year 1873*, pp 26, 43; *Forty-first report . . . for the year 1874*, pp 20–1; *Forty-second report . . . for the year 1875*, pp 28, 42; *Forty-third report . . . for the year 1876*, p. 38; *Forty-fourth report . . . for the year 1877*, p. 38; *Forty-fifth report . . . for the year 1878*, pp 24, 36; *Forty-sixth report . . . for the year 1879*, p. 32; *Forty-seventh report . . . for the year 1880*, pp 26, 34; *Forty-ninth report . . . for the year 1882*, pp 32, 36; *Fiftieth report . . . for the year 1883*, p. 32; *Fifty-first report . . . for the year 1884*, p. 38; *Fifty-second report . . . for the year 1885*, p. 40; *Fifty-fourth report . . . for the year 1887*, pp 29, 40; *Fifty-fifth report . . . for the year 1888*, pp 39, 56; *Fifty-sixth report . . . for the year 1889*, pp 36, 54.

the part of one commissioner. In the mid-1890s, the commissioners requested that a commission be appointed by the lord lieutenant to look into the position of practical work in the national schools. The lord lieutenant wanted the commissioners to do it themselves, but the commissioners objected upon the grounds that no one would pay any attention to them. Lord Chief Baron Palles fired off a most irritated letter to the lord lieutenant denouncing the stranglehold the treasury held upon the throat of Irish national education. He pointed out that seven years had been occupied by correspondence between the treasury and the commissioners of national education about the commissioners' desire to introduce a kindergarten system into Ireland, and that on five occasions the commissioners had been balked by the refusals of the treasury to allow the kindergartens to be created because of the anticipated cost, and that on seven additional occasions the same request, when made by the Irish government, was also refused sanction. 'So, it should not be imagined,' the lord chief baron concluded, 'that the national board had the control of education in Ireland. No doubt the public believes they had ... but when they came to examine that power they found they had not got it. They were curtailed by a higher power.'[41]

Although it would be inaccurate to see the civil service commissioners as a great threat to the autonomy of the commissioners of national education, they did reinforce the treasury's activities in reducing the commissioners' freedom of action. After 1870, the civil service commissioners were responsible for bringing uniform entrance standards and organizational procedures into most of the British civil service. From 1871 onwards, a qualifying examination conducted by the civil service commissioners was the normal mode of entry into the government service. On some jobs, however, the national education commissioners maintained certain controls. For example, candidates for inspectorships were selected by limited competition examinations, rather than by open examinations.[42] Further, the commissioners had a good deal to say about what was covered in examinations for the higher ranks in their service. In 1895 the civil service commissioners and the commissioners of

[41] M.C.N.E.I., 19 Aug. 1896.
[42] McDowell, p. 37.

national education had a tussle about the commissioners' right to determine what the test for inspectors should cover. The civil service commissioners expressed disapproval of the electricity examination included in the national education commissioners' programme for the examination of prospective inspectors,[43] but the education commissioners were obdurate about the value of electricity and, in addition, refused to accept a proposal made by the civil service commissioners that would have taken from the education commissioners their right to set the tests and qualifications they required for inspectors.[44]

Such a battle with the civil service commissioners was minor compared to the commissioners' great fight with the treasury from 1894 to 1896. Under the provisions of the English local government act of 1888 and of the Probate Duties (Scotland and Ireland) Act, 1888, a plan was worked out for the sharing of the probate duties between England, Scotland, and Ireland for the purpose of relieving local taxation through funds from the imperial exchequer. The ratio for dividing the funds was eighty per cent for England, eleven per cent for Scotland, and nine per cent for Ireland, this division being on the basis of the proportional contribution made by each country to the imperial exchequer. The 80–11–9 division was also used in the customs and excise duties act of 1890, which provided funds for education. In 1891 English school fees were effectively abolished through a special grant from the exchequer, and Scotland and Ireland naturally demanded their fair share. The English grant was determined upon the basis of a capitation grant of ten shillings for each child in average daily attendance. In theory, these grants were in relief of local taxation. Rather than make a ten shillings grant per child to the Scottish and the Irish schools, the chancellor of the exchequer, George Goschen, suggested that an 'equivalent grant' from the customs and excise money be made to Scotland and Ireland of eleven per cent and nine per cent, respectively, of the grant made to England.[45] It is significant that in advocating this policy, Goschen was looking on the

[43] M.C.N.E.I., 19 Feb. 1895.

[44] M.C.N.E.I., 19 Feb. 1895.

[45] 'School grants, Ireland and Scotland', P.R.O.L., CAB 37/42, 1896, no. 29, pp 1–3; *Sixty-second report of the commissioners of national education in Ireland, for the year 1895*, pp 23–7.

grant not as a function of the educational needs of the three nations, but as a product of their abilities to contribute to the exchequer. Thus, both Ireland and Scotland were cheated of a good deal of money which would have been theirs if the capitation grants had been extended to these countries, for each of the countries had a larger proportion of the children of the British Isles receiving education than they had money to contribute to the imperial exchequer. Goschen's plan saved the government considerable money, but resulted in the rich becoming richer.

Whatever the inequities of this arrangement, the commissioners of national education did not complain, for they were promised more money. Unfortunately, they basked in the promise of the increased grants without finding out how the plan of 'equivalent grants' operated. The Scottish and Irish acts, it is important to note, did not actually prescribe that the equivalent grant from customs and excise revenue be divided in the ratio of 80–11–9 for every year but only for the first year of the acts' operation. The Irish act provided for a grant of £210,000 which was 9/80ths of the English grant from the customs money for the same year, but it did not specify that the Irish grant should permanently be 9/80ths of the English grant. Nevertheless, it did not prescribe any other method of calculation nor any special steps to be taken for increasing the grant if the English grant increased. Unhappily for the national system, the commissioners assumed that they would automatically receive nine per cent of the English grant each year and that no action was necessary on their part. Such was not the case, for the treasury's interpretation of the law was that although the Irish were entitled to nine per cent of any English grant, they would receive it only if they asked for it. The Scottish board of education realized that this was the meaning of the identical provision in the Scottish education act of 1892, and from the first year of the act's operation annually demanded a fixed proportion, eleven per cent, of the English grant from customs revenues. The treasury tried to block the increase to the Scottish education department in 1893–4, but the Scottish office insisted upon a grant in proportion to the newly increased English grant. The treasury, although it did not give in in principle, agreed in all subsequent years to the department's demands for its eleven per cent. This amount, it should be noted, was calculated as a per centage of the original English estimate and did not include funds from supplemental estimates.[46]

Although the commissioners of national education in Ireland lacked the alertness of the Scottish education department and did not apply for increased funds when the English grants rose, it is unclear whether or not the commissioners were primarily at fault for Ireland's not getting her share of the money. The commissioners took no steps to claim for Ireland anything more than the £210,000 fixed for Ireland under the act, even though they were aware that the English grants were rising. Near the end of 1893 they became aware that they were not receiving the full benefit of the proportionate principle, but even then all they did was write the treasury asking the treasury to clarify the situation. Upon receiving the treasury's reply, they let the matter drop and applied for only £210,000 for 1894–5.[47]

The commissioners blamed the loss upon difficulties in providing estimates, for it was impossible for them, they correctly noted, to know at the time of submitting their own estimates precisely what the English estimate would be for that year: 'The amount of the grant, in our view of the case was to be determined by the amount of the English grant simply as a matter of proportion. And of the amount of the English grant for the coming year we know nothing.'[48] Granted that the commissioners would not be expected to be clairvoyant, the compelling rejoinder from their opponents was that they could simply have left this part of their estimate blank, as did the Scottish education department, to be filled in by the treasury on the basis of the proportionate calculation.[49]

Clearly, the Irish commissioners could be faulted for failure to keep abreast of their financial responsibilities at least during the first year of the equivalent grants. After the first year, however, the treasury must bear the brunt of the blame. In a letter of 20 October 1893, their lordships replied to the commissioners' request for information about the basis on which the

[46] 'School grants, Ireland and Scotland', p. 3.
[47] Ibid., pp 23–4.
[48] *Sixty-second report of the commissioners of national education in Ireland, for the year 1895*, p. 35.
[49] 'School grants, Ireland and Scotland', p. 24.

request for money from the equivalent fund should be calculated that, 'if parliament should so determine, an increase or decrease should be made in the Irish grant in the event of any increase or decrease being made in the English fee grant'.[50] The implication of this statement was that the Irish commissioners of national education could not receive any additional money from the equivalent grant above the fixed £210,000 without parliamentary sanction, an implication that even the treasury's defenders had to admit was inaccurate and misleading.[51] The national education commissioners took this as the final word and settled for £210,000 in the estimates for 1894–5.[52]

The combination of treasury skulduggery and the commissioners' inertia brought silence for a short time, but then the commissioners became restive. While receiving only £210,000 in 1894, they came to realize that if the proportionate principle had been in operation they would have received £248,962.[53] On 21 August 1894, the chief secretary, John Morley, was confronted in the commons with the question of the injustice being done to Irish education by the policy concerning the equivalent grant from the customs and excise revenues. Morley indicated that he was himself uncertain about the meaning of the original legislation and that he was doing his best to ascertain the correct legal interpretation of the act.[54]

Encouraged by the question's being raised in parliament, the commissioners addressed a letter to the treasury on 28 November 1894, pressing for their rightful share of the equivalent grant. In arguing their case the commissioners pointed out that the wordings of the Scottish and the Irish acts were identical regarding the method by which the amount of the grants to the two countries was to be determined. Because the Scottish grants had been increased the Irish commissioners had a *prima facie* case for their demand. Specifically, they requested £234,000 for 1895–96 and noted that 'a higher figure may be required to maintain the due proportion to be claimed for Ireland'.[55] The commissioners also tentatively submitted a claim for £37,000 in arrears

[50] Ibid., p. 30.   [51] Ibid., p. 24.   [52] Ibid., p. 24.
[53] *Sixty-second report of the commissioners of national education in Ireland, for the year 1895*, p. 34.
[54] Ibid., p. 34; *Freeman's Journal*, 21 July 1896.
[55] 'School grants, Ireland and Scotland', p. 30.

for the years 1893–95. At this point, the treasury beat a truculent retreat, and, in January 1895, admitted the first principle argued by the Irish commissioners. In early February 1895, the treasury granted the commissioners of national education £234,000 for the financial year 1895–6, this being equivalent to 11/80 of the original English estimate out of the equivalent grant.[56]

Another question remained: were the national education commissioners entitled to 9/80 of the money from the equivalent grant from customs and excise revenues that the English committee of council received from its supplementary estimates, as well as their proportion of the original estimate? The national education commissioners thought that the answer should be 'yes' and in February 1896 pressed their demands. The Irish administration backed the commissioners and in April the treasury, after several refusals, gave in.[57]

Having given in on the two proportionate questions, the treasury tried to hold firm on a third: 'should the commissioners of national education be compensated for arrears, that is, for the amount of money they had lost in the years 1893 to 1895, before the proportionate principle was fully acknowledged?' The commissioners had raised the question as early as November 1894, and in January 1895 had submitted the request for arrears to the Irish government. The government merely forwarded the letter to the treasury, which pointed out to the Irish administration that it had not supported the commissioners' claim, but that it could not be granted even if the administration did support it. Thereupon, in February 1895, the administration decided to support the claim.[58]

The commissioners were so angry about the situation that they took the extraordinary step of devoting eighteen pages of their report for the year 1895 to the equivalent grants questions, concluding their summary with the assertion that, 'it seems clear to us that when provision is thus being made for the payment of the amount unpaid in 1895–96, provision should also be made for the amounts similarly unpaid in the previous

[56] Ibid., pp 25, 31.   [57] Ibid., pp 25, 32.
[58] Ibid., p. 25.

years'.[59] William Walsh, the Roman Catholic archbishop of Dublin and an able and active commissioner of national education from 1895 to 1901, wrote a number of letters to the public press exposing the treasury's deceitfulness.[60] The matter was of sufficient importance to merit attention by the cabinet and a lengthy cabinet paper was drawn up on the subject in July 1896. The paper's basic argument was that the commissioners of national education in Ireland were not entitled to the arrears because, although entitled to the money in principle, they had been asleep to their own interests and in not asking for the money at the proper time they had tacitly given up all rights to the money. This argument was buttressed by reference to the principle of treasury procedure that precluded the reopening of a case closed in former years.[61] Finally, however, the treasury gave in and agreed to make up the arrears. The amount paid was approximately £108,000, of which about £13,000 was to go to convent and monastery schools and the rest to the teacher's pensions fund. The commissioners accepted this offer.[62] The equivalent grants affair was the only time in the years 1870–1900 that the commissioners stood up to the treasury on an important issue. Ironically, after all the fighting about the equivalent grants, the government and the treasury decided to calculate the grants from the customs and excise money for the financial year 1896–7 and succeeding years on the basis of a capitation grant of ten shillings a head for each child in average daily attendance.[63]

3

When we turn to general administrative developments in the last three decades of the nineteenth century we do not expect to find many dramatic changes, since the bureaucracy of national education was by then a mature, stable organization. The bureaucracy went along with its usual mixture of general competence

[59] *Sixty-second report of the commissioners of national education in Ireland, for the year 1895*, p. 40.
[60] See, for example, *Freeman's Journal*, 21 July 1896.
[61] 'School Grants, Ireland and Scotland', pp 21–6.
[62] M.C.N.E.I., 16 Feb. 1897.
[63] M.C.N.E.I., 16 Feb. 1897; *Hansard 4*, xlvii, 283, 22 Jan. 1897.

salted with specific inefficiencies and difficulties. Alexander Macdonnell resigned as resident commissioner in 1871 and was replaced by Patrick Keenan who held the office into the 1890s. As had been true in the preceding decades, the inspectors were the most difficult of the groups which Keenan had to control. In May 1884, A. Purse, secretary to the 'committee of district inspectors', wrote a letter to G. O. Trevelyan, the chief secretary, complaining of inadequate salaries. In his statement, Purse pointed out that on 4 July 1873 the house of commons had resolved that the salaries of civil servants in Ireland were, in general, inadequate and that this situation should be redressed as soon as possible. Hence in 1874 the inspectors' salaries were raised by a small amount. Purse's memorandum voiced two grievances. First, that the increment had not sufficiently compensated for the increase of work placed upon the inspectors by the results system. Second, that the salaries for Irish inspectors remained at a level considerably below those of British school inspectors (Scottish and English wages were the same). The minimum salary of a British inspector was £400, that of an Irish inspector £250. A Scottish or English inspector could look forward to a maximum salary of £800 a year, an Irish inspector to only £500. The commissioners of national education were unhappy at the news that their inspectors had gone over the commissioners' heads in petitioning the chief secretary about their grievances, and they reacted by expressing regret at the inspectors' action and by doing nothing about the inadequate salaries.[64]

It may be that the inspectors deserved their inferior salaries, since there is considerable evidence that their department was inefficient, although this was more the fault of the chiefs of inspection than of the inspectors themselves. The chiefs of inspection seem to have been generally lazy. In the early 1890s, Keenan was forced to deal with their inefficiency; the majority of the reports submitted to the chiefs of inspection were being dealt with by the clerical staff of the board, rather than receiving the personal attention of the chiefs of inspection. Keenan de-

---

[64] *Copy of any circular or document conveying to the inspectors of national schools in Ireland a reprimand in connection with the agitation for increased remuneration, passim,* H.C. 1884–5 (22), lxi; M.C.N.E.I., covering 5 Feb. 1884 to 17 Nov. 1885, insert between pp 158 and 159.

manded that the chiefs make their own decisions on cases submitted to them, although it was of course proper for them to rely
on the clerks for information useful in making their decisions.
The chiefs of inspection circumvented Keenan's intentions by
having the clerks make the recommendations for action upon
slips of paper that could be destroyed, rather than directly upon
the reports. The chiefs then simply copied out the clerks' suggestions as their own.[65]

A serious case of administrative bungling occurred in 1895
when a number of teachers complained that the examinations
used for determining whether or not a teacher should be promoted had been marked much too severely and that a number
of questions had not been set properly. When the commissioners raised the question with the senior officials in charge of this
work, the head inspector and the chiefs of inspection, the officials
were very reluctant to change their work. The upshot of the
affair was that some of the commissioners had to take a hand in
re-marking the papers.[66] Although it would be a mistake to
infer too much from this episode, the fact that civil servants
would dare to question the commissioners' orders, and the fact
that the commissioners themselves were forced to mark papers,
suggest that the commissioners were not, at the century's end,
commanding a very taut ship.

When William Starkie became resident commissioner in
February 1899, things began to change rapidly. (Starkie succeeded C. T. Redington, who had taken Keenan's place after
Keenan's death in 1894.) It was clear that the inspectorate
needed reorganization. Not only were some of the head inspectors and chiefs of inspection insubordinate and slack in doing
their office duties, but even the best of them rarely had time to
visit schools. After 1880 the head inspectors were assigned specific
areas of ten inspection districts apiece, but they still spent little
time in the field: in 1898 two of the head inspectors made only
six check inspections and another made none at all. Although
most of the head inspectors were not distinguished for their
energy, much of the blame must lie with the organization of the
department; these senior officials were chosen from the ranks of
the inspectors after twenty to thirty years of service and were
usually too advanced in years, especially after doing nothing but

[65] McDowell, p. 254.   [66] Ibid., pp 254–5.

routine inspections for decades, to adapt themselves to the requirements and pace of the central office.

In 1900, Starkie wrought four major changes. First, he rearranged the country's inspection districts, reducing the sixty districts then in operation to twenty-two. Each of these districts was placed under a senior inspector, with two junior inspectors as his aides. Second, Starkie re-titled the chiefs of inspection as 'chief inspectors', and redefined their duties. Whereas they had previously spent their time in the office reading inspectors' reports, he now sent them into the field to oversee the inspection process. In doing this Starkie was protecting his own position as resident commissioner, for he was thus able to remove from Dublin the two men who had been habitually insubordinate and who clearly threatened his control of the central establishment. Moreover, he specifically established that the two men were directly responsible to him for maintaining the proper operation of the system of inspection. Third, Starkie created the new post of 'examiner' in the central office to deal with paper work previously done by the chiefs of inspection. Fourth, although the records on the move are unclear, it is probable that at this time he also abolished the posts of head inspector, probably shifting the incumbents to senior inspectorships.[67] These changes went down very badly with the former chiefs of inspection who felt that they had been demoted in rank. They argued that they should not be mere inspectors but that they were actually heads of a department. Both of the chief inspectors were suspended and forced to apologize before returning to office.[68] Thus, at the end of the century the most mutinous segment of the crew had been whipped into line.

One arm of the board withered in the years 1870–1900, and that was the agricultural school department. In addition to the Albert National Agricultural Training College at Glasnevin

[67] Ibid., pp 250, 255; *Vice-regal committee of enquiry into primary education (Ireland), 1913: Final Report of the committee*, pp 6–9 [Cd 7235], H.C. 1914, xxviii.

The statement that the head inspectors' positions were abolished at this time is based on the facts that they existed at least up to 1899, that in 1914 there were no head inspectors upon the staff, and that the only reorganization on a major scale to take place between 1899 and 1914 took place in 1900.

[68] McDowell, p. 256.

(opened in 1838) and the Munster Model Farm near Cork (opened in 1853), the commissioners leased, usually in connection with a local manager, a number of farms as model agricultural schools, of which there were twenty in 1856. Also, the commissioners recognized as ordinary agricultural schools, national schools with farms attached. In 1875 there were 228 farms of various sorts attached to national schools, of which nineteen were model agricultural schools.[69] The commissioners' attempt at agricultural education was an expensive one, both because of the cost of leasing and managing the farms and because of the special demands upon the central establishment as regards the inspection and management. The Powis commission took a very sceptical view of the value of the model agricultural schools and recommended that the Albert Institution be continued but that the number of model agricultural schools should be reduced. On the other hand, the Powis commission felt that the ordinary agricultural schools under local management should be encouraged.[70]

Teeth were put in the Powis recommendation about the model agricultural schools by a treasury committee under the chairmanship of W. H. Gladstone, that inquired into the Board in 1873 and 1874.[71] Hence, by 1881 the commissioners had divested themselves of all the model agricultural schools save the Albert and the Munster institutions. In April 1900, these establishments were transferred to the newly-created department of agricultural and technical instruction.[72] During the 1890s the number of school farms in connection with national schools was sharply reduced, the farms becoming school gardens. In 1895 the number of schools with farms was only forty-six, while gardens were connected with forty-three. In 1899 thirty-eight farms remained, but the number of gardens had risen to 116.[73] The ordinary agricultural schools were following the model agricultural schools into extinction, leaving scores of garden plots as their memorial.

[69] Balfour, p. 105.
[70] *Royal commission of inquiry into primary education (Ireland)*, vol. i, pt 1; *Report of the commissioners*, pp 531–3, [C 6], H.C. 1870, xxviii, pt i.
[71] *Hansard 3*, ccxl, 1036, 31 May 1878.
[72] McDowell, p. 253.
[73] Balfour, p. 105; *Report of the council of education* [Pr. 2583], p. 54.

The biggest challenge the Irish administration and the commissioners of national education faced in the last three decades of the century was to keep pace with their English contemporaries. The payment of a capitation grant of ten shillings for each child in average daily attendance from the customs and excise revenues meant that English elementary schools were, after 1891, effectively free. The Irish act of 1892 followed the English precedent and used customs and excise funds to abolish fees in all national schools in which the average fee for pupils had been six shillings or less a year. Only in schools in which the fee had exceeded that amount could any fee be charged and then only the difference between that amount and the six shillings. Most teachers were compensated for their loss by receiving a twenty per cent increase in their class salaries. In those convent and monastery schools still paid on a capitation basis, each teacher received an additional three shillings and six pence per head. Bonuses were also paid to assistant teachers and monitors to compensate for their loss.[74] In 1900, 8,371 of the 8,684 schools in operation were free of school fees.[75]

But the Irish commissioners and the Irish administration had another English precedent to emulate, namely the introduction of compulsory education. Since 1880 compulsory attendance had been required in England for children of five to fifteen, albeit with exemptions for beneficial employment. Therefore, it is not surprising that the act which made Irish primary education effectively free contained provisions for compulsion as well. Under the terms of the act (55 and 56 Victoria, c. 42) parents in areas covered by the terms of the act were required to send children between the ages of six and fourteen to school for at least seventy-five days a year. Attendance could be made at a national school or other efficient school. The act, however, was riddled with absurdities and inadequacies, such as the provision that any child over eleven years of age who received a certificate of proficiency in reading, writing, and arithmetic of the fourth programme level would be excused from attendance.

[74] Balfour, p. 103; *Irish Free State*, report of the department of education, *the school year 1924–25, and the financial and administrative years 1924–25–26* (Dublin, 1926), p. 16.
[75] *Sixty-seventh report of the commissioners of national education in Ireland, for the year 1900*, pp 12–13.

Children were also excused during periods when their labour was needed in fishing, husbandry, or other seasonal industry. The act contained a prohibition on the employment, in places covered by the act, of all children under eleven, and of any child between the ages of eleven and fourteen who did not have a certificate of proficiency in reading, writing, and arithmetic. Here too, the major provisions were undercut by a set of minor exclusions which added up to a considerable body of exceptions. The child-labour section did not apply to the planting of potatoes, to hay-making, or to harvesting. Moreover, it did not apply to any employment that by reason of being done during school holidays or during the hours that schools were not open, could be conducted without interference with the child's schooling. Nothing prevented an employer from working a child weekends and evenings, as long as the child spent the days in a school.

The agencies for enforcing school attendance were school attendance committees, local bodies composed of six to ten persons, at least one half of whom were appointed from among the patrons and managers of the schools within the attendance committees' boundaries. After duly warning parents who refused to comply with the law, the committee was to ask that a school attendance order be drawn up by a court of summary jurisdiction and served upon the parents. If the parents still refused to comply, that court could fine the parents up to five shillings, including costs. This was hardly a terrifying sum and a questionable deterrent to violators. Mild as those provisions were, they only applied—and all the provisions of the act only applied—to towns and cities governed by a town council or commissioners. Rural areas were left totally outside the boundaries of the law. At the time of the act's passage there were no county councils in Ireland, and the act weakly provided that should county councils be established by some future parliament, each council could enforce the compulsory attendance provisions in its domain if it so desired.[76]

The statistics of national school attendance for the last fifteen years of the nineteenth century indicate that the Irish education

[76] *Appendix to the sixtieth report of the commissioners of national education in Ireland, for the year 1893,* pp 3–10 [C 7457–I], H.C., 1894, xxx, pt ii.

act of 1892 certainly did not bring about any sharp change in the Irish national system of education:[77]

Year	No. of children making at least one attendance in the year	No. attending at least once in fortnight before enumeration	Average no. on roll	Average daily attendance	% of average no. no rolls in average daily attendance	No. of schools in operation
1886	1,071,791	705,585	848,347	490,484	57·8%	8,024
1887	1,071,768	715,740	853,091	515,388	60·4%	8,112
1888	1,060,895	711,035	846,433	493,883	58·3%	8,196
1889	1,053,399	710,489	839,603	507,865	60·5%	8,251
1890	1,037,102	694,832	828,520	489,144	59·0%	8,298
1891	1,022,361	700,670	824,818	506,336	61·4%	8,346
1892	N/A	694,294	815,972	495,254	60·7%	8,403
1893	1,032,287	721,092	832,545	527,060	63·3%	8,459
1894	1,028,281	720,977	832,821	525,547	63·1%	8,505
1895	1,018,408	N/A	826,046	519,515	62·9%	8,557
1896	808,939	N/A	815,248	534,957	65·6%	8,606
1897	798,972	N/A	816,001	521,141	63·9%	8,631
1898	794,818	N/A	808,467	518,799	64·2%	8,651
1899	785,139	N/A	796,163	513,852	64·5%	8,670
1900	745,861	N/A	770,622	478,224	62·0%	8,684

The commissioners of national education did their best to bring the compulsory attendance clauses into effect, but the difficulties were considerable. In January 1894, they submitted a tired and discouraged minute on the subject to the chief secretary. In that minute they pointed out that of the 118 municipal bodies empowered to act as local attendance authorities under the act, eighty-eight had taken steps to comply, but that the remaining thirty places had done nothing effectual in this direction, and that Dublin, Cork, Limerick, and Waterford were numbered among the delinquents. The commissioners

[77] Compiled from, *Fifty-third report of the commissioners of national education in Ireland, for the year 1886*, pp 3–4; *Fifty-fourth report . . . for the year 1887*, pp 3–4; *Fifty-fifth report . . . for the year 1888*, p. 4; *Fifty-sixth report . . . for the year 1889*, p. 5; *Fifty-seventh report . . . for the year 1890*, p. 5; *Fifty-eighth report . . . for the year 1891*, p. 5; *Fifty-ninth report . . . for the year 1892*, p. 6; *Sixtieth report . . . for the year 1893*, pp 5–6; *Sixty-first report . . . for the year 1894*, p. 8; *Sixty-second report . . . for the year 1895*, p. 9; *Sixty-third report . . . for the year 1896–97*, p. 9; *Sixty-fourth report . . . for the year 1897–98*, p. 9; *Sixty-fifth report . . . for the year 1898–99*, p. 9; *Sixty-sixth report . . . for the year 1899–1900*, p. 9; *Sixty-seventh report . . . for the year 1900*, p. 12.

also pointed out that although the act purported to give the commissioners powers to take over the school attendance responsibilities in any area in which the local authorities were negligent in their duty, the act nowhere provided for the commissioners of national education to defray the expense such enforcement would necessarily involve. Hence, either the local authorities implemented the act of their own accord, or the act was ignored. Moreover, the commissioners reported, each local authority was completely free to choose its half of the members of the school attendance committee in any way it liked, the commissioners having no right to interfere in this matter. (The commissioners nominated half of the members of the committee, the local authority the other half.) The commissioners had been under the impression that the rule requiring that at least one half of the persons appointed to the committees be managers or patrons of national schools was binding both upon themselves and upon the local authority. When they called this opinion to the attention of the various local authorities they encountered considerable disrespect. In Londonderry, for example, the local authority chose to appoint as its five members of the ten man committee, five protestants, none of whom were school managers or patrons. The commissioners were justifiably worried that appointments on this pattern would prevent harmony on any school attendance committee, for if the responsibility of appointing the managers and patrons for each group, and of protecting the rights of the religious groups not in control of the local town government, fell solely upon the commissioners, school attendance committees would be automatically split into two hostile groups, one of laymen of one denomination, the other of managers and patrons of the other. In some cases the commissioners had chosen, in the interests of religious harmony, not to appoint the full complement of patrons and managers. The commissioners concluded by stating that no further steps could be taken under the act until its provisions were so amended as to make it workable.[78]

[78] M.C.N.E.I., 30 Jan. 1894; *Sixtieth report of the commissioners of national education in Ireland, for the year 1893*, pp 7–11; *Return of copy of correspondence between the commissioners of national education in Ireland and the Irish government on the subject of the difficulties experienced by the commissioners in bringing into operation the Irish education act, 1892*, pp 3–5, H.C. 1893–4 (508), lxviii.

One reason for the failure of the act that the commissioners did not mention was that it had the disapprobation of the Roman Catholic hierarchy. The prelates were opposed in principle to compulsory education as an infringement on parental right.[79] This stand was reinforced by the fact that the Irish education act of 1892 did not provide financial aid to the Christian Brothers schools and similar institutions. The bishops were backed by a considerable number of town councils. John Morley, the chief secretary, estimated in February 1895, that upwards of twenty of the local authorities refused to put the act in operation so long as 'certain classes of schools were excluded from participation in the grants'.[80] Since no modification was made in the grant rules, the prelates unanimously resolved in May 1896 to oppose the amending act introduced in that year.[81] The prelates were successful, and the 1892 Irish education act remained unamended at century's end. In 1898, the Local Government (Ireland) Act created county and rural district councils and thus implicitly extended the 1892 education act to rural Ireland. In 1901 there were school attendance committees operating in forty-three rural districts.[82]

Although compulsory attendance laws were eventually to be successful, there is no evidence that the law had much impact during the nineteenth century. The commissioners of national education were fond of pointing out that the attendance in areas in which the act had been in continuous operation were higher than in other areas: in 1899, the average daily attendance expressed as a percentage of the average number on national school rolls was 71·2 % in areas in which the act had been in continuous operation, and 64·5 % in the national schools

[79] 'Resolutions of the assembled archbishops and bishops of Ireland on the education bill', *Irish Ecclesiastical Record*, 3 ser., xiii (May 1892), pp 472–7. If opposed to compulsion as an infringement upon parental rights, the hierarchy approved 'indirect compulsion', by which they meant such things as child labour laws which would indirectly compel children to go to school, for lack of other alternatives.

[80] John Morley to commissioners of national education in Ireland, 6 Feb. 1895, S.P.O.I., Chief Secretary's Office, Registered Papers, 2637/1895.

[81] *Daily Express*, 30 May 1896; 'Important declarations of the bishops of Ireland on the Irish education bill', *Irish Ecclesiastical Record*, 3 ser., xvii (July 1896), p. 643.

[82] Balfour, p. 104.

generally.[83] These figures are not meaningful as an index of the effectiveness of the 1892 act, however, because the difference is easily accounted for by the fact that the schools in compulsory attendance areas were mostly in urban areas. The figures, then, tell something about the difference between urban and rural Ireland, but little about the effectiveness of the act.

Before leaving our discussion of the administrative arrangements for Irish primary education during the period 1870–1900, the relationship between the national system and the systems of intermediate and technical education should be briefly described. In 1878, a system of intermediate education was created, under the control of seven unpaid commissioners. The intermediate system was endowed with the interest on £1,000,000 that had been appropriated from the funds of the late established church. The income at the commissioners disposal ranged from £27,500 to £32,000 a year. Unlike the commissioners of national education, the commissioners of intermediate education had no power to found schools or in any way to regulate the conduct of intermediate education. Rather they were limited to acting as an examining body and to paying premiums to schools on the basis of the results of their examinations. A second major difference between the intermediate system and the system of national education was that the intermediate system gave funds to denominational schools. The only limit on religious teaching in any school receiving aid from the commissioners of intermediate education was that a conscience clause be observed forbidding any pupil to attend religious instruction which his parents and guardians had not sanctioned, and that the time for religious instruction be so fixed so that no pupil absenting himself from religious instruction for reasons of conscience should be excluded, either directly or indirectly, from the advantages of the secular education given in the school.

Not only were the intermediate and the national systems sharply divergent as administrative organizations, but the men running the two systems seem to have gone blithely along, making no effort mutually to coordinate their activities. The worst aspect of this mutual ignorance was that each group of commissioners set its own examinations and curricula without

[83] *Sixty-sixth report of the commissioners of national education in Ireland, for the year 1899–1900*, p. 13.

reference to the other. This meant that in some cases there was unnecessary overlapping of effort, such as in the subjects for which the commissioners of national education paid extra fees for advanced work. In the more common case there was a considerable gulf between the termination of the education given in the local national school and the level of attainment expected upon entry into an intermediate school. And even where overlapping or educational gaps did not occur, there was no effort made to see that there was any logical relationship in subject or approach between the work done in the national school and in the intermediate school.[84]

The commissioners of intermediate education were at least located in Dublin, but the science and art department governed their Irish charges from South Kensington. In 1852 a department of practical art was established in London and, in 1853, a department of science was added, both of these divisions being under the board of trade. In 1856, the science and art department was transferred to the control of the committee on education. The department served chiefly as an examining body which distributed grants encouraging the study of scientific subjects. Ireland shared in the science and art department grants from the very beginning and came under the London administration. The department allocated its grants on the basis of examinations, although capitation grants were also made. Grants were paid to teachers and prizes to pupils according to how the pupils did upon the department's tests. During the 1890s, the science and art department in London also administered the money allotted for technical education in Ireland. In 1899 both agricultural and technical education were united in a department of agricultural and technical instruction, serving as an Irish department. At no time during the period that the science and art department ruled Irish technical instruction was there any effort to co-ordinate the activities of that body with those of the commissioners of national education. At the

[84] Balfour, pp 205–9; Arnold F. Graves, 'On the reorganization of Irish education departments and the appointment of a minister of education', *Journal of the Statistical and Social Inquiry Society of Ireland* (Aug. 1882), pp 350–9; McDowell, pp 238–9; *Report of the department of education, the school year 1924–25 and the financial and administrative years 1924–25–26*, pp 44–6.

turn of the century things seemed to be improving somewhat for one representative of the commissioners of national education was named as a member of the department of agricultural and technical instruction.[85] Certainly it would not have been amiss if someone had argued for a single ministry of education to oversee and co-ordinate all Irish education efforts.

4

Although the government did not at once adopt all the recommendations of the Powis commission with regard to religion, the commission's recommendations favourable to the Roman Catholics gradually found their way into practice. For example, the commissioners voted eleven to two in December 1880, to abolish the rule forbidding the use of national schools as places for divine worship.[86] During the 1880s, the commissioners became increasingly lax about enforcing the rules regarding religious emblems and devotional pictures. In several cases they allowed crosses built into the gables of Roman Catholic national schools to remain. They also allowed scripture verses to be left hanging on the walls throughout the school day and permitted religious pictures depicting biblical scenes to stay upon the wall during the hours of combined literary instruction.[87] By the end of the century the commissioners were unwilling to rule that the making of the sign of the cross during the hours of literary instruction was prohibited, although their printed regulation on the subject remained unaltered. They simply dodged the issue, refusing, in the case of the Drogheda Convent National School, to state whether or not the making of the sign of the cross by the children on each hour was a religious exercise.[88] By refusing to rule on such cases, they implicitly sanctioned the practice, even if they did not officially modify their rules.

The commissioners slowly bent to Roman Catholic wishes about the use of religious names on national schools. In schools

---

[85] Balfour, pp 155, 201–5; *Report of the department of education, the school year 1924–25 and the financial administrative years 1924–25–26*, pp 55–6.

[86] M.C.N.E.I., 7 Dec. 1880.

[87] See, for example, M.C.N.E.I., 11 Dec. 1883, 18 Dec. 1883, 1 Nov. 1887.

[88] M.C.N.E.I., 12 Jan. 1899.

with several rooms, they condoned the practice of naming the rooms, if the names were nondenominational in character. Thus, they ruled in 1887 that rooms could not be named 'Ave Maria', 'St Mary's', 'Alma Mater', 'Sedes Sapientiae'.[89] True to form, however, they soon back-tracked on the question of naming rooms and allowed rooms to be affixed with the following names: 'St Mary's', 'St Joseph's', 'St Michael', 'St Patrick's', and 'St Francis", although 'St Aloysius", and 'St Angela's', were banned, probably because the two latter names are not saints recognized by the Church of Ireland.[90] The commissioners clung to their rule that no title of a school should be permitted if that title made it appear that the school was open to only one denomination, yet they modified their interpretation of the rule to allow the name of a convent or monastery that was supporting the school to be included in the national school's name.[91]

The lot of the monastic and convent schools was considerably improved after 1870. The 1855 regulation excluding monastic schools from connection with the national system was rescinded in February 1882, upon the motion of Sir Robert Kane. The motion passed by a majority of ten to two, and the lord lieutenant approved the change at once.[92] Although the Christian Brothers held aloof from the national system, a number of schools associated with other orders did join, there being forty-five monastic schools in connection with the national system in 1899.[93]

The rules relating to convent schools were also considerably liberalized. The specific changes seem to have been caused by the resolutions of the Irish Roman Catholic bishops passed in October 1884, complaining that the convent schools had been unfairly treated since the founding of the national system. Specifically, the bishops objected to the rule restricting the number of national schools in connection with an individual convent and to the system of capitation grants to convent national schools.[94] The Irish administration reacted quickly. The chief secretary,

[89] M.C.N.E.I., 1 Nov. 1887.   [90] M.C.N.E.I., 10 June 1890.
[91] M.C.N.E.I., 4 Dec. 1900.
[92] M.C.N.E.I., 24 Jan., 7 Feb., 28 Mar., 1882.
[93] *Sixty-sixth report of the commissioners of national education in Ireland, for the year 1899–1900*, p. 18.
[94] 'Resolutions of the Irish bishops', *Irish Ecclesiastical Record*, 3 ser., v (Nov. 1884), p. 745.

Campbell-Bannerman, wrote to the commissioners in mid-November, 1884, making a number of suggestions on behalf of the administration. Campbell-Bannerman recommended that the commissioners' rules be so modified as to allow nuns and monks to teach in vested schools, they having previously been limited to teaching in non-vested schools. Further, he suggested that the rule forbidding the granting of aid to more than one school in connection with the same convent or monastery be abandoned. He also favoured abolishing the rule that the teacher of an industrial department in a convent national school had to be a lay person. Campbell-Bannerman desired that convent schools be eligible for building grants, a benefit from which they had been excluded since the national system's foundation. He also suggested that the existing practice of paying the convent and monastery teachers results-fees on the same terms as teachers in ordinary national schools be continued. In addition, he felt the convent and monastery teachers should have the right to choose either to be tested and classified for basic salary purposes, as were all other national school teachers, or to receive a capitation grant of twelve shillings per head for children in average daily attendance, when the results examination was entirely satisfactory, and ten shillings a head when it was only fair or passable. In effect, the proposals offered convent and monastery teachers the right to be paid in perfect equality with all other teachers, or, if they scrupled at fitting themselves into the commissioners' system of teacher classification, to be able to refuse without great financial penalty. The commissioners of national education agreed to all these suggestions and most of the grievances of the monastic and convent schools disappeared.[95] Thereafter the only thing the prelates could find to complain about was that the rate of the capitation grant was too low.[96]

Another major recommendation of the Powis commission, that denominational training colleges be sanctioned, was effected in 1883. On the fifth of November 1874, the chief secretary, Sir Michael Hicks-Beach, had directed half a dozen questions at the commissioners of national education, one of which dealt with the vast number of untrained teachers employed in the

[95] M.C.N.E.I., 25 Nov. 1884.
[96] 'Resolutions of the assembled archbishops and bishops of Ireland on the education bill', p. 476.

national schools. In their reply, the commissioners produced a set of statistics that indicated that the majority of Irish national school teachers were untrained and that the problem was especially acute among Roman Catholic teachers:[97]

TRAINED

	Males		Females		Total		
Religious Denominations	*Principals*	*Assistants*	*Principals*	*Assistants*	*Principals*	*Assistants*	*Total*
R.C.	1,666	73	728	173	2,394	246	2,640
E.C.	229	19	121	57	350	76	426
Presby.	455	22	165	78	620	100	720
Others	29		19	8	48	8	56
Totals	2,379	114	1,033	316	3,412	430	3,842

UNTRAINED

	Males		Females		Total		
Religious Denominations	*Principals*	*Assistants*	*Principals*	*Assistants*	*Principals*	*Assistants*	*Total*
R.C.	1,633	545	1,269	1,560	2,902	2,105	5,007
E.C.	167	15	79	119	246	134	380
Presby.	197	27	100	326	297	353	650
Others	28	1	13	39	41	40	81
Totals	2,025	588	1,461	2,044	3,486	2,632	6,118

To solve this problem the commissioners repeated the suggestion made by chief secretary Fortescue in 1866 and by the Powis commissioners in 1870: that 'non-vested training colleges' be created. By this they meant that in addition to their model schools and to the Marlborough Street training colleges, the commissioners would grant aid to training schools under de-

[97] Secretaries to commissioners of national education to Sir Michael Hicks-Beach, 10 Dec. 1874, reproduced in M.C.N.E.I., 8 Dec. 1874. (The dating is correct. The letter as approved by the commissioners was postdated.)

nominational auspices. The commissioners proposed that a non-vested training college be defined as a college for instructing candidates for the office of national school teacher in which secular teaching was available to all religious denominations. Such a school was to be required to conduct secular business at least six hours a day. A practising school was to be connected with each college and operated and aided on the same terms as all other national schools. Aid was to be granted to the schools at the rate of £100 for each master and £70 for each mistress who, after attaining a first class training certificate, taught for two years in a national school. The grants for those achieving a second class training certificate and teaching for two years were to be £80 and £56, for men and women, respectively. The training course was to last for two years, but if the candidate was trained for only one year, the training college was to receive one half of the above grants. The total grants earned by any training college were not to exceed seventy-five per cent of the actual expenditure of the college in any given year. The amount payable to the training colleges was to be paid quarterly at the rate of £6 for males and £5 for females and the balance due paid at the end of each year.[98] The proposals did not raise much public excitement, although the National Education League and the elementary education committee of the general assembly of the presbyterian church in Ireland protested against the proposed encroachment upon the 'fundamental principles' of the national system.[99] The government seems to have lost interest in the proposals and they were quietly ignored.

The situation did not improve while it was being ignored. In January 1883, the commissioners called the government's attention to the problem by submitting to the government a letter containing a resolution recently passed by the general synod of the Church of Ireland to the effect that the system in force in the the Marlborough Street schools might be modified to allow

---

[98] Ibid.

[99] *Copy of memorials from the council of the National Education League for Ireland, addressed to his grace the duke of Abercorn, lord lieutenant, etc., on the subject of inroads made and contemplated upon the fundamental principle of the national system of education in Ireland; and from the elementary education committee of the general assembly of the presbyterian church in Ireland, addressed to his grace the lord lieutenant, on the subject of non-vested training colleges*, passim, H.C. 1875 (201), lix.

students to reside, at public expense, in boarding houses under the superintendence of a clergyman of their own denomination. The commissioners also provided the chief secretary with a summary of past efforts at introducing denominational training colleges and with information which led the chief secretary, G. O Trevelyan, to express regret that in this matter the educational interest of the people of Ireland had been so long deferred. He was especially disturbed that the commissioners' last report revealed that sixty-six per cent of the teachers in national schools were untrained. Of the Roman Catholic teachers, only twenty-seven per cent were trained, the figures for protestant teachers being fifty-two per cent. The injustice of not allowing grants to denominational training colleges seemed especially apparent to Trevelyan when he compared the Irish situation to that prevailing in England and Scotland, for in each of those countries government grants were made to denominational training institutions. Ireland was also being ill-treated financially, for the estimates for 1882–3 provided £110,500 to support forty-two training colleges in England and Wales, enrolling 3,150 students, and £27,000 to support seven Scottish colleges, enrolling 851 students; Ireland, on the other hand, was receiving only £7,755 in aid of Marlborough Street, with its 220 candidates. Trevelyan, therefore, expressed his approval of the suggestions that training colleges under local management be created and granted governmental aid.[100]

The commissioners agreed to the Church of Ireland's proposals that students at Marlborough Street colleges be allowed to board in private residences under denominational sanction and proceeded to draw up a scheme for denominational training colleges closely modelled upon the English system.[101] The proposals were essentially those of 1874. Students admitted into recognized training colleges were to be called 'Queen's scholars' and were to receive either a one or two year course. The one year course was to be open to certificated teachers who had not

[100] G. O. Trevelyan to commissioners of national education, 6 Mar.1883, reproduced in M.C.N.E.I., 30 Mar. 1883, and in *Fiftieth report of the commissioners of national education in Ireland, for the year 1883*, pp 15–18.

[101] M.C.N.E.I., 30 Mar. 1883: W. H. Newell to G. O. Trevelyan, 2 Apr. 1883, reproduced in *Fiftieth report of the commissioners of national education in Ireland, for the year 1883*, pp 18–19.

previously been trained, while the two year course was for all other candidates. The financial arrangements were almost precisely those of the 1874 proposals, being £100 for each master and £70 for each mistress (payable to the college) who taught for two years in a national school after being trained for two years, and £50 for each man and £35 for each woman who taught for two years after the one year training course. Grants were to be limited to seventy-five per cent of the colleges' expenditures for any given year. Each training college was to receive £12 for each man and £8 for each woman in training (payable thrice annually) the balance to be paid after the colleges' accounts for the year had been audited.[102] The presbyterians sent a deputation to the lord lieutenant to try to block the innovations,[103] but to no avail, and they became effective almost at once.

The denominationalists and especially the Roman Catholics were gratified, but not satisfied, by the new regulations. St Patrick's Training College, Drumcondra (for men) and Our Lady of Mercy Training College, Dublin (for women) were opened by the Roman Catholics in 1883 and the Church of Ireland brought its Kildare Place Training College for men and women into connection with the commissioners in 1884.[104] Archbishop Walsh, the Roman Catholic archbishop of Dublin, wrote a considerable volume on catholic educational grievances which appeared in 1890. The first of his complaints was that the cost of buildings and premises had to be borne by the managers of the denominational training colleges, with no aid being granted by the commissioners. In contrast, the entire cost of purchasing the site and erecting the buildings for the Marlborough Street Training College was borne by the commissioners themselves. Second, Walsh complained that the entire cost of furnishing the denominational colleges fell upon their managers, while the furnishing expenses of the commissioners' 'mixed' school in Marlborough Street were borne entirely out of the public purse. Third, whereas maintenance and

[102] *Fiftieth report of the commissioners of national education in Ireland, for the ear 1883,* pp 19–22.

[103] *Irish Times,* 10 Apr., 1883.

[104] *Fifty-seventh report of the commissioners of national education in Ireland, for the new year 1890,* p. 21.

repair fees were borne in their entirety by the commissioners in
the case of their Dublin training school, at least one-fourth, and
perhaps more, of the similar expenses for denominational training schools had to come out of the managers' pocket. This was
because the commissioners treated maintenance expenses as
part of the ordinary school expenses towards which the commissioners would contribute only three quarters of the amount
spent. In this instance Walsh did not object to paying the one-
fourth so much as he wished that the commissioners would pay
only three-fourths in the Marlborough Schools. This was a mali-
cious suggestion since the Marlborough Street training colleges
had no patron except the commissioners, and if the commissioners were barred from paying more than three fourths of the
maintenance expenses, there would be no way for them to be
paid. Fourth, Walsh objected to the general limitation of
seventy-five per cent of the total expenses of denominational
training colleges being borne by the state.[105]

In harping upon the inequality between the mixed institutions in Marlborough Street and the denominational training
colleges, Walsh was upon good grounds as a propagandist, but
poor grounds logically. Granted, the mixed school in Dublin
received more government money, but in return it was completely under the control of the commissioners of national education. Walsh refused to admit that freedom had its price. He
was on much better ground when criticizing the seventy-five
per cent rule, for the real issue was simply that the denominational colleges needed more money.

In his complaints, Walsh had the backing of the anglican
communion. The Church of Ireland had begun criticizing the
financial arrangements as early as 1885, when the synod of
Dublin had complained about the 'inequality' of the seventy-
five per cent grant. At that time, the commissioners of
national education had expressed their opinion that the inequali-
ties should be removed, but nothing was done. Finally, in
November 1890, the chief secretary, A. J. Balfour, wrote to the
commissioners suggesting that a fixed grant in all training
colleges (including Marlborough Street) of £50 a year be paid

[105] William Walsh, *Statement of the chief grievances of Irish catholics in the
matter of education, primary, intermediate and university* (Dublin, 1890), pp
124–9.

for each male in training and £35 for each female, regardless of whether or not they completed the course or served as a national school teacher. In addition to this training grant he recommended that after two years of service a diploma bonus of £10 be granted for males and £7 for females for each year they were trained. Significantly, Balfour suggested that all training colleges be allowed to receive grants to an amount equal to their actual certified expenditure. Balfour further proposed that each of the training colleges should have a 'free home'. With this end in view the government was to make a valuation of the buildings and valuation of each of the colleges, and to authorize a loan from the board of works to the manager of each college equal to the full amount of the valuation, repayable in thirty-five years at five per cent interest. Upon a manager's presenting the commissioners of national education with the receipt for the annual charge, he was to be reimbursed by the commissioners. Thus, the loan was to become a gift.[106] The suggestions were immediately agreed to by the commissioners, and their rules regarding training colleges were revised at once.[107] By century's end, two additional Roman Catholic training colleges had come into connection, one, the De La Salle College in Waterford, for men, the other, St Mary's in Belfast, for women.[108]

With each successive acceptance of the Powis commissioners' suggestions, the national system became even more denominational in character than it was in 1870. The catholic prelates came to realize that the national system was not a mixed system, but in practice a denominational one. As early as 1866 a joint letter of the prelates indicates some awareness that most schools were *de facto* denominational institutions, for they argued for denominational education for the great mass of the Irish people on the following grounds:

This would be simply to recognize the fact that these schools are

[106] A. J. Balfour to commissioners of national education, 25 Nov. 1890, reproduced in *Fifty-seventh report of the commissioners of national education in Ireland, for the year 1890*, pp 23–6.

[107] *Fifty-seventh report of the commissioners of national education in Ireland, for the year 1890*, p. 26.

[108] Irish Free State, *Report of the department of education, the school year 1924–25 and the financial and administrative years 1924–25–26*, pp 33–4.

denominational and to change the rules of the board so as to deal with them as such—rules which, so far as regards religious instruction in this large class of schools, are not merely vexatious but absurd; for they prohibit the fulness of religious teaching and all religious teaching during the hours of secular instruction, upon the assumption that the schools are mixed, whereas the pupils are exclusively of one religion or another.[109]

At the national synod of 1900 the bishops gave thanks that the national system had undergone a great change since its foundation, and instead of spreading secularism, was in the greater part of Ireland as denominational as could be desired. The system, they noted, was a help rather than a hindrance to the Roman Catholic church.[110] The growing awareness that the national system was very close to being a denominational system guaranteed that the prelates would not seriously entertain the idea of severing connection with it, but it did not mean that they would stop trying to modify it. Indeed, the fact that the system was largely denominational merely spurred on the prelates' efforts to make it completely denominational.

5

By 1891 the only grievance important enough to concern most of the catholic prelates and a significant number of the laity was the refusal of the commissioners of national education to grant aid to the Christian Brothers' schools. The Christian Brothers had received aid in the national system's early years, but had withdrawn rather than submit to the commissioners' religious rules, most notably those prohibiting devotional exercises at intervals throughout the day. The Powis Commission had recommended that they be granted aid, but the matter lay dormant until the last decade of the nineteenth century. When it became clear, however, that the government would introduce a bill providing for a fee grant to make the national schools effectively free, and providing for compulsory education in the towns and cities, the Christian Brothers issue reappeared.

[109] Quoted in Walsh, pp 37–8.
[110] Peadar MacSuibhne, *Paul Cullen and his contemporaries, with their letters from 1820–1902* (Naas, 1961), i, 16.

Dublin Castle was bombarded with petitions praying that the benefits of state aid be extended to the schools of the Christian Brothers.[111] When the actual contents of the bill became known the petitions asked that the Christian Brothers be explicitly included in its benefits. Protestant bodies protested vigorously.[112]

The principle of compulsion as embodied in the Irish education act of 1892 was accepted in practice (if protested against in theory) by the Roman Catholic hierarchy upon the condition that the government would attempt to modify the national system to enable the Christian Brothers to participate.[113] In a cabinet paper, John Morley, chief secretary from late August 1892 to July 1895, stated that the reasons the Christian Brothers were excluded from the grant were that they did not accept the conscience clause of the commissioners of national education, that they exhibited religious emblems during all hours of instruction, and that they used books impregnated with 'sectarian colour'. According to Morley, it was understood that the Christian Brothers would accept a conscience clause usually known as the 'intermediate education conscience clause' as the basis for joining the national system.[114] Hence, on 11 August 1892, William Jackson, chief secretary from November 1891 to late August 1892, had sent a letter to the commissioners of national education suggesting that they should consider whether or not the conscience clause from the intermediate education act could conveniently be embodied in their regulations.[115]

---

[111] The petitions came from boards of guardians, trades councils, county commissioners, etc. Twenty-four petitions were received in the first six months of 1891 from such bodies. S.P.O.I., Chief Secretary's Office, Registered Papers, 6999/1896.

[112] See the petitions in S.P.O.I., Chief Secretary's Office, Registered Papers, 6999/1896.

[113] John Morley, 'National education in Ireland, regulations as to religious instruction', P.R.O.L., CAB 37/32, 1892, no. 38, p. 1.

[114] Ibid., p. 1.

[115] *Ibid* p. 2; *Copy of correspondence between the Irish government and the commissioners of national education for Ireland, with extracts from minutes of the proceedings of the commissioners in relation to certain proposed changes in the rules under which grants are made by Parliament for elementary education in Ireland*, pp 3–5, H.C. 1893–94, [55], lxviii; M.C.N.E.I., 16 March 1892, 25 Oct. 1892; W. L. Jackson to commissioners of national education, 11 Aug. 1892, S.P.O.I., Chief Secretary's Office, Registered Papers, 6999/1896 (copy).

The form of the proposed rule was that in any school district in which there had been operated for three years two or more schools, of which one was protestant, the other Roman Catholic, having an average attendance of not less than twenty-five children, the national commissioners might aid the school without requiring any religious rules whatsoever, save the following version of the intermediate education conscience clause:

(I) No pupil attending the school shall be permitted to remain in attendance during the time of any religious instruction which the parents or guardians of such pupil shall not have sanctioned.

(II) The time for giving religious instruction shall be so fixed that no pupil not remaining in attendance shall be excluded directly or indirectly from the advantages of the secular education given in the school.[116]

The rule was moved on 25 October 1892, by the lord chief baron, the Rt Hon. Christopher Palles, but an amendment was promptly proposed by Rev. Dr Wilson, stating that the clauses in the lord chief baron's motion were inadequate safeguards against proselytism. Wilson moved that the intermediate education conscience clause should be allowed as an alternative to the existing one only if all the other religious regulations remained unchanged. Specifically, he wished to leave intact the rules separating religious from secular instruction, those requiring that school books sanctioned by the commissioners and free of sectarian bias be used, and those prohibiting all denominational images and rites during the hours of literary instruction. The commissioners adjourned after Wilson's lengthy motion and when they returned the next day the amendment was lost by a vote of ten to five, with two abstentions. Thereupon, Rev. Dr Evans attempted an amendment that would have blocked the adoption of the intermediate conscience clause, an attempt which failed by an eleven to five vote, with one abstention. Next, Lord Justice Fitzgibbon introduced an amendment whose effect would have been to introduce the intermediate education conscience clause and to allow denominational schools to receive aid, but which would have subjected such schools to inspections, and their books, timetable, and regulations to the commissioners' approval. This was lost by a

[116] M.C.N.E.I., 25 Oct. 1892; *Copy of correspondence . . .* p. 8.

vote of twelve to five. Finally, a slightly amended version of the lord chief baron's motion was approved eleven to six and a letter sent to the chief secretary requesting his approval of the proposed change.[117]

This put Morley in a difficult position for the suggestion that the rule be changed was not his, but his predecessor's. In the cabinet minute of 2 November 1892, he spelled out the difficulties. One of these was that the commissioners had gone further than his predecessor had intended. Jackson's request had mentioned the introduction of the conscience clause from the intermediate education act, but the commissioners had placed the clause within the context of a complete revocation of the existing rules prohibiting the practice of pious rituals and the exhibition of emblems during the hours of secular instruction. The previous government had explicitly forbidden opening, either directly or indirectly, the question of religious emblems. Morley was especially pained by the commissioners' actions since it had been understood that on the question of school books the Christian Brothers were prepared to give way and use only those approved by the commissioners. Thus, in advancing into an area that they had been warned to avoid, the commissioners had destroyed the possibility that the Christian Brothers would quietly join the national system. After the commissioners had indicated that they were willing to radically revise their religious rules, the Christian Brothers would have been publicly shamed if they settled for anything less than that revision. The suggested revision of the religious rules was politically dangerous, for the parliamentary opposition was apt to join the band of strong anti-denominationalists upon the liberal benches in censoring the change. Morley's position was all the more embarrassing because the majority among the commissioners of national education in Ireland that supported the change was composed of a strong and unyielding alliance of Roman Catholic commissioners and anglican commissioners, with the presbyterians being the only source of serious objection. The few differences existing between the Roman Catholics and the anglicans would, Morley felt, be adjusted by negotiation between the two groups.

Morley saw only three possible courses of action. First, the

[117] M.C.N.E.I., 25 Oct. 1892, 26 Oct. 1892; *Copy of correspondence* . . . pp 4–13.

government could decline to sanction the proposed rule changes on the same grounds on which the presbyterians had objected to them: that they involved a destruction of the existing non-denominational system. Second, the government could admit the substance of the new rules on the 'home rule principle' that the Irish should decide these things for themselves. A decision to approve the changes could also be buttressed by reference to English precedent, for none of the English education acts or codes prohibited the exhibition of religious emblems during the hours of secular instruction. Third, the government could abstain from dissenting on principle, could express a sense of general desire in Ireland to include as many schools as possible in the national system, and could then refer the matter back to the commissioners of national education to consider whether they could devise further protections for religious minorities. Suggestion number one, Morley forlornly noted, would bitterly offend the Roman Catholics, while numbers two and three would raise presbyterian disfavour, and, it might be added, would be politically painful at Westminster.[118]

On the tenth of November Morley wrote the commissioners informing them that the question called for a period of 'counsel and deliberation', because the commissioners' proposals had not been carried with so near an approach to unanimity as their importance would require.[119] The commissioners took this as a mandate for further discussion on their part, and they created a committee of six members to reconsider the modifications and to suggest changes which would yield greater unanimity among the commissioners. The committee was given specific power to inquire of the Christian Brothers and of the heads of the Church Education Society what changes in their existing regulations they would be prepared to make in their respective schools.[120]

The committee reported on 16 January, their report being approved by five of the six members. If Morley had expected any significant changes from the original proposals he was

[118] Morley, as above, pp 3–5.
[119] John Morley to commissioners of national education, 10 Nov. 1892, reproduced in M.C.N.E.I., 15 Nov. 1892, and in *Copy of correspondence . . .* p. 15.
[120] M.C.N.E.I., 15, 22 Nov. 1892; *Copy of correspondence . . .* pp 15–18.

rudely surprised, for the committee recommended that in areas with two schools of three years' standing, one catholic and the other protestant, each having thirty-five children in average daily attendance, the commissioners should be permitted to grant aid to any school which, within the preceding twelve months, had not had a mixed attendance. Such schools were not to be subjected to the commissioners' religious rules. The conscience clause to operate in such schools was essentially that of the intermediate education act of 1878. There were only three important changes from the previous proposals. The first of these was that the new proposal provided that if there were a model school in the area, and either an exclusively catholic or an exclusively protestant national school in the area, that either of the latter schools could operate as denominational schools. This proposal was essentially an attempt to remove Roman Catholic grievances against the model schools and was hardly likely to be acceptable to Morley. The second difference was that under the new plan schools would have had to have had an average daily attendance of thirty-five, rather than twenty-five, to be eligible for denominational status. The third change was that a school would have had to have been totally unmixed in the year preceding its recognition as a denominational school, this provision clearly being an attempt to meet Morley's concern for minority rights. The commissioners as a whole approved a proposal for a new rule based upon the committee's report by a vote of twelve to seven. The decision was then reported to Morley.[121]

Morley was advised by David Harrell, Irish under-secretary, that the new rule should not be sanctioned. Harrell argued that the successful working of the newly proposed rule depended upon so many different contingencies as to make it unlikely that it would greatly improve Irish primary education. He noted that the Church Education Society had decisively declined to assent to any change which would have made the rule applicable to their schools. The Christian Brothers continued to refuse to give up their emblems, and on the question of school books refused to give up their own books. The Christian Brothers' sole motion for compromise was an offer to submit a specially approved edition of their books for use by the protestant

[121] M.C.N.E.*I.*, 16 Jan. 1893; *Copy of correspondence* . . . pp 20–26.

children in their schools for the commissioners' approval. Further, Harrell pointed out that the proposed rule was objectionable on legal grounds, for the term 'locality', was undefined and open to legions of interpretations. He concluded by saying that there was not as yet sufficient unanimity among the commissioners to make it incumbent on the administration to take decisive action.[122]

Decisive action was one thing Morley was not inclined to take in this matter. Indeed, it appears that he really did not know what the powers of the Irish administration were regarding the national system, for he caused a telegram to be sent from the Irish office to the chief secretary's office asking that the attorney general be questioned regarding the legal powers of the lord lieutenant as to the fundamental rules of the national system being changed by the commissioners of national education.[123] Morley simply did nothing, and in the confusion concerning the administration of the Irish education act of 1892, the Christian Brothers' question temporarily disappeared.

In early 1895, however, Morley reopened the issue with a letter to the commissioners suggesting that they again consider the rules bearing upon aid to efficient schools not in connection with the national system. Morley was forced to make the request because the compulsory attendances clauses of the 1892 education act were not working; one of the reasons local authorities were refusing to enforce the act was that 'certain schools' were excluded from participation in the grants. He commended to the commissioners' attention the task of revising their rules so as to admit an extension of state aid to efficient schools not previously receiving aid.[124] By this he meant that

[122] [David]H[arrel] to John Morley, 31 Jan. 1893, S.P.O.I., Chief Secretary's Office, Registered Papers, 6999/1896.

[123] Dowdall to the attorney general, 2 Feb. 1893, S.P.O.I., Chief Secretary's Office, Registered Papers, 4381/1893 (copy).

[124] John Morley to Commissioners of National Education, 6 Feb. 1895, S.P.O.I., Chief Secretary's Office, Registered Papers, 2637/1895 (copy); also reproduced in M.C.N.E.I., 25 Feb. 1895, and in, *Copy of correspondence in the year 1895 between the Irish government and the commissioners of national education for Ireland, with extracts from minutes of the proceedings of the commissioners, in relation to certain proposed changes in the rules under which grants are made by parliament for elementary education in Ireland*, p. 4, H.C.1895 (324), lxxvii.

the commissioners should think of some politic way for the Christian Brothers to be given aid. The commissioners met on 25 February 1895, and after dispensing with two delaying motions, proceeded to the motion of Lord Chief Baron Palles. Under the terms of Palles' motion, the forty-fourth recommendation of the Powis commission was to be invoked and denominational schools recognized for purposes of aid, subject only to the religious restrictions of the conscience clause of the intermediate education act. This was almost precisely what the commissioners had recommended in 1892. Palles' motion was slightly amended and the amended version sent to Morley in the form of resolutions by the commissioners of national education.[125]

Characteristically, Morley refused to act upon the recommendation that the Powis recommendation should be the basis for a change in the commissioners' rules. Rather than dealing with the abstract principle, he wished to see the proposed rule changes explicitly framed before passing judgement. He therefore requested that a committee of commissioners draw up the new regulation,[126] and, in the middle of April 1895, the entire body of commissioners considered the committee's report. With minor changes, the report was approved by a twelve to four vote. The report suggested that the commissioners should recognize separate denominational schools and aid those schools, subject to a series of provisos. One of these was that adequate provision exist in the neighbourhood of the denominational schools for children of other denominations. It also recommended that all books to be used in denominational schools should be presented to the commissioners for their approval and that no books should be used without their sanction. The report suggested remarkably few limitations upon religious teaching in such schools. Inevitably, of course, the intermediate education act's conscience clause was the chief of these. In order to prevent proselytism, the manager of a denominational school in which the children were all catholic could not admit a protestant without giving the commissioners fourteen days notice of

[125] M.C.N.E.I., 25 Feb. 1895; *Copy of correspondence in the year 1895* . . . pp 3–11.
[126] John Morley to commissioners of national education, 2 Mar. 1895, reproduced in M.C.N.E.I., 17 Apr. 1895, and in *Copy of correspondence in the year 1895* . . . p. 13.

this intention in advance, nor could protestant managers of all-protestant schools admit a catholic without giving the same notice. Moreover, it was suggested that in protestant schools filled with children of several protestant denominations no religious instruction save Bible reading was to be given to any child unless his parents gave written permission for him to attend doctrinal instruction. Nowhere did the report suggest that there should be any limit upon the use of emblems, nor upon the performance of rites by any religious group.[127]

Realizing at last that his own immobility would not budge the commissioners even if it could block them, Morley responded with some ideas of his own. He was clearly unnerved by the commissioners' dealing with 'large issues' as they had done and he tried to focus their attention upon a narrower purpose: 'the object of the government is to devise some expedient for removing the obstacle to the full working of an act of parliament of the highest importance to the educational advancement of this country, which arises from the exclusion of schools, rather less in all than one hundred in number of both denominations. An expedient of this kind ought to be attainable without at the same time attempting to settle questions of such wide compass as are raised in the scheme now submitted for the approval of his excellency the lord lieutenant.'[128] He then proposed that the commissioners modify their rules so as to allow existing efficient schools in the areas covered by the 1892 act to receive a capitation grant on the basis of their average daily attendance. The conditions for this grant should be, he thought, that the school was a primary school, free for all children between three and fifteen, open for inspection and examination to test its efficiency, and its manager willing to accept a conscience clause. The grant to such a school, Morley felt, should be smaller than that to the national schools, in view of the fewer restrictions placed upon them.

The commissioners replied with a strongly worded resolution (passed only by a vote of eight to five), telling Morley that they could not undertake afresh the task of framing new rules for the

[127] M.C.N.E.I., 17 Apr. 1895; *Copy of correspondence in the year 1895* . . . pp 13–20.

[128] John Morley to commissioners of national education, 14 May 1895. reproduced in M.C.N.E.I., and in, *Copy of correspondence in the year 1895* . . , pp 25–6.

extension of state aid, that the principle espoused by Morley was unacceptable, and criticizing him for introducing his new principle at this late date after three sets of rules had been submitted to the government by the commissioners.[129] Morley responded with a defence of his capitation plan on the grounds that it was convenient and meant no alteration in the principles of the national system. On the other hand, the commissioners' suggested rules, especially that rule requiring the exclusion of the children of one denomination from schools of another, were clearly a departure from the national system's fundamental principles and thus unacceptable.[130] In this instance, Morley was being unfair, for the payment of money to denominational schools in the form of capitation grants was just as much a departure from the national system's fundamental principles as were the commissioners' suggestions. The real difference, it would seem, was that Morley's idea might have been politically feasible, but the commissioners' would almost inevitably have been blocked at Westminster. The commissioners sent Morley a twenty-six point resolution pointing out fallacies in Morley's reasoning and arguing for equality of payment to all schools receiving any government aid. They staunchly stood by the recommendation that schools having full denominational freedom should not be allowed to enroll children of other denominations. They refused to frame any more new rules.[131] Morley attempted to bring this crude minuet to a graceful close by sending the commissioners a letter stating that if the matter of compulsory exclusion could be settled, he saw no reason why the entire problem could not be solved. In his letter he enclosed an extensive list of the modifications he thought necessary in the commissioners' rules.[132]

Shortly after writing the letter, and before the commissioners

[129] M.C.N.E.I., 20 May 1895; *Copy of correspondence in the year 1895* . . . pp 26–8.

[130] John Morley to commissioners of national education, 8 June 1895, reproduced in M.C.N.E.I., 18 June 1895, and in *Copy of correspondence in the year 1895* . . . pp 31–2.

[131] M.C.N.E.I., 18 June 1895; *Copy of correspondence in the year 1895* . . . pp 32–6.

[132] John Morley to commissioners of national education, 24 June 1895, reproduced in M.C.N.E.I., 25 June, and in, *Copy of correspondence in the year 1895* . . . pp 37–44.

could act upon it, Morley left office and was replaced by the conservative G. W. Balfour. The commissioners provided Balfour with a lengthy summary of the course of events to date and submitted essentially the same proposals they had presented to Morley.[133] Balfour brought the train of correspondence to an abrupt end by refusing to sanction the changes proposed by the commissioners. He informed the commissioners that the question of finding a way to bring the excluded schools into connection with the national system had been raised not on account of any grievance by the Christian Brothers or the Church Education Society, but because of the difficulty of making the compulsory clause of the 1892 education act effective. Balfour saw no answer to this problem in the commissioners' new rules and even doubted if the rules would satisfy the societies whose scruples they were designed to satisfy.[134] Chilled by this letter, the commissioners let the matter drop.

The Powis report's recommendation upon denominational schools was the only one of its recommendations not to be effected by century's end, and the only important issue on which the Roman Catholic bishops were thwarted between 1870 and 1900. In this case the source of the bishops' frustration was the Irish administration, not the commissioners of national education; indeed, the irony of the proceedings on the subject was that the Irish government was placed in the position of defending the fundamental principles of the national system from change, while the commissioners acted as agents of the proponents of denominationalism.

While the Roman Catholic bishops were demanding and receiving concession after concession, the Church of Ireland clergy were quietly giving in and joining the national system. The anglican church in Ireland was disestablished by an act passed in 1869 that became effective in 1871. The church received some financial compensation under the act, but all politi-

[133] J. C. Taylor and M. S. Seymour to G. W. Balfour, 1 Aug. 1895, reproduced in, M.C.N.E.I., 1 Aug. 1895, and in, *Copy of further correspondence between the Irish government and the commissioners of national education in Ireland; with extracts from minutes of the proceedings of the commissioners, in relation to certain proposed changes in the rules under which grants are made by parliament for elementary education in Ireland*, pp 13–17, H.C. 1896 (89), lxvi.

[134] G. W. Balfour to commissioners of national education, 12 Feb. 1896, reproduced in, *Copy of further correspondence . . . p. 23.*

cal connection between the church and the state was severed and the Church of Ireland became a voluntary body. Inevitably, the church entered into a time of financial stringency and political unimportance. After 1870 there was no chance that the church could force the commissioners of national education to bend to its demands. During the last three decades of the century, it was clear that the Church Education Society could hope for a government grant only if anglican demands coincided with the catholic demands.

The Church Education Society shrivelled after 1870. By the century's end, the once proud system of anglican schools consisted of few schools and drew almost no income. The society's report for the year 1884 stated that 'although some feared that the society was dead, and others feared that it was dying, your committee was enabled to distribute in January last the sum of £367 10'.[135] At the society's annual meeting in April 1896, it was reported that there were 200 schools in connection with the society, having 5,000 children on the rolls and an average attendance of approximately 3,000.[136] A complementary development was the increasing adherence of anglicans to the national system. The following data indicates that by century's end the proportion of anglicans in the national schools population came close to equaling the proportion of anglicans in the overall population:[137]

Anglicans on national school rolls as % of total no. on rolls		Anglicans as % of total population	
1860	5·63	1861	11·96
1870	7·44	1871	12·34
1880	9·4	1881	12·36
1890	10·7	1891	12·75
1900	11·9	1901	13·03

Since it was inevitable that the majority of anglican clergymen

---

[135] *Forty-fifth annual report of the Church Education Society for Ireland, for the year 1884* (Dublin, 1885), p. 5.

[136] *Daily Express*, 17 Apr. 1896.

[137] Compiled from, *Census of Ireland, 1901*, pt II: *General report with illustrated maps, diagrams, tables and appendix*, p. 50 [Cd 1190], H.C., 1902, cxxix; *Twenty-seventh report of the commissioners of national education in Ireland, for the year 1860*, pp 5, 8 [2873], H.C. 1861, xx; *Thirty-seventh report . . . for the year 1870*, pp 9, 12, 13; *Forty-seventh report . . . for the year 1880*, pp 3, 4, 6, 7; *Fifty-seventh report . . . for the year 1890*, pp 6, 9; *Sixty-seventh report . . . for the year 1900*, p. 13.

would place their schools under the national system, a mechanism was established allowing the church some control over the religious education given in anglican national schools. After disestablishment a board of education was created by the general synod of the Church of Ireland, consisting of the two archbishops, ten bishops, thirty-six elected members, most of whom were laymen, eleven co-opted members, and a secretary. This body served as an executive committee to supervise religious instruction of teachers in training, to examine teachers already teaching in anglican schools, and to keep general superintendence over the religious education of anglican children. To this end an educational inspector was appointed for each diocese. The inspector reported to a diocesan board of education which was directly responsible for religious and primary education in each diocese. Vicars who had schools in connection with the national commissioners could 'join' the diocesan board for purposes of examinations in religious teaching, the diocesan inspector thus serving the same purpose for religious instruction that the national school inspector served for literary instruction.[138] Thus, by the end of the century, the anglican church in Ireland had adapted itself to the realities of its disestablished position, its clergy by and large had joined the national system, and the church had worked out means of accommodating the demands of the national commissioners while preserving its own religious interests.

6

For all its troubles, the system of national education closed the nineteenth century upon a hopeful note. This tone was sounded by the commission on manual and practical instruction in primary schools under the board of national education in Ireland, usually known as the 'Belmore commission'. Actually, as Lord Monteagle remarked, it might well have been called the 'Walsh commission' for Archbishop Walsh was largely responsible for its creation.[139] By the middle 1890s,

[138] Church of Ireland, *Board of Religious Education, report, 1878* (Dublin, 1878), pp 1–3; *Daily Express,* 30 Aug. 1873; H. Kingsmill Moore, *The education work of the Church of Ireland* (Dublin, 1885), pp 9–15.

[139] Patrick J. Walsh, *William J. Walsh, archbishop of Dublin* (Cork and Dublin, 1928), p. 508.

Walsh and two other leading commissioners, Lord Chief Baron Palles and Professor Fitzgerald, had become convinced that a radical change in the national school curriculum was necessary. They were concerned that the curriculum was too narrow and bookish, a tendency accentuated by the system of payment by results. In March 1896, Walsh introduced a resolution, which the commissioners passed unanimously, sending a deputation to wait on the lord lieutenant on the subject of manual and practical instruction.[140] The lord lieutenant responded by suggesting that the commissioners form themselves into a committee and investigate the problem themselves. This the commissioners were loath to do because they felt, probably correctly, that no one would pay any attention to recommendations if they were made solely upon the authority of the commissioners of national education in Ireland.[141] They later changed their minds and said they would do the report if the lord lieutenant would provide them with four assistant commissioners.[142]

The lord lieutenant's solution was to create a commission of fourteen members, ten of whom were commissioners of national education. Under the lord lieutenant's warrant of 25 January 1897 the following national commissioners were appointed to the manual and practical instruction commission: Archbishop Plunket, Archbishop Walsh, Chief Baron Palles, C. T. Redington, Judge Shaw, Rev. Henry Evans, Rev. Hamilton Wilson, Professor George Fitzgerald, Stanley Harrington, and William Molloy. In addition to these commissioners of national education, the lord lieutenant appointed the earl of Belmore as chairman, and T. B. Shaw, an inspector of science and art in England, J. Struthers, inspector of schools in Scotland, and Monsignor Molloy as members.[143] This arrangement

---

[140] *Vice-regal committee of inquiry into primary education (Ireland), 1913: Final report*, p. 5 [Cd 7235], H.C. 1914, xxviii.

[141] See, M.C.N.E.I., 18 Aug. 1896.

[142] Commissioners of national education to lord lieutenant, 3 Sept. 1896; 'Minutes of the proceedings of the commissioners of national education from 5 May 1896 to 13 April 1897,' insert between pp 167 and 168.

[143] *Commission on manual and practical instruction in primary schools under the board of national education in Ireland: Final report of the commissioners*, pp iv–v [C 8923], H.C. 1898: xliv, see also *Return giving the names, appointments, and attendances, 1890–1900, of the commissioners of national education in Ireland*, pp 1–2.

was a politically wise one, for it allowed the commissioners of national education to produce a report of their own design which would bear the prestige of having been produced by a commission of public appointment, chaired by a noble name.

The commission's approach was nothing if not meticulous. It held ninety-three meetings, took formal evidence from 186 persons, and visited 119 different schools. It began by holding meetings in Dublin, then proceeded to England, inspecting schools in London, Birmingham, Liverpool, and other cities. A quorum went to Sweden and Denmark. The report was submitted to the lord lieutenant on 25 June 1898.[144] The commission's recommendations were not dramatic but we should not suppose they were insignificant. It began at the beginning, recommending that the kindergarten system, with its attendant methods and principles, be extended as far as possible to all schools attended by very young children. It recommended that in the first three grades of ordinary national schools, educational handwork be introduced in the form of cardboard work, clay-modelling, and similar exercises. It felt that drawing as a subject should be compulsory in all national schools. The commission suggested that elementary science should form a part of the normal course in the national schools. Significantly, it rejected the idea that agriculture, in the sense of practical farming, was a subject properly belonging to the elementary school. In place of the theory of agriculture course given in most rural agricultural schools, the commission proposed that the elementary science course be so taught in rural areas as to include illustrations of the application of simple scientific principles to farming. It recommended that the Glasnevin and Munster model farms be transferred to an Irish agricultural department, whenever such a department was established. Cooking and needlework for girls were emphasized as useful, but compulsion was shunned. Singing, the commission stated, could very properly be brought within the curriculum of the Irish national school. The commission mentioned its most important point almost in passing: the above recommendation on manual and practical instruc-

[144] *Commission of manual and practical instruction in primary schools under the board of national education in Ireland: Final report of the commissioners*, pp iv, 59.

tion could be effected only if the system of payment by results
was not extended to these subjects.[145]

The effect of the commission's report was to bring about a
complete revision of the Irish national schools curriculum, and,
most noteworthy, a complete abandonment of the results system. In October, 1898, a committee of national education commissioners was appointed to consider the arrangements to be
made, and in April 1900 William Starkie introduced the 'revised programme' of national education. Under this programme
the system of results examinations was replaced by regular inspections of a more general sort. Since teachers were no longer
paid according to how well their students did on tests, the entire
method of paying teachers was restructured. The new programme
was distinguished by a flexibility made possible by the breaking
of the bonds of the results examinations, and by an emphasis
upon the subjects recommended by the Belmore commission, in
addition to the traditional ones of reading, arithmetic, and writing.[146] Like any new programme, the revised programme was
found in time to have its faults, but in 1900 it seemed to the
more optimistic observers of the national system that a new day
was dawning.

[145] Ibid., 3–4.
[146] *Vice-regal committee of inquiry into primary education (Ireland), 1913*, pp
5–6; *Department of education, report of the council of education* [Pr. 2583], pp
58–60.

IX

CONCLUSION

~~~~~~~~~~~~~~~~~~~~~~~~~~~~~~~~~~~~

I

UP TO THIS POINT our discussion of the Irish national system
of education has focused directly upon the creation, structure,
and evolution of the system. We have seen that the system was
shaped by the religious, social, and political realities of nineteenth-century Ireland. Given this fact, it would be easy to
ignore a reciprocal fact: that the national system of education
had important effects upon the Irish nation. The most important
of these was that it was the chief means by which the country
was transformed from one in which illiteracy predominated to
one in which most persons, even the poorest, could read and
write. Accurate census data upon literacy were first assembled
in 1841. The percentage of persons five years and above neither
able to read nor write at each decennial census is given below.[1]

	1841	*1851*	*1861*	*1871*	*1881*	*1891*	*1901*
Ireland	53	47	39	33	25	18	14
Leinster	44	39	31	27	20	15	11
Munster	61	55	46	39	28	20	14
Ulster	40	35	30	27	20	15	12
Connaught	72	66	57	49	38	27	21

The following table indicates that of the major denominations the greatest relative benefits accrued to the catholic population:[2]

[1] *Census of Ireland, 1901*, pt II: *General report with illustrative maps, diagrams
tables and appendix*, p. 527 [Cd 1190], H.C. 1902, cxxix.

[2] Compiled from *Census of Ireland, 1901*, as above, p. 59.

Conclusion

Proportion neither able to read nor write
(5 years and above)

Denominations	1861	1871	1881	1891	1901
Roman Catholic	45·8%	39·9%	31·0%	22·0%	16·4%
Anglican	16·0	14·2	10·9	8·6	7·3
Presbyterian	11·1	9·6	7·1	5·6	4·9
Methodist	9·0	6·7	5·5	4·4	4·1
All others	9·6	8·1	5·3	5·0	4·7

Throughout the century Ireland had the highest percentage of illiteracy of the three countries in the British Isles, but the differential diminished as the years passed. The table below is taken from the registrar-general's returns, and indicates the percentage of persons who signed the marriage register by mark:[3]

	England and Wales		Ireland		Scotland	
Year	Men	Women	Men	Women	Men	Women
1841	32·7%	48·9%	......	......	......	......
1851	30·7	45·2	......	......	......	......
1861	24·6	34·7	......	......	10·6%	21·3%
1871	19·4	26·8	37·5%	45·2%	10·0	19·6
1881	13·5	17·7	26·1	30·7	7·1	13·9
1891	6·4	7·3	19·4	19·4	3·4	5·3
1901	2·8	3·2	13·2	10·7	......	......

Admittedly, it would be possible to become coy intellectually and argue that these figures do not prove that the national system was responsible for sharply reducing illiteracy, but only that they indicate illiteracy was on the wane at the same time that the national schools were in full bloom. Although we may grant the statisticians' argument that correlation does not prove causation, the fact of the matter is that in nineteenth-century Ireland the only system of schools teaching a significant proportion of the population was the national system, and that credit must therefore be given to it for wiping out mass illiteracy.

This conclusion has especially sharp implications in regard to the catholic population. Those romantics who claim that the national system supplanted a vigorous, democratic, and efficient system of catholic hedge schools should be reminded that the data indicate that prior to mid-century the majority of the Irish populace was illiterate, that the catholic population had a higher

[3] Graham Balfour, *The educational systems of Great Britain and Ireland* (Oxford, second ed., 1903), p. 289.

proportion of illiteracy than did any other religious group, and that under the tutelage of the national system, the catholics showed the greatest relative increase in literacy of any religious group.

If it was through the national system that the Irish nation was given the blessing of literacy, it is important to note that the system taught the nation to read and write English, not Irish. The entire issue of the Irish language is wrapped in emotion and sentimentality, and thus is a difficult one with which to deal. To understand the effect of the national system upon the national language, three questions must be asked. First, to what extent did the Irish language decline in the nineteenth century? Second, to what extent must that decline be ascribed to the national system of education? Third, if the national system was a mechanism for the extermination of Irish, to what degree was this a conscious policy of the Irish administration and of the commissioners of national education, and to what degree was it a result of a desire upon the part of the Irish peasant to replace Irish with the more useful and more prestigious English tongue?

Turning to the first question, we find that statistics on the precise extent to which Irish was used are unavailable prior to the year 1851. From 1851 onwards accurate statistics are available and they suggest that Irish had ceased to be the national language long before mid-century.[4]

	Leinster	Munster	Ulster	Connaught	Ireland
Year 1851					
Total population	1,672,738	1,857,736	2,011,880	1,010,031	6,552,385
No. who spoke Irish only	200	146,336	35,783	137,283	319,602
% of total pop. who spoke only Irish	·01%	7·9%	1·8%	13·6%	4·9%
No. who spoke Irish and English	58,976	669,449	100,693	375,566	1,204,684
Total who could speak Irish	59,176	815,785	136,476	512,849	1,524,286
% of pop. who could speak Irish	3·5%	43·9%	6·8%	50·8%	23·3%

[4] Derived from, *Census of Ireland for the year 1851*, pt vi: *General report, etc.*, p. xlvii [2134], H.C. 1856, xxxi; *Census of Ireland, 1871* pt iii: *General report, etc.*, p. 189 [C 1377], H.C. 1876, lxxxi; *Census of Ireland, 1901*, pt ii: *General report, etc.*, pp 170, 575.

	Leinster	Munster	Ulster	Connaught	Ireland
Year 1861					
Total population	1,457,635	1,513,558	1,914,236	913,135	5,798,564
No. who spoke Irish only	238	62,039	23,180	77,818	163,275
% of total pop. who spoke only Irish	·02%	4·1%	1·2%	8·5%	2·1%
No. who spoke Irish and English	35,466	483,492	91,639	331,664	942,261
Total who could speak Irish	35,704	545,531	114,819	409,482	1,105,536
% of pop. who could speak Irish	2·5%	36·3%	6·0%	44·9%	19·1%
Year 1871					
Total population	1,339,451	1,393,485	1,833,228	846,213	5,412,377
No. who spoke Irish only	374	33,967	19,067	50,154	103,562
% of total pop. who spoke only Irish	·02%	2·4%	1·0%	5·9%	1·9%
No. who spoke Irish and English	15,873	352,527	65,856	280,057	714,313
Total who could speak Irish	16,247	386,494	84,923	330,211	817,875
% of pop. who could speak Irish	1·2%	27·7%	4·6%	39·0%	15·1%
Year 1881					
Total population	1,278,989	1,331,115	1,743,075	821,657	5,174,836
No. who spoke Irish only	50	18,422	12,360	33,335	64,167
% of total pop. who spoke only Irish	·004%	1·4%	·7%	4·1%	1·3%
No. who spoke Irish and English	27,402	427,344	98,163	332,856	885,765
Total who could speak Irish	27,452	445,766	110,523	336,191	949,932
% of pop. who could speak Irish	2·1%	33·5%	6·3%	44·6%	18·2%
Year 1891					
Total population	1,187,760	1,172,402	1,619,814	724,774	4,704,750
No. who spoke Irish only	8	9,060	7,053	22,071	38,192
% of total pop. who spoke only Irish	·0007%	·8%	·4%	3·0%	·8%
No. who spoke Irish and English	13,669	298,573	77,099	252,712	642,053

N*

	Leinster	Munster	Ulster	Connaught	Ireland
Total who could speak Irish	13,677	307,633	84,152	274,783	680,245
% of pop. who could speak Irish	1·2%	26·2%	5·2%	37·8%	14·5%
Year 1901					
Total population	1,152,829	1,076,188	1,582,826	646,932	4,458,775
No. who spoke Irish only	7	4,387	4,456	12,103	20,953
% of total pop. who spoke only Irish	·0006%	·4%	·3%	1·9%	·5%
No. who spoke Irish and English	26,429	271,881	88,402	233,477	620,189
Total who could speak Irish	26,436	276,268	92,858	245,580	641,142
% of pop. who could speak Irish	2·3%	25·7%	5·9%	38·0%	14·4%

If we can project the trend indicated in these figures back into the period before 1851, it would appear altogether probable that the majority of the population was not able to speak Irish in 1841, and it even appears questionable if Irish was understood by most Irishmen as early as 1831. Thus, it is clear that the national system of education cannot be blamed for the abandonment of Irish by the overwhelming majority of Irishmen, for most Irishmen had probably ceased to understand the language even before the system was founded. Although speculation about the real cause for the decline of Irish is out of place in a discussion focusing on the national system of education, it might be suggested that the obvious economic advantages of speaking English and the insistence of the Roman Catholic clergy upon the use of English were largely responsible for the decline of the language.

In refusing to lay primary responsibility for the decline of the Irish language to the charge of the commissioners of national education, we should not leap to the conclusion that the national system had nothing to do with English replacing Irish as the vernacular tongue. The national system served as a vehicle which furthered a process begun before its foundation. After 1831 the national schools provided a convenient place for the peasant's children to acquire the much valued English language. Throughout most of the nineteenth century the rules of the national system concerning the use of Irish were noteworthy for their non-existence. The commissioners were not hostile to the Irish language so much as unaware of it. There was no rule against its use, but hardly anyone seems to have even considered that it might be used. Between 1831 and 1870 the minutes of the commissioners of national education contain only two mentions of the use of the Irish language. One of these occurred in the minutes for 1834 when application was made for a teacher of Irish to be appointed in a national school. The commissioners refused on the grounds that the request did not come within the framework of their plan of education. The second mention occurred in the minutes for 1844, when a clerical manager asked permission to teach Irish during the hours of secular instruction and to use the spelling and reading books of the London Irish Society. The commissioners declined the request.[5] Before the 1870s, the closest the Irish language came to official consideration by the commissioners was in 1855, 1857, and 1858, when Patrick Keenan, then a head inspector, presented in his inspectorial reports a strong case for the use of Irish in the schools in Irish-speaking areas.[6] Nothing was done about his proposals, and Keenan himself seems to have lost enthusiasm for the use of Irish, for, in 1881, when serving as resident commissioner, he argued that a knowledge of Irish was not necessary for teachers serving in Irish-speaking localities.[7]

In 1879, the commissioners began to pay results-fees for Irish when taught as an extra subject for advanced pupils, that is, when taught outside of school hours. John Morley replied to a question in the house on the arrangements by explaining: 'In order to encourage teachers to instruct their pupils in Irish the result-fee allowed by the commissioners for a pass therein as an extra branch to pupils of the fifth class and above is ten shillings, or double the fee allowed for French.'[8] The effectiveness

---

[5] M.C.N.E.I., 9 Jan. 1834, 27 June 1844; T. Ó'Raifeartaigh, 'The state's administration of education', *Administration*, ii (Winter, 1954–55), p. 74.

[6] *Appendix to the twenty-second report of the commissioners of national education in Ireland, for the year 1855*, pp 72–3 [2142–11], H.C. 1856, xxvii, pt. ii; *Twenty-fourth report . . . for the year 1857*, p. 135 [2456–1], H.C. 1859, vii; *Twenty-fifth report . . . for the year 1858*, p. 180 [2593], H.C. 1860, xxv.

[7] *Forty-seventh report . . . for the year 1880*, p. 12 [C 2925], H.C. 1881, xxxiv.

[8] *Hansard 4*, xxviii, 452, 18 Aug. 1894.

of the scheme was doubtlessly reduced by the requirement that before any teacher could earn results-fees for teaching Irish, he had to pass an examination in the subject, even if he were a native speaker.[9] Irish as an extra subject was taught in less than one hundred national schools, a number hardly amounting to a language revival.[10]

The commissioners did add a section to their rules in 1883 stating:

If there are Irish-speaking pupils in a school, the teacher, if acquainted with the Irish language should, whenever practicable, employ the vernacular as an aid to the elucidation and acquisition of the English language. Inspectors are at liberty to employ the vernacular in the conduct of their examinations if they think it desirable to do so.[11]

The rule does not seem to have been universally understood, however, for one Gaelic League writer claimed that up to the turn of the century most people including national school teachers, managers, and even inspectors, believed that the use of Irish within school hours was prohibited.[12] In 1900, the 'revised programme' appeared and it explicitly, if mildly, encouraged the use of the language. That programme allowed Irish to be taught as an optional branch during ordinary school hours, provided this did not interfere with other instruction. Moreover, although the abolition of payment by results meant the abolition of results-fees for extra subjects, the commissioners convinced the treasury that the ten-shilling grant for Irish as an extra subject taught outside of school hours should be continued.[13]

Clearly the national system served as a mechanism by which the Irish peasant replaced his Irish with English. It has been

[9] *Hansard 3*, cclv, 1096, 24 Aug. 1880.

[10] Irish Free State, *Report of the department of education, the school year 1924–25 and the financial and administrative years 1924–25–26* (Dublin, 1926), p. 28.

[11] *The case for bilingual education in the Irish-speaking districts* (Dublin, undated, *c.* 1899), p. 2.

[12] M. P. O'Hickey, *The future of Irish in the national schools* (Dublin, 1900), p. 6.

[13] Irish Free State, *Report of the department of education, the school year 1924–25, and the financial and administrative years 1924–25–26*, p. 29; *Seventy-second report of the commissioners of national education in Ireland, for the year 1905–06*, p. 22 [Cd 3699], H.C. 1907, xxii.

established, however, that the system was only a part of the process and that its overseers were not the initiators of the process. Granted, then, that the system contributed in some degree to the decline of the Irish language, we must ask whether the commissioners of national education were part of a conspiracy against the Irish language or were merely acting upon generally held opinions. The fact that the Irish language was raised before the commissioners only twice before the 1870s, and then only as a matter affecting specific national schools, not as a subject to be discussed as a general principle, destroys any suggestion that the commissioners consciously espoused a policy of destroying the Irish language against the wishes of the Irish people. The commissioners for their first four decades hardly gave the language a thought, and in this indifference they were abetted by the parents of national school children, the national school teachers, and the national school managers. Even before the national system was founded, it had been clearly established that if the Irish peasantry were seriously aggrieved about something they could make a loud and often very effective noise about it. Yet, there are no instances of peasants petitioning the commissioners or parliament or holding meetings in favour of adding Irish to the national school curriculum. With the exception of the two cases mentioned earlier, until the 1870s there were no petitions on the part of teachers or managers concerning the use of Irish in the schools. Yet, these same teachers and managers felt perfectly free to submit petitions and requests to the commissioners on any subject connected with the national schools. The only reasonable conclusion is that those in charge of the schools were satisfied with the commissioners' non-policy regarding the Irish language. Only after 1870 did petitions and agitation about the Irish language begin, and then the petitioners were not peasants nor school teachers nor managers, but groups of middle-class intellectuals such as the Society for the Preservation of the Irish Language, the Gaelic Union, and the Gaelic League. Thus, if the national system of education contributed in some degree to the decline of the Irish language, it did so with the tacit approval of the great majority of Irishmen.

In the earlier chapter on the curriculum of the national schools, it was established that the national system's curriculum contained almost no material on Ireland as a nation and as a culture. The country was recognized as a geographical unit and as little else, a situation that led the *Nation* to state tartly in December 1867, that 'it has been unofficially announced that the reading books of the Irish national schools are being revised, and that one object of the revision is to introduce into them some acknowledgement of the existence of such a country as Ireland . . .'.[14] Not only were the school books culturally antiseptic concerning Ireland, but school teachers were enjoined from making nationalistic departures from the texts. Loyalty to the British crown was of course taught in the schools. Granted that the national schools were non-nationalistic ('anti-nationalistic' being too strong a word), it is impossible to determine what effect this had upon the Irish people. The British authorities would have liked to have thought that the schools were reinforcing their control over the country, but one wonders how realistic this hope was. Despite their being unfavourable to the nationalist viewpoint, the national schools aided the job of nationalist propagandist and agitator by providing a populace that could read and hence could be reached by newspaper and by pamphlet; when the Irish revolution eventually took place it was not a revolution conducted by or for illiterate men.

The national system had a number of effects upon the Irish religious situation. One of these was that it saved the various denominations a great deal of money. When the system was twisted from its original non-sectarian moorings to a tacitly denominational position, the need for individual denominations to conduct schools financed from their own treasuries disappeared. Not all denominations appreciated this at once: the anglicans did not take full advantage of the system until after 1870. Nor did all denominations benefit equally. The Roman Catholic church was saved the largest amount of money simply because it had the largest number of members of school age. The importance of the savings for the catholic church can be easily recognized if one compares the present-day Roman Catholic educational system in the United States with that in Ireland. In America the church is forced to spend vast amounts of money in maintaining a parochial school system, almost every cent of the expenditure coming from the church's own coffers. In Ireland,

[14] *Nation*, 27 Dec. 1867.

in contrast, the great bulk of educational expenditure is paid by the central government, and has been paid ever since the middle of the nineteenth century.

The second important effect upon the Irish religious situation was that, in addition to saving the churches considerable money, the national system delivered a great deal of patronage into their hands. Not only were the schools made acceptable to the clergy but on the local level they were controlled by the clerics. Once again the logic of numbers meant that the Roman Catholic church benefited most by this arrangement. Each year several hundred thousand pounds, and near the end of the century more than a million pounds, was voted by parliament for Irish education. Some of this money went for the upkeep of the central administration, but most of it was disbursed to the local level, where it was parcelled out by the clerical authorities. Besides providing financial patronage for clerical use, the national system also placed control of a considerable amount of local jobbery in denominational hands: each school manager, almost inevitably a clergyman, was given control over valuable local preferments, such as principal and assistant teacherships and monitorships in national schools.

The third major effect the national schools had upon the Irish religious structure was to reinforce the walls between the denominations. The intention of the founders of the system had been that children of varying faiths would study together during the hours of literary instruction, and that this would provide the basis for toleration and understanding between religious groups. In reality, the national system became a denominational system and fraternization between children of different faiths was slight. It is hard to see how the religious apartheid policy that prevailed under the national system could have done anything but strengthen the barriers that separated catholic and protestant in nineteenth-century Ireland.

2

Returning to the central issue of the evolution and structure of the national system, three points bear reiteration. The first of these is that the creation of the system came at a surprisingly early date: it was a product of a constellation of characteristics peculiar to nineteenth-century Ireland. Herein lies one of the chief points on which a history of the Irish national system is significant to the educational historian. Most historians of education in the western world have concluded that state systems of popular education can appear and operate successfully only in economically advanced countries. Discussions of educational development often point out that educational institutions, in common with most other social institutions, have grown out of the family. These discussions suggest that education in most pre-industrial societies took place within a world which was an extension of the home. In agrarian societies the parish blended in perceptibly with the household. Children were socialized not through formal schooling, but through participation in the economic and social activities of the family. Only when the closely knit rural order was disturbed, most notably by a shift of the economy from an agrarian to an industrial base, did the family prove unable to fully educate the child.

The economic changes which affected Great Britain and western Europe in the nineteenth and twentieth centuries produced a series of major social changes, many of which had direct educational implications. The development of an industrial economy implied the concentration of materials and labourers in one place, with the result that most workers came to live in cities. In most instances, the extended family typical of rural cultures was replaced by the nuclear family. The community ceased to be an organization of intermarried families, and became an aggregate of independent and unrelated units. In such a situation the educational function of the family was sharply reduced, for in an urban society the child can only be introduced into the constricted confines of the family circle, not into a brotherhood of related families like that which characterized the rural parish. Further, the occupational structure of most industrial communities has demanded the employment of at least one parent in a factory or workshop. Hence, the informal learning which took place with the child at his father's side in agricultural and domestic industry has been lost. Moreover, the knowledge demanded in industrialized societies has become too complicated to be transmitted within the average family. Clearly, the pressure of events has made necessary the introduction of formal schooling.

Conclusion

Although it is dangerous to become too schematic, it appears that a society is most apt to rely first upon formal schools which are supported by voluntary philanthropy, and only at a later stage of development is it apt to aid educational enterprise with government funds. Only at a very high stage of development is the state likely to both create and maintain at its own expense a system of education for the mass of its citizenry. Hence, the development of state systems of education in England and in Scotland which was outlined in chapter I serves not only as a framework within which to view the history of the Irish national system of education, but as a template which applies to the educational history of much of the western world.

Yet, when we look at Ireland, a country possessing a state-created and supported system of education as early as 1831, we are viewing a country which was painfully pre-industrial. The typical Irishman of the time did not live in a town. Most likely he lived in a small village where his ancestors had lived for generations, and in which he was related by blood or marriage to the majority of his neighbours. The cultural and family life of this community was intact and there was no sign of any breakdown in the structure of the Irish family. The peasant's children worked at his side in the field or home and learned crafts from their parents just as the parents had learned them from their own parents. In other words, Ireland was a poor, stable nation whose social and economic structure was much closer to that of the middle ages than to that of the industrial revolution. It is an almost perfect example of the kind of society which one would expect to be adequately served by informal means of education and expect to have neither the need nor the ability to evolve a network of formal education institutions.

The value of a study of the creation of the national system of education in Ireland, then, is that its creation and its subsequent success provide a shattering exception to the generalization that advanced educational systems can develop only in economically and socially advanced societies. This does not mean that the generalization is useless, but that it tells only part of the story. The Irish case makes it clear that the main lines of educational history can be determined not only by economic and social development, but by cultural, political, and religious influences as well. Specifically, we have seen that the relationship of Ireland to England was one which allowed the English rulers of Ireland to approach Irish social problems in a relatively freewheeling manner. Because Irish parliaments had been regularly legislating in educational matters since the sixteenth century, this meant that it was easy for radical educational legislation to be proposed and passed. Unlike the English situation, a consensus of official opinion on the topic of Irish education developed early in the nineteenth century. The opinions of the Roman Catholic hierarchy were woven into that consensus. The Irish peasantry was enthusiastic for any kind of schooling. Strikingly, this set of circumstances produced the same sort of state controlled network of popular schools that usually emerges as the result of a society becoming urbanized and industrialized. In some ways the creation and success of the Irish national system of education is a comforting phenomenon, for it may be interpreted, at least in part, as a victory of the spirit over the material, an occurrence of considerable rarity.

The relationship of Ireland and England in the creation of the national system is illuminating if ironic. It is highly questionable if the system would have been founded without intervention by the English government in Irish affairs. Paradoxically, if Ireland could not have created a system of education by itself, England in the 1830s could not create one for itself, torn as it was by religious problems. Hence, the rise of the national system stands as another instance of the predictive value of Irish history for the English historian: in this, as in so many other instances, the lines of future English development were first sketched in Ireland.

We should be very careful, however, to avoid uncritically transferring the lessons of the Irish national system into the twentieth century. It is tempting to conclude that if a people are willing to sacrifice to support education institutions, and that if they possess leaders willing to press for intelligent and acceptable forms of state action in the educational field, a viable system of national education can be created, even if the nation is economically backward. Granted, that it would be gratifying to find some underdeveloped African or Asian country establishing a state system of popular education on the scale of the Irish national system, our analysis of the national system indicates that a vital component in the creation of the national system was the effectively colonial relationship of Ireland and England. In achieving independence modern under-developed countries have cut themselves off from benevolent intervention in their affairs by a superior power and are thus left with the difficult task of lifting themselves by their own bootstraps.

The second important point to be made about the national system in the last century is that its development was a continual process of adaptation to the religious and political realities of nineteenth-century Ireland. This is not to say that those in charge of the system consciously and conscientiously tried to bring it into line with the wishes of the dominant groups, for they often opposed those wishes. It is to say that the voices of power within the community eventually prevailed. Thus, the system was created because of the generalized attitude of the peasantry in favour of education, and because of the specific demands of the catholic hierarchy for a religiously neutral system of state schools. At the time of its creation, the system assumed a stance of religious neutrality, this stance being indicative of a rough equality of power between the protestant groups and their political allies, and the Roman Catholic church and its associates. As the century progressed the system slowly changed into a system of denominational schools. This transformation was partially the product of demographic factors, but also of the failure of the commissioners to resist the pressures of the religious groups for religiously separate schooling. In 1840, the presbyterians were able to force the government to tacitly sanction denominationalism, but from 1850 onwards, it was the Roman Catholic hierarchy which pressed for separate schools. As the hierarchy grew stronger, and as the government's position throughout Ireland grew less secure, the commissioners of national education granted concession after concession to the catholic bishops until, at century's end, the only major demand of the bishops that had gone unmet was the cry for aid to the Christian Brothers' schools. Thus, the state system of non-denominational education that was founded in 1831 had become, by 1900, a state system of denominational education. At our present point in history it is still too early to judge whether this chain of events constitutes a morality play or an Irish tragedy.

A third point of general interest about the Irish national system is that the system serves as a case study in the British civil administration of Ireland. The national system was originally controlled root and branch by a group of unpaid commissioners who were given virtually a free hand by Dublin Castle. During the century, however, the independence of these commissioners was gradually nibbled away. One reason was the increasing size and complexity of the national system which meant that the commissioners had to take their civil servants' word for things, rather than supervise them themselves. Another reason for this was that from the 1850s to the 1890s the higher dignitaries of the Roman Catholic church refused to serve as commissioners. More important, the Roman Catholic hierarchy became increasingly aggressive after 1850. Since the Castle eventually agreed to give one-half the seats among the commissioners to Roman Catholics (and thus to give the Roman Catholics an effective majority), it was highly unlikely that the commissioners would stand firm against the prelates, especially since the day was passed when a catholic layman could stand out against the church without paying the price for his insubordination. While the hierarchy cut away at the commissioners from one side, the treasury slashed at the other. This process is especially interesting, for it suggests that in the latter portion of the nineteenth century the English government was seeking closer control over certain aspects of Irish affairs, but, for reasons that are worthy of conjecture, it chose to gain that control through quiet means. Rather than do something obvious such as replace the commissioners with a board of paid civil servants, control over the national system was asserted by having the treasury quietly press its thumb across the system's financial windpipe. Thus, at century's end national education was ostensibly under the control of the commissioners of national education, but actually dominated by the proclamations of the Roman Catholic hierarchy, and by the English treasury.

The Irish national system of education that evolved in the nineteenth century has been preserved, as if in amber, in the Irish Republic's schools of the twentieth century. The system remained unchanged until independence. Thereafter, the connection between the systems of primary and of secondary education was clearly articulated so that a child could go from one to the other without inconvenience, but there reform stopped. The schools now inculcate Irish patriotism instead of British history, and drum the Irish language into the heads of Irish children. But structurally little has changed. To this day Irish primary schools remain small, clerically-managed institutions in which Roman Catholic rarely meets protestant. Primary and secondary education remain distinct and secondary education is not compulsory. Advanced as the Irish national system may have been for the first half of the nineteenth century, it is a brittle fossil in the second half of the twentieth.

APPENDIX

The two versions of Lord Stanley's letter to the duke of Leinster are reproduced below. 'Version A' was published in the *Dublin Gazette*, in Parliamentary Papers for 1831–2, and in the report of the 1837 select committee on the progress and operation of the Irish national system of education. It was copied into the very first volume of the minutes of the commissioners of national education. The Powis commissioners claimed to have found the original of this version in the Irish Office. 'Version B' was published in the annual reports of the commissioners of national education until 1841. The two versions reproduced below are taken from the Powis report of 1870, with discrepancies underlined. The marginal notes are those of the Powis report.[1]

'Version A'	*'Version B'*
Irish Office, London	Irish Office, London
October 1831	October 1831

MY LORD—His majesty's government having come to the determination of empowering the lord lieutenant to constitute a board for the superintendence of a system of national education in Ireland, and parliament having so far sanctioned the arrangement as to appropriate a sum of money in the present year as an experiment of the probable success of the proposed system, I

[Identical]

---

[1] *Royal commission of inquiry into primary education (Ireland)*, vol. I, pt 1: *Report of the Commissioners*, pp 22–6, [C 6] H.C. 1870, xxviii, pt i.

am directed by his excellency to acquaint your grace that it is his intention, with your consent, to constitute you the president of the new board: and I have it further in command to lay before your grace the motives of the government in constituting this board, the powers which it is intended to confer upon it, and the objects which it is expected that it will bear in view, and carry into effect.

The commissioners in 1812 recommended the appointment of a board of this description to superintend a system of education from which should be banished even the suspicion of proselytism, and which, admitting children of all religious persuasions, should not interfere with the peculiar tenets of any. The government of the day imagined that they had found a superintending body, acting upon a system such as was recommended, and entrusted the distribution of the national grants to the care of the Kildare Street Society. His majesty's present government are of opinion that no private society, deriving a part, however small, of their annual income from private sources, and only made the channel of the munificence of the legislature, without being subject to any direct responsibility, could adequately and satisfactorily accomplish the end proposed; and while they do full justice to the liberal views with which that society was

The commissioners in 1812 recommended the appointment of a board of this description, to superintend a system of education, from which should be banished even the suspicion of proselytism, and which, admitting children of all religious persuasions, should not interfere with the peculiar tenets of any. The government of the day imagined that they had found a superintending body, acting upon a system such as was recommended, and entrusted the distribution of the national grants to the care of the Kildare Street Society. His majesty's present government are of opinion that no private society, deriving a part, however small, of their annual income from private sources, and only made a channel of the munificence of the legislature, without being subject to any direct responsibility, could adequately and satisfactorily accomplish the end proposed; and while they do full justice to the liberal views with which that society was originally instituted,

Clause inserted in B	originally instituted, they cannot but be sensible that one of its leading principles was calculated to defeat its avowed objects, as experience has subsequently proved that it has. The determination to enforce in all their schools the reading of the holy scriptures without note or comment was undoubtedly taken with the purest motives; with the wish at once to connect religious with moral and literary education, and, at the same time, not to run the risk of wounding the peculiar feelings of any sect by catechetical instruction or comments which might tend to subjects of polemical controversy. But it seems to have been overlooked that the principles of the Roman Catholic church (to which, in any system intended for general diffusion throughout Ireland, the bulk of the pupils must necessarily belong) were totally at variance with this principle; and that the *indiscriminate* reading of the holy scriptures without note or comment by children, must be peculiarly obnoxious to a church which denies, even to adults, the right of unaided private interpretation of the sacred volume *with respect to* articles of religious belief.	*as well as to the fairness with which they have, in most instances, endeavoured to carry their views into effect,* they cannot but be sensible that one of the leading principles of that society was calculated to defeat its avowed objects, as experience has subsequently proved that it has. The determination to enforce in all their schools the reading of the holy scriptures without note or comment, was undoubtedly taken with the purest motives; with the wish at once to connect religious with moral and literary education, and, at the same time, not to run the risk of wounding the peculiar feelings of any sect, by catechetical instruction, or comments which might tend to subjects of polemical controversy. But it seems to have been overlooked that the principles of the Roman Catholic church (to which, in any system intended for general diffusion throughout Ireland, the bulk of the pupils must necessarily belong) were totally at variance with this principle; and that the reading of the holy scriptures without note or comment, by children, must be peculiarly obnoxious to a church which denies, even to adults, the right of unaided private interpretation of the sacred volume *in* articles of religious belief.

Indiscriminate omitted in B (margin note) — Verbal variations (margin note)

Shortly after its institution, although the Society prospered and extended its operations under the fostering care of the	*[Identical]*

legislature, this vital defect began to be noticed, and the Roman Catholic clergy began to exert themselves with energy and success against a system to which they were on principle opposed, and which they feared might lead in its results to proselytism, even although no such object were contemplated by its promoters. When this opposition arose, founded on such grounds, it soon became manifest that the system could not become one of national education.

The commissioners of education in 1824-5, sensible of the defects of the system and of the ground as well as the strength of the objection taken, recommended the appointment of two teachers in every school, one protestant and the other Roman Catholic, to superintend separately the religious education of the children; and they hoped to have been able to agree upon a selection from the scriptures which might have been generally acquiesced in by both persuasions. But it was soon found that these schemes were impracticable; and in 1828 a committee of the house of commons, to which were referred the various reports of the commissioners of education, recommended a system to be adopted which should afford, if possible, a combined literary and a separate religious education, and should be capable of being so far adapted to the views of the religious persuasions *which prevail in* Ireland,

The commissioners of education in 1824-5, sensible of the defects of the system, and of the ground, as well as the strength of the objection taken, recommended the appointment of two teachers in every school, one protestant and the other Roman Catholic, to superintend separately the religious education of the children; and they hoped to have been able to agree upon a selection from the scriptures which might have been generally acquiesced in by both persuasions. But it was soon found that these schemes were impracticable; and in 1828 a committee of the house of commons, to which were referred the various reports of the commissioners of education, recommended a system to be adopted which should afford, if possible, a combined literary, and a separate religious education, and should be capable of being so far adapted to the views of the religious persuasions which *divide* Ireland, as to render it, in truth, a system of National education for the *poorer* classes of the community.

For the success of the undertaking much must depend upon the character of the individuals who compose the board; and upon the security thereby afforded to the country, that while the interests of religion are not overlooked, the most scrupulous care should be taken not to interfere with the peculiar tenets of any description of Christian pupils.

To attain the first object, it appears essential that the board should be composed of men of high personal character, *including individuals* of exalted station in the church; to attain the latter, that it should consist of persons professing different religious opinions.

It is the intention of the government that the board should exercise a complete control over the various schools which may be erected under its auspices, or which, having been already established, may hereafter place themselves under its management and submit to its regulations. Subject to these, applications for aid will be admissible from Christians of all denominations; but as one of the main objects must be to unite in one system children of different creeds, and as much must depend upon the co-operation of the resident clergy, the board will probably look with peculiar

to render it, in truth, a system of National education for the *lower* classes of the community.

[*Identical*]

To attain the first object, it appears essential that *a portion* of the board should be composed of men of high personal character, *and* of exalted station in the church; for the latter, that it should consist *in part* of persons professing different religious opinions.

[*Identical*]

favour upon applications proceeding either from —

1st the protestant and Roman
   Catholic clergy of the parish;
   or
2nd one of the clergymen, and
   a certain number of parishioners professing the opposite
   creed; or
3rd parishioners of both denominations.

Where the application pro-
ceeds exclusively from protestants or exclusively from Roman
Catholics, it will be proper for
the board to make inquiry as to
the circumstances which lead to
the absence of any names of the
persuasion which does not appear.

[*Identical*]

The board will note all applications for aid, whether granted
or refused, with the grounds of
the decision, and annually submit to parliament a report of
their proceedings.

[*Identical*]

They will invariably require,
as a condition not to be departed
from, that local funds shall be
aised, upon which any aid from
the public will be dependent.

[*Identical*]

They will refuse all applications in which the following
objects are not locally provided
for —

They will refuse all applications in which the following
objects are not locally provided
for —

1st, a fund sufficient for the
   annual repairs of the school-
   house and furniture;
2nd, a permanent salary for the
   master not less than ......
   pounds;
3rd, a sum sufficient to purchase

1st, a fund sufficient for the
   annual repairs of the school-
   house and furniture;
2nd, a permanent salary for the
   master, not less than ......
   pounds;
3rd, a sum sufficient to purchase

books and school requisites at half price;

4th, where aid is *sought* from the commissioners for building a school-house it is required that at least one-third of the estimated expense be subscribed, a site for building, to be approved of by the commissioners, be granted *for the purpose*, and that the school-house, when finished, be vested in *trustees, to be also approved of by them.*

They will require that the schools be kept open for a certain number of hours, on four or five days of the week, at the discretion of the commissioners, for moral and literary education only; and that the remaining one or two days in the week be set apart for giving, separately, such religious education to the children as may be approved by the clergy of their respective persuasions.

They will also permit and encourage the clergy to give religious instruction to the children of their respective persuasions, either before or after the ordinary school hours, on the other days of the week.

They will exercise the most entire control over all books to be used in the schools, whether in the combined *moral and* literary or separate religious instruction; none to be employed in the first except under the sanction of the board, nor in the latter but with the approbation

---

books and school requisites at half price, *and books of separate religious instruction at prime cost*;

4th, where aid is *required* from the commissioners for building a school-house, it is required that at least one-third of the estimated expense be subscribed, a site for building, to be approved of by the commissioners, be granted *to them*, and the school-house, when finished, to be vested in *them.*

[*Identical*]

[*Identical*]

They will exercise the most entire control over all books to be used in the schools, whether in the combined literary or separate religious instruction; none to be employed in the first except under the sanction of the board, nor in the latter but with the approbation of *the* members of *those* members of the board who are of the same religious persuasion with those for *whose use* they are intended. *Although it is not designed to exclude from the list of books for the combined instruction such portions of sacred history or of religious and moral teaching as may be approved of by the board, it is to be understood that this is by no means intended to convey a perfect and sufficient religious education, or to supersede the necessity of separate religious instruction on the day set apart for that purpose.*

They will require that a register shall be kept in the schools, in which shall be entered the attendance or non-attendance of each child on divine worship on Sundays.

They will at various times, either by themselves or by their inspectors, visit and examine into the state of each school, and report their observations to the board.

They will allow to the individuals or bodies applying for aid the appointment of their own teacher, subject to the following restrictions and regulations:

ıst He (or she) shall be liable to be fined, suspended, or removed altogether by the authority of the commissioners, who shall, however, record their reasons.

2nd He shall have received previous instruction in a model school in Dublin *to be sanctioned by the board.*

---

of the board of the persuasion of those *for whom* they are intended.

[*Identical*]

[*Identical*]

They will allow to the individuals or bodies applying for aid, the appointment of their own teacher, subject to the following restrictions and regulations:

ıst He (or she) shall be liable to be fined, suspended, or removed altogether, by the authority of the commissioners, who shall, however, record their reasons.

2nd He shall have received previous instruction in a model school, *to be established in Dublin.*

Verbal

Important proviso omitted in B

Change as to training school

o   399

N.B. It is not intended that this regulation should apply to prevent the admission of masters or mistresses of schools already established, who may be approved of by the commissioners.

3rd He shall have received testimonials of good conduct and of general fitness for the situation from the board.

The board will be entrusted with the absolute control over the funds which may be annually voted by parliament, which they shall apply to the following purposes:

1st, granting aid for the erection of schools, subject to the conditions hereinbefore specified;

2nd, paying inspectors for visiting and reporting upon schools;

3rd, gratuities to teachers of schools conducted under the rules laid down not exceeding ...... pounds each;

4th, establishing and maintaining a model school in Dublin and training teachers for country schools;

5th, editing and printing such books of moral and literary education as may be approved of for the use of the schools, and supplying them

N.B. It is not intended that this regulation should apply to prevent the admission of masters or mistresses of schools already established, who may be approved of by the commissioners, *nor of such as the board may think fit to appoint, before the proposed model school may come into full operation.*

3rd He shall have received testimonials of good conduct and of general fitness for the situation, from the board *or the persons employed by them to conduct the model school.*

The board will be entrusted with the absolute control over the funds which may be annually voted by parliament, which they shall apply to the following purposes:

1st, granting aid for the erection of schools, subject to the conditions hereinbefore specified;

2nd, paying inspectors for visiting and reporting upon schools;

3rd, gratuities to teachers of schools conducted under the rules laid down, not exceeding ...... pounds each;

4th, establishing and maintaining a model school in Dublin and training teachers for country schools;

5th, editing and printing such books of moral and literary education as may be approved of for the use of the schools, and supplying them

Marginal notes:

Provisional masters sanctioned by B

Power of granting testimonials extended by B

One purpose of grant omitted in B

and school necessaries at not lower than half price;

6th, *defraying all necessary contingent expenses of the board.*

I have thus stated the objects which his majesty's government have in view, and the principal regulations by which they think those objects may be most effectually promoted; and I am directed by the lord lieutenant to express his excellency's earnest wish that the one and the other may be found such as to procure for the board the sanction of your grace's name and the benefit of your grace's attendance.

A full power will, of course, be given to the board to make such regulations upon matters of detail, not inconsistent with the spirit of these instructions, as they may judge best qualified to carry into effect the intentions of the government and the legislature. Parliament has already placed at his excellency's disposal a sum which may be available even in the course of the present year; and as soon as the board can be formed it will be highly desirable that no time should be lost, with a view of the estimates of the ensuing year, in enabling such schools, already established, as are willing to subscribe to the conditions imposed, to put in their claims for protection and assistance; and in receiving applications from parties desirous to avail themselves of the munificence of the

and school necessaries at not lower than half price.

[*Identical*]

legislature in fouding new schools
under your regulations.

I have the honour to be, &c.,
(Signed) E. G. STANLEY
Irish Office, London, 23rd Feb.
1832.

(A true copy)
GEORGE TRUNDLE

I have the honour to be, my
lord,
Your grace's most obedient
servant,

E. G. STANLEY

To his grace the duke of Leinster
&c., &c.

The Powis report contained a sound summary of the differences between the two versions.[2] First, 'Version A' was less complimentary to the Kildare Place Society than was its counterpart. Second, 'Version A' made clear the commissioners' right to publish non-dogmatic works of moral teaching and sacred history, while 'Version B' did not. Third, 'Version B' omitted Stanley's declaration that the new system was 'by no means intended to convey a perfect and sufficient religious education, or to supersede the necessity of separate religious instruction on the day set apart for that purpose'. Fourth, 'Version A' provided for the vesting of schoolhouses in approved trustees, while 'Version B' required that schoolhouses be vested in the commissioners. Fifth, 'Version A' spoke of 'a model school in Dublin, to be sanctioned by the board', while its counterpart mentioned 'a model school to be established in Dublin'. Sixth, 'Version B' gave the commissioners power to provide books for separate religious instruction at prime cost, a power not mentioned in 'Version A'. In addition, there were other minor differences as noted in the marginal comments.

[2] Ibid., p. 26.

BIBLIOGRAPHY*

~~~~~~

I MANUSCRIPT MATERIAL

Belfast
  Public Record Office
    Anglesey Papers.

Dublin
  National Library of Ireland
    Bonaparte-Wyse Papers.
    Harrington Papers.
    Larcom Papers.
    Minutes of the commissioners of national education in Ireland,
       1831–1900 (Feb. 1837–June 1840, missing).
    Monsell Papers.
    Monteagle Papers.

* With the exception of a few important items, it has been necessary to limit entries in the bibliography to items directly cited in the text.

Bibliography

MS 8401; n. 4036/p. 3707; n. 4038/p. 3709. Photostats and microfilms of correspondence of the second earl Grey, from the originals in the library of the University of Durham.

Public Record Office
  Chief Secretary's Office, Registered Papers:
    carton 621, doc. 3688/1822; carton 1119, doc. 11, 551/1825.
    carton 1123, doc. 12,702/1826; carton 1145, doc. 14,439/1826.
  'Circular Letters to Inspectors, 2 January 1861 to 21 September 1872.'
  Minutes of royal commission on primary education, 1868–1879. 3 vols 1a–50–36.

State Paper Office
  Chief Secretary's Office, Country Letterbooks:
    Volumes 144, 148, 157, 167.
  Chief Secretary's Office, Government Correspondence Books: Volumes 72, 78.
  Chief Secretary's Office, Irish Department Book. 23 March 1866–29 December 1866.
  Chief Secretary's Office, Official Papers, Unregistered (miscellaneous) Papers: 140/1833, 9/1858.
  Chief Secretary's Office, Registered Papers:
    1691/1832, 16/1834 354/1834, 1687/1834, 30/1835, 376/1835, 3731/1835, 3858/1835, 313/1836, 68/1837, 48–10757/1839, 48–3268/1839, 0–382/1845, 0–21032/1846, 0–22100/1846, 4764/1855, 12695/1866, 114/1870, 12782/1873, 1869/1877, 4381/1893, 12559/1894, 2637/1895, 6999/1896.
  Irish Department Books
    Volumes 3, 6.

Representative Church Body
  Notes by H. Cotten on title page of 'Scripture extracts'.

Royal Irish Academy
  Mathew Horgan, 'Catholic poor schools at Cove, 1829'.

Leyburn, Yorkshire
  Bolton Manuscripts. In possession of the Right Hon. Lord Bolton, Bolton Hall.

London
  British Museum
    Gladstone Papers. Add. MS 44,443, f. 237; Add. MS 44, 727 ff., 12–25.
  Public Record Office
    CAB 37/42, 1892, no. 38; CAB 37/42, 1896, no. 29.

Bibliography

Oxford
  Bodleian Library
    MS Top Ireland, d.2, d.3.

II UNPRINTED THESES

Bradley, William J., 'Sir Thomas Wyse—Irish pioneer in education re form', University of Dublin, Ph.D. 1947.

Connolly, Helen M., 'The operation of the national education system of Ireland between 1831 and 1837', University College, Dublin, M.A. 1958.

Hamilton, William D., 'The development of education in the county of Londonderry from 1800 to 1922', Queen's University, Belfast, M.A. 1963.

Jacques, William, 'The chief factors determining the developments in primary education, Ireland, 1831–1947', Queen's University, Belfast, Ph.D. 1952.

Kennedy, Cuthbert, 'Survey of the history of education in Corca Laughdhe (Diocese of Ross) from earliest times to 1825', University College, Cork, M.A. 1942.

Lynch, Michael A., 'The Kildare Place Society (1811–1831)', University College, Cork, M.A. 1958.

Sullivan, James J., 'The education of Irish catholics, 1782–1831', Queen's University, Belfast, Ph.D. 1959.

III BRITISH PARLIAMENTARY PAPERS

(A) Reports of the commissioners of national education in Ireland (in chronological order)

First report of the commissioners appointed by the lord lieutenant to administer funds voted by parliament for the education of the poor of Ireland, H.C. 1834 [70], xl.

Second report of the commissioners of national education in Ireland, for the year ending 31st March 1835, H.C. 1835 [300], xxxv.

Third report . . ., for the year ending 31st March 1836, [44], H.C. 1836, xxxvi.

Fourth report . . ., for the year ending 31st March 1837 [110], H.C. 1837–8, xxviii.

Fifth report . . ., for the year ending 31st March 1838 [160], H.C. 1839, xvi.

Sixth report . . ., for the year 1839, [246], H.C. 1840, xxviii.

Seventh report . . ., for the year 1840, [353], H.C. 1842, xxiii.

Eighth report . . ., for the year 1841, [398], H.C. 1842, xxiii.

Ninth report . . ., for the year 1842, [471], H.C. 1843, xxviii.

Tenth report . . ., for the year 1843, [569], H.C. 1844, xxx.

Eleventh report . . ., for the year 1844, [629], H.C. 1845, xxvi.

Appendix to the eleventh report . . ., for the year 1844, [650], H.C. 1845, xxvi.

Twelfth report . . ., for the year 1845, [711], H.C. 1846, xxii.

Thirteenth report . . ., for the year 1846, [832], H.C. 1847, xvii.

Fourteenth report . . ., for the year 1847, [981], H.C. 1847–48, xxix.

Fifteenth report . . ., *for the year 1848*, [1066], H.C. 1849, xxiii.

Sixteenth report . . ., *for the year 1849*, 2 vols [1231], [1231–II], H.C., 1805, xxv.

Seventeenth report . . ., *for the year 1850*, [1405], H.C. 1851, xxiv, pt i.

Appendix to the seventeenth report . . ., *for the year 1850*, [1405–11], H.C. 1851, xxiv, pt i.

Eighteenth report . . ., *for the year 1851*, [1582], H.C. 1852–3, xlii.

Nineteenth report . . ., *for the year 1852*, [1688], H.C. 1852–53, xliii, pt i.

Twentieth report . . ., *for the year 1853*, [1834], H.C. 1854, xxx, pt i.

Twenty-first report . . ., *for the year 1854*, [1950], H.C. 1854–5, xxiii, pt i.

Twenty-second report . . ., *for the year 1855*, [2142–1], H.C. 1856, xxvii, pt i.

Appendix to the twenty-second report . . ., *for the year 1855*, [2142–11], H.C. 1856, xxvii, pt ii.

Twenty-third report . . ., *for the year 1856*, [2304], H.C. 1857–8, xx.

Twenty-fourth report. . ., *for the year 1857*, [2456–1], H.C. 1859, vii.

Twenty-fifth report . . ., *for the year 1858*, [2593], H.C. 1860, xxv.

Twenty-sixth report . . ., *for the year 1859*, [2706], H.C. 1860, xxvi.

Twenty-seventh report . . ., *for the year 1860*, [2873], H.C. 1861, xx.

Twenty-eighth report . . . *for the year 1861*, [3026], H.C. 1862, xx.

Twenty-ninth report . . ., *for the year 1862*, [3235], H.C. 1863, xvii, pt i.

Thirtieth report . . ., *for the year 1863*, [3351], H.C. 1864, xix, pt ii.

Thirty-first report . . ., *for the year 1864*, [3496], H.C. 1865, xix.

Thirty-second report . . ., *for the year 1865*, [3713], H.C. 1866, xxix.

Thirty-third report . . ., *for the year 1866*, [3905], H.C. 1867, xxiv.

Thirty-fourth report . . ., *for the year 1867*, [4026], H.C. 1867–68, xxvi.

Thirty-fifth report . . ., *for the year 1868*, [4193], H.C. 1868–69, xxi.

Thirty-sixth report . . ., *for the year 1869*, 2 vols. [C 119, C. 120], H.C. 1870 xxiii

Thirty-seventh report . . ., *for the year 1870*, [C 360], H.C. 1871, xxiii.

Thirty-eighth report . . ., *for the year 1871*, [C 599], H.C. 1872, xxiii.

Thirty-ninth report . . ., *for the year 1872*, [C 805], H.C. 1873, xxv.

Fortieth report . ., *for the year 1873*, [C 965], H.C. 1874, xix.

Forty-first report . . ., *for the year 1874*, [C 1228], H.C. 1875, xxv.

Forty-second report . . ., *for the year 1875*, [C 1503], H.C. 1876, xxiv.

Forty-third report . . . *for the year 1876*, [C 1757], H.C. 1877, xxxi.

Forty-fourth report . . ., *for the year 1877*, [C 2031], H.C. 1878, xxix.

Forty-fifth report . . ., *for the year 1878*, [C 2312], H.C. 1878–79, xxiv.

Forty-sixth report . . ., *for the year 1879*, [C 2592], H.C. 1880, xxiii.

Forty-seventh report . . ., *for the year 1880*, [C 2925], H.C. 1881, xxxiv.

Forty-eighth report . . ., *for the year 1881*, [C 3243], H.C. 1882, xxiv.

Forty-ninth report . . ., *for the year 1882*, [C 3651], H.C., 1883, xxvi.

Fiftieth report . . ., *for the year 1883*, [C 4053], 1884, xxv.

Fifty-first report . . ., *for the year 1884*, [C 4458], H.C. 1884–85, xxiv.

Fifty-second report . . ., *for the year 1885*, [C 4800], H.C. 1886, xxvii.

Fifty-third report . . ., *for the year 1886*, [C 5082], H.C. 1887, xxxi.

Fifty-fourth report . . ., *for the year 1887*, [C 5406], H.C. 1888, xl.

Fifty-fifth report . . ., *for the year 1888*, [C 5738], H.C. 1889, xxxi.

Fifty-sixth report . . ., for the year 1889, [C 6074], H.C. 1890, xxx.
Fifty-seventh report . . ., for the year 1890, [C 6411], H.C. 1890–91, xxix.
Fifty-eighth report . . ., for the year 1891, [C 6788], H.C. 1892, xxx.
Fifty-ninth report . . ., for the year 1892, [C 7124], H.C. 1893–94, xxvii.
Sixtieth report . . ., for the year 1893, [C 7457], 1894, xxx, pt ii.
Sixty-first report . . ., for the year 1894, [C 7796], H.C., 1895, xxix.
Sixty-second report . . ., for the year 1895, [C 8142], H.C. 1896, xxviii.
Sixty-third report . . ., for the year 1896–97, [C 8600], H.C. 1897, xxviii.
Sixty-fourth report . . ., for the year 1897–98, [C 9038], 1898, xxvii.
Sixty-fifth report . . ., for the year 1898–99, [C 9446], H.C. 1899, xxiv.
Sixty-sixth report . . ., for the year 1899–1900, [Cd 285], H.C. 1900, xxiii.
Sixty-seventh report . . ., for the year 1900, [Cd 704], H.C. 1901, xxi.
Seventy-second report . . ., for the school year 1905–06, [Cd 3699], H.C. 1907, xxii.

(B) *Other parliamentary papers (in chronological order).*
Reports from the commissioners of the board of education in Ireland:

First report . .: Free schools of royal foundation, H.C. 1809 (142), vii.
Second report . . .: Schools of Navan and Ballyroan, of private foundation, H.C. 1809 (142), vii.
Third report . .: The protestant charter schools, H.C. 1809 (142), vii.
Fourth report . . : Diocesan free schools, H.C. 1810 (174), x.
Fifth report . . .: Wilson's hospital, H.C. 1810 (175), x.
Sixth report . . .: Blue-coat hospital, H.C. 1810 (176), x.
Seventh report . . .: Hibernian school in the Phoenix Park, H.C. 1810 (177), x.
Eighth report . . .: Fondling hospital, H.C. 1810 (193), x.
Ninth report . . .: Schools founded by Erasmus Smith, Esq., H.C. 1910 (194), x
Tenth report . . .: Hibernian marine school, H.C. 1810 (242), x.
Eleventh report . . .: Parish schools, H.C. 1810–11 (107), vi; reprinted, H.C. 1821 (743), xi.
Twelfth report . . .: Classical schools, of private foundation, H.C. 1812 (218), v.
Thirteenth report . . .: English schools of private foundation, H.C. 1812 (219), v.
Fourteenth report . . .: View of the chief foundations, with some general remarks, and result of deliberations, H.C. 1812–13 (21), vi.
The fourteen reports as enumerated above are reprinted with an index in H.C. 1813–14 (47), v.

The report of the commissioners of education in Ireland to his excellency the lord lieutenant of the proceedings of their board, from the 18th of November, 1813 to the 25th of March, 1814, H.C. 1814–15 (29), vi.
A statement of the grants voted by parliament on account of miscellaneous services for Ireland in 1818; of the estimates for the like services laid before parliament in 1819; and of the sums voted thereupon; with a comparative view of the increase and decrease under each head in those years; and the total decrease upon the whole, H.C. 1819 (515), xv.
First report of the commissioners of Irish education inquiry, H.C. 1825 (400), xii.
Second report . . ., H.C. 1826–7 (12), xii.
Third report . . ., H. C. 1826–7 (13), xiii.

Bibliography

Fourth report . . ., H.C. 1826–7 (89), xiii.

Fifth report . . ., H.C. 1826–7 (441), xiii.

Sixth report . . ., H.C. 1826–7 (442), xiii.

Seventh report . . ., H.C. 1826–7 (443), xiii.

Eighth report . . ., H.C. 1826–7 (509), xiii.

Ninth report . . ., H.C. 1826–7 (516), xiii.

Report from the select committee to whom the reports on the subject of education in Ireland were referred, H.C. 1828 (341), iv; reprinted H.C. 1829 (80), iv.

Report from the select committee appointed to take into consideration the state of the poorer classes in Ireland, H.C. 1830 (667), vii.

Estimate of miscellaneous services: for the year 1830, H.C. 1830–1 (11), vi.

A bill for the establishment and maintenance of parochial schools, and the advancement of the education of the people in Ireland, H.C. 1831 (286), 1.

A return from the different diocesan and other endowed schools under the superintendence of the commissioners of education in Ireland; of the number of scholars taught in each school, at the period of January 1831, specifying the number of those from whose education, board, and lodging, payment is made from private means, and the number of those who are free scholars taught gratuitously at each school; with an account of the salary and emolument attached to such schools from their foundation or establishment, H.C. 1831 (106), xv.

Return of the total number of children in the charter schools of Ireland, in the years 1826, 1827, 1828, 1829, and 1830, H.C. 1831 (157), xv.

Copy of a letter from the chief secretary for Ireland to the duke of Leinster, on the formation of a board of commissioners for education in Ireland, H.C. 1831–2 (196), xxix.

A bill for the establishment of a board of national education, and the advancement of elementary education in Ireland, H.C. 1835 (285), ii.

First report of the commissioners of public instruction, Ireland, (45 and 46), H.C. 1835, xxxiii.

Second report of the commissioners of public instruction, Ireland, (47), H.C. 1835, xxxiv.

A report of the select committee of the house of lords on the plan of education in Ireland; with minutes of evidence, H.C. 1837 (543–1), viii, pt i.

Minutes of evidence taken before the select committee of the house of lords on the plan of education in Ireland, H.C. 1837 (543–11), viii, pt ii.

Report from the select committee appointed to inquire into the progress and operation of the new plan of education in Ireland, H.C. 1837 (485), ix.

Report from the select committee on foundation schools and education in Ireland, H.C. 1837–8 (701), vii.

Copies of any applications made by clergymen of the synod of Ulster to the board of education in Ireland, for aid to schools connected with the synod, since the recent conference between the deputation from the synod and the board, in presence of the lord lieutenant of Ireland; and, of any answers returned to such applications, or of any minutes made or resolutions entered into by the board in relation thereto, H.C. 1840 (110), xl.

A copy of the charter of incorporation lately granted by her majesty to the board of national education in Ireland, H.C. 1846 (193), xlii.

Copy of a resolution lately adopted by the board of national education in Ireland, ex-

cluding the use of certain books for the schools under their management, H.C. 1852–3 (826), xciv.

Copies of correspondence of education commissioners (Ireland), relative to school books, with Mr Tottenham, in 1840; return of books now in use in each of the several model schools; copies of memorandums addressed to the education board by the archbishop of Dublin, complaining of the innovations introduced in some of the model schools without the sanction of the commissioners, and the answers thereto, and his grace's replies to the defence of the irregularity; together with his notice of withdrawal from the board; and of proceedings of special meeting of education commissioners held on the 17th day of June 1853, with reference to rule 8, sect. 2, referred to in the proceedings of the 8th day of July 1853 (826), H.C. 1852–3 (972), xciv.

Report from the select committee of the house of lords appointed to inquire into the practical working of the system of national education in Ireland, 2 pts. H.C. 1854 (525), xv.

Census of Ireland for the year 1851; Part vi: General report, [2134], H.C. 1856, xxxi.

Report of her majesty's commissioners appointed to inquire into the endowments, funds, and actual condition of all schools endowed for the purpose of education in Ireland, [2336–I], H.C. 1857–8, xxii, pt i.

Evidence taken before her majesty's commissioners of inquiry into the state of the endowed schools in Ireland, vol. i [2336–II], H.C. 1857–8, xxii, pt ii.

Evidence taken before her majesty's commissioners of inquiry into the state of the endowed schools in Ireland, vol. ii [2336–III], H.C., 1857–8, xxii, pt iii.

Papers accompanying the report of her majesty's commissioners for inquiring into endowed schools in Ireland, vol. iii [2336–IV], 1857–8, xxii, pt iv.

Copies of report of the committee of the national board of education in Ireland, appointed on the 11th day of September 1857, to inquire into the conduct of J. Kavanagh, Esq., head inspector of national schools; of appendices to the foregoing report, marked (A), (B), (C), (D), (E), (F), (G), (H); extracts from the minutes of the proceedings of the 17th day of November 1857, with reference to the report of the committee appointed to inquire into the conduct of J. Kavanagh, Esq., head inspector of national schools; and statement of further proceedings connected with J. Kavanagh, Esq., subsequent to the order of the board, dated the 27th day of November 1857, depressing him from the rank of head inspector to district inspector of the first class, H.C., 1857–8 (386), xlvi.

A copy of all correspondence, from the 1st day of July 1857 to the present date, which passed between the commissioners of national education in Ireland and Mr James Kavanagh, head inspector of national schools, omitting such only as is of a mere routine nature, or not bearing upon any matter in dispute between Mr Kavanagh and any other party, excluding also the returns respecting the Ballandine national schools, and so much of the correspondence, etc., as is contained in parliamentary papers, no. 386, of last session; and return of the names of the members appointed on the special committee of the 11th day of September 1857, in reference to Mr Kavanagh, with the names of those subsequently added; the precise matters which the committee was first appointed to investigate, with a statement of any others afterwards added; the dates of the several sittings of the committee, with the members present at each: And, copy of the minutes of the business transacted;

of the report of the committee, with the names of those members (as laid before the board on the 27th day of November 1857) of the committee present when it was adopted; of the names of the commissioners present at the board's meeting of the 27th day of November 1857; and of all communications which the members of the board or other public parties may have forwarded to the commissioners, or to the resident commissioner, in reference to the case of Mr Kavanagh, within the whole of the above period, H.C. 1859 (sess. 1, 254), xxi, part ii.

Copy of the memorial of the Roman Catholic prelates relative to national education in Ireland, and of the reply thereto of the chief secretary for Ireland, dated 28th November 1859, H.C. 1860 (26), liii.

Further correspondence relative to national education in Ireland (presented in continuation of parliamentary paper no. 26 of the present session), H.C. 1860 (206), liii.

Copy of a letter on the subject of national education in Ireland, addressed to the chief secretary in the month of July last by certain members of parliament, H.C. 1861 (212), xlviii.

Return of the amount of money voted each year by parliament for the purpose of national education in Ireland, from the commencement of the system to the year 1861; and of the amount of local contributions each year in aid of teachers' salaries, of the building, fitting and inclosing of schools, and the amount of money contributed by the board towards the building of schools; also the number of schools in connexion with the board, built by local subscriptions, without any aid from parliament; and also the amount of any pecuniary assistance or other voluntary contributions in sustainment of the national system, H.C. 1861 (532), xlviii.

Copy of a memorial lately presented to the lord lieutenant of Ireland by the lord bishop of Down, Connor, and Dromore, on behalf of certain clergy and laity of his diocese, on the subject of national education in Ireland; of the statement read by the bishop on presenting such memorial; and of any correspondence which has since taken place between the lord lieutenant and the bishop on the subject, H.C. 1862 (347), xliii.

Census of Ireland for the year 1861, report on religion and education, [3204–III], H.C. 1863, lix.

Copy of any correspondence between the chief secretary for Ireland, and the chief commissioner of national education in Ireland, relative to the recent alterations in the rules of the board, H.C. 1864 (181), xlvi.

Copy of any new or altered rule on the subject of religious teaching made in May 1866 by the commissioners of national education (Ireland), with the names of the commissioners present when the same was adopted, and the protests, if any, H.C. 1866 (407), lv.

Return showing the cost of last revision of the school books published by the commissioners of national education in Ireland; and time occupied in said revisions; copies of any statement or memorial on the subject of these revised books presented to the lord lieutenant or the commissioners of education by the elementary education committee of the general assembly of the presbyterian church in Ireland; of any letter or protest of any member or members of the national board regarding said books; and of the final resolution of the commissioners with respect to them, H.C. 1867–8 (363), liii.

Bibliography

Report from the commission on the science and art department in Ireland, vol. i: *Report*, [4103], H.C. 1868–9, xxiv; vol. ii, *Minutes of evidence, appendix, and index*, [4103–I], H.C. 1868–9, xxiv.

Royal commission of inquiry into primary education (Ireland), vol. i, pt i: *Report of the commissioners*, [C 6], H.C. 1870, xxviii, pt i.

——, vol. i, pt ii: *Appendix to the report and also special report by royal commissioners on model schools (district and minor), the central training institution, etc., Dublin, and on agricultural schools*, [C 6a], H.C. 1870, xxviii, pt ii.

——, vol. ii; *Reports of assistant commissioners*, [C 6–I], H.C. 1870, xxviii, pt ii.

——, vol. iii: *Minutes of evidence taken before the commissioners, from March 12th to October 30th, 1868*, [C 6–II], H.C. 1870, xxviii, pt iii.

——, vol. iv: *Minutes of evidence taken before the commissioners, from November 24th, 1868 to May 29th, 1869* [C 6–III]. 1870, xxviii, pt iii.

——, vol. v, *Analysis of evidence; and index to minutes of evidence, and appendices*, [C 6–IV], H.C. 1870, xxviii, pt iv.

——, vol. vi, *Educational census: returns showing number of children actually present in each primary school, 25 June 1868, with introductory observations and analytical index*, [C 6–V]., H.C. 1870, xxviii, pt v.

——, vol. vii, *Returns furnished by the national board*, [C 6–VI], H.C. 1870, xxviii, pt v.

——, vol. viii, *Miscellaneous papers and returns*, [C 6–VII], H.C. 1870, xxviii, pt v.

Copy of all minutes and proceedings from the 1st day of May 1866 to the present time, relating to changes of rules or of practice as to religious instruction: date when the certificate book of religious instruction was first brought into active operation, copy of such book, and copy of circulars to patrons and inspectors relating thereto; copy of query, if any, introduced into the form of inspector's report, with a view to record the observance or neglect of the rules as to the certificate book; and returns of all schools in which certificates have been used, etc, H.C. 1872, (416), xlvi.

Copy of memorials from the council of the national education league for Ireland, addressed to his grace the duke of Abercorn, lord lieutenant etc., on the subject of inroads made and contemplated upon the fundamental principle of the national system of education in Ireland; and from the elementary education committee of the general assembly of the presbyterian church in Ireland, addressed to his grace the lord lieutenant, on the subject of non-vested training colleges, H.C. 1875 (201), lix.

Census of Ireland, 1871, pt. III; General report with illustrative maps and diagrams, summary tables, and appendix [C 1377], 1876, lxxxi.

Copy of any circular or document conveying to the inspectors of national schools in Ireland, a reprimand in connection with the agitation for increased remuneration, H.C. 1884–5 (22), lxi.

Copy of a memorial presented to the lord lieutenant by certain catholic bishops upon the subject of elementary education, and which was alluded to by the chief secretary in introducing a bill upon the subject, H.C. 1884–5 (229), lxi.

A bill to improve national education in Ireland, H.C. 1892 (234), iv.

A bill (as amended in committee) to improve national education in Ireland, H.C. 1892 (420), iv.

A bill to amend the Irish education act, 1892, H.C. 1893-4 (297), iii.

A bill to amend the Irish education act, 1892, H.C. 1893-4 (344), iii.

A bill for the better regulation of national education in Ireland, H.C. 1893-4 (4), vi.

Copy of correspondence between the Irish government and the commissioners of national education for Ireland, with extracts from minutes of the proceedings of the commissioners, in relation to certain proposed changes in the rules under which grants are made by parliament for elementary education in Ireland, H.C. 1893-4 (55), lxviii.

Return showing the number of monastic schools in Ireland under the national board of education, with the name of each; the number of children on the roll of each school; the number of children in average daily attendance at each; the number of teachers employed; and the names of the several religious orders to which they belong; and copies of the form of application for the school to be taken under the board, and of the form in the quarterly returns certifying that the rules of the board have been duly observed, H.C. 1893-4 (243), lxviii.

Return of copy of correspondence between the commissioners of national education in Ireland and the Irish government on the subject of the difficulties experienced by the commissioners in bringing into operation the Irish education act, 1892, H.C. 1893-4 (508), lxviii.

A bill to amend the Irish education act, 1892, H.C. 1894 (107), iv.

Copy of correspondence in the year 1895 between the Irish government and the commissioners of national education for Ireland, with extracts from minutes of the proceedings of the commissioners, in relation to certain proposed changes in the rules under which grants are made by parliament for elementary education in Ireland, H.C. 1895 (324), lxxvii.

A bill to amend and explain the Irish education act, 1892, H.C. 1896 (214), iii.

Copy of further correspondence between the Irish government and the commissioners of national education in Ireland; with extracts from minutes of the proceedings of the commissioners, in relation to certain proposed changes in the rules under which grants are made by parliament for elementary education in Ireland, H.C. 1896 (89), lxvi.

Commission on manual and practical instruction in primary schools under the board of national education in Ireland: First report of the commissioners and minutes of evidence taken at the first seven public sittings, [C 8383], H.C. 1897, xliii.

——: *Second report of the commissioners*, [C 8532], H.C. 1897, xliii.

——: *Second volume of evidence, comprising that taken in England between March 18 and April 9, 1897, being a supplement to the second report of the commissioners*, [C 8532], H.C. 1897, xliii.

——: *Third report of the commissioners*, [C 8618], H.C. 1897, xliii.

——: *Third volume of minutes of evidence, comprising that taken between April 29 and July 21, 1898, being a supplement to the third report of the commissioners*, [C 8619], H.C. 1897, xliii.

——: *Final report of the commissioners*, [C 8923], H.C. 1898, xliv.

——: *Fourth volume of minutes of evidence, comprising that taken between Sep-*

tember 29 and December 17, 1897, being a supplement to the final report of the commissioners, [C 8924], H.C. 1898, xliv.

———: *Appendices to the reports of the commissioners*, [C 8925], H.C. 1898, xliv.

A bill for establishing a department of agriculture and other industries and technical instruction in Ireland, and for other purposes connected therewith, H.C. 1899 (180), i.

A bill (as amended by the standing committee on trade, etc.) for establishing a department of agriculture and other industries and technical instruction in Ireland, and for other purposes connected therewith, H.C. 1899 (280), i.

Lords' amendments to the agriculture and technical instruction (Ireland) bill, H.C. 1899 (300), i.

Report from the standing committee on trade (including agriculture and fishing), shipping and manufactures, on the agriculture and technical instruction (Ireland) bill; with the proceedings of the committee, H.C. 1899 (284), viii.

New rules and regulations [national education], 1900–1, [Cd 601], H.C. 1901, lvii.

Return giving the names, appointment and attendances, 1890–1900, of the commissioners of national education in Ireland, H.C. 1901 (305), lvii.

Census of Ireland, 1901, pt. ii: *General report, with illustrative maps, diagrams, tables, and appendix*, [Cd 1190], 1902, cxxix.

Report of Mr F. H. Dale, his majesty's inspector of schools, board of education, on primary education in Ireland, [Cd 1891], H.C. 1904, xx.

Vice-regal committee of inquiry into primary education (Ireland), 1913: First report of the committee, [Cd 6828], H.C. 1913, xxii.

———: *Appendix to the first report of the committee. Minutes of evidence, 13th February–12th March 1913*, [Cd 6829], H.C. 1913, xxii.

———: *Second report of the committee*, [Cd 7228], H.C. 1914, xxviii.

———: *Appendix to the second report of the committee. Minutes of evidence, 13th March–25th June 1913*, [Cd 7229], 1914, xxviii.

———: *Third report of the committee*, [Cd 7478], H.C. 1914, xxviii.

———: *Appendix to the third report of the committee. Minutes of evidence, 26th June 17th September, 1913*, [Cd 7480], H.C. 1914, xxviii.

———: *Final report of the committee*, [Cd 7235], H.C. 1914, xxviii.

Vice-regal committee of inquiry into primary education (Ireland), 1918. Final report of the committee, vol. i: *Report*, [Cmd 60], H.C. 1919, xxi.

———: *Report of the committee*, vol. ii: *Summaries of evidence, memoranda, and returns*, [Cmd 178], H.C. 1919, xxi.

IV IRISH NATIONAL SCHOOL-BOOKS AND ASSOCIATED
PUBLICATIONS

Agricultural class book; or, how best to cultivate a small farm and garden: together with hints on domestic economy, Dublin, 1848.

An analysis of the school books published; by authority of the commissioners of national education in Ireland, Dublin, 1853.

Fifth book of lessons for the use of the Irish national schools, Dublin, 1835 and 1852.

Bibliography

First book of lessons for the use of schools, Dublin, 1836 and 1847.

Fourth book of lessons for the use of the Irish national schools, Dublin, 1835 and 1853.

Joyce, Patrick W., *A handbook of school management and methods of teaching*, Dublin, 1863.

Lessons on the truth of christianity, being an appendix to the fourth book of lessons for the use of the schools, Dublin, 1846 and 1850.

Natural philosophy for the use of teachers and schools: electricity-galvanism-magnetism-electro-magnetism-heat-the steam-engine, Dublin, 1860.

Sacred poetry adapted to the understanding of children and youth for the use of schools, Dublin, 1860.

Sacred poetry adapted to the understanding of children and youth for the use of schools, Dublin, 1845.

Scripture lessons, adapted for the use of schools: no. 1, Old Testament, Dublin, 1832.

Scripture lessons, for the use of schools: Old Testament, no. II, Dublin, 1846.

Scripture lessons: New Testament, no. I, for the use of the Irish national schools, Dublin, 1834.

Scripture lessons: New Testament, no. II, for the use of the Irish national schools, Dublin, 1835.

Second book of lessons for the use of the Irish national schools, Dublin, 1836, 1837 and 1846.

Sequel No. I to the second book of lessons, Dublin, 1853.

Sequel No. II to the second book of lessons for the use of schools, Dublin, 1853.

Sequel to the second book of lessons for the use of schools, Dublin, 1846.

Sixth reading book, Dublin, 1897.

Third book of lessons for the use of the Irish national schools, Dublin, 1835.

V PUBLICATIONS OF THE IRISH FREE STATE AND OF THE RE-
PUBLIC OF IRELAND

Report of the department of education, the school year 1924–25, and the financial and administrative years 1924–25–26, Dublin, 1926.

Report of the council of education [Pr. 2583], Dublin, 1954.

VI NEWSPAPERS

(A) *Newspapers*
Belfast Newsletter, 1831–42.
Dublin Evening Mail, 1835–42.
Dublin Evening Post, 1824–42.
Freeman's Journal, 1815–51.
Northern Whig, 1831–42
The Times, 1815–1900.

(B) *Clipping collections*
National Library of Ireland: Larcom Papers, collection of newspaper clippings on Irish affairs during mid-nineteenth century, including national education.

414

Public Record Office of Ireland: collection of newspaper clippings on Irish education during the last three decades of the nineteenth century.

VII   PRINTED COLLECTIONS OF LETTERS AND PAPERS

Cloncurry, Valentine, *Personal recollections of the life and times, with extracts from the correspondence of Valentine, Lord Cloncurry*, 2nd ed., Dublin, 1850.

Fitzpatrick, William J., *The life, times, and correspondence of the Right Rev. Dr Doyle, bishop of Kildare and Leighlin*, 2 vols, Dublin, 1861.

Historical Manuscripts Commission, national register of archives, *Bolton MSS (part I)*, London, 1962.

Historical Manuscripts Commission, *Twelfth report*, appendix, pt IX; *Manuscripts of the duke of Beaufort, K.G., the earl of Donoughmore, and others*, [C 6338–I] H.C. 1890–1, xlvi.

MacSuibhne, Peadar, *Paul Cullen and his contemporaries, with their letters from 1820–1902*, 3 vols, Naas, 1961.

O'Donoghue, David J., *The life of William Carleton: being his autobiography and letters; and an account of his life and writings, from the point at which the autobiography breaks off*, 2 vols, London, 1896.

O'Reilly, Bernard, *John MacHale, archbishop of Tuam: his life, times and correspondence*, 2 vols, New York and Cincinnati 1890.

Whately, E. Jane, *Life and correspondence of Richard Whately, D.D., late archbishop of Dublin*, 2 vols, London, 1866.

Wyse, Winifrede M., *Notes on education reform in Ireland during the first half of the 19th century, compiled from the speeches, letters, etc., contained in the unpublished memoirs of the Rt Hon. Sir Thomas Wyse, K.C.B.*, Waterford, 1901.

Young, G. M. and W. D. Handcock, (ed.), *English historical documents, 1833–1874*, London, 1956.

VIII PAMPHLETS, TREATISES, REPORTS AND OTHER WORKS

(A) Published before 1900

'Admonition addressed by the bishops to the catholic national school teachers', *Irish Ecclesiastical Record*, 3 ser., xvii, pp 762–3 (Aug. 1896).

Anderson, William, *The opposition to the national system of education, considered in its effect upon the established church in Ireland, with remarks upon a pamphlet recently published*, Belfast, 1858.

Association for Discountenancing Vice, *The report of the Association Incorporated for Discountenancing Vice and Promoting the Knowledge and Practice of the Christian Religion*, Dublin, 1826.

Baptist Society for Promoting the Gospel in Ireland, *Second annual report of the Baptist Society for Promoting the Gospel in Ireland by establishing schools for teaching the native Irish, for itinerant preaching, etc,*, London, 1816.

'Board of national education', *Christian Examiner and Church of Ireland Magazine*, 2 ser., iv, 681–92 (Oct. 1835).

'Board of national education', *Christian Examiner and Church of Ireland Magazine*, 2 ser., iv, 855–63 (Dec. 1835).

Butt, Isaac, *The liberty of teaching vindicated*, London and Dublin, 1865.

——, *National education in Ireland: a speech delivered at a meeting of the Church Education Society in Youghal, on Monday, October 16, 1854*, Dublin, 1854.

——, *The problem of Irish education: an attempt at its solution*, London, 1875.

Carleton, William, *Amusing Irish tales*, new ed., London and Glasgow, 1892.

——, *Traits and stories of the Irish peasantry*, 2 vols, tenth ed., London, 1854.

The case for bilingual education in the Irish-speaking districts, Dublin, undated, c. 1899.

'The control of the schools', *Irish Ecclesiastical Record*, 3 ser., xiii, 1141–2 (Dec. 1892).

Church Education Society for Ireland, *First annual report of the Church Education Society for Ireland*, Dublin, 1840.

——, *Second annual report . . .*, Dublin, 1841.

——, *Third annual report . . .*, Dublin, 1842.

——, *Fourth annual report . . .*, Dublin, 1843.

——, *Sixth annual report . . .*, Dublin, 1845.

——, *Seventh annual report . . .*, Dublin, 1846.

——, *Eighth annual report . . .*, Dublin, 1848.

——, *Ninth annual report . . .*, Dublin, 1849.

——, *Tenth annual report . . .*, Dublin, 1850.

——, *Thirteenth annual report . . .*, Dublin, 1853.

——, *Sixteenth annual report . . .*, Dublin, 1856.

——, *Twenty-fourth annual report . . .*, Dublin, 1864.

——, *Thirty-first annual report . . .*, Dublin, 1871.

——, *Forty-fifth annual report . . .*, Dublin, 1885.

Church of Ireland, *Board of Religious Education, report, 1878*, Dublin, 1878.

Comerford, M., *Collections relating to the diocese of Kildare and Leighlin*, Dublin, 1883.

Commissioners of national education, *Reports of the commissioners of national education in Ireland for the years 1834, 1835, and 1836*, Dublin, 1836.

Cooke, Henry, *National education: a sermon, preached in the presbyterian church, May Street, Belfast, upon Sunday the 15th of January 1832*, Belfast, 1832.

Cullen, Paul, *Pastoral letter of his eminence Cardinal Cullen, catholic archbishop of Dublin, etc., for the festival of St Patrick*, Dublin, 1867.

Declaration in favour of united secular education in Ireland by members of the United Church of England and Ireland; with the list of signatures, Dublin, 1866.

'Derry and Raphoe address on national education', *Christian Examiner and Church of Ireland Magazine*, 3 ser., ii, 18–30 (Jan. 1837).

The Derry and Raphoe propositions, the Church Education Society, the national board schools compared, with remarks, Dublin, 1849.

Devine, F. Pius, 'John MacHale, archbishop of Tuam', *Dublin Review*, cix, 27–40 (July 1891).

Digest of the evidence before the committees of the house of lords and commons, in the year 1837 on the national system of education in Ireland, London, 1838.

Doyle, James, *Letters on the state of Ireland, addressed by J.K.L. to a friend in England*, Dublin, 1825.

——, *Unpublished essay by Dr Doyle: an essay on education and the state of Ireland by an Irish catholic*, Dublin, 1880.

Dunlop, Durham, *A review of the administration of the board of national educa-*

tion in Ireland, from its establishment in 1831 to 1841; with suggestions for its improved administration, London, Edinburgh, and Dublin, 1843.

Dutton, Hely, *A statistical survey of the county of Clare, with observations on the means of improvement; drawn up for the consideration, and by the direction of the Dublin Society*, Dublin, 1808.

Elrington, Charles, *A few suggestions addressed to the clergy upon the present state of the question respecting national education in Ireland*, second ed., Dublin, 1847.

Foster, Benjamin F., *Education reform: a review of Wyse on the necessity of a national system of education, comprising the substance of that work, so far as relates to common school and popular education*, New York, 1837.

Garrett, John, *Education in Ireland; comparison of the advice given in two addresses, recently issued by his grace the lord primate of all Ireland, and the lord bishop of Ossory, Ferns and Leighlin, embodying an address to the archbishops, bishops and clergy of the Church of Ireland*, London and Dublin, 1860.

Godkin, James, *Education in Ireland; its history, institutions, system, statistics and progress, from the earliest times to the present*, London and Dublin, 1862.

Graves, Arnold F., 'On the reorganisation of Irish education departments and the appointment of a minister of education', *Journal of the Statistical and Social Inquiry Society of Ireland*, viii, 350–9 (Aug. 1882).

Gregory, Alfred, *Robert Raikes, journalist and philanthropist*, London, 1877.

'Important declarations of the bishops of Ireland on the Irish education bill', *Irish Ecclesiastical Record*, 3 ser., xvii, 643 (July 1896).

'Important resolutions of the Irish hierarchy', *Irish Ecclesiastical Record*, 4 ser., xvi (Nov. 1904).

'Important resolution of the Irish hierarchy on the education question', *Irish Ecclesiastical Record*, 3 ser., xiii, 285 (Mar. 1892).

Incorporated Society for Promoting English Protestant Schools in Ireland, *A brief review of the rise and progress of the Incorporated Society in Dublin for Promoting English Protestant Schools in Ireland, from the opening of his majesty's royal charter, February 6th, 1733 to November 2nd, 1748*, Dublin, 1748.

'An Irish hedge school', *Dublin University Magazine*, lx, 600–16 (Nov. 1862).

[Kavanagh, James], *Mixed education, the catholic case stated; or, principles, working, and results of the system of national education, with suggestions for the settlement of the education question, most respectfully dedicated to the catholic archbishops and bishops of Ireland*, London and Dublin, 1859.

Kavanagh, James, *Popular education in Ireland; sketch of the rise, progress and present prospects, being a paper read before the British Association for the Advancement of Science at the twenty-seventh meeting, Dublin, September 1st, 1858, with notes and appendix*, Dublin, 1858.

——, *Six letters to a cabinet minister upon the education crisis in Ireland*, Dublin, 1859.

Kebbel, Thomas E., *Life of the earl of Derby, K.G.*, second ed., London, 1893.

King, Anthony, *Thoughts on the expediency of adopting a system of national education more immediately suited to the policy of this country; with certain brief remarks on that class of free schools, commonly distinguished by the name of diocesan free schools*, Dublin, 1793.

[Kirkpatrick, Thomas], *Agricultural education in Ireland: its organization and efficiency with a reply to recent criticisms*, Dublin, 1858.

Lecky, William E. H., *A history of Ireland in the eighteenth century*, vol. i, London, new impression, 1912.

Lee, Alfred T., *Facts respecting the present state of the Church of Ireland*, third ed., London and Belfast, 1865.

Letters on national education in Ireland, containing suggestions with a view of obtaining the co-operation of the clergy of the established church with the incorporated national board, Dublin, 1846.

MacDonagh, Michael, *Bishop Doyle: a biographical and historical study*, London and Dublin, 1896.

McEvoy, John, *Statistical survey of the county of Tyrone, with observations on the means of improvement; drawn up in the years 1801 and 1802, for the consideration and under the direction of The Dublin Society*, Dublin, 1802.

MacNeill, John G. S., *The Irish parliament: what it was and what it did*, third ed., London, 1886.

Madden, R., *Historical notice of penal laws against Roman Catholics, their operation and relation during the past century; of partial measures of relief in 1779, 1782, 1793, 1829; and of penal laws which remain unrepealed, or have been rendered more stringent by the latest so-called emancipation act*, London, 1865.

Martin, J. C., *A defense of the Irish clergy and a view of the past and present duty with respect to the system of national education in Ireland*, Dublin, 1844.

Moore, H. Kingsmill, *The education work of the Church of Ireland*, Dublin, 1885.

O'Brien, R. Barry, *Fifty years of concessions to Ireland, 1831–1881*, 2 vols, London, 1885.

Orde, Thomas, *Mr Orde's plan of an improved system of education in Ireland; submitted to the house of commons, April 12, 1787; with the debate which arose thereon, reported by John Giffard*, Dublin, 1787.

'Parliamentary evidence on national education in Ireland', *Christian Examiner and Church of Ireland Magazine*, 3 ser., ii, 867–83 (Nov. 1837).

'Parliamentary evidence on national education in Ireland', *Christian Examiner and Church of Ireland Magazine*, 3 ser., iii, 52–8 (Jan. 1838).

'Pastoral address of the Irish bishops on the managerships of catholic schools', *Irish Ecclesiastical Record*, 4 ser., iv, 75–8 (July 1898).

Porter, J. L., *Life and times of Henry Cooke, D.D., LL.D.*, 'People's edition', Belfast, 1875.

General assembly of the presbyterian church in Ireland, *Report on elementary education adopted by the general assembly of the presbyterian church in Ireland, at its meeting in Dublin in June, 1871, etc.*, Belfast, 1871.

Pros and cons, being a digest and impartial analysis of all the principal reasons that have been given, and arguments used for and against the national board of education; with brief remarks by 'Clericus Armachanus', Dublin, 1848.

Reply of his grace the archbishop of Dublin to the address of the clergy of the diocese of Dublin, and Glandalough on the government plan for national education in Ireland; to which are added, the above-mentioned address, and the observations of some of the archbishops and bishops of the United Church of England and Ireland on the same subject, London, 1832.

'Report of the select committee of the house of commons, appointed to examine the reports on Irish education', *Christian Examiner and Church of Ireland Magazine*, viii, 43–60 (July 1828).

Rescript of his holiness Pope Gregory XVI to the four archbishops of Ireland, in reply to the appeal to the holy see on the subject of the national system of education in Ireland, Dublin, 1841.

'Resolutions of the assembled archbishops and bishops of Ireland on the education bill', *Irish Ecclesiastical Record*, 3 ser., xiii, 472–7 (May 1892).

'Resolutions of the Irish bishops', *Irish Ecclesiastical Record*, 3 ser., v, 744–6 (Nov. 1884).

A review of the scripture lessons for the use of the Irish national schools, London and Dublin, 1836.

'The right to educate: to whom does it belong?', *Irish Ecclesiastical Record*, iii, 281–94 (Mar. 1867).

'The right to educate: to whom does it belong?' *Irish Ecclesiastical Record*, iii, 410–18 (May 1867).

'The right to educate: to whom does it belong?', *Irish Ecclesiastical Record*, iii, 541–4 (Aug. 1867).

Sadler, Michael (ed.), *Special reports on education subjects, 1896–1897*, London, 1897.

Saintsbury, George, *The earl of Derby*, London, 1892.

Scully, Denys, *A statement of the penal laws which aggrieve the catholics of Ireland; with commentaries*, 2 vols, Dublin, 1812.

Smyth, George L., *Ireland: historical and statistical*, 3 vols, London, 1844.

Society of United Irishmen, *Report of a committee appointed by the Society of United Irishmen of Dublin, 'to enquire and report the popery laws in force in this realm'*, Dublin, 1792.

A speech delivered by the lord bishop of Ossory and Ferns, at the annual meeting of the Church Education Society for Ireland, held in the Rotunda, Dublin, on Thursday, April 15, 1852, Dublin, 1852.

Stopford, Edward A., *A report to the lord bishop of Meath on the state of elementary schools in the diocese and the opinion of the clergy respecting the question of national education*, Dublin, 1845.

Tighe, Robert S., *A letter addressed to Mr Orde upon the education of the people*, Dublin, 1787.

Townsend, T. S., *The policy of a separate grant for education in Ireland, considered; with some remarks on the ninth annual meeting of the Church Education Society held in Dublin on the 12th April, 1849, at the Rotunda*, Dublin, 1849.

Wakefield, Edward, *An account of Ireland, statistical and political*, 2 vols, London, 1812.

Walsh, William, *Statement of the chief grievances of Irish catholics in the matter of education, primary, intermediate and university*, Dublin, 1890.

Whately, Richard, *Address to the clergy of the diocese of Dublin and Glandalagh and Kildare on the recent changes on the system of Irish national education*, London and Dublin, 1853.

——, *Speech of the most reverend his grace the archbishop of Dublin on presentation of petition respecting education (Ireland) in the house of lords on Tuesday, March 19, 1833*, London, 1833.

Wright, Alexander, *The history of education and of the old parish schools of Scotland*, Edinburgh, 1898.

Wyse, Thomas, *Education reform, or, the necessity of a national system of education*, London, 1836.

——, *Speech of Thomas Wyse, Esq., M.P., in the house of commons on Tuesday, May 19, 1835 on moving for leave to bring in a bill for the establishment of a board of national education, and for the advancement of elementary education in Ireland*, Dublin, 1835.

(B) Twentieth-century publications

Auchmuty, James J., *Irish education, a historical survey*, London and Dublin, 1937.

——s J., *Sir Thomas Wyse, 1791–1862: the life and career of an educator and diplomat*, London, 1939.

Balfour, Graham, *The educational systems of Great Britain and Ireland*, second ed., Oxford, 1903.

Barkley, John M., *A short history of the presbyterian church in Ireland*, Belfast, 1959.

Barnard, H. C., *A history of English education, from 1760*, second ed., London, 1961.

Barry, P. C., 'The holy see and the Irish national schools', *Irish Ecclesiastical Record*, 5 ser., xcii, 90–105 (Aug. 1959).

Batterberry, Richard P. J., *Sir Thomas Wyse, 1791–1862, an advocate of a 'mixed education' policy over Ireland*, Dublin, 1939.

——, 'The synod of Ulster and the national board', *Irish Ecclesiastical Record*, 5 ser., lvi, 548–61 (Dec. 1940).

——, 'The synod of Ulster and the national board—II', *Irish Ecclesiastical Record*, 5 ser., lviii, 16–28 (July 1941).

——, 'The synod of Ulster and the national board—III', *Irish Ecclesiastical Record*, 5 ser., lix, 61–73 (Jan. 1942).

Beckett, J. C., 'The Irish parliament in the eighteenth century', *Belfast Natur. Hist. Soc. Proc.*, 2 ser., iv, 17–37 (1950–55).

——, *The making of modern Ireland*, 1603–1923, London, 1966.

Breathnach, Michael, 'The infancy of school inspection', *Irish School Weekly*, lv, 487–9, 501 (7, 14 Nov. 1953).

Brenan, Martin, *Schools of Kildare and Leighlin*, A.D. 1775–1835, Dublin, 1935.

Britain, an official handbook, London, 1964.

Burns, Robert E., 'The Irish penal code and some of its historians', *Review of Politics*, xxi, 276–9 (Jan. 1959).

——, 'The Irish popery laws: a study of eighteenth-century legislation and behavior', *Review of Politics*, xxiv, 495–508 (Oct. 1962).

Cahill, Edward, 'English education in Ireland during the penal era (1691–1800)', *Irish Ecclesiastical Record*, 5 ser., liv, 627–43 (Dec. 1939).

'Catholic Clerical Managers' Association', *Irish Ecclesiastical Record*, 4 ser., xvi, 76–81 (July 1904).

Clark, G. Kitson, *The making of Victorian England*, London, and Cambridge, Mass., 1962.

Clarke, Desmond, *The ingenious Mr Edgeworth*, London, 1965.

Corcoran, Timothy, *The catholic schools of Ireland, primary, secondary, university*, Dublin, 1931.

——, 'Catholic teachers and the penal law of 1782', *Irish Monthly*, lix 422–5 (July 1931).

——, 'Chronicle: T. M. Healy and Irish education', *Studies*, xx, 306–16 (June 1931).

——, 'The civil law and Irish education, A.D., 1795–1799', *Irish Monthly*, lix, 620–24 (Oct. 1931).

——, 'The Dublin education bill of 1787', *Irish Monthly*, lix, 495–500 (Aug. 1931).

——, 'Education in the Dublin acts of 1792–93', *Irish Monthly*, lix, 541–6 (Sept. 1931).

——, 'Education policy after the union', *Irish Monthly*, lx, 686–90 (Nov. 1931).

——, *Education systems in Ireland, from the close of the middle ages*, Dublin, 1928.

——, 'Enforcing the penal code on education', *Irish Monthly*, lix, 149–54 (Mar. 1931).

——, 'Financing the Kildare Place schools', *Irish Monthly*, lx, 808–12 (Jan. 1932).

——, 'The Irish language in the Irish schools', *Studies*, xiv, 377–88 (Sept. 1925).

——, 'The Kildare Place Education Society', *Irish Monthly*, lix, 748–52 (Dec. 1931).

——, 'The Kildare Place schools—their defined purposes', *Irish Monthly*, lx, 160–5 (Mar. 1932).

——, 'Legal repression of catholic education, A.D. 1740–1760', Irish Monthly, lix, 290–3 (May 1931).

——, 'Making an education act: College Green, Dublin, 1782', *Irish Monthly*, lix, 371–5 (June 1931).

——, *O'Connell and catholic education*, Dublin 1929.

——, 'Our schools and teachers (1820–1825)', *Irish Monthly*, lx, 228–33 (Apr. 1932).

——, 'Popular education in the Ireland of 1825', *Studies*, xiv, 34–45 (Mar. 1925).

——, 'The proselytising schools (1800–1830)', *Irish Monthly*, ix, 427–33 (July 1932).

——, 'The quality of our schools (1823–1830)', *Irish Monthly*, lx, 286–92 (May 1932).

——, *Some lists of catholic lay teachers and their illegal schools in the later penal times*, Dublin, 1932.

——, *State policy in Irish education, A.D. 1536 to 1816*, Dublin, 1916.

Costello, Nuala, *John MacHale, archbishop of Tuam*, Dublin, 1939.

Delany, V. T. H., *Christopher Palles*, Dublin, 1960.

Dowling, Patrick J., 'The catholic clergy and popular education in Ireland in 1825', *Tablet*, clxi, 654–5 (27 May 1933).

——, *The hedge schools of Ireland*, London, 1935.

Dunlop, O. Jocelyn, *English apprenticeship and child labour*, London, 1912.

Edwards, R. Dudley, and Williams, T. Desmond (ed.). *The great famine*, Dublin, 1956.

Fenton, Seamus, *It all happened*, Dublin, 1949.

Fitzpatrick, J. D., *Edmund Rice, founder and first superior general of the brothers of the christian schools of Ireland (Christian Brothers)*, Dublin, 1945.

Gallagher, Anthony M., *Education in Ireland*, Washington, D.C. 1948.

Gibson, William J., *Education in Scotland, a sketch of the past and the present*, London, 1912.

Goldstrom, J. M., 'Richard Whately and political economy in school books', *Irish Historical Studies*, xv, 131–46 (Sept. 1966).

Halevy, Elie, *England in 1815*, trans. E. I. Watkin and D. A. Barker, New York, 1961; original edition 1913.

'Important statement of the Irish hierarchy', *Irish Ecclesiastical Record*, 4 ser., xvi, 171–6 (Aug. 1904).

Jamieson, John, *The history of the Royal Belfast Academical Institution 1810–1960*, Belfast, 1959.

Johnston, Edith M., *Great Britain and Ireland, 1760–1800: a study in political administration*, Edinburgh, 1963.

Johnston, Thomas J., Robinson, John L., and Jackson, Robert W., *A history of the Church of Ireland*, Dublin, 1953.

Jones, M. G., *The charity school movement, a study of eighteenth century puritanism in action*, London, 1964; originally published, 1938.

Jones, Wilbur D., *Lord Derby and victorian conservatism*, Oxford, 1956.

Kennedy, David, 'Robert Park's account of schools in Ballymoney parish', *Irish Historical Studies*, vi., no 21, pp 23–43 (Mar. 1948).

Kennedy, David, *Toward a university*, Belfast, 1946.

Kerr, Anthony J. C., *Schools of Scotland*, Glasgow, 1962.

Kerr, John, *Scottish education, school and university, from early times to 1908*, Cambridge, Eng., 1910.

Kiely, Benedict, *Poor scholar: a study of the works and days of William Carleton (1794–1869)*, London, 1947.

Knox, Henry M., *Two hundred and fifty years of Scottish education, 1696–1946*, Edinburgh, 1953.

Larkin, Emmet, 'Church and state in Ireland in the nineteenth century', *Church History*, xxxi, 294–306 (Sept. 1962).

——, *The quarrel among the Roman Catholic hierarchy over the national system of education in Ireland, 1838–41*, Cambridge, Mass., 1965; originally published in *The Celtic Cross*, 1964.

Latimer, William T., *A history of the Irish presbyterians*, second ed., Belfast, 1902.

Lynam Joseph D. ('Jacques' *pseud.*), *Irish education as it is and as it should be*, Dublin, 1906.

Lyons, F. S. L., *The Irish parliamentary party, 1890–1910*, London, 1951.

McDowell, R. B., *The Irish administration, 1801–1914*, London and Toronto, 1964.

——, 'The Irish executive in the nineteenth century', *Irish Historical Studies*, ix, 264–80 (Mar. 1955).

——, *Irish public opinion, 1750–1800*, London, 1944.

——, *Public opinion and government policy in Ireland, 1801–1846*, London, 1952.

——, (ed.), *Social life in Ireland, 1800–1845*, Dublin, 1957.

McElligott, T. J., *Education in Ireland*, Dublin, 1966.

McGrath, Fergal, *Newman's university, idea and reality*, London, 1951.

Mahaffy, John, *An epoch in Irish history, Trinity College, Dublin: its foundation and early fortunes, 1591–1660*, London, 1903.

Maxwell, Constantia, *A history of Trinity College, Dublin, 1591–1892*, Dublin, 1946.

Mechie, Stewart, *The church and Scottish social development, 1780–1870*, London, 1960.

Meghen, P. J., *A short history of the public service in Ireland*, Dublin, 1962.

Mescal, John, *Religion in the Irish system of education*, London and Dublin, 1957.

Moody, T. W., *The Londonderry plantation, 1609–41*, Belfast, 1939.

Moody, T. W., and Beckett, J. C., *Queen's Belfast, 1845–1949: the history of a university*, 2 vols, London, 1959.

——, (ed.), *Ulster since 1800: a political and economic survey*, London, 1955; corrected impression, 1957.

——, *Ulster since 1800: a social survey*, London, 1957; corrected impression, 1958.

Moore, H. Kingsmill, *An unwritten chapter on the history of education, being the history of the Society for the Education of the Poor of Ireland, generally known as the Kildare Place Society*, London, 1904.

Morgan, Alexander, *Rise and progress of Scottish education*, Edinburgh, 1927.

Mowat, Charles L., *Britain between the wars, 1918–1940*, Chicago, 1955.

Murphy, Harold L., *A history of Trinity College, Dublin, from first foundation to 1702*, Dublin, 1951.

Murphy, James, *The religious problem in English education: the crucial experiment*, Liverpool, 1959.

Norman, Edward R., *The catholic church and Ireland in the age of rebellion, 1859–1873*, London, 1965.

Nowlan, Kevin B., *The politics of repeal: a study in the relations between Great Britain and Ireland, 1841–50*, London and Toronto, 1965.

O'Brien, R. Barry, *Dublin Castle and the Irish people*, London, 1909.

O'Connell, Philip, *The schools and scholars of Breifne*, Dublin, 1942.

Ó Heidan, Eustas, *National school inspection in Ireland: the beginnings*, Dublin, 1967.

——(Hayden, Eustace), 'National school inspection and the Kildare Place Society', *Irish Ecclesiastical Record*, 5 ser., lxxxvii, 241–51 (Apr. 1957).

——, 'National school inspection and the Kildare Place Socity—II', *Irish Ecclesiastical Record*, 5 ser., lxxxvii, 343–54 (May 1957).

O'Hickey, M. P., *The future of Irish in the national schools*, Dublin, 1900.

O'Meara, John J., *Education in the Republic of Ireland*, London, 1965.

Ó'Raifeartaigh, T., 'Mixed education and the synod of Ulster, 1831–40', *Irish Historical Studies*, ix, 281–99 (Mar. 1955).

——, 'The state's administration of education', *Administration*, ii, 67–77 (Winter 1954–5).

Phillips, Walter A. (ed.), *History of the Church of Ireland from the earliest times to the present day*, vol. iii: *The modern church*, London, 1933.

Pryde, George S., *Central and local government in Scotland since 1707*, London, 1960.

Bibliography

——, *Scotland from 1603 to the present day*, London, 1962.

Quane, Michael, 'The diocesan schools—1570–1870', *Journal of the Cork Historical and Archaeological Society*, 2 ser., lxvi, 26–49 (Jan.–June 1961).

Quigley, E. J., 'Saints, scholars and others', *Irish Ecclesiastical Record*, 5 ser., xxiii, 445–60 (May 1924); xxiii, 601–13 (June 1924); xxiv, 23–34 (July 1924); xxiv, 165–76 (Aug. 1924); xxiv, 372–83 (Oct. 1924); xxiv, 511–20 (Nov. 1924).

Reid, John M., *Scotland, past and present*, London, 1959.

'Report on the state of popery, Ireland, 1731', *Archivium Hibernicum*, i, 10–27 (1912).

Reynolds, James A., *The catholic emancipation crisis in Ireland, 1823–1829*, New Haven, 1954.

Ryan, Desmond, *The sword of light, from the four masters to Douglas Hyde, 1636–1938*, London, 1939.

Savage, Roland, *A valiant Dublin woman: the story of George's Hill (1766–1940)*, Dublin, 1940.

Schroder, Anna-Magdalena, *Das religionsproblem in der Irisch-Englischen schulpolitik*, Charlottenburg, 1935.

Sheehy, Edward, 'The philomath sings', *Ireland Today*, i, 19–25 (Aug. 1936).

Trevelyan, George M., *Lord Grey of the reform bill, being the life of Charles, second earl Grey*, second ed., London, 1929.

Wade, Newman A., *Post-primary education in the primary schools of Scotland, 1872–1936*, London, 1939.

Wall, Maureen, *The penal laws, 1681–1760*, Dundalk, 1967, originally published 1961.

Walsh, Louis J., 'Some Irish schoolmasters', *The Catholic World*, cxxxv, 582–7 (Aug. 1932).

Walsh, Patrick J., *William J. Walsh, archbishop of Dublin*, Cork and Dublin, 1928.

Walsh, Timothy J., *Nano Nagle and the Presentation Sisters*, Dublin, 1959.

Webb, John J., *Municipal government in Ireland, medieval and modern*, Dublin, 1918.

INDEX